Runaway religious were monks, canons and friars who had taken vows of religion and who, with benefit of neither permission nor dispensation, fled their monasteries and returned to a life in the world. This book is the first to tell their story.

Not only the normal tugs of the world drew them away: other less obvious yet equally human motives, such as boredom, led to a return to the world. No legal exit for the discontented was permitted – religious vows were like marriage vows in this respect – until the financial crisis caused by the Great Schism created a market in dispensations for priests in religious orders to leave, take benefices and live as secular priests. The church therefore pursued runaways with her severest penalty, excommunication, in the express hope that penalties would lead to the return of the straying sheep. The secular arm, at the behest of religious superiors, sent out hundreds of writs to royal officials to effect the arrest and return of runaway religious. Once back, whether by free choice or by force, the runaway was received not with a feast for a prodigal but, in a rite of stark severity, with the imposition of penalties deemed suitable for a sinner. The story ends only when the religious houses, great and small, were emptied of their inhabitants in the sixteenth century.

Cambridge Studies in Medieval Life and Thought

RUNAWAY RELIGIOUS IN MEDIEVAL
ENGLAND, *c.* 1240–1540

Cambridge Studies in Medieval Life and Thought
Fourth series

General Editor:

D. E. LUSCOMBE

Professor of Medieval History, University of Sheffield

Advisory Editors:

R. B. DOBSON

Professor of Medieval History, University of Cambridge, and Fellow of Christ's College

ROSAMOND MCKITTERICK

Reader in Early Medieval European History, University of Cambridge, and Fellow of Newnham College

The series Cambridge Studies in Medieval Life and Thought was inaugurated by G. G. Coulton in 1921. Professor D. E. Luscombe now acts as General Editor of the Fourth Series, with Professor R. B. Dobson and Dr Rosamond McKitterick as Advisory Editors. The series brings together outstanding work by medieval scholars over a wide range of human endeavour extending from political economy to the history of ideas.

For a list of titles in the series, see end of book.

RUNAWAY RELIGIOUS IN MEDIEVAL ENGLAND
c. 1240–1540

F. DONALD LOGAN

Professor Emeritus of History
Emmanuel College, Boston

CAMBRIDGE
UNIVERSITY PRESS

Published by the Press Syndicate of the University of Cambridge
The Pitt Building, Trumpington Street, Cambridge CB2 1RP
40 West 20th Street, New York, NY 10011–4211, USA
10 Stamford Road, Oakleigh, Melbourne 3166, Australia

First published 1996

Printed in Great Britain by Redwood Books, Kennet Way, Trowbridge, Wiltshire

A catalogue record for this book is available from the British Library

Library of Congress cataloguing in publication data
Logan, F. Donald.
Runaway religious in England, *c.* 1240–1540 / F. Donald Logan.
p.   cm. – (Cambridge studies in medieval life and thought;
4th ser.)
Includes bibliographical references and indexes.
ISBN 0 521 47502 3 (hc)
1. Monasticism and religious orders – England. 2. Monasticism and
religious orders – History. Middle Ages, 600–1500. 3. England –
Church history – 1066–1485. I. Title. II. Series.
BX2592.L64 1996
271'.00942'0902 – dc20   95–31970   CIP

ISBN 0 521 47502 3 hardback

In Memory of My Parents

CONTENTS

Contents

Contents

PLATES, FIGURE AND TABLES

PREFACE

Few books end up exactly as they were originally planned. This book is no exception. Several decades ago, while studying the use of the secular arm against English excommunicates, I noticed that there was a parallel procedure for the use of the secular arm against runaway religious. As one does, I marked it out in my mind as a subject worth returning to. Many years and other projects intervening, I was able to focus on this subject only in the early 1990s. I discovered that runaway religious was a subject untreated in a specific way by the historians of the medieval religious orders, and, rather than concentrate merely on the use of the secular power to effect the return of runaway religious, I decided to do the subject as a whole for the period from the mid-thirteenth century to the end of the religious orders in England. Consequently, what would have been an article has now become a book.

A word of self-exculpation must be given to explain the absence of the word 'Wales' in the title of this book. I could say that during this period the four Welsh dioceses fell within the juris-diction of the archbishop of Canterbury, who was their metro-politan. But, more importantly, it must be sadly admitted that, although there were dozens of religious houses in Wales, the evidence regarding them for this subject is unfortunately exiguous. To include 'Wales' in the title might cause a misunderstanding of the book's contents. Of course, Welsh references are given and the names of all Welsh runaways encountered in this study are included in the register.

The generosity and helpfulness of other scholars have greatly assisted me in the preparation of this book, and it is a pleasure to record my gratitude. Large sections of the text were read by Christopher Harper-Bill, C. H. Lawrence and David M. Smith, and their comments have measurably improved the finished text. Charles Donahue alerted me to several cases and made perceptive comments on the first chapter. I have profited much from discussions with Claire Cross and Joan Greatrex about Yorkshire nuns and cathedral priories. When I had specific questions about English Carmelites, Keith J. Egan promptly and graciously replied from his unrivalled knowledge of the subject. Likewise, Dr Michael Robson, OFM Conv., sent me information culled from the files of medieval Franciscans made by the late Bishop John Moorman. At a moment when I feared I would be unable to wait for the appearance of volume 17 of the *Calendar of Papal Letters*, its editor, Anne P. Fuller, in an act of great kindness, photocopied her page-proofs and mailed them to me. To no scholar do I owe more than to Paul Brand, who read the entire text. He gave the text the benefit of his broad erudition and sound historical judgement, and he gave the author much appreciated words of encouragement. I greatly value the suggestions of all these scholars and have departed from them rarely and then, I fear, to my own peril.

Without the quietly efficient help of librarians and archivists this work could never have been completed. Mention should be made of the staffs of the Borthwick Institute (York), British Library, Emmanuel College Library (Boston), Institute of Historical Research, Public Record Office and St John's Seminary Library (Boston), where Rev. Laurence W. McGrath made available his great fund of knowledge.

Several audiences have heard from me about this subject, and their responses have helped to shape this work. Convenors and organizers have made this possible: at Boston University, Harvard Law School, the Institute of Historical Research, University of Michigan and at meetings of the Midwest Conference on British Studies and of the New England Historical Association.

Throughout, where surnames are English place-names, these have been silently modernized where it seems reasonable (e.g., 'Lincolne' is rendered 'Lincoln'). Also, English quotations from contemporary texts have been given modern spelling and punctuation. Transcripts of crown-copyright records in the Public Record Office appear by permission of the Controller of HM Stationery Office. The British Library Board and the Courtauld Institute of Art have given permission to reproduce material from their collections.

Caveat lector. The persons discussed in this book had one thing in common: they had abandoned the religious life. Perhaps, at the distance of half a thousand years or so, the tragedy of their human situations does not impress itself on our sensibilities as forcefully as it should, and the historian must remind himself that human tragedy commands respect. To drag up stories of human failure and misery merely as entertaining anecdotes or, worse, to satisfy prurient interests is not particularly historical: it runs the real danger of distorting and, perhaps, misrepresenting the past. The historian must describe the past as fairly as possible, never accepting the lurid as necessarily more representative than the dull, never dwelling beyond the demands of the subject on areas of human weakness. *Qui sine peccato est . . .*

ABBREVIATIONS

Amundesham	*Johannis Amundesham, monachi monasterii S. Albani, annales* (ed. H. T. Riley; 2 vols.; RS; London, 1870–1).
Ann. mon.	*Annales monastici* (ed. H. R. Luard; RS; 5 vols; London, 1864–9).
BIHR	*Bulletin of the Institute of Historical Research.*
BL	British Library.
Blythe's Vis.	*Bishop Geoffrey Blythe's Visitation, c. 1515–1525* (ed. Peter Heath; Staffordshire Record Society, Collections, 4th ser., 7, 1973).
BRUC	A. B. Emden, *A Biographical Register of the University of Cambridge to AD 1500* (Cambridge, 1963).
BRUO	A. B. Emden, *A Biographical Register of the University of Oxford to AD 1500* (3 vols.; Oxford, 1957–9).
Bullarium romanum	*Bullarium diplomatum et privilegiorum sanctorum Romanorum pontificum Taurinensis editio* (ed. A. Tomassetti; 25 vols.; Turin, 1857–72).
Canivez, *Statuta*	*Statuta capitulorum generalium ordinis Cisterciensis ab anno 1116 ad annum 1786* (ed. J. M. Canivez; 6 vols.; Louvain, 1933–41).
CAP	*Collectanea Anglo-Premonstratensia* (ed. F. A. Gasquet; 3 vols.; Camden Soc., 3rd ser., vols. 6, 10, 12, 1904–6).
CCM	*Corpus consuetudinum monasticarum* (vols.; Sieburg, 1963–).
CCR	*Calendar of Close Rolls* (London, 1902–).

Chron. S. Mary's York	*The Chronicle of St Mary's Abbey, York* (ed. H. H. E. Craster and M. E. Thornton; Surtees Soc., 148, 1934).
Clem.	*Constitutiones* of Pope Clement V.
Councils and Synods	*Councils and Synods with Other Documents relating to the English Church*. Vol. 1, *AD 871–1204* (2 pts; eds. D. Whitelock, M. Brett and C. N. L. Brooke; Oxford, 1981). Vol. 2, *AD 1205–1313* (2 pts; eds. F. M. Powicke and C. R. Cheney; Oxford, 1964).
CPL	*Calendar of the Entries in the Papal Registers relating to Great Britain and Ireland: Papal Letters* (London and Dublin, 1894–).
CPP	*Calendar of the Entries in the Papal Registers relating to Great Britain and Ireland: Petitions to the Pope* (London, 1897).
CPR	*Calendar of Patent Rolls* (London, 1901–).
EHR	*English Historical Review.*
Epp. Jo. Peckham	*Registrum epistolarum fratris Johannis Peckham archiepiscopi Cantuariensis* (ed. C. T. Martin; RS; 3 vols.; London, 1882–5).
Fac. Off. Reg.	*Faculty Office Registers, 1534–1549* (ed. David S. Chambers; Oxford, 1966).
Gesta abbatum	Thomas Walsingham, *Gesta abbatum monasterii S. Albani* (ed. H. T. Riley; RS; 3 vols.; London, 1867–9).
JEH	*Journal of Ecclesiastical History.*
KH	David Knowles and R. Neville Hadcock, *Medieval Religious Houses: England and Wales* (2nd edn; London, 1971).
Knowles, *RO*	David Knowles, *The Religious Orders in England* (3 vols.; Cambridge, 1948–59).
Linc. Vis.	*Visitations of Religious Houses in the Diocese of Lincoln* (ed. A. H. Thompson; 2 vols. in 3; Lincoln Rec. Soc. 7 (1914), 14 (1918), 21 (1929).
Lit. Cant.	*Literae Cantuarienses* (ed. J. B. Sheppard; RS; 3 vols.; London, 1886–9).

LP	*Letters and Papers Foreign and Domestic of the Reign of Henry VIII* (21 vols.; London, 1862–1910).
Mon. Franc.	*Monumenta Franciscana* (eds. J. S. Brewer and R. Howlett; RS; 2 vols.; London, 1858–82).
Pantin, *Chapters*	*Documents Illustrating the Activities of the General and Provincial Chapters of the English Black Monks, 1215–1540* (ed. W. A. Pantin; 3 vols.; Camden Soc., 3rd ser., 45, 47, 54, 1931–7).
PL	*Patrologiae cursus completus . . . series latina* (Paris, 1844–64).
Power, *Nunneries*	Eileen Power, *Medieval English Nunneries* (Cambridge, 1922).
Prynne	William Prynne, *The History of King John, King Henry III, and the Most Illustrious King Edward the I* (London, 1670).
Reg. Pal. Dunelm.	*Registrum Palatinum Dunelmense* (ed. T. D. Hardy; RS; 4 vols.; 1873–8).
Reg. ____	Bishops' registers are referred to with the name of the bishop and diocese (e.g., *Reg. Chichele, Canterbury*); specific references can be found in E. L. C. Mullins, *Texts and Calendars: An Analytical Guide to Serial Publications* (2 vols.; London, 1958–83) and in David M. Smith, *Guide to Bishops' Registers of England and Wales* (London, 1981).
RS	Rolls Series (*Rerum Britannicarum Medii Aevi Scriptores or Chronicles and Memorials of Great Britain and Ireland during the Middle Ages*; 99 vols.; London, 1858–97).
Rymer, *Foedera*	T. Rymer, ed., *Foedera, conventiones, literae*, etc. (new edn; Adam Clark *et al.*, eds.; 7 vols.; London, 1816–69).
Salter, *Chapters*	*Chapters of the Augustinian Canons* (ed. H. E. Salter; Canterbury and York Soc. 29, 1922).
Searle, *Lists*	*Christ Church, Canterbury*, vol. 2, *Lists of the Deans, Priors, and Monks of Christ*

	Church, Canterbury (ed. W. G. Searle; Cambridge Antiquarian Soc., octavo ser., 34 1902).
Statutes	*Statutes of the Realm* (eds. A. Luders *et al.*; London, 1810–28).
Talbot, *Letters*	*Letters from the English Abbots to the Chapter at Cîteaux, 1442–1521* (ed. C. H. Talbot; Camden Soc., 4th ser., 4, 1967).
VCH	*Victoria History of the Counties of England* (individual counties are referred to by abbreviated county name, e.g., *Lincs.*).
VI°	*Liber sextus* of Pope Boniface VIII.
Vis. Dioc. Linc.	*Visitations in the Diocese of Lincoln, 1517–1531* (ed. A. H. Thompson; 3 vols.; Lincoln Record Soc., 33, 35, 37, 1940–7).
Vis. Norwich	*Visitations of the Diocese of Norwich, AD 1492–1532* (ed. A. Jessopp; Camden Soc., new ser., 43, 1888).
Wilkins, *Concilia*	*Concilia Magnae Britanniae et Hiberniae, AD 446–1718* (ed. D. Wilkins; 4 vols.; London, 1737).
Wright	*Three Chapters of Letters Relating to the Suppression of Monasteries* (ed. Thomas Wright; Camden Soc., 26, 1843).
X	*Decretales* of Pope Gregory IX.
YAJ	*Yorkshire Archaeological Journal.*

All archival references, unless otherwise stated, are to the Public Record Office, London. The traditional counties of England and Wales are referred to by their conventional abbreviations (e.g., Lancs. for Lancashire).

INTRODUCTION

This book is about runaway religious. It is about those men and women who had taken vows to lead the religious life as monks, canons, friars or nuns and who without dispensation left that life and returned to the world. In doing so they usually abandoned the religious habit, the outward sign of their inner commitment. They had 'climbed over the wall', if only metaphorically. Some were like Peter Dene, who did in fact climb over the wall at St Augustine's, Canterbury, with the assistance of a local rector.[1] Others simply walked out through gates, seldom secured during the day and frequently providing easy egress at night. The physical restraints against flight were few and scarcely ever insuperable. More imposing were the moral restraints of vows and conscience and, in some cases, fear of punishment, that rose wall-like around the individual religious. When the feeling of personal dissatisfaction and unhappiness became particularly intense, a religious might climb over these walls.

The vows taken, whether explicitly or implicitly, bound the religious for life with virtually no possibility of dispensation – even Pope Innocent III said he did not have the power! – until the 1390s, when honourable withdrawal became possible but only for some men. That a religious might feel entrapped should not surprise the modern reader. Likewise, that such entrapment might lead to flight should not seem novel to us. Yet in the world of Christian Europe in the middle ages, society viewed such an action as a cause of acute public scandal and the church saw it as a peril to the runaway's soul. Excommunication and efforts to seek the runaway's return logically followed.

The runaway religious must be firmly distinguished from others who abandoned commitments made before God and who might

---

[1] See below, pp. 34–41.

appear similar to runaways. The cleric, especially one in major orders, who left his clerical state was in a radically different canonical situation, for, unlike the religious, he had never taken formal vows to lead a clerical life: he entered the clerical life and was then subject to the positive, man–made laws of the church binding clerics, which laws he violated by abandoning the clerical state. Similarly, obligations were taken by those entering the married state, which, it might be argued, resembled those taken by a religious and the abandonment of a marriage by one of the parties closely paralleled the abandonment of the religious life. Despite superficial similarities, there were substantial differences in these two cases: the married state was entered into by a contract made by two consenting parties *coram deo*. The abandonment of a marriage constituted the violation of this contract. Religious, on the other hand, did not enter into a contract with God but freely (*sponte*) promised God to live the religious life. The abandonment of this promise (*votum*) constituted the nature of the deed attributed to the men and women encountered in these pages. Further, the runaway religious must be distinguished from the wandering monk, who, while not having abandoned the religious life, wandered from monastery to monastery as, in Hugh Lawrence's phrase, 'the professional guest'.[2] These *gyrovagi* were vehemently condemned by St Benedict and can be seen in various guises until the twelfth century, but by the period here under review they had largely disappeared from the scene and are not the subjects of this study.[3]

Runaway religious, although never a sizeable percentage of professed religious, were recognizable figures in the ecclesiastical landscape of medieval Europe and can be seen, sometimes in vivid detail, in England in the three hundred years before the dissolution of the religious houses by Henry VIII. It is this 300-year period that is here under study. The *termini* – *c.* 1240 and 1540 – require comment. The *terminus ad quem* marks the year of the dissolution of the last religious houses. With the surrender of Holy Cross Abbey, Waltham (Essex), on 23 March 1540 the long history of religious communities in England came to an end. The *terminus a quo* might appear somewhat arbitrary, and, indeed, in some sense it

---

[2] C. H. Lawrence, *Medieval Monasticism* (2nd edn; London, 1989), p. 27.
[3] The classic description is in Helen Waddell, *The Wandering Scholars* (7th edn; London, 1934), chap. 8.

is. It is clearly not the beginning: to begin in the beginning one would have to go back to the monasteries established by Augustine at Canterbury in 597 and Aidan at Lindisfarne in 635. The year 1240, then, is admittedly arbitrary, but not wholly so. Before that date there are, indeed, references to runaway religious, but from *c.* 1240 the evidence is of such a nature that we can go beyond the anecdotal and proceed to analysis. From this time written records survive in richer abundance. The bishops' registers begin to appear in the thirteenth century. The acts of Lincoln diocese, the largest in size and population, were registered as early as *c.* 1215 and those of York, the second largest diocese, from 1225. Others followed: in the 1250s the dioceses of Coventry and Lichfield, Exeter and Rochester; in the 1260s the dioceses of Bath and Wells, Norwich, Winchester and Worcester; and before the century's end all the other dioceses of England – including the great sees of Canterbury, London and Durham. Registers for Ely diocese survive from the early fourteenth century, although earlier registers were kept, and the surviving evidence from the Welsh church is unfortunately exiguous.[4] The long, unrivalled series of central government records also begins to appear at this time, particularly the records of the royal chancery and courts. In addition, the work of a hundred years, initially under the aegis of the Public Record Office (London) and now of the Irish Manuscripts Commission, has made the papal registers accessible in calendar form for Great Britain and Ireland from the pontificate of Innocent III (1198–1216) into the sixteenth century. These three *fontes principales* are supplemented for this period by records of religious orders and reports of visitations of houses as well as by chronicles of individual monasteries.

In addition, by the 1240s almost all the religious orders were now in England. The last to come were the friars. Gilbert de Fresney and twelve other Dominicans landed at Dover in early August 1221, and by the end of the 1240s there were twenty-four houses of the Black Friars from as far north as Carlisle and Newcastle upon Tyne to as far south as Exeter and Canterbury.[5] The Franciscans were at Canterbury, London and Oxford in 1224

---

4 David M. Smith, *Guide to Bishops' Registers of England and Wales* (London, 1981), p. vii.
5 William A. Hinnebusch, *The Early English Friars Preachers* (Rome, 1951), pp. 494–5; KH, pp. 213–14.

and in the next twenty years established thirty-four houses. It was in the 1240s that the other two orders of mendicant friars came to England: the Carmelites were at Aylesford (Kent) in 1242 and by the decade's end at five other places, while the Austin friars, the smallest of the mendicant orders, arrived at Clare (Suffolk) in the last years of this decade. Thus, from the 1240s the full roster of religious orders can be seen in England, excepting only the Bridgettine nuns, who were to come to Twickenham (Middlesex) in 1415.

Moreover, the appearance in 1234 of the greatest medieval collection of canon law, the Decretals of Gregory IX, provides a clear milestone, its promulgation a *maximum momentum* in the history of the church. The papal bull *Rex pacificus* promulgated this systematic, authentic, universal, exclusive collection of law. The canon law for the Western church was now, in a sense, fixed: it was no longer necessary to consult disparate collections of papal decrees and conciliar canons, for they were at hand in this new collection. The Decretals of Gregory IX – as, indeed, the law for religious which this collection contained – would be added to by subsequent popes, yet these were but additions to the definitive text. It was to remain the principal text of canon law until 1918.

To begin this study *c.* 1240 should not imply that the abandonment of the religious life was a phenomenon of more striking significance from then than it had been in previous centuries. Near the dawn of Western monasticism the straying monk can be seen. When John Cassian, from his monastic experiences in the East and in Gaul, wrote his Institutes (417–18), he recognized that a monk, like a slave, might try to slip away from his monastery at night under cover of darkness.[6] In the life of St Benedict, attributed to St Gregory the Great (590–604), we see at Subiaco the monk who was led away from his prayers by the devil.[7] The *locus classicus* is in the rule itself, where we see the straying monk who left his community: he is to be received back, taking the lowest place among the monks, even to a third time but not beyond. The rule distinguished him from the monk expelled for bad conduct, although the returning *eiectus* was to be treated in the same way as

---

[6] *Instituta* 4. 6 (*PL* 49. 159).

[7] 'Nunquid non aspicitis quis est qui istum monachum foras trahit?' (*Dialoga* 2. 4; *PL* 66. 142). For the authorship see Francis Clark, *The Pseudo-Gregorian Dialogues* (2 vols.; Leiden, 1987).

the returning runaway. The words used to describe the latter are instructive: he was a monk who left through his own fault ('frater qui proprio uitio egreditur').[8] This passage was to be read aloud to generations and generations of monks, many of whom would commit it to memory. Influential commentaries on the rule glossed this passage. The monastic capitulary of Aachen (817), associated with Benedict Aniane, decreed that monks wishing to take flight be sent to another monastery.[9] (Canonists would later call this *exsilium*.) Likewise, Smaragdus, later in that century, quoted approvingly those who would require a monastery to seek out its runaways and who would forbid other monasteries to take them in, for, it was said, if no one takes them in, they will feel compelled to return to their own monastery.[10] Here, then, are the two elements which were to remain consistent in the long history of monasticism: (1) the runaway who had committed a grave misdeed by his flight and (2) the insistence that he be received back.

The monastic literature was supplemented by conciliar and papal decrees and the teaching of canonists. From the time of Gratian's *Decretum* the runaway religious appears as a figure whose conduct was considered criminal and who was subject to ecclesiastical penalties, which in the form of excommunication became automatic from 1298.[11] Forbidden by monastic rules and by canon law from abandoning the religious life, the runaway religious was clearly seen as a deviant person in medieval society, a violator of vows and a scandal to the faithful. Yet Dante encountered two such nuns in paradise.[12]

England was no exception to the general experience of other lands where religious became deviant and sought release from the religious life through flight. Two great tenth-century monastic reformers, Dunstan and Ethelwold, were themselves ordained with

---

[8] Cap. 29 (Rudolph Hanslik, ed., *Benedicti regula* (rev. edn; *Corpus scriptorum ecclesiasticorum latinorum*, Vienna, vol. 75, 1977), pp. 93–4).

[9] J. Semmler, ed., 'Legislatio Aquisgranensis', *CCM* 1. 524.

[10] A. Spannagel and P. Engelbert, eds., *Smaragdi abbatis expositio in regulam sancti Benedicti* (*CCM* 8, 1974), pp. 233–4. In an extremely severe interpretation of monastic stability Pope Gregory II wrote to St Boniface in 726 that, in the event of a contagious disease or plague, monks not yet afflicted were not free to flee: 'we declare this to be the height of folly; for no one can escape from the hand of God'(*The Letters of Saint Boniface* (tr. Ephraim Emerton; New York, 1940), p. 55).

[11] See chap. 1 for further elaboration of the canon law. For a useful summary see J. Bouché, 'Apostasie de religion', *Dictionnaire de droit canonique* 1. 564–74.

[12] *Paradiso*, canto 3.

a priest who was to abandon the monk's habit 'and ended his life amid the stinking of luxury'.[13] Anglo-Saxon law dealt with the fugitive religious. The bishops in synodal canons (1008) decreed that runaway monks and nuns, if found, should return and that their monasteries should receive them, imposing suitable punishment.[14] Not long thereafter, King Cnut threatened such offenders with banishment from the realm.[15] St Dunstan features, albeit posthumously, in the tale of a late eleventh-century incident at Christ Church, Canterbury. At that time Edward, archdeacon of London, responded to an inner calling and entered that monastery, where he soon became secretary. Fervour, however, gave way to torpor, and correction was not cheerfully accepted. Flight by night was Brother Edward's response to his situation. The night of his planned departure, he stopped at Dunstan's tomb to ask the saint's permission. As he then proceeded to leave, his way was blocked by a severe-looking monk, who bade him return to the tomb and pray again. Dissatisfied with Edward's reaction, the monk revealed himself as St Dunstan and said, 'You shall never leave with my permission, but you shall remain here and die here.'[16]

By the time St Anselm came to Canterbury as archbishop (1093), he was already familiar with the problem. In one well-known instance, a fugitive monk of Christ Church, Canterbury, came to Bec, where Abbot Anselm received him kindly, and, when the monk repented and asked to be reconciled with his community, Anselm sent him back accompanied by a most affecting letter on his behalf.[17] In England, as archbishop, Anselm encountered two royal princesses at Wilton Abbey, whose attachment to the religious life was much in question. In 1094, he required Matilda,

---

[13] Wulfstan of Winchester, *The Life of St Aethelwold* (eds. Michael Lapidge and Michael Winterbottom; Oxford, 1991), chap. 8 (pp. 12–13).

[14] V Ethelred 5–6 (*Councils and Synods* 1. 1. pp. 347–8); for an English translation see *English Historical Documents* 1. 406.

[15] II Cnut 4a.1 (F. Liebermann, ed., *Die Gesetze der Angelsachsen* (3 vols.; Halle, 1903–16), p. 310).

[16] Eadmer, 'Vita S. Dunstani', *Memorials of St Dunstan, Archbishop of Canterbury* (ed. William Stubbs; RS, 1874), pp. 241–5. For a revisionist approach to the tenth-century monastic reforms see Antonia Gransden, 'Traditionalism and Continuity during the Last Century of Anglo-Saxon Monasticism', *JEH* 40 (1989) 159–207.

[17] Ep. 40. The text is in F. S. Schmitt, ed., *Sancti Anselmi Cantuariensis archiepiscopi opera omnia* (6 vols.; Edinburgh, 1946–51) 3. 285–7. For an English translation see Walter Frohlich, tr., *The Letters of St Anselm of Canterbury* (2 vols.; Kalamazoo, 1990–3) 1. 322–4.

daughter of King Malcom III of Scotland, to return to her abbey, where she had worn the religious habit.[18] Nearly a decade later, when Henry I wished to marry Matilda, Anselm endorsed the expected decision which he had left to the English bishops: since she had neither read her profession nor been blessed by a bishop, she was free to marry the king. A ceremony followed, at which Anselm himself officiated. It was as controversial then as now.[19] He had perhaps greater success with Gunhilda, the daughter of the last Anglo-Saxon king: she had left Wilton Abbey to be the wife or mistress of a great northern baron. Although you have never read profession or been blessed by a bishop, he wrote, you have privately and publicly worn the nun's habit and have affirmed to all those who saw you that you were dedicated to God. 'It is impossible to be saved unless you return.' And return she apparently did.[20]

In incidents such as these, perhaps not so dramatic nor involving such high-born persons, and in other fleeting references runaway religious appear in the surviving records of the next centuries. A few examples may be cited. Theobald, one of Anselm's successors (1139–61) in the see of Canterbury, concerned himself with what should happen to returning runaways, and his response resonates with the familiar prescriptions of the rule.[21] Under Becket's successor at Canterbury, Richard de Dover (1174–84), we catch the glimpse of the abbot of Tewkesbury (Gloucestershire) being advised to take back one of his monks.[22] A lay brother of the Cistercian abbey of Garendon (Leicestershire) was said to be fugitive, no later than 1202.[23] At about the same time, Alice Clement can be seen in royal and ecclesiastical courts, attempting to establish that she had never been a nun of Ankerwyke nunnery (Buckinghamshire), could not be a fugitive and could legally

---

[18] Ep. 177 (Schmitt 3. 60–1; Frohlich 2. 91–2).

[19] Eadmer's *History of Recent Events in England: Historia novorum in Anglia* (tr. Geoffrey Bosanquet; London, 1964), pp. 126–31. See Sally Vaughn, *Anselm of Bec and Robert of Meulan* (Berkeley, 1987), pp. 223–5, and R.W. Southern, *Saint Anselm: A Portrait in a Landscape* (Cambridge, 1990), pp. 260–2.

[20] Epp. 168, 169 (Schmitt 4. 43–50; Frohlich 2. 64–74). See Southern, pp. 262–4.

[21] Avrom Saltman, *Theobald, Archbishop of Canterbury* (London, 1956), no. 31; text is also in *Lit. Cant.* 3. 354–5.

[22] C. R. Cheney and B. E. A. Jones, eds., *English Episcopal Acta* II, *Canterbury, 1162–1190* (London, 1986), no. 214.

[23] *VCH, Leics.* 2. 6.

inherit from her father.[24] From such incidents and anecdotes a bridge stretches across the first half of the thirteenth century and deposits us where detail is richer and analysis more possible. *Pontem transeamus.*

---

[24] The case first surfaced in the mid-1180s and was not settled until 1221 (see Elizabeth Vodola, *Excommunication in the Middle Ages* (Berkeley, 1986), pp. 102–10).

Chapter 1

A QUESTION OF TERMS

The runaway religious, who are the subject of this book, were variously described by their contemporaries. *Fugitivi* they were called, and *vagabundi* and *vagantes*. Yet the word used most frequently by contemporaries – perhaps as much as 95 per cent of the time – was none of these. To popes and bishops, to heads of religious houses, to canon and secular lawyers, they were simply *apostatae* (i.e., apostates). The understanding of the English word 'apostate' in another sense in modern times makes it hazardous to use the word without explanation: a book entitled *Apostate Religious* might understandably lead the reader to believe that it deals with the rejection of the Christian faith, which it does not. Twelfth-century commentators on the *Decretum* of Gratian (1140) recognized two uses of the word 'apostasy': they distinguished between *apostasia a fide*, by which a baptized person rejects the Christian faith (like Julian the Apostate), and *apostasia a religione*, by which a professed religious abandons the religious life and returns to the world. Stephen of Tournai, writing about 1160, commented that 'today we mean by an apostate a person who, after taking the religious habit, returns to a life in the world'.[1] In this sense there is no implication of abandoning the Christian faith, which is the modern meaning, but merely the abandonment of the religious life.[2] The word 'religion' itself merits comment: the runaways were

---

[1] 'Hodie etiam apostata dicitur qui post susceptum religionis habitum ad secularem conversationem revertitur' (J. F. von Schulte, ed., *Die Summa des Stephanus Tornacensis* (Giessen, 1891), p. 76). The principal texts in the *Decretum* are D.50. c.69; C.16. q.1. cc.11, 12, 17; C.20. q.3. cc.1–4; C.27. q.1. cc.1, 18, 19. Many later commentators added a third kind of apostasy: *apostasia inobedientiae*, which was a setting of one's self in the most wilful way against authority itself (e.g., Adam and Eve); see Hostiensis, *Summa aurea* (Lyons, 1548), fo. 241, and, in England, William Lyndwode, *Provinciale* (Oxford, 1679), 5.6.1 s.v. *apostasia*.

[2] The Latin word is a transliteration of ἀποστασία, which was a late classical form of ἀπόστασις, and means standing apart from. Hostiensis said that the etymological meaning of apostate was *retro-stans*, which implies not merely a standing apart from but

9

said to be guilty of 'apostasy from religion'. In this sense, religion means nothing more than the religious life or a religious order or a religious house. It refers to monks, canons, friars and nuns as well as to lay brothers and sisters of religious orders.[3] Apostasy from religion was viewed as a crime both by the general law of the church and by the constitutions of individual orders. Before 1298 excommunication was the penalty that could be imposed on apostates, and from 1298 excommunication was incurred *ipso facto*.[4] Apostates from religion, then, are the subject of this book.

The definition seems clear enough: an apostate is a professed religious who abandons the religious life and returns to the world. Complexities, however, will soon become apparent. In general, the definition has two elements: one, that the person be a professed religious and, the other, that the person abandon the religious life and return to the world. If either of these elements is absent, there is no apostasy. They need to be discussed in turn.

RELIGIOUS PROFESSION

In the first place, it is said that an apostate had to have been a professed religious. If profession never took place or if, for some reason, the profession was not a true profession, then there was no apostasy and there were none of the dire consequences, including automatic excommunication and, in England, liability to arrest by the secular arm. In a word, if no profession, then no apostasy. To be a true profession it was necessary that the profession be made freely by an unmarried person who had reached the age of discretion and who was *compos mentis*. That these constituted the

---

a return to where one previously stood (see preceding note). John Wyclif, on the other hand, believed (wrongly) that it derived from *apos-stolo* (presumably ἀποστέλλω) meaning *retro-missio*, a sending back to where one had been (M. H. Dziewick, ed., *Tractatus de apostasia* (Wyclif Soc., London, 1889), p. 1).

[3] Writing about 1441, Lorenzo Valla took objection to the use of the word 'religious' to apply to those who took vows as well as to the implication that such people had a higher form of the Christian life ('In professione religiosorum', *Sitzungsberichte der philosophisch-historischen Classe der kaiserlichen Akademie der Wissenschaften* 61–2, Vienna, 1869; reprinted in L. Valla, *Opera omnia* (Turin, 1962) 2. 287–322). Similar sentiments had been expressed by John Wyclif in his work on apostasy, written probably in 1383 (pp. 9–10).

[4] According to the *Decretals* of Gregory IX (1234) obdurate apostates ought to be excommunicated by their superiors (X.3.31.24), but Boniface VIII in the *Liber sextus* (1298) decreed apostates automatically excommunicate (3.24.2 in VI°). See Albert J. Riesner, *Apostates and Fugitives from Religious Houses* (Catholic University of America, Canon Law Studies, no. 168, Washington, 1942), pp. 29–31.

1 *Apostate monk and abbot*. From 'Omne bonum', BL, Royal MS 6E.VI, fo. 115ʳ
(photo: The British Library)

essential elements of profession had long been held, and they were crystallized in the Decretals; subsequently there were but clarifications as well as extensions to the mendicant orders.

The rule for age was clear. The age of discretion for entering a religious house was the same as the age of discretion for marriage: the age of legal puberty, twelve for girls and fourteen for boys. It was not enough to be in the twelfth or fourteenth year; the twelfth or fourteenth birthday had to be reached. It must be emphasized that this was the minimum age for entering the novitiate of a religious house not the minimum age for religious profession. Since a year of probation was required, the minimum age for profession was thirteen and fifteen.[5] By this period, the oblate (i.e., the child offered – *oblatus* – to a religious house by its parents) was a thing of the past, but the admission and profession of underage children, particularly in orders of friars and nuns, was not uncommon in England.[6]

The practice of the friars was defended in a treatise by the Franciscan John Pecham, Parisian master of theology, during the controversy about this question in the thirteenth century.[7] As archbishop of Canterbury (1279–92), Pecham supported this view in practice. In one noteworthy instance he tried to impose on the unwilling nunnery at Stratford-at-Bow (Middlesex) an underage girl and replied to the objecting prioress that 'because of her youth she would be better suited to learn and accept the discipline of the order'.[8] The practice was condemned strongly by Richard Fitzralph in a memorable sermon given at Avignon in 1357. He recounted the story of how he was accosted that very day on his way to the papal palace by an Englishman whose 12-year-old son had been seduced by the friars while a student at Oxford. In the following year the University of Oxford took strong action against

---

[5] Theoretically it was possible for a novice during the year of probation to make an absolute profession of conversion of soul. Such professions were not to be presumed and had to be proven, since the assumption was that entry was conditional and that the first year was a year of probation. The present writer has not found any instance of this spontaneous conversion. For the pertinent texts see X.3.31.16, 20, 23; 3.14.2 in VI°.

[6] For the decline of the practice of child oblation see C. H. Lawrence, *Medieval Monasticism* (2nd edn; London, 1989), pp. 37–8.

[7] For the question generally see L. Oliger, 'De pueris oblatis in ordine minorum', *Archivum Franciscanum Historicum* 8 (1915) 389–447; an edition of the Pecham treatise is on pp. 414–39.

[8] 'propter minoritatem huiusmodi habilior sit et capacior ad discendum et recipiendum ea quae tui ordinis respiciunt disciplinam' (*Epp. Jo. Peckham* 1. 356; see too p. 366).

the friars for this practice: the friars were forbidden, under pain of banishment from university activities, from recruiting university students under the age of eighteen.[9] The practice provided Wyclif's followers with ample ammunition. Jacke Upland, writing in 1404, asked

> Why steal ye mens children
> for to make hem of your sect,
> since that theft is against God's hestes
> and sith your sect is not perfect?

To which Friar Daw Topias feebly replied,

> I hold it no theft
> but if thou calle Christ a theef
> that did the same . . .
> it ne is no robbery,
> but Christ appreved thefte.[10]

In 1401 parliament addressed this issue, but the statute that emerged did not forbid the friars from taking underage boys. What it did was to forbid such boys being taken without the consent of their parents or others responsible for them.[11] The church, too, tried to stop the practice. Pope Martin V in 1430 condemned the practice.[12] Yet both before and after parliamentary statute and papal decree the practice existed, although, to be sure, not in every house of every order of friars, and it is not always evident whether parental consent was given. In any event, the profession – as distinct from the admission – of underage boys by the friars was clearly *contra legem* and such professions invalid. This factor of age in profession and consequently in apostasy appears in cases throughout the period here under study.

---

[9] Pope Urban V in 1365 ordered the university to revoke these statutes. For these matters see Katherine Walsh, *A Fourteenth-Century Scholar and Primate: Richard Fitzralph in Oxford, Avignon and Armagh* (Oxford, 1981), pp. 424–6; Hastings Rashdall, *The Universities of Europe in the Middle Ages* (new edn, F. M. Powicke and A. B. Emden; Oxford, 1936), 3. 74–6. Also, see Janet Coleman, 'FitzRalph's Antimendicant "proposicio" (1350) and the Politics of the Papal Court at Avignon', *JEH* 35 (1984) 376–90.

[10] Thomas Wright, ed., *Political Poems and Songs* (RS; 2 vols.; London, 1859–61), 2. 22, 83–4. For the charge of the anti-mendicants that the friars 'stole' children see Carolly M. Erikson, 'The Fourteenth-Century Franciscans and their Critics', *Franciscan Studies* 35 (1975) 112–13.

[11] 4 Henry IV, c. 17 (*Statutes* 2. 138). The Commons had asked for a minimum age of twenty-one (*Rotuli Parliamentorum* 3. 502).

[12] Even the pope allowed some exceptions (*Bullarium romanum* 4. 737).

The Dominican friars of Gloucester, in 1327, took an 11-year-old boy, William le Botiler, from his *patria* by gifts and promises and clothed him in the habit of their order without his father's consent. His father, John le Botiler, discovering what had happened, hurried to Gloucester, where he saw his little son clothed as a friar and crying. The prior adamantly refused the father's request to take his boy home. The bishop of Worcester, at the father's behest, wrote sternly to the prior:

We, who support your order, ask you to consider what honour there is for you in keeping this boy, a boy so clearly underage in the year of probation, a boy who is illiterate or nearly so. It is no small wonder that a boy who is unable to govern himself should be removed from the control of his father and placed among strangers who do not know him . . . It is our wish, under God, that you return the boy to his father, at least until he reaches the age of discretion.

The outraged reaction of Bishop Cobham, no doubt intensified by his friendship with the boy's father, was, in any case, directed against the admission of an underage child.[13]

Less fortunate than William le Botiler was Richard, son of John de Thornton, citizen and spicer of York. In 1358, Thornton claimed that his son had been ensnared by the Carmelites of York, who took his profession before he was fourteen, and, although Richard also left before he was fourteen, the friars called him an apostate and sought his arrest by the secular arm. The king intervened and took young Thornton under his protection, pending further investigation, and arrest was thus forestalled. If Thornton's account of his son's encounter with the Carmelites is true, then the boy had not been truly professed and, hence, could be subject neither to apostasy nor to arrest for apostasy.[14]

---

13 The Latin text of this letter is in *Reg. Cobham, Worcester*, p. 215. The bishop said that he intervened at the request 'of our special long-time friend'. John le Botiler, who told Cobham that his son was taken away while he was preoccupied with threats to his property and person, may have been the same John le Botiler of Llantwyt, who was involved at this time with the party of Hugh Despenser (see entries listed in indexes to *CPR, 1324–27; 1327–30; CCR, 1327–30*). See E.H. Pearce, *Thomas de Cobham, Bishop of Worcester, 1317–1327* (London, 1923), pp. 243–4, where le Botiler is mistakenly called le Bouler.

14 *CPR, 1358–61*, p. 19. Not dissimilar was the case of William Heydok, who, in the late fourteenth century, entered the Austin friars (possibly at one of the Norfolk houses) at the age of nine and made his profession at the age of twelve, clearly in violation of the canons and against the wishes of his family. He later went to university – the *relatio* says

The London Carmelites were involved in a similar dispute, when, in 1443, John Hawteyn (alias Scharynton) claimed that he had been placed in the London priory at the age of eight. When he had run away, he was brought back by his mother and was imprisoned by order of Thomas Netter of Walden, the prior provincial. Later the boy was held at Oxford. Although the Carmelites claimed that they never violated the statute by receiving any boys under the age of fourteen, they nevertheless did not pursue the matter, and the sentence given in 1447 found against them: Hawteyn was free to leave the order.[15]

The pope, in 1490, intervened on behalf of John Sillow, who, at the age of about seven and under the care of his stepmother, was induced to enter the Franciscan friars, which he did 'with childish levity'. At fourteen he tried to leave, but the friars would not allow it, and he was forced to make profession. He later (*c.* 1476) fled and was obviously considered an apostate by the Franciscans. Now the pope cleared him of any taint of apostasy for, in his judgement, profession had been made by virtue of force and fear.[16] In many ways this case parallels the case of Henry Hill, who entered the Franciscans as a boy and, although he protested at the age of fifteen, he was not allowed to leave and in time was ordained priest there. Because Hill had been forced to remain after he was fifteen, the pope, in 1518, dispensed him to live as a secular priest.[17]

Nunneries, although not the subject of legislation similar to the friars in this respect, were known on occasion to accept the professions of underage girls. In 1383, Clarissa Styl, at the age of eight, entered the preceptory of the sisters of the Order of Knights Hospitallers at Buckland (Somerset), having been brought there by the rector of Northleigh in Devon. Two months after her entry she made her profession according to the tradition of that house which allowed youthful profession provided the girl was at least seven years old, in patent violation of the canons.[18] In another case,

---

a year and a half after profession – where he put off the religious habit and was ordained a priest of the Norwich diocese (*CPL* 4. 352).

[15] *VCH, London* 1. 509. Hawteyn was said to have made his profession to Netter, who was prior provincial from 1414 till his death in 1430 (*BRUO* 2. 1344). Another London Carmelite, John Lethinard, claimed in 1391 that he had been forced at the age of twelve to enter and was intimidated into making profession (*VCH, London* 1. 508).

[16] *CPL* 14. 38–9.

[17] *Reg. Bothe, Hereford,* pp. 115–16.

[18] E135/6/173. She was found to have been truly professed, since she remained there even at the age of fourteen; she was thus judged to be disinherited.

Agnes, wife of Richard Clivedon, claimed, in 1392, that she was
not a professed nun. What seems to have happened was that she
had entered Shaftesbury Abbey at the age of seven, made religious
profession and remained there for nine years, leaving in 1374
apparently to claim an inheritance.[19] Likewise, in 1402 a royal
inquiry by Henry IV concerning Isabel, one of the daughters of
Thomas, duke of Gloucester, revealed that, as an underage girl, she
had entered the nunnery of Poor Clares outside Aldgate, London,
where she was professed, and where (the abbess reported) she
remained as a pious nun.[20]

In all this, the impression should not be left that friars and nuns
routinely and against the laws of the church accepted the profession
of underage children; such was not the case. The examples given
here serve another purpose: they underline the truth of the
proposition that profession, under the age of discretion, was not
true profession.[21]

Being of age was not of itself enough; it was necessary that
the professed not be bound by a present marriage. The law was
unambiguous: entry into the religious life was limited to single
persons, to widows and widowers. One exception was allowed: a
husband and wife could by mutual and free agreement both enter
the religious life.[22] The general requirement had practical

[19] C269/8/12; E135/6/76.

[20] C269/9/5. She was one of the heirs of her sister Joan, who had died in 1400. In 1401
the pope ordered the bishop of London to go to the nunnery with the archbishop of
Canterbury to determine whether Isabel wanted to remain, for the archbishop had said
that she had been placed there as an infant and had never professed and that now, with
her brothers and sisters dead, the inheritance might go to strangers (*CPL* 5. 385).
Although the pope said that she could leave if she so wished, Isabel was still at Aldgate
in 1403 (*CPR, 1401–05*, p. 248) and later became abbess (*VCH, London* 1. 519).

[21] Quite another, though related, issue concerns the actual age at which profession was
made. We may never feel secure in generalizing about this. In his important study
of Christ Church Priory, Canterbury, John Hatcher estimates that the average age of
admission between 1486 and 1507 was 16.8 and that the entrants all fell between the ages
of 15 and 21; for the longer period from 1395 to 1505 the mean age was about 18. See
'Mortality in the Fifteenth Century: Some New Evidence', *Economic History Review*, 2nd
ser., 39 (1986) 26–7. At Westminster Abbey for the years from 1390 to 1529 the age at
entry was normally older than 18 (Barbara Harvey, *Living and Dying in England,
1100–1540: The Monastic Experience* (Oxford, 1993), p. 118). At St Mary's Abbey,
Winchester, in 1524 it was reported that six girls were professed: five were aged 15 and
one was aged 16 (Diana Coldicott, *Hampshire Nunneries* (Chichester, 1989), p. 40). For a
discussion of the evidence for the age of admission at Durham, see R. B. Dobson,
Durham Priory, 1400–1450 (Cambridge, 1973), p. 61.

[22] See Elizabeth M. Makowski, 'The Conjugal Debt and Medieval Canon Law', *Journal of
Medieval History* 3 (1977) 109–10, and reprinted in *Equally in God's Image: Women in the*

consequences, and incidents are far from wanting which demonstrate its impact. John de Beverley, for example, entered St Mary's Abbey, York, in 1268, but during his probationary year he admitted to the abbot that he had contracted and consummated marriage. And, so, he left. That was quite straightforward.[23] Less straightforward, however, was a similar claim made by Robert Trone, who, after being a professed Franciscan friar for nine years and having been priested, confessed in 1284 that he had been previously married; he was thus stripped of his religious habit. Trone then lived with the woman he said was his wife but – alas! – not happily ever after: in 1285 and, again, in 1289 writs were issued for his arrest as an apostate and, according to the chronicler, he was imprisoned. Very puzzling, indeed. One wonders whether he was found to have lied about his previous marriage.[24] Similarly, in 1311, Agnes de Flixthorpe alias de Wissenden, confined to her cell at St Michael's convent, Stamford (Northamptonshire), because of apostasy and refusal to resume the religious habit, claimed that she was not professed and that, before entering the nunnery, she had married a man who was still living.[25]

An unhappy religious who wanted to leave without incurring apostasy, *ipso facto* excommunication and possible arrest could allege prior marriage. Thus, the Augustinian canon, Thomas de Melton of Hexham Priory in Northumberland, in order to leave without odour of apostasy, lied to his superiors and told them that he had been married before profession, and he was then invited to leave, without apostasy. He later appeared (in 1350) repentant and seeking reconciliation.[26] More complex was the situation that developed at the nearby Cistercian abbey of Newminster. Sometime about the year 1300 a monk of that abbey, Walter de Witton, left without permission and was apostate for eight weeks. Contrite, he returned, but, instead of receiving a warm welcome, he was beaten by the cellarer and his servants and then imprisoned.

Middle Ages (eds. J. B. Holloway, C. S. Wright and J. Bechtold; New York, 1990), p. 136. An apparent violation of this law at the nearby hospital of St James so disturbed the abbot of Westminster in 1322 that he ordered the expulsion on these grounds of such people (*VCH, London* 1. 543n.).

23 *Chron. S. Mary's York*, p. 12.
24 Chronicle of Dunstable (*Ann. mon.* 3. 314). For requests for writs of capture see C81/1792/11, 13.
25 Lincs. Archives Office, Episc. Reg. III, fos. 180ᵛ, 228. See below, pp. 257–8.
26 *CPL* 3. 393.

Witton broke out of prison and wandered apostate for ten years. He then attempted another return, but the penance imposed on him, he felt, was so insupportable that, in desperation, he announced falsely that he had contracted marriage before his profession. The abbot had no alternative but to remove Witton's habit, clothe him in secular garb and cast him out into the world. The story does not end there. After a while, Witton returned yet again and now confessed his lie. The abbot, his patience tried beyond endurance, refused to have him back in his monastery. At length, Witton, ever resourceful, appealed to the Holy See and, in 1311, received papal letters, but these failed to stir the abbot to change his mind. The bishop of Durham intervened, probably with effect, but one feels certain that there was no fatted calf awaiting Walter de Witton at Newminster.[27] Obviously, as these cases show, in practice it was impossible to prove the negative of never having been married; then (as now) oaths under pain of perjury were required. What these examples illustrate is that prior marriage rendered profession invalid and apostasy impossible.

External pressures could invalidate religious profession: if a forced profession, then not a true profession. Although some examples of this occur, they are not so numerous as those claiming lack of age or prior marriage. The force of parental pressures is difficult for us of a different culture to calculate. If freedom of choice meant that the individual acted independently of parental wishes, then perhaps few marriages could stand the test, and *a pari* few religious professions. The line between societally acceptable and societally unacceptable parental force is difficult for us to draw.[28] There was the Augustinian canon of Kirkham Priory (Yorkshire), John Strother, who claimed that he entered the priory because of his father's threats and who, in 1372, was given leave by the archbishop of York to go to Avignon to seek release from his vows.[29] In an unusual case at Jervaulx Abbey (Yorkshire) in the sixteenth century, a man said he had been sold to the abbot by the master to whom he was apprenticed and that the abbot tonsured him and clothed him as a Cistercian monk. After a career that saw him in at least three other monasteries, he moved to

---

[27] *Reg. Pal. Dunelm.* 1. 13–16.
[28] For perceptive remarks on this issue see Penelope D. Johnson, *Equal in Monastic Profession: Religious Women in Medieval France* (Chicago, 1991), pp. 13–18.
[29] *VCH, Yorks.* 3. 222.

Colchester, married and lived as a layman. To charges made against him he responded that he was not an apostate. If his story is reliable, then he may indeed not have been freely professed and, hence, not apostate.[30]

No doubt other religious houses used a procedure similar to that used at Christ Church Priory, Canterbury, whereby candidates about to enter the monastery as novices had to answer, under oath, a series of questions.[31] Some concerned issues affecting their canonical eligibility: had they contracted marriage? were they excommunicate? Others were concerned with suitability: were they in debt? were they suffering from incurable illness or contagious disease? It was only after satisfactory answers had been given to these and other questions that the prior admitted each candidate to his year of probation.[32]

How did profession take place? The answer is not so simple as might appear at first sight. One obvious answer is that, at the end of the year of probation, a ceremony was held, at which the novice made an oral profession, generally to the abbot of the abbey or the prior of the priory or frequently, in the case of women religious, a bishop. The novice read aloud the words of profession, or, if the novice did not have letters, he or she was suitably prompted. Then the newly professed signed a cross to the profession.[33] What was vowed was a life of obedience, chastity and poverty. The officiating prelate then blessed the habit, and the ceremony of profession was over. This was all done in public: the vows of obedience to the house or order, of life-long celibacy and of renunciation of property were not private vows (or simple vows, as the canonists would have said); they were solemn vows, i.e., vows solemnized by ritual. The form of the profession would have

---

[30] For this case see James E. Oxley, *The Reformation in Essex to the Death of Mary* (Manchester, 1965), p. 57.

[31] *Lit. Cant.* 1. 321–2. This can also be seen, for example, in the rite of admission of novices at St Augustine's, Canterbury (E. M. Thompson, ed., *Customary of the Benedictine Monasteries of Saint Augustine, Canterbury, and Saint Peter, Westminster* 1 (Henry Bradshaw Society 23, 1902) 6.) For the questions asked of a postulant at the Carthusian priory of Sheen see *VCH, Surrey* 2. 90–1.

[32] 'In nomine Sanctae Trinitatis nos recipimus et admittimus te ad ordinem Sancti Benedicti et ad habitum monachalem portandum in Ecclesia tempore probacionis, et ulterius solempniter profitendum, juxta observancias regulares et canonicas sanctiones' (*Lit. Cant.* 1. 322).

[33] The form of reception was outlined in the Rule of St Benedict, chap. 58 (Rudolph Hanslik, ed., *Benedicti regula (Corpus scriptorum ecclesiasticorum latinorum* 75; Vienna, 1977), pp. 133–8).

been similar to that taken by a nun named Joan, who in 1416 professed at Easebourne Priory in Sussex:

I, Sister Joan, do hereby promise stability, moral conversion and obedience according to the rule of St Augustine before God and his saints in this monastery, which is dedicated to St Mary, in the presence of the lord bishop of Selymbria, suffragan of Chichester, and in the presence of Dame Margery, prioress of Easebourne, and her sisters. To Prioress Margery and her successors I promise to live without my own goods and in chastity until death.

And, we are told, Sister Joan made her mark with a cross.[34] Lists of professions were no doubt expected to be kept by the religious houses, and some still exist.[35] When inquiries were later made about the details of profession, accurate information could be promptly produced.[36]

There is another answer to the question of how religious profession took place. It was quite possible for persons to become professed religious without ceremony, without words, without blessing: they simply had to remain in the religious house for more than a year. When the year of probation ended, the novice became professed merely by remaining and continuing to wear the religious habit. Indeed, a ceremony might also take place, but the continued presence in the house, the continued wearing of the religious habit and the failure to leave – these of themselves constituted profession, which in law was as binding as profession with ceremony, words and blessing. The canonists called this tacit profession.[37] To leave the religious life after tacit profession was every bit as much apostasy as leaving after express profession. The Council of Lambeth in 1281 observed that some nuns foolishly

---

[34] *Reg. Chichele, Canterbury* 3. 454–5, where it is given in Latin. English-language professions for nuns were probably more common. The rite of profession can be found in ordinal books of monasteries: for Westminster Abbey, e.g., see J.W. Legg, ed., *Missale ad usum ecclesie Westmonasteriensis* (Henry Bradshaw Soc. 5 (1893) cols. 1187–1216), which contains separate ceremonies for monks and for nuns; also for Eynsham Abbey see Antonia Gransden, ed., *The Customary of the Benedictine Abbey of Eynsham in Oxfordshire* (*CCM* 2; Sieburg, 1963), pp. 58–66.

[35] Two such lists can be seen in W. G. Searle, ed., *Christ Church, Canterbury*, I, *The Chronicle of John Stone*; II, *Lists of the Deans, Priors, and Monks of Christ Church, Canterbury* (Cambridge Antiquarian Soc., octavo ser., 34, 1902), pp. 162–96. For the lists in the Durham Liber Vitae see R. B. Dobson, *Durham Priory, 1400–1450* (Cambridge, 1973), p. 56.

[36] See the case of Simon le Chamberlain (below, p. 23).

[37] For remarks about tacit profession, see Wolfgang N. Frey, *The Act of Religious Profession* (Catholic University of America, Canon Law Studies, 63; Washington, 1931), pp. 23–31.

think that after a year they are free to return to the world simply because they have not solemnized their vows and received a bishop's blessing: they are *ipso facto* professed and not allowed to return to the world without apostasy. This applies, the bishops went on to say, to monks and to other religious, and, if they leave after tacit profession, they are guilty of apostasy and are to be compelled to return to their houses.[38] The English bishops were not creating new law: they were merely repeating the general law of the church. Pope Honorius III (1216–27) had pronounced on this question. It was a cause of great embarrassment, he said, that some men have worn the religious habit for many years without making religious profession and that they felt themselves bound neither to poverty nor to chastity. Honorius decreed that, after wearing the habit for a year, they were to be considered professed and bound by the rule of their order. This decretal found its way into the Decretals in 1234 and so remained the universal law of the church until the nineteenth century and for religious women until 1918.[39] It was echoed by the bishops at Lambeth in 1281 and by generations of canonists, including the English canonist William Lyndwode, who, in 1430, wrote two long glosses on the subject.[40]

It was clearly desirable, despite the canonically binding force of tacit profession, to have the religious make an express profession with its solemnization of vows and appropriate blessing: it would mark a significant moment in the life of the individual and in the common life of the religious community. For example, in 1397, Bishop Braybrook of London received the profession of fourteen nuns of Barking Abbey (Essex), and in 1414 Philip Repingdon, bishop of Lincoln, commissioned a suffragan to receive the express profession of seven nuns at Markyate Priory, who were already tacitly professed.[41] It is interesting to note that, when Archbishop Warham visited Davington Priory in Kent in 1511, he found two non-professed nuns who had been there for ten and fifteen years

---

[38] *Councils and Synods* 2. 2. 912.

[39] The text is in X.3.31.22 (Potthast 7811). It was promptly incorporated in the legatine statutes for the English Black Monks in 1238 (*Councils and Synods* 2. 1. 254; Matthew Paris, *Chronica maiora* (ed. H.R. Luard; RS; 7 vols.; London, 1872–84) 3. 504). For its life into modern times, see Frey, *Act of Religious Profession*, pp. 30–1.

[40] *Provinciale* (Oxford, 1679), 3.17.2, s.vv. 'nullatenus permittantur' and 'religionis habitum'.

[41] *VCH, Essex* 2. 118; *Reg. Repingdon, Lincoln* 3. 33–4. In Dec. 1337 Bishop Hempnall of Worcester received the profession of eighteen religious women of the Order of Fontevrault at Westwood Priory (*VCH, Worcs.* 2. 149).

respectively: they were obviously two tacitly but not expressly professed nuns.[42] When the reforming statutes of the Augustinian canons were issued in 1339, they required each novice, having completed his year of probation, to make express profession.[43] What seems to have generally happened in practice was this: if the novice stayed beyond the year of probation, he or she was considered professed and, at some point thereafter, in a matter of months rather than, as at Davington Priory, a matter of years, there would be held the ceremony of express profession and the blessing of the habit. To sum up, when it is said 'no profession, therefore no apostasy', profession means either express profession or tacit profession.

The fact of profession was central to other issues. The English bishops, in 1300, complained that the royal courts were admitting pleas of inheritance from nuns who had apostasized after express or tacit profession. The king replied (probably in 1301) that in such cases his courts allowed exceptions to be made which alleged religious profession, and, when that happened, his judges straight away remitted the matter to the local bishop in order to determine whether profession had occurred.[44] What was at issue here was that a professed religious by virtue of the vow of poverty could not inherit and exceptions alleging religious profession could be used to thwart a claim to an inheritance. In most instances, such an exception constituted a charge of apostasy. Among cases of this sort was the dispute brought before the king's justices in 1274 about the rightful heir of Roger de Wykes, a nephew claiming that Roger's sister Godhuda could not inherit since she had been a nun of Kilburn Priory for over thirty years, a claim supported by information supplied by the abbot of Westminster.[45] In another context, we have already met Clarissa Styl, who, in 1383, at the age of eight

---

[42] Mary Bateson, 'Archbishop Warham's Visitation of Monasteries, 1511', *EHR* 6 (1891) 28. Also, in 1464, Wilton Abbey (Wilts.) had 23 professed nuns and 17 nuns awaiting profession (*VCH, Wilts.* 3. 239).

[43] If he requested express profession and the superior who should receive it refuses or delays unreasonably, the novice is treated as if he had expressly professed; not so if he fails to make express profession through his own fault (Salter, *Chapters*, pp. 216–17).

[44] *Councils and Synods* 2. 2. 1215. Bracton had said that, when the exception of religious profession was made in inheritance suits, reference is to be had to the bishop, who can determine whether the person had worn the habit of probation or the habit of profession (*Bracton on the Laws and Customs of England* (G. E. Woodbine, ed.; S. E. Thorne, tr. and rev.; 4 vols. (Cambridge, MA, 1968–77) 4. 310–11).

[45] CP 40/105, m. 142. The case was reopened in 1294 without apparent success. I am grateful to Dr Paul Brand for bringing this case to my attention.

was professed with the Hospitallers at Buckland in Somerset. The reason why an inquiry was held was that a wardship of her was claimed in an inheritance question. The validity of her profession was in dispute. In the event, the royal courts referred the question of her alleged profession to the bishop of Bath and Wells, who held that, although she professed as a minor, Clarissa had nevertheless remained at Buckland for two years beyond her twelfth birthday, where, he said, she is still content (1389). Although the bishop did not say it in so many words, this constituted tacit profession.[46] Similarly, in 1409, the royal courts referred the allegation that Grace and Agnes, sisters and heirs of Emery Nowers, were professed nuns, to the bishop of Lincoln, who found that they had been professed earlier that year (in fact, within a month of his writing!) at St Giles Abbey in Flamstead (Hertfordshire).[47] A particularly nasty family feud erupted between the brothers Chamberlain in 1298. Henry le Chamberlain, in an attempt to disinherit his elder brother, Simon, claimed that Simon was a professed monk of Little Malvern Priory in Worcestershire, who had apostasized and was living in an adulterous union. The matter was referred to Archbishop Winchelsey, who, in turn, required the prior of Little Malvern to provide him with the facts, which were that Simon had entered the priory on 25 November 1289 and announced on the following 16 September his intention to leave, which he did about the time of All Saints (1 November 1290), less than a year after his entry. The prior concluded that Simon le Chamberlain was professed neither by deed (i.e., expressly) nor by law (i.e., tacitly). His brother Henry persisted: he appealed the case in the church courts, invoked the king's court and secured a certificate that Simon had been ordained subdeacon while a monk of Little Malvern.[48] There the trail ends.

Cases of this sort could be multiplied, but perhaps one further case may be summarized. It concerns the Lovedays of Suffolk. In 1287, Roger Loveday died, leaving two sons: Roger, junior, by his

---

[46] E.135/6/173; *Year Book of 12 Richard II* (ed. G. F. Deiser; Ames Foundation, Cambridge, MA, 1914) pp. 71–8, 150–3. For details of this case – including the alleged threat by the nuns that, if Clarissa were to leave the nunnery, the devil would take her away – see Power, *Nunneries*, pp. 36–8; also see above, p. 15.

[47] C269/9/24. Agnes Nowers of Knossington (Leics.) was signified for arrest as an excommunicate by the bishop of Lincoln in 1372 and again, in 1373, after she had failed to prosecute an appeal in the Arches (C85/107/13, 15).

[48] The affair can be seen at different points in *Reg. Winchelsey, Canterbury* 1. 347–8; *Reg. Giffard, Worcester* 2. 499, 503–5; and *CPR, 1292–1301*, p. 370.

first wife, and Richard, by his widow. The issue came to the royal courts in 1300, when Roger claimed his inheritance. His claim was countered by the allegation by Richard that Roger was, in fact, a professed member of the Templars and had been so for more than eight years during his father's lifetime and for two more years after his father's death, when he apostasized and began to wear secular clothes. In a particularly vivid moment in King's Bench, Richard was asked where his half-brother had been professed, and he replied at Temple Bruer in Lincolnshire; to which Roger replied that he was 'homo secularis' and of 'secularis status'. Was Roger Loveday a layman and heir to his father's estate or a professed Templar and apostate? Although a mandate was sent to the bishop of Lincoln to certify concerning the religious profession of Roger Loveday, no certificate was returned.[49]

Proof of non-profession could also be used to counter the writ for one's capture as an apostate.[50] Of the more than five hundred cases in which apostates were pursued by the writ for their arrest only two cases have come to light in which the alleged apostate countered the writ with the claim of non-profession. In the first case, the Master of the Order of Sempringham (the Gilbertines), on 17 November 1366 requested a writ for the capture of Alice, daughter of John Everingham, a professed nun of Haverholme Priory in Lincolnshire, who, he said, had apostasized and was living in sin with James de Huthulle.[51] Alice fought the matter in the royal chancery, claiming that she could not be arrested as an apostate since she was not a professed nun. A hearing was held, at which the Master and Alice's attorney made contradictory statements. The question was referred to the bishop of Lincoln, who, after examining Alice, the nuns and brothers of Haverholme as well as others, found that she was not a nun and had never been professed.[52]

In like manner, Richard Bengeworth (alias de Evesham) held that he was not a professed religious of St Mary's Hospital at

---

[49] KB 27/174, m. 69; see, also, BL, Stow MS 386, fos. 215v–216 and Add. MS 5925, fo. 6v; *Calendar of Inquisitions Post Mortem*, 2 (1906) no. 643; 3 (1912) no. 486. I am grateful to Dr Paul Brand for bringing this case and these references to my attention.

[50] The whole subject is treated in chapter 4.

[51] C81/1791/2. The writ was issued on 12 Dec. 1366 (*CPR, 1364–67*, p. 369).

[52] C269/4/29 and dorse. The bishop had commissioned two canons of Lincoln to hear the case. The matter did not end there, for the Master appealed to the Roman court (*CPL* 4. 69–70).

Ospringe in Kent. In 1386 the Master of St Mary's claimed that Bengeworth had taken the habit on St Martin's Day (11 November) 1358, wore it for more than three years and then rashly left: 'we do not know whether he was [expressly] professed'. The archbishop of Canterbury confirmed the Master's testimony.[53] In the following year the Master requested Bengeworth's arrest.[54] One wonders what, after twenty-four unbothered years, brought him to the attention of his superiors. As with Alice Everingham, profession was at the heart of the matter, although Bengeworth was apparently less successful. The two cases cited here, exceptional perhaps in themselves, serve to emphasize the absolute necessity of prior profession in the definition of apostasy.

ABANDONMENT OF THE RELIGIOUS LIFE

The second element in defining an apostate is rejection of the religious life and return to the world. This meant that the religious left the religious house without permission, not just for an evening's excursion to the local village, but had left with the intention of rejecting the religious life, with the intention of not returning and with the intention of returning to the world.

A clear sign of the abandonment of the religious life was the abandonment of the religious habit. There was a medieval commonplace that the habit does not make the monk ('habitus non facit monachum'). It meant that to be a good monk one needed to do more than merely wear the monastic habit, that there had to be an inner conversion, a genuine commitment to the interior life of the spirit. The phrase 'habitus non facit monachum' was understood as an exhortation for the monk to clothe his soul as well as his body in the monastic life.

In another sense, we may say 'habitus facit monachum', in the sense that, as we have seen, after a year of wearing the habit (with or without interior conversion), the wearer became a monk.[55] And so, conversely, the non-wearing of the habit was seen as the unmaking of the monk, as a clear sign of his rejection of the

[53] C269/7/17, 23.
[54] C81/1796/12.
[55] For the significance of the habit in becoming a religious in an earlier period see Giles Constable, 'The Ceremonies and Symbolism of Entering Religious Life and Taking the Monastic Habit, from the Fourth to the Twelfth Century', *Settimane di studio del centro italiano de studi sull'alto medioeva* 33 (Spoleto, 1987), 771–834.

religious life, and his wearing secular clothes a clear sign of his embracing the life of the world. Dare we say, 'monachus sine habitu non est monachus'? Time and time again, almost like stock phrases, apostates are said to have abandoned their habits and taken on secular clothes. The form commonly used in requesting the writ for the capture of an apostate and in the writ itself was that the apostate had spurned the habit of his order ('spreto habitu ordinis sui') and was going about 'in habitu seculari'. As a rule of thumb, then, abandonment of the religious habit and the wearing of secular clothes established the presumption of apostasy, but this does not mean that in every case of apostasy the religious habit was abandoned. The essential element was that the professed religious had abandoned the authority of the religious order by physically leaving the religious house with no intention of returning. Continued wearing of the habit while apostate merely added to the *scandalum publicum* of the deed. For example, the Augustinian canon William Homet was described in papal letters of 1352 as an apostate still wearing his habit.[56] The common lawyer Anthony Fitzherbert noted this phenomenon in his *Novel Natura Brevium*, published in 1534, where he wrote that the phrases about spurning the religious habit and going about in secular clothes are used in the writ even if the apostate continued to wear his habit, 'for these are but words of form and not of substance, for the habit of religion is the obedience and profession which he hath made', and, if he leaves, 'it seemeth that he doth relinquish the habit'.[57] Fitzherbert reached the heart of the matter: the leaving stripped the monk of his spiritual 'habit', the commitment to the religious life.[58]

The word 'apostate' was applied in practice to a wide range of religious men and women who did not conform to the letter of the definition, who had not necessarily abandoned the religious life and who had no intention of returning to the world. Charges of apostasy were made against many such religious, and they give us a sense of the widening application of the term and, indeed, its misapplication in practice.

In a curious turn of events in the early fourteenth century,

---

[56] *CPL* 3. 470.

[57] Quoted from the English edition, London, 1677, p. 520. In a similar way, Joannes Andreae distinguished the habit of conversion from the habit of probation and the habit of profession (*In tertium decretalium librum novella commentaria* (Venice, 1581) 3.31.13).

[58] For a description of the habit and clothing of the Black Monks see Barbara F. Harvey, *Monastic Dress in the Middle Ages: Precept and Practice* (Canterbury, 1988).

professed members of a religious order, trying to be faithful to their vows and habit, found themselves involved in charges of apostasy and excommunication. Such was the case with the Order of Knights Templars at the time of their trial and dissolution. The sad tale can be seen with some vivid detail in the North of England. At this time there were 135 members of the order in England, about 40 of them in the northern province.[59] Proceedings in England moved slowly against the Templars. Although the first royal writs were issued on 20 December 1307, it was not until the spring of 1310 that proceedings actually began in York.[60] Many Templars had evaded arrest, prompting the king, on 14 December 1309, to issue writs to all the sheriffs of his realm to arrest Templars, who were apostate, wandering about in secular clothes.[61] The sheriff of York was later chided for lax custody at York Castle of those arrested by these writs.[62] Although one 'apostate' Templar returned, eight other northern Templars were still 'apostate' when the initial inquiries began in April 1310, and Archbishop Greenfield duly excommunicated them.[63] Of these eight apostates of the spring and summer of 1310, only one later surfaces to our attention: Stephen de Staplebridge was captured at Salisbury and reconciled, probably after having been tortured, at London in the summer of 1311.[64] Meanwhile, in the North during that same summer, Staplebridge's former *confratres* were intimidated into abjuration and then assigned to religious houses (e.g., Selby, Jervaulx, Whitby) for penance. Despite these assignments, many of the Templars failed to go to their places of penance and continued to wear the habit of their orders. Others had gone to the places assigned them but had returned. Roger Sheffield had fled from Kirkstall Abbey, and others had problems at Rievaulx and Fountains.[65] When the papal bull was published in York on

---

[59] In general, see C. Perkins, 'The Trial of the Knights Templars in England', *EHR* 24 (1909) 432–47; T. W. Parker, *The Knights Templars in England* (Tucson, 1963), pp. 91–8; Malcom Barber, *The Trial of the Templars* (Cambridge, 1978), pp. 193–204. More specifically for the North see E. J. Martin, 'The Templars in Yorkshire', *YAJ* 30 (1931) 140–50; A. Hamilton Thompson's introduction, *Reg. Greenfield, York*, 5. xxxii–xl; R. M. T. Hill, 'Fourpenny Retirement: The Yorkshire Templars in the Fourteenth Century', *Studies in Church History* 24 (1987) 123–8.
[60] For the writ ordering their capture see *CCR, 1307–13*, p. 14.
[61] The text is in Rymer, *Foedera* 2. 1. 100; see *CCR, 1307–13*, p. 189.
[62] *Foedera* 2. 1. 105; see *CCR, 1307–13*, p. 206.
[63] *Reg. Greenfield, York* 4. nos. 2271, 2294.
[64] *CCR, 1307–13*, pp. 316–17; *Councils and Synods* 2. 2. 1307–10.
[65] *Reg. Greenfield, York* 5. no. 2354.

15 August 1312, Sheffield and at least fourteen other former Templars were still free and still wearing the Templar habit.[66] The bull of suppression explicitly forbade, under pain of excommunication, the wearing of the Templar habit. During the next six weeks, Sheffield and the others were absolved by the archbishop from the excommunication which they had incurred by continuing to wear the habit in which they had been professed.[67] These fifteen former Templars, unlike their brothers who had earlier evaded trial, were not called abandoners of the habit and apostates, but wearers of the habit and excommunicates.[68]

Briefly, in the 1390s, the word 'apostate' was applied to another group of religious who scarcely conform to stereotypical runaways. We catch only glimpses of them: friars who left England to study and take degrees abroad. As early as December 1390 the English Dominicans complained to the king that some friars were vicious, apostate and condemned to prisons of their order for crossing the sea and for deceitfully and fraudulently acquiring the degree of Master and other exemptions, whereas English Dominicans by custom take their degrees at Oxford or Cambridge. The king replied by denying such friars the customary liberties, honours and graces accorded to masters.[69] The mendicant orders joined to bring the matter before parliament on 22 January 1397, where they complained that friars were taking theological degrees at foreign universities without permission. It was therefore ordained that no friar should leave the country without permission under penalty of losing the king's protection; those who had returned with foreign degrees must renounce them.[70] Whether moved by this ordinance or some other force, Geoffrey Launde, a Dominican friar, recently returned from the University of Cologne as a master of theology,

---

[66] For publication at York, see ibid., no. 2362. The bull *Vox in excelso* had been issued on 22 March 1312. Archbishop Winchelsey complained in 1312 about a similar problem of former Templars (unnamed) wandering about in his province (*Reg. Winchelsey, Canterbury* 2. 1240–1).

[67] *Reg. Greenfield, York* 5. no. 2364 and n.

[68] As late as 1318 Pope John XXII was complaining about Templars who were wearing lay clothes and acting as laymen – some even contracting matrimony – mindless of their vows which bind perpetually, the suppression of their order notwithstanding (York, Borthwick Institute, Register Melton, fos. 633v–634).

[69] The text is in Rymer, *Foedera* 3. 4. 65 (*CPR, 1388–92*, pp. 330–1). An exemplification was entered on the patent rolls in 1403 (ibid., *1401–05*, p. 313).

[70] *Rotuli parliamentorum* 3. 341–2. Exemplifications were made on the patent rolls by the Dominicans and Carmelites in April and May 1397 (*CPR, 1396–99*, pp. 107, 114).

in 1398 protested that he had papal permission to study at Cologne and that the General Chapter of the order held at Frankfurt had confirmed him in all the privileges pertaining to that degree. The king pardoned him from the consequences of the parliamentary statute of the previous year: he need not renounce the degree nor its privileges.[71] What lay behind all this is not apparent, but this brief concern of the friars shows yet another extension of the word 'apostate', here to doctors of theology who took degrees at foreign universities, allegedly without permission.[72]

And pilgrims became apostates. The Holy Year of 1350 was the occasion. When Boniface VIII announced the first Holy Year (for 1300), his bull *Antiquorum habet* called for the celebration of a Holy Year at 100-year intervals.[73] Pope Clement VI reduced the interval to fifty years and declared 1350 a Holy Year.[74] It opened at Christmas 1349 and by Easter more than 1,200,000 pilgrims had come to Rome (including the poet Petrarch), many in thanksgiving for surviving the Plague. Among these pilgrims were pilgrims from England – 'innumerabilis multitudo', according to one chronicler – and among these pilgrims from England were apostate religious.[75] These were religious in good standing who asked for permission to go to Rome as pilgrims, were refused and went anyway or who were given permission and overstayed their leave or, having been given permission, travelled in secular clothes.[76] In no case is there any suggestion that they had

---

[71] Ibid., p. 425.

[72] A century earlier the *Liber sextus* of Boniface VIII *ipso facto* excommunicated religious who went to *studia* without permission as well as religious who, while there, rashly abandoned the religious habit (3.24.2 in VI°).

[73] The text is in *Bullarium romanum* 4. 156–7. See Joseph Lecler, 'Boniface VIII et le jubilé de 1300', *Etudes* 264 (1950) 145–57, and the more general article by E. Jombart, 'Jubilé', *Dictionnaire de droit canonique* 6. 191–203.

[74] See Diana Wood, *Clement VI: The Pontificate and Ideas of an Avignon Pope* (Cambridge, 1989), pp. 90–5.

[75] E. Venables, ed., *Chronicon abbatie de Parco Lude* (Lincoln, 1891), p. 29. Parks conservatively estimated that about 400 English pilgrims went to Rome during this Holy Year (George B. Parks, *The English Traveler to Italy* (Rome, 1954), pp. 356–7). Royal permission was required to make the pilgrimage, and a list of 377 who received royal licences is in *Foedera* 3. 1. 203–4, but none of the 'apostates' is among them.

[76] There were, of course, pilgrim religious who went from England to Rome with permission and who did not overstay their leave; e.g., Henry de Lisle, prior of the Augustinian priory of Horsley in Glos. (*Sede vacante Reg., Worcester*, p. 245). Richard Fitzralph, archbishop of Armagh, acting for Edward III, had tried without success to convince Clement VI in August 1349 to allow cloistered religious from England to gain the jubilee indulgence without having to undergo the hazards of a journey to Rome (see

abandoned the religious life and returned to the world with the intention of not returning to their order. That in some cases they wore secular clothes while travelling should not be surprising, for, when the newly elected abbot of St Albans travelled to Avignon for confirmation in 1349, the monks travelling with him separated at Calais and donned secular clothes 'because of the discord between the kingdoms'.[77] The offence of the pilgrim-apostates was not abandonment of the religious life but simply that they had left without permission or dallied at Rome without permission or dressed as laymen.

Eighteen of these pilgrim-apostates appear in the papal registers because, before returning to England, they sought absolution. Two of these – Nicholas de Stanton, a Cistercian monk of Grace Dieu Abbey (Monmouthshire), and Peter de Hereford, a Benedictine monk of Crowland Abbey (Lincolnshire) – stayed longer than permitted, Hereford at least until May 1351.[78] Among the others was the prior of Westminster Abbey, Benedict de Chertsey, who said that it was for safety's sake that he had worn lay clothes.[79] Worcester priory had sent one of its monks, Walter de Winforton, to Avignon on business, but, once at Avignon, Winforton decided to go on to Rome for the Jubilee indulgence.[80] Three monks left Peterborough Abbey for Rome without permission in October 1350 and became apostates.[81]

The eighteen pilgrim-apostates are known to us because they sought reconciliation according to the constitution *Pastor bonus* of Benedict XII (1335).[82] For each of these apostates two papal documents were drawn up: one was a grant given to the apostate, while he was in Rome, permitting him to return to his religious house, and the other was a mandate to three (named) English ecclesiastics to effect his return and reconciliation. How many English pilgrim-apostates did not use this procedure we may never

---

Katherine Walsh, *A Fourteenth-Century Scholar and Primate: Richard Fitzralph in Oxford, Avignon and Armagh* (Oxford, 1981), pp. 288–96; Guillaume Mollat, 'Le jubilé de 1350', *Journal des savants* 1963, p. 192). For modern Holy Years, professed religious could gain the Jubilee indulgence without leaving their houses (see. E. Jombart, 'Le jubilé de 1950', *Nouvelle revue théologique* 71 (1949) 932–3).

[77] 'quia tunc orta fuit discordia inter regna' (*Gesta abbatum* 2. 383). Also, a monk and four nuns, mistakenly thought to be English while travelling through France at this time, were arrested and imprisoned (Mollat, 'Le jubilé', p. 194).

[78] *CPL* 3. 385, 429.

[79] Ibid., 3. 384, 387.   [80] Ibid., 3. 388.

[81] Ibid., 3. 382.   [82] See below, pp. 123–5.

know. The eighteen received their papal letters between April 1350 and July 1351. After that time none appears until 1390, when Pope Boniface IX absolved John Wyom, a Cistercian monk of Kirkstead Abbey (Lincolnshire), from apostasy in connection with the Holy Year called by Urban VI for 1389, a solitary echo of the events of mid-century.[83]

The extension of the word apostate to include the Templars, student friars and Holy Year pilgrims must be distinguished from the misuse of the word or, at the least, the use in a sense beyond the canonical sense. A popular, non-canonical usage broadened the meaning of apostate to include anyone leaving a religious house without permission. The traditional view of the canon law and the canonists was that rejection of the religious life was essential for apostasy. This rejection could be seen in the Templars refusing to appear for questioning and apparently – for so they were charged – for wearing secular clothes. Pilgrims leaving England and going to Rome for what had to be months – some even travelling in secular clothes – can be seen as an extension of the classical meaning. Also, friars who abandoned their English friaries and travelled without permission to continental universities can be seen in this broad context. But now we see, in practice, the calling of any monk absent without permission an apostate. The modern military distinction between deserting and going AWOL (absent without official leave) exactly parallels this situation. The religious who left his house without permission and went to the village for a night's entertainment had not abandoned the religious life. He was absent without leave and disobedient and possibly mischievous as well, but he had not deserted the religious life. Yet, in the late middle ages, he stood in peril of being called an apostate. The canonist Joannes Andreae, writing in the middle of the fourteenth century, recognized that the word 'apostate' had a broad as well as a strict meaning and that the broad sense was not the canonical meaning.[84] Also, particular orders might use for their purposes a broader definition. The Carmelites, for example, in 1357 adopted this broad approach: any friar who, without permission, left his

---

[83] In 1450 Katherine Thornyf, a nun of Wykeham Priory (Yorks.), without permission, left with another nun on a Jubilee pilgrimage to Rome. The other nun died on the journey, and Katherine Thornyf was said to have been living with a married man in London. Repentant, she approached the archbishop of York, who ordered her readmission (*VCH, Yorks.* 3. 183).

[84] *In tertium decretalium librum novella commentaria* (Venice, 1581), 3.31.5.

convent, whether by day or night, was considered apostate even if he returned the same day or night. Also, a friar who had permission to leave but who failed to return at the assigned time was considered apostate.[85] The examples of *apostasia late dicta* given here are drawn from the visitations of the English Premonstratensian houses by the reforming Bishop Redman during the last two decades or so of the fifteenth century.

Redman remained abbot of Shap (Westmorland) even after he became bishop of St Asaph in 1471 and undertook with diligence and seriousness the arduous task of visiting between 1475 and 1503, perhaps as many as nine times, the thirty-two houses of his order, which required him to travel from the Scottish Borders to deepest Devon. And he found what he called 'apostates'.[86] No doubt he found true canonical apostates, i.e., apostates who had returned to the world. Such were Thomas Ledley, canon of Tupholme Abbey in Lincolnshire, who pleaded for mercy in 1482, and William Darntone of Beauchief Abbey in Derbyshire, whom Redman declared excommunicate in 1500.[87] There may have been other true apostates among over sixty canons called apostate by Bishop Redman, but this conclusion is far from necessary. One gets a strong hint of something else happening here. In 1488 at St Radegund's Abbey in Kent the visitor described Richard Beltone as apostate and, what is worse, wearing secular clothes and living in the world, to which Beltone replied that he had permission and, in the event, had returned.[88] Yet, at that same visitation at St Radegund's, Redman made it very clear what he meant by apostasy: 'We strictly order under pain of apostasy that none of the brothers should presume to go outside the monastic enclosure without the permission of his own superior.'[89] Three years later, while visiting the abbey at Torre in Devon, Redman used similar words.[90] For him, it is quite clear, apostasy meant leaving the monastery without permission, pure and simple. And

---

[85] Paul F. Robinson, ed., *The Carmelite Constitutions of 1357* (Rome, 1992), p. 303.

[86] For a general analysis of Redman's visitation see Knowles, *RO* 3, chap. 4. The visitation records are found in F. A. Gasquet, ed., *CAP* (3 vols.; Camden Soc., 3rd ser., vols. 6, 10, 12, 1904–6) as corrected by H. M. Colvin, *The White Canons in England* (Oxford, 1951), pp. 389–91.

[87] *CAP* 3. 159; 2. 69–70.

[88] Ibid., 3. 101–2.

[89] 'Precipimus eciam districte, sub pena apostasie, ne aliquis fratrum extra septa monasterii exire presumat, sine licencia sui proprii prelati' (ibid., 3. 99–100).

[90] Ibid., 3. 150.

so he used this definition in practice. At Titchfield Abbey in Hampshire, William Gloucester was declared apostate for staying outside the monastery all night, unbeknown to his abbot, drinking and brawling.[91] William Hankyn, a canon of Welbeck in Nottinghamshire, became apostate by eating meat in the houses of laymen night and day and being unable to rise to sing Matins.[92] Thomas Prestone of Bayham Abbey in Sussex went out secretly at night to meet Agnes Skinner, and, Richard Wolfet, a canon of Beauchief Abbey in Derbyshire, went out for secret assignations with Joan Stevyne. To Redman, both canons were apostates.[93] All of these 'apostates' presumably returned after their adventures, perhaps very late at night or during the next day. John York of Newbo Abbey in Lincolnshire did not even stay out over night: although the abbot had refused him permission, he left anyway but had second thoughts and returned the same day, yet he was called apostate.[94] None of these Premonstratensian canons had abandoned the religious life and returned to the world. They were not truly apostate, in the strict canonical sense of the term, yet the reforming visitor used a broad brush and, in doing so, blurred the distinction between absence without permission, even if that absence involved unmonk-like behaviour, and the abandonment of the religious life itself. These canons were not fugitives or vagabonds, but disobedient religious who returned, perhaps wearied and possibly even repentant, from their misdeeds, but return they did. Contemporary canonists would have recognized that Redman in his reforming zeal was using the term broadly. The canonists who in 1535 drew up the proposed new English ecclesiastical laws gave a traditional definition: 'He is considered apostate who, although he has not been properly dispensed, wanders about outside the monastic enclosure, either having abandoned the religious habit or acting without the permission of his superior.'[95]

This chapter has been an exploration of the meaning of apostasy as seen in the dynamics of a living institution. It has also been an attempt to rescue apostasy from the stereotype that pictures the

[91] Ibid., 3. 128.   [92] Ibid., 3. 189–90.
[93] Ibid., 2. 78; 2. 66–7.   [94] Ibid., 3. 65.
[95] 'Apostata uero reputatur qui absque licita dispensatione uel abiecto sue religionis habitu uel sine sui superioris assensu extra cepta monasterii sui uagatur' (London, BL, Add. MS 48040, fo. 30r). For this collection see F. Donald Logan, 'The Henrician Canons', *BIHR* 47 (1974) 99–103.

apostate solely in terms of the monk fleeing by night over monastic walls, the abbey's silver in his bag and the neighbour's daughter waiting on the other side. One can find such apostates, but apostasy meant much more, as this book will endeavour to show. Before exploring alternatives to apostasy, let us consider an actual case that exhibits some of the points raised in this chapter.

THE CASE OF THE QUESTIONABLE MONK OF CANTERBURY

Something very strange indeed happened at St Augustine's Abbey, Canterbury, on 2 April 1322. It had to do with the admission into that Benedictine community of Dr Peter Dene, secular priest of Chichester diocese and well known canon lawyer.[96] By that time Dr Dene's relationship with St Augustine's had extended over two decades. In 1300 he had appeared before the monks in their chapter house and, in return for receiving an annual retainer of £10 to represent the interests of the abbey, particularly in affairs touching the archbishop, the archdeacon of Canterbury and the prior of Canterbury Cathedral priory, he promised on oath to be faithful to St Augustine's 'omnibus diebus vitae suae'.[97] The reader, at the end of the story, may render a judgement about Dene's keeping of his oath.

In the years after the taking of this oath Dene pursued a career that brought him into conflict with Archbishop Winchelsey, who in 1302 attempted to deprive him of his ecclesiastical benefices. Dene, however, continued to show considerable skill in acquiring benefices, and by the time of the principal events to be narrated here he claimed canonries in the cathedral churches of York, London and Wells as well as in the collegiate churches of Southwell and Wimborne.[98] He was an influential cleric at York, where, in addition to holding the prebend of Grindale (probably to 1322), he also served as Archbishop Greenfield's vicar-general in 1309 and in 1313. He also donated a window in the north nave aisle

---

[96] He was *doctor utriusque iuris*, whose university Dr Emden was unable to determine (*BRUO* 3. 2168–9).

[97] Roger Twysden, ed., 'Chronica Guillielmi Thorne', *Historiae Anglicanae scriptores decem* (London, 1652), col. 1979, which may be more accessible in A. H. Davis's English translation, *William Thorne's Chronicle of St Augustine's Abbey, Canterbury* (Oxford, 1934), p. 348. Hereafter, they will be cited as Twysden and *Thorne's Chronicle* respectively.

[98] For these details see *BRUO*.

at York Minster, where he is depicted (Plate 2).[99] His wealth allowed him not only to donate a window at York but also allowed him to make generous gifts to St Augustine's and to build houses there within the monastic walls, presumably for himself and his household.[100]

Not one to disdain political involvement, Dene supported the party of Thomas, earl of Lancaster, against King Edward II. With the defeat of Lancaster on 16 March 1322 at Boroughbridge and his execution at Pontefract a week later, Dene, 'being threatened with arrest, imprisonment, loss of position, the seizure of all his property and even with death', fled south and took refuge in St Augustine's and in the Benedictine habit of that monastery.[101] He arrived at the monastery on 30 March, a scarce two weeks after Boroughbridge, received the monastic habit on that very day and three days later – on 2 April 1322 – Peter Dene made his profession as a monk of St Augustine's. No wait of a year of probation for the frightened Dr Dene, now Brother Peter, the almost instant monk. But was he truly a monk or merely, as the translator of the chronicle calls him, 'a sham monk'?[102] This was a question frequently raised in the years to come.

Many unusual circumstances attended his profession, beside his fleeing dire threats and his almost instantaneous profession. First, there was the disposition made of his earthly goods. On the day of his profession, no doubt before the act of profession itself, Peter Dene drew up his last will and testament.[103] He left all his goods, not already promised otherwise, to the monastery of St Augustine's, Canterbury, with only one not insignificant condition, that he would continue to have use of them. He bequeathed his canon law library, which included Gratian's *Decretum*, the Decretals of Gregory IX, and commentaries by

---

99 See G. E. Aylmer and Reginald Cant, *A History of York Minster* (Oxford, 1977), pp. 349–50. I am grateful to Dr David Smith for calling this window to my attention.

100 Twysden, cols. 2012–13; *Thorne's Chronicle*, pp. 399–400.

101 Twysden, col. 2055; *Thorne's Chronicle*, pp. 463–4. Dene may have been allied with Bartholomew, lord of Badlesmere, against whom the king issued a writ for judgement at Canterbury on 25 March 1322 (*CPR, 1321–24*, p. 149) and who was executed on 14 April 1322 at Bleen near Canterbury (Cambridge, Trinity College MS R.5.41, fo. 118; see also *Flores historiarum* (ed. H. R. Luard; 3 vols.; RS, 1890) 3. 207). I am grateful to Professor J. R. S. Phillips for the reference to Badlesmere's execution.

102 *Thorne's Chronicle*, p. 704.

103 The text of the testament and accompanying indenture is in Twysden, cols. 2037–8, and in *Thorne's Chronicle*, pp. 436–9.

Hostiensis, Innocent IV, Guido de Baysio, William Durandus, Joannes Monachus and Joannes Andreae, and, in addition, a five-volume collection of Roman law texts.[104] He remitted to the monastery the sum of 350 marks owed to him in repayment of a loan and also a further 150 marks, which he had deposited in the monastery. In addition, Dene bequeathed to the monastery 95 Florentine florins, 5 *moutons d'or* and 10 *florins de Mas*. A considerable amount of silver, carefully described in an indenture deposited the previous October in the care of the monastery, completed the bequest. Thus, since he had disposed of his goods, Dene could proceed to religious profession. All of these things, it should be repeated, he would continue to have *ad usum suum*.[105] The canonist had cleverly exercised his skills.

The canonist's work did not end with this cleverness, if we can believe Dene's later recounting, which the chronicler appears to have believed. He then turned his skills to the profession itself. Dene contrived that his religious profession would not be the usual simple, unconditional commitment to the monastic life. He hedged it in, as the chronicler relates, 'under many conditions, qualifications and terms, which were openly expressed by him and accepted and granted by those amongst whom he was admitted both before and at his entrance'.[106] The terms – if we should believe the unfriendly chronicler – in effect allowed him to live a free and independent life. He would, of course, wear the habit and live at the monastery, yet he would not live in the dormitory but, rather, with his household in the houses which he had built north of the infirmary. Besides, he would not be expected to join with the other monks in church, chapter, refectory or elsewhere for singing the divine office or for anything else. He was to be free to do as he pleased, or, rather, 'as the Lord should inspire him and as it pleased Peter'.[107] More significantly than these cosy

---

[104] His other books, those kept in the monastery and elsewhere, he had already given as donations *inter vivos*.

[105] His goods passed immediately upon his profession to the monastery since 'when a man becomes "professed in religion", his heir at once inherits from him any land that he has, and, if he has made a will, it takes effect at once as though he were naturally dead' (F. Pollock and F. W. Maitland, *The History of English Law before the Time of Edward I* (2nd edn, reissued with introduction by S. F. C. Milsom; 2 vols.; Cambridge, 1968) 1. 434). It was this provision of law that allowed the monastery later to charge him with theft.

[106] Twysden, col. 2055; *Thorne's Chronicle*, p. 464.

[107] 'prout sibi dominus inspiraret et de ipsius Petri libera procederet voluntate' (Twysden, col. 2055).

2 *Dr Peter Dene*. From heraldic window (n23), north nave aisle, York Minster
(Photo: The Conway Library, Courtauld Institute of Art)

arrangements, Peter Dene made what must have been a public statement: he declared, we are told, that by taking this profession he did not intend to bind himself in any way to regular observance. No matter that he wore the habit, no matter that he actually made a religious profession, no matter how long he would continue to live in the monastery, or, indeed, no matter anything else, he neither intended nor wanted to be bound by the religious life. Did he, then, become a monk? Was this religious profession true, genuine and valid? Had he not attached to it explicitly stated conditions which vitiated the profession itself? Was it not tantamount to his saying, 'Although I may say the words, I do not intend them to mean what they say'? The questions were to be raised, even at the Roman curia.

Questions were raised, for eight years later Peter Dene fled the monastery. The monks of St Augustine's said that he was an apostate, but he was to deny this, since how could he be an apostate if he was not really a monk. The story is known in some detail to us, and, although the sources present somewhat conflicting narratives, the broad outlines are quite clear.

The monastery's chronicle says that it was eight years after his entry – it may, in fact, have been nine years – that Peter Dene, feeling that the threat to his goods and person had abated, informed the abbot that he wanted to leave. When no serious attention seemed to be given to his request, he devised a plan of escape.[108] On a winter's night in December 1331, he told the servant not to waken him in the morning, because he would sleep in.[109] Just before midnight Dene threw off his monkish habit, put on secular clothes, took with him some of his silver and made his way to the monastic wall just opposite the church of St Martin. There the rector with accomplices, by prearrangement, was waiting on the other side. Dene alerted the rector by throwing a stone over the wall. The men on the other side had two ladders; they climbed up one and lowered the other into the monastic garden. Soon Dene was over the wall and on his way by horse to Bishopsbourne, about four miles away. His flight discovered, search parties were sent off, even to the coast. Not only were the monks actively searching for

---

[108] This narrative follows the account found in Twysden, cols. 2056–60, and *Thorne's Chronicle*, pp. 465–7.

[109] The date given by the monastic chronicler is 1330, but the chronicler, elsewhere in his account, is one year off and the year 1331 seems to the present writer to fit in better with the narrative.

him, but also a royal party, no doubt responding to the writ for the capture of an apostate. At length, it was the latter, led by William Reculver, steward of the archbishop's liberty, which discovered Dene. Before Reculver could bring him to the royal jail at Maidstone, Reculver's party was overtaken by three monks of St Augustine's, who snatched Dene and brought their apostate back to his monastery. They led him triumphantly into the great abbatial church, while the monks were singing Vespers.[110]

The unsympathetic chronicler states that Dene, once back at St Augustine's and facing a harsh and severely restricted life with the concessions made to him at his entry about to be withdrawn, issued a statement that he truly was a monk and had made his profession absolutely.[111] When the immediate threats disappeared, the canonist secretly appealed to the pope, and, on 1 July 1332, Pope John XXII responded by repeating the essence of Dene's argument and by appointing three papal commissioners to investigate.[112] The substance of Dene's appeal was that he had made his religious profession *simulate* (i.e., he had only gone through the motions) out of fear of his enemies: he had been play-acting. The abbot, he said, understood this: Dene had expressly declared his intention in front of the community in chapter. He wore the monastic habit merely as a pretence and with the intention, once it was safe, to return to the world. Yet, when he did leave, he was violently seized, virtually imprisoned in his house, deprived of food and allowed neither to attend Mass nor to receive the Eucharist.

The question to be determined was clearly a question of fact:

---

[110] Royal pardons were given on 26 January 1332 to the three monks who seized Dene from Reculver (*CPR, 1330–34*, p. 239), and on the same day a pardon was given to Dene from charges of theft, which had been brought by the monastery (ibid.). The suit against Dene had apparently been brought before Justice Geoffrey le Scrope in King's Bench (Twysden, col. 2066; *Thorne's Chronicle*, p. 480), where, on 31 March 1332, Richard Wilughby was ordered to supersede the monastery's plea of robbery against Dene since he had been pardoned (*CCR, 1330–33*, p. 549).

[111] The texts of two recantations, different from each other, suggest two separate events. Besides that given in the chronicle (Twysden, cols. 2058–9; *Thorne's Chronicle*, pp. 469–70), which was probably made shortly after his return, there is the recantation referred to in a letter by the prior of Christ Church, which was made after Dene had appealed *ad curiam Romanam* (*Lit. Cant.* 2. 9–10).

[112] *CPL* 2. 369. The text is given in full in the monastic chronicle (Twysden, cols. 2060–2; *Thorne's Chronicle*, pp. 472–4). In the meantime, a report had been brought that Henry, the new earl of Lancaster, suspected Dene of stealing from the treasury of his deceased brother and of concealing it in the monastery. At this time the bishops of Norwich and Worcester, on their way to France on royal business, were staying at St Augustine's and giving advice to the monks about the Dene affair (*CPR, 1330–34*, pp. 466–7).

did Peter Dene make religious profession on 2 April 1322 unconditionally and, hence, validly or conditionally and hence invalidly? It was to determine this question of fact that the pope appointed three commissioners: Richard de Oxenden, the new prior of Christ Church, Canterbury, Dr William Reynham, canon of St Paul's, London, and Master Henry de Iddesworth, official of the court of Canterbury (i.e., the Court of Arches). Their task was to go to St Augustine's Abbey, interview Dene privately and, if his story was true, free him from the monastery. Obstacles dogged their mission. Iddesworth was unable to go to Canterbury, and thus it was Oxenden and Reynham who on 14 November 1332 presented themselves at the monastery. The monastery would not accept the papal letters: forged, they said, and, besides, there was, over erasures, new writing in a different hand and with different ink. In addition, even if the document was authentic, several clauses were so ambiguous as to admit of several meanings. There the matter rested for the moment. One can sense Oxenden's unease. Within the next three months he wrote for counsel to Archbishop Mepham, to Reynham (now, it seems, unwilling to return to Canterbury), to Iddesworth (no more anxious now than before to get involved), and, finally, in apparent desperation, to his old Oxford teacher, Master John de Offord, now Dean of Arches.[113]

The decisive day came. Delaying and obfuscating tactics now past, on 23 February 1333 Prior Oxenden, unaccompanied by his fellow papal commissioners but emboldened by a large crowd ('in multitudine copiosa'), made up of monks from the cathedral priory and others as well, approached the great gate to the monastery. It was closed to them and chained against their breaking through, and inside were guards, who allowed Oxenden and a number of his companions to enter by a wicket door one by one. Left outside were about two hundred men. Prior Oxenden, at the head of this small band, came to the great west door of the church itself. It too was closed against them, and, again, they entered through a tiny wicket. One by one, they trickled into the massive monastic church. The scenes that followed must have been related, generation after generation, by the monks of St Augustine's. Not quite murder in the cathedral, but high drama at least.

[113] For these letters see *Lit. Cant.* 2. 7–10, 17–19, 40–3. See also *Ninth Report of the Royal Commission on Historical Manuscripts*, pt 1, appendix, p. 81.

Prior Oxenden went to different parts of the church and read out the papal letters containing his commission. Entering, no doubt from the north, cloister side, came a party led by the prior of St Augustine's, Stephen Hakynton, and including Peter Dene, eight other monks and a large group of clergy and laity. They would not allow Prior Oxenden to come close to Dene, and, in fact, they formed a circle about Dene so that Oxenden could converse with him only in the hearing of all. There was much shouting as the St Augustine's party tried to drown out the reading of the papal letters. Oxenden demanded access to Dene, but the shouting continued, and, even with the papal commissioner threatening excommunication, Dene was removed from the church and taken back into the monastery.

On the following day (24 February 1333) Prior Oxenden returned and found entrance only through the open cemetery gate. Guards, lined up shoulder to shoulder on either side, formed a way for him to the church. Once inside, he repeated his commission and demanded a private interview with Dene. The monastery wanted its own notaries to take down Dene's testimony. Dene, at first, probably intimidated, agreed, but Oxenden insisted on a private interview, and the monks moved away from Dene, not far away, only fourteen to twenty feet away. Dene gave his answers, at times, *sotto voce* and, at other times, *alto voce*. In the latter he shouted for the benefit of the monks that he was a truly professed monk, wanted to remain so and, if he were asked questions until nightfall, he would give the same answer. When Oxenden told him in a subdued voice that he would release him so that he could pursue his appeal to the Roman court, Dene replied quietly that he would pursue the matter if he were younger in years and stronger in body. Then, raising his voice for all to hear, Dene spoke of the wrongs done to him by Oxenden and his companions.

There he stayed at St Augustine's Abbey, this questionable monk, the question of his profession and apostasy undecided and his body and spirit perhaps broken. But who knows how unhappily? In the year following the events in the abbatial church, the monks selected a seven-monk committee to choose a new abbot, and the list of selectors was led by the name of Peter Dene.[114]

---

[114] *CPL* 2. 405. Prior Stephen Hakynton and another monk of St Augustine's were absolved from excommunications incurred at the time of Prior Oxenden's visit (*Lit. Cant.* 2. 19–20).

Chapter 2

LEGAL ALTERNATIVES

Once professed, could a religious leave without becoming apostate? Was a legal and honourable departure an option for a dissatisfied religious? Did the system have a safety valve? The presence of alternatives could have ameliorated the situation in which the religious life had become a great burden to discontented religious and the discontented in turn, perhaps, an even greater burden to their fellow religious. The possibility of leaving the religious life without committing the crime of apostasy, without incurring excommunication and without being subject to arrest might be seen by modern eyes as a way of enhancing the quality of the religious life itself rather than diminishing it. Medieval eyes, however, viewed the situation differently: vows taken at religious profession, somewhat analogous to marriage vows, were considered permanent. That having been said, what could the discontented religious do? The question merits enquiry.

Was dispensation a practical possibility? Could a profoundly unhappy Carmelite friar of Nottingham or nun of Godstow or monk of Tintern be released from the solemn vows they had professed? How dispensable, if at all, were these vows? That great exponent of papal power, Pope Innocent III, answered that not even the pope himself could dispense from solemn vows. His decretal *Nec aestimet* (1202) held that the rejection of property and a life of chastity were so essential to the monastic life 'ut contra ea nec summus pontifex possit indulgentiam indulgere'.[1] The rigour of this view did not prevail, particularly after Innocent IV (1243–54), writing not as pope but as canonist, expressed the view that he could conceive of a monk with property and with a wife: poverty and chastity were not intrinsically but only positively connected to the monastic state. Hence for great and true causes the pope can dispense. For him, there was understood in every vow

---

[1] X.3.36.6.

the phrase 'unless it pleases God otherwise', and, of course, the Vicar of Christ can decide what pleases God.[2] This more lenient view was to become the accepted teaching henceforward.[3] Theory and the teaching of the canonists apart, what actually happened in practice? One can point to some extremely rare cases where dispensations were granted for *raisons d'état*; for example, the papal dispensation granted in 1391 to the Cistercian monk who had become king of Portugal that allowed him to marry the daughter of John of Gaunt.[4] These are not our present concern. The question here relates to the practical possibility of dispensation for members of the religious order in medieval England – for the discontented Carmelite friar, Benedictine nun or Cistercian monk – and asks how possible it was for a religious to be dispensed and return to the world. In a word, such full dispensations were simply not granted. There were only three possible avenues of legal departure: a change of house or order, appointment as an honorary papal chaplain or dispensation to hold a benefice. Of these three only the first was open to all religious, women as well as men, and the second and third only to male religious and, for them, only in the fifteenth and sixteenth centuries. These three will be examined in turn.

TRANSITUS – TRANSFER

To gain release from the religious life was difficult for all and impossible for many, yet the discontented religious could seek a transfer. The principle was established by a decretal of Innocent III of 1206.[5] The canonists called it *transitus*. It was based on the premise that one's profession was, at root, a profession to the religious life in general and not merely to its manifestation in a single house or a single order. The classical phrase was *transitus ad ordinem strictiorem* or *arctiorem*, which, on the face of it, seems to mean a transfer from an order with a less severe rule to an order with a more severe rule. Canonists, however, would distinguish

---

[2] 'nisi aliter deo placeat' (*Commentaria . . . super libros quinque decretalium* (Frankfurt, 1570) 3.36.6).
[3] For the general subject of dispensation see J. Brys, *De dispensatione in iure canonico praesertim apud decretistas et decretalistas usque ad medium saeculum decimum quartum* (Bruges, 1925), pp. 209–20.
[4] *CPL* 4. 367.
[5] It was included in the Decretals in 1234 (X.3.31.18).

between the historical severity of the rule itself and the actual
severity of a particular house here and now. The rule of the
Augustinian canons, for example, might be seen historically as less
severe than the rule of the Benedictine monks, but, in practice, a
monk transferring from a specific house of monks to a specific
house of canons could be transferring to a stricter religion.[6]

Restrictions and rules limited the *transitus*. The Cistercian order,
in particular, seemed wary of this whole process. As early as 1195
the General Chapter forbade the reception of Carthusians and
also the transfer of their own monks to the Carthusians unless
permission were given by the order *a quo*.[7] In 1233 the Cistercians
decreed that any of their monks transferring to the Dominican or
Franciscan friars was to be considered an apostate, and in 1266 they
further decreed that friars from these orders would not be received
unless the General Chapter itself gave permission.[8] This Cistercian
xenophobia was not limited to the mendicants. In 1251, they
sensed a great danger from their monks transferring to the
Benedictine order and, indeed, to other orders and decreed their
excommunication.[9] The mendicants, besides being restricted in
receiving religious from other orders, were themselves restricted
in transferring to other orders. Papal bulls to the Franciscans and
Dominicans required the consent of the superiors of transferees.[10]
The Council of Vienne, in 1312, decreed that friars who became
monks could never hold office in their monastery nor have a voice
in chapter.[11] In 1335, Pope Benedict XII, recognizing that such
transfers could cause great disturbance, ordered that henceforth a
friar would require papal permission to become a monk.[12] In the
same year, Benedict XII labelled as apostates those religious of
any order who transfer to another religion and to another habit

---

[6] This is summed up by the fifteenth-century canonist Panormitanus, citing earlier
teaching (*Commentaria in tertium decretalium librum* (Lyons, 1586) 3.31.10).

[7] Canivez, *Statuta* 1. 187–8.

[8] Ibid., 2. 24.

[9] Ibid., 2. 361.

[10] See Luke Wadding, *Annales minorum* (2nd edn; 25 vols.; Rome, 1731–1886) 2. 400,
433–44, etc., and William A. Hinnebusch, *The Early English Friars Preachers* (Rome,
1951), pp. 268–71.

[11] J. Aberigo *et al.*, eds., *Conciliorum oecumenicorum decreta* (Basle, 1962), p. 346; also 3.9.1 in
Clem. For the experience of the Premonstratensians with *transitus*, particularly in the
twelfth century, see Douglas Roby, 'Philip of Harvengt's Contribution to the Question
of Passage from One Religious Order to Another', *Analecta Praemonstratensia* 49 (1973)
69–100.

[12] *Bullarium romanum* 4. 328–9.

without papal or other necessary permission.[13] In the context of dire warnings and threats and of fluctuating regulations, what seems to have happened in practice was that a religious desiring to transfer would get permission from the superior *a quo* (abbot, prior, abbess, prioress, etc.), frequently in the form of letters dimissory, and would also get permission from the superior *ad quem*.[14] The latter would not be necessary if, as occasionally happened, a general letter was given, allowing *transitus ad aliquem*. If one's own superior refused, letters from the local bishop or from the pope could be sought. Archbishop Chichele in 1425 gave permission for William Christmas, a monk of Christ Church, Canterbury, to transfer to any other monastery of equal or stricter severity; in the event, Christmas migrated to the Cluniac priory of Monkton Farleigh in Wiltshire.[15] Numerous examples of papal letters permitting transfer can be seen in the calendars of papal registers. On occasion, these letters, whether episcopal or papal, would be general, allowing the religious to transfer to any order of stricter observance or, frequently, of equally severe observance or, even at times, of less severe observance. By the fifteenth century canonists, including William Lyndwode, held that there could be *transitus ad ordinem laxiorem*, since the profession was to the religious life of poverty, chastity and obedience and since these elements were present wherever the religious life was practised, even in less severe orders.[16] Thus, in 1429, a brother of Syon Abbey in Middlesex was permitted by papal letters to transfer to a less severe order because of his physical infirmities.[17]

The presence, then, of a transferred religious in a religious house was probably a fairly common occurrence. Almost as a matter of fact, the St Albans chronicler notes that the saintly Abbot de la Mare (1349–96) granted permission for four of his monks to

[13] Ibid., 4. 327. In a most unusual case, a royal writ was sent in 1255 to all abbots and priors, ordering them not to receive any of the monks of Winchester Cathedral Priory, 'many of whom are wandering about all over England', without the permission of the bishop-elect or the prior (*CPR, 1247–58*, p. 439). The cathedral priory was in turmoil at this time over the election of Aylmer of Valence as bishop; the new bishop deprived the prior and expelled others. See *Ann. mon.* 2. 95; *CPL* 1. 305; *VCH, Hants.* 2. 18–19, 109.

[14] The changing regulations, particularly for the friars, are summarized in William A. Hinnebusch, *The History of the Dominican Order*, vol. 1 (New York, 1966), pp. 321–6.

[15] *Reg. Chichele, Canterbury* 4. 263.

[16] Lyndwode, *Provinciale* (Oxford, 1679), 5.6.1. s.v. *laxiorem*.

[17] *CPL* 8. 174–5. See also ibid. 3. 429, where, in 1351, John Kemp, a Carmelite, was granted permission to transfer to the Benedictine abbey of St Mary's, York, because of physical weakness.

transfer.[18] We can even catch a glimpse of the occasional religious who transferred and then transferred back. For example, Nicholas de Aldeburi, a Dominican friar, transferred to Dunstable Priory of Augustinian canons in Bedfordshire and then, in 1274, returned to the Dominicans.[19] At Durham Priory, Prior Wessinton, many of his monks dissenting, gave permission to Robert Erghowe to enter the Dominican priory at Bamburgh. When the Dominicans at Bamburgh refused him admission, Erghowe went to their priory at Berwick, where he spent a fortnight, only to leave and attempt readmission to Durham. A new prior at Durham was adamant, and this unfortunate monk and would-be friar was not taken back.[20] More extreme, indeed, was the case of Avice de Beverley, a nun of Nunburnholme in the East Riding of Yorkshire, who, it was reported in 1285, had during her thirty years as a nun of that nunnery left three times to lead a stricter life and each time returned and who, on the fourth return, was not welcomed. The archbishop of York intervened at that point, but to what effect is not clear.[21]

In 1394, on his way home from the funeral of Queen Anne at Westminster Abbey, the abbot of Glastonbury encountered at Thatcham, Berkshire, a monk of Rochester Priory, who, in the abbot's words, was 'without companion, money or a book from which to read the canonical hours'.[22] The hapless monk showed the great abbot a very general letter allowing him to transfer to a stricter order. The abbot sent him to the Carthusians, who refused to accept him, for they knew what the abbot presumably did not know, that the hapless monk had tried several times to transfer to

[18] Thomas Banstede to Bradwell Priory (Bucks.) and John Folsham to Rochester Priory, both Benedictine houses; Stephen Hertford to the Franciscans and Robert Astone to the Cistercian Abbey at Warden (Beds.) (*Gesta abbatum* 2. 416).

[19] *Ann. mon.* 3. 261.

[20] For the description of this case and other cases of *transitus* see R. B. Dobson, *Durham Priory, 1400–1450* (Cambridge, 1973), p. 76

[21] *Reg. Wickwane, York*, no. 308. In 1306 an Avice de Beverley, possibly the same woman, was elected prioress of Nunburnholme (*VCH, Yorks.* 3. 118). In the late fourteenth century, Richard Lyming, a Trinitarian, incurred apostasy and excommunication by leaving Moatenden and transferring to the Cistercians at Boxley, both in Kent, but he later returned and was reconciled at Moatenden (*CPL* 5. 276). Similarly, Richard Lek, an Augustinian canon of Kyme Priory (Lincs.), left his priory about 1430 without permission and entered the Franciscans and was considered apostate by the Augustinians. In 1440, repentant, he asked to be readmitted to Kyme Priory (*Linc. Vis.* 2. 169).

[22] 'sine comite, sine expensis et sine libro in quo persolveret horas canonicas et debitas Deo laudes' (Pantin, *Chapters* 3. 84–7). Pantin (p. 86n.) suggests that this migrating monk was John Craye.

different Carthusian houses and, when given permission, remained only a month or so before returning to Rochester. This same monk also tried his vocation with the Cluniacs at Bermondsey, and finally, given permission to transfer to the Franciscans at Cambridge, he instead journeyed to Rome, where he received papal letters restoring him to his former place at Rochester Priory. He probably migrated yet again in 1401. This is but an admittedly extreme example that illustrates the general point that the procedure of transfer formed part of the religious life as it was actually lived.

Misunderstandings frequently occurred, and a religious migrating without the immediate superior's permission, which in some circumstances he could legally do, might stand in peril of being called an apostate. The early attraction of the newly arrived friars in England prompted such difficulties. In 1233, for example, two Augustinian canons of Dunstable Priory in Bedfordshire, acting without permission, left their priory through a broken window, scaled the walls and went to Oxford to join the Franciscans, taking with them books and cloth fabric.[23] Also among those attracted to the Franciscans at this time was John, the abbot of Osney Abbey outside Oxford, who, in 1235, became a friar at Northampton.[24] In 1290, the Franciscan friar William de Pershore, formerly a monk of Pershore Abbey (Worcestershire), left his new order without permission and was received by the Benedictine monks at Abingdon Abbey (Berkshire); he was pursued by cries of 'apostasy' and by sentences of excommunication. The abbot and monks of Westminster were also excommunicated because they had given Pershore shelter. In the settlement of this celebrated dispute, the abbot of Westminster agreed to help the Franciscans recover William and also to pay the friars the sum of 60 marks.[25]

---

[23] *Ann. mon.* 4. 133–4. The prior had them denounced as excommunicates. One of the canons returned in the company of three friars and was physically and verbally punished and forced to return what he had stolen; he could remain with the friars for a year, at the end of which, if he determined their life stricter than the Augustinian, he could stay there. The prior found the other canon in London, who, instead of returning with the prior to Dunstable, went to Rome.

[24] Ibid., 4. 82. Earlier (in 1218), the prior of Merton Priory in Surrey, seeking solitude and quiet, had become a Carthusian (ibid., 2. 290). In 1273 the Master of St Mark's Hospital, Billeswick (near Bristol), received permission to enter the Carthusian house at Hinton, Somerset (*Reg. Giffard, Worcester* 2. 59).

[25] *Epp. Jo. Peckham* 3. 971–4; *Reg. Pecham, Canterbury* 2. 246; *Reg. Giffard, Worcester* 2. 372; *Mon. Franc.* 2. xiv–xvi, 31–62; *Fourth Report of the Royal Commission of Historical Manuscripts* (London, 1874), pp. 178–9. An incomplete summary is in *VCH, London* 1. 441.

The Carmelite theologian Thomas Netter of Walden, as prior provincial of his order in England, took strong exception to the claim of John Buxhale, a friar of Hitchin Priory (Hertfordshire), who said that he could not live a sufficiently spiritual life at Hitchin and who thus wanted to become a Carthusian at Sheen Priory (Surrey). Netter, a man not reluctant to state his views firmly, as Wyclifites discovered, wrote with some passion to the prior of Sheen:

If he had wished to be good, he [Buxhale] could most assuredly have been so. Let him speak the truth. Is it not amongst us that he has learned to subdue the passions and overcome the appetites of youth? Where did he begin to see the beauty of holiness and hold the world in contempt if it was not with us? Where, I demand to know, where, if not here, was he taught to practise chastity and the golden rule? From his youth up, has he not lived with us? I need bring no other witness but myself to recall to brother John how much of the world's contumely we have together endured, how many years we have shed side by side in daily confession, how many a time and oft he and I have spent half the night in prayer and, worn out with watching, have stretched our frozen limbs along the cold stone floor. Brought up as he certainly was in this austere school, is he not ashamed to pretend that he cannot be good amongst us? But let me ask your forgiveness that I should thus allow myself to be offended. The good brother John need not be alarmed. I, for my part, shall be very beholden to you, most venerable father and beloved brother in the faith, if you succeed in making him good, since with us he can be nothing of the kind. Nay more, in order to disburthen myself of all my responsibilities, I propose to send you for their betterment forty more of our brethren, of whom not one shall be any worse or any better than brother John. Tell me, if you will, what you think of my plan.[26]

Should one not see in Netter's over-reaction to a friar seeking *transitus* to a stricter order a large element of inter-order rivalry?[27]

A case which may have involved more than the records reveal concerns Arnold Lym. He first appears in 1335 as an apostate Dominican friar of Guildford Priory who secured papal letters reconciling him. The reconciled Lym is next seen at the Dominican house at Winchester. He then appears, about 1337, as a monk of nearby Hyde Abbey, a Benedictine monastery in

[26] *Monumenta historica Carmelitana* (ed. Benedict Zimmerman; Lerins, 1905), p. 442. The translation is by Reginald L. Hine, *The History of Hitchin* (2 vols.; 1927–9), I. 137–8.

[27] For an example of *transitus* and Benedictine inter-monastery rivalry see the case of William Pouns of St Albans (below, pp. 63–5).

Winchester. Was this *transitus* or an unusual form of the penalty *exsilium*? This question was to become pivotal. According to Lym, the papal letters of reconciliation were confiscated at the time of his move from the Dominican to the Benedictine house at Winchester. Lym fled Hyde Abbey. A writ was issued for his arrest early in 1341; he was captured and returned to Hyde Abbey. The far from passive Lym pursued the matter in the king's court, maintaining that the writ for his capture was invalid because he was not an apostate Benedictine. The royal justices recognized that the essential question – was Arnold Lym a Dominican or Benedictine? – pertained to another jurisdiction and referred the question to the ecclesiastical authorities. Feelings were running so high that monks of Hyde appear to have assaulted Lym in the very Hall of Westminster itself and then imprisoned him for three days. In 1348, Bishop Edington of Winchester found that Lym at the time in question was a professed monk of Hyde Abbey, which implies that Lym's move to Hyde was by way of transfer and not exile.[28]

The cry of apostasy was also heard in Yorkshire, where Thurstan Lofthous alias Watson left the Cistercian abbey of Kirkstall and transferred without permission to the Carthusians at Mount Grace, where after a year's probation he was professed and continued to live for several more years. Lofthous then left and returned to Kirkstall. The matter went to the abbot of Fountains and thence, in 1485, to the abbot of Cîteaux. Lofthous, it appears, returned to Mount Grace, and the abbot of Kirkstall, not content to declare Lofthous apostate and thus excommunicate, secured papal letters in 1490 to rehabilitate him. Lofthous, however, was still with the Carthusians in 1490 and received papal permission to remain there as a Carthusian.[29]

Transitus of another (uncanonical) sort could occur when the religious not only left his house without permission and entered another house, but when he did so without telling the second

---

[28] Glimpses of this case can be seen in *CPL* 2. 530; C81/1786/21; Year Book, Hilary 22 Edw. III, no. 14 (*Le second part de le reports del cases in ley* (London, 1619), pp. 2–3); *Reg. Edington, Winchester* 2, nos. 47, 652, 654; *Rotuli parliamentorum* 2. 186–7. In 1347, Lym, called a Dominican, received a royal pardon for his good services during the war in France (*CPR, 1345–48*, p. 524).

[29] *CPL* 15. nos. 320, 577. He was no doubt the same person as Thurston Watson, similarly described at the same time (Talbot, *Letters*, nos. 38, 66; Canivez, *Statuta* 5. 501, no. 26).

house that he had already been professed elsewhere. Such a one was the Augustinian canon Thomas de Ellingham of Thremhall Priory in Essex, who, although professed and a subdeacon, left without his prior's permission and wandered, obviously apostate, for two years. He then presented himself at Ixworth Priory in Suffolk, a house of the same order, but failed to reveal his past. There he again professed and was again ordained subdeacon. At length, his conscience did not allow him to continue the ruse, and, in 1363, he confessed his misdeeds and received papal absolution and permission to remain a canon of Ixworth.[30]

What should be remembered in all this is that, despite the various circumstances which occurred, *transitus* was an option for some discontented religious. The fact that very few examples of women religious appear in the records suggests that access to this procedure may have been easier for male religious. There were the two Benedictine nuns of Barrow Gurney in Somerset who, in 1398, transferred without permission to a Benedictine nunnery in Wales – they said – on account of poverty and were allowed to return.[31] Quite different was the transfer of Maud de Lancaster in 1364. She was the widow of the knight Ralph Dufford and had become an Augustinian canoness of Campsey Ash in Suffolk. She petitioned and, through the support of the king of France, received papal permission to transfer to the Minoresses (the Poor Clares). Her reasons were two: first, before her marriage she had intended to enter this order and, second, there were too many nobles visiting Campsey Ash and distracting her from her religious life.[32] Whether for men or for women, *transitus* was but one remedy for discontent. It did not resolve all problems: there were obviously many whose discontent had to do with the religious life itself and not merely with the *locus* where it was lived or with the relative strictness or laxity of the house. Two other avenues of departure opened up in the last decade of the fourteenth century. Neither of these applied to women for reasons which will be quickly apparent. It is to them that we now turn.

---

30 *CPP* 1. 459–60.
31 *CPL* 5. 162.
32 Ibid., 4. 37–8. Among other examples of women religious taking advantage of *transitus* are two nuns of Davington Priory to whom Archbishop Chichele in 1424 gave permission to transfer to Higham Priory, both Benedictine nunneries in Kent (*Reg. Chichele, Canterbury* 4. 254).

Legal alternatives

HONORARY PAPAL CHAPLAINS

In January 1390 William Oliver, a Cistercian monk of Cleeve Abbey in Somerset, was made an honorary papal chaplain.[33] By January 1415 at least 325 other members of religious orders had become honorary papal chaplains. Papal chaplains were clerics who served the pope in a real capacity and whose positions gave them special privileges; honorary papal chaplains were priests outside the papal curia, secular as well as religious, who shared many of these privileges.[34] What was implied in a religious becoming an honorary papal chaplain? The granting of an honorary papal chaplaincy with all its privileges and *non obstantibus* clauses exempted the holder from the regular life and from obedience to religious superiors. Its attraction was obvious for those male religious looking for a legal way out. Although some English papal chaplains had been created earlier in the fourteenth century, honorary papal chaplaincies became easily available only from the late 1380s. Thomas Walsingham in the *Gesta abbatum* of St Albans Abbey pointed to the desperate need of Pope Urban VI for revenues during the schism. He noted that in 1386 a Carmelite friar, Walter Disse, was empowered by a papal bull to create fifty honorary papal chaplains to support the Lancastrian crusade in Spain. Walsingham recounted how White Monks, Black Monks, canons and friars of all orders, in order to free themselves from the obedience of their superiors, sent money to Rome to gain this honour and exemption; the chronicler added 'mirabiliter, immo miserabiliter'.[35] For twenty years 'astonishingly and wretchedly' members of every major order from all parts of the country took advantage of this loophole. At least 83 Augustinian canons, 48 Cistercian monks, 38 Benedictine and Cluniac monks and 12 Premonstratensian canons as well as 129

---

[33] *CPL* 4. 274.

[34] On honorary papal chaplains see Bernard Guillemain, 'Les chapelains d'honneur des papes d'Avignon', *Mélange d'archéologie et d'histoire* 64 (1952) 217–38; Charles Burns, 'Vatican Sources and the Honorary Papal Chaplains of the Fourteenth Century', *Römische Kurie, kirchliche Finanzen* (ed. Erwin Gatz; 2 vols.; Pontificia Universitas Gregoriana, Misc. Historiae Pontificiae, 45 and 46, 1979) 1. 65–95.

[35] *Gesta abbatum* 2. 417–18, and, more briefly, in *Historia Anglicana* (ed. H. T. Riley; RS; 2 vols.; London, 1863–4) 2. 157. The 'crusade' was published at St Paul's on 18 Feb. 1386 with Disse among those given authority (*Polychronicon Ranulphi Higden monachi Cestrensis* (eds. C. Babbington and J. R. Lumby; RS; 9 vols.; London, 1865–86) 9. 81–2. See P. E. Russell, *The English Intervention in Spain and Portugal in the Time of Edward III and Richard II* (Oxford, 1955), pp. 409, 492.

friars from the four mendicant orders were among those who became papal chaplains in England; there were even some from small hospitals such as St Mary's at Newcastle upon Tyne. The matter had moved beyond Disse and had become a source of revenue for the hard-pressed pope at Rome, deprived as he was of income from vast parts of Christendom.

Such a sizeable defection from the religious life did not go unchallenged. Individual heads of religious houses took action. At St Albans the abbot was confronted by three young monks and an aged monk (Ralph Whichchurche, who, after fifty years as a monk there, 'made a great spectacle of himself'), all of whom claimed that, as papal chaplains, they were exempt from his jurisdiction.[36] The abbot refused to allow these monks to live in any of the houses of the monastery, except old Whichchurche, who was then staying at Belvoir Priory and who, indeed, held the parish church of Gunby, Lincolnshire. Nearly forty years later, one of the Young Turks, John Scheppeye, approached the gates of St Albans, humbly repentant, and asked to be taken back; and Abbot Wethamstede prepared a great feast for the prodigal papal chaplain.[37] Also, the abbot of St Mary's, York, complained to the pope about two of his monks who had become papal chaplains in 1397 and who then refused him obedience.[38] In another instance, the prior of St Frideswide, Oxford, in 1399 asked the pope for assistance with John Wodestock, one of his canons, who, as a papal chaplain, simply left the priory and was living dissolutely.[39] In 1402 the abbot of Peterborough told the pope that a number of his monks, alleging exemption because they were papal chaplains, refused to obey him, wore secular clothes and wandered freely in the world.[40] Not only did individual heads of houses complain but from the early 1390s onward the heads of orders voiced their concerns. In 1393, the Dominicans had Richard II endorse their complaints, as did the Franciscans in the following year.[41] In 1395, the English

[36] 'de se grande fecit spectaculum' (*Gesta abbatum* 2. 418, where these events are described).
[37] Amundesham 1. 86–8; 2. xvii–xx.
[38] *CPL* 5. 153.
[39] Ibid., 5. 286.
[40] Ibid., 5. 546.
[41] *CPL* 4. 444, 508. The General Chapter of the Dominican order, in 1397, worried about disquiet caused by (unspecified) papal bulls obtained by individual friars, ordered that such bulls not be given credence until examined by the Master General (B. M. Reichert, ed., *Acta capitulorum generalium ordinis praedicatorum*, vol. 3 (*Monumenta ordinis fratrum praedicatorum historica* 8, 1898) 96).

Carmelites were empowered by the pope to correct errant friars.[42] Within a month in 1399 both the Carmelites and the Austin friars secured the help of the secular arm in bringing their papal chaplains/apostates back to obedience.[43] The Carmelites were active against individual friars, suing writs for the arrest of Thomas Bumpstead of their Cambridge house in 1393 and Nicholas Weston of their Northampton house about the same time.[44] In 1401, the provincial of the Carmelites sued a writ for the arrest of the apostate Richard Trenance, who claimed a chaplaincy and was said to be wandering in Devon.[45] Also in 1401, the Augustinian canons in England taxed their houses in order to combat the personal privileges obtained by canons.[46] In the following year the Master of the Order of Sempringham (Gilbertines) invoked the secular arm against six apostate canons from four different houses, 'who, claiming to be chaplains of the apostolic see, put off their habits and wander about in lay clothes'.[47]

The Master's charges merely echoed those of his colleagues: the papal chaplains failed to obey their superiors, exempted themselves from attendance at divine services, wore lay clothes and left their houses at will. Boniface IX (1389–1404), the creator of the market in papal chaplaincies, invariably replied to complaints that such chaplains should obey their superiors, should be present at divine services, should not leave without permission and, in general, should act as if they were not papal chaplains.[48] This response of Boniface IX, the chronicler John Capgrave (himself an Austin friar) said, 'pleased well the four orders of Mendicants, for they pulled many a man that was of full evil rule.'[49] Such papal prohibitions, however, did not solve the problem, for an inventive papal

---

[42] Thomas Rymer, ed., *Foedera, conventiones, literae*, etc. (10 vols.; The Hague, 1737–45) 3. 4. 107.

[43] *CPR, 1399–1401*, pp. 123–4, 148. Also, in a statute of the southern province in that same year it was said that some religious apostates were acting as officials of archdeacons and as chaplains in parish churches. To gain their return even the local bishop was to have the power to capture and imprison apostates (Wilkins, *Concilia* 3. 241). Should we see here newly created papal chaplains who found employment with archdeacons and as parochial rectors and vicars?

[44] C81/1793/27, 29.   [45] C81/1793/21.

[46] Salter, *Chapters*, pp. 79–80.

[47] C81/1791/7; *CPR, 1401–05*, p. 196.

[48] Boniface was merely repeating the general reply given to similar complaints, apparently from other countries, by Gregory XI in 1373 (*Bullarium romanum* 4. 565–6), who, in turn, was repeating a bull of Urban V of 1363.

[49] *Chronicle of England* (ed. F. C. Hingeston; RS; London, 1858), p. 262.

bureaucracy merely added to the *non obstantibus* clauses a new clause referring to these very prohibitions. The market continued to flourish, and, where it is possible to determine the presence of such exclusionary clauses, at least 80 per cent of the newly created papal chaplains availed themselves of such exclusions.

The window of opportunity was open for about twenty-five years. It had opened abruptly in the late 1380s and closed just as abruptly in 1415. In the following half century only four honorary chaplaincies were granted to Englishmen, a trickle compared with the 326 of the flood years. The procedure, as we have seen, was not without its problems. The new papal chaplain stood in danger of being treated as an apostate and perhaps even arrested. Besides, how would a religious, thus freed from his religious house, support himself? Could he secure a benefice or, at least, employment as a chaplain or curate without benefice? Many of these uncertainties could be resolved by another procedure that affected the status of religious, the procedure of actual dispensation.

DISPENSATION TO HOLD A BENEFICE

From the mid-1390s until the time of the dissolution there was available another papal procedure, more straightforward and less fraught with difficulties than the procedure just discussed.[50] It provided male members of religious orders a dispensation that allowed them, in effect, to leave their order and to live as secular priests, free from the authority of their order and free to hold property. This procedure, like the appointment of papal chaplains, was a creature of the Great Schism. There is a single instance in 1389 in favour of an Augustinian canon, who had apparently supported the pope against his enemies, and then another instance in 1392 in favour of a leprous Franciscan forced to live apart from his order without support.[51] The possibilities suggested by these rare dispensations were seized upon, and by 1395 the procedure was in full swing: 21 dispensations for England were granted in that year alone. And so they continued to be granted decade after decade and by 1513 (when the calendars of the papal registers now end) a total of at least 810 dispensations had been granted to

---

[50] See the remarks of Knowles, *RO* 2. 172–3, and Alfred H. Sweet, 'Papal Privileges Granted to Individual Religious', *Speculum* 31 (1956) 602–10.
[51] *CPL* 4. 324, 45. The leper was Thomas Wyke, a master of theology.

English religious to leave their religious houses without committing the crime of apostasy. The actual total was probably higher, given the non-survival of many registers.

This papal dispensation, in its usual wording, permitted the monk, canon or friar to hold a benefice with or without cure of souls as long as he lived, even a benefice usually held by a secular priest, even a benefice with a lay patron, and to exchange his benefice for another as often as he liked.[52] In other words, he could, in practice, if collated to a benefice, live like a secular priest, bound neither to obedience to his religious superior – since as rector or vicar he would be subject to the local bishop – nor to poverty of life – since he could keep the income from his benefice. The dispensation, then, was a dispensation from the vows of obedience and poverty. He still technically remained a professed religious but a religious now no longer bound to his order: to use a more modern expression, he was exclaustrated (living *extra claustrum*). He was a clear part of the ecclesiastical landscape of the fifteenth century.

This was not an absolute dispensation: the religious to whom it was granted was not automatically dispensed from these vows. It was, rather, a conditional dispensation: the dispensation took effect only on condition that the religious receive a benefice. Until he was instituted to a benefice, he was still bound by these vows. Thus, one cannot conclude that all of the 810 religious who received these (conditional) dispensations found patrons to present them to benefices and actually left the religious life. Yet it seems highly unlikely that a religious would go to the trouble and expense (probably amounting to as much as £2, if not more, when hidden fees were added to curial fees), unless there was a genuine hope of being instituted to a benefice. Far from complete as the institution lists for this period are, they nevertheless contain scores and scores of such religious being instituted to secular benefices by virtue of dispensations granted by papal letters. For example, in 1446 the bishop of Bath and Wells, Thomas Beckington, instituted the Austin friar William Wenlock as rector of Pill near Bristol.[53] In 1460 Beckington instituted Robert Ady, a Cistercian from Grace

---

[52] For the text of a dispensation see the bull granted to John Bristol, Cistercian monk of Hailes (later vicar of Radbourne Craven), by Pope Paul II on 12 May 1468 (Talbot, *Letters*, no. 25); for more on this case see *CPL* 12. 632; Canivez 5, 404, no. 37.

[53] He had received the dispensation over a year and a half previously (*Reg. Beckington, Bath and Wells* 1. no. 246).

Dieu Abbey in Monmouthshire, as perpetual vicar of Puriton, Somerset.[54] In 1463 he instituted Owen Smyth, an Augustinian canon of Carmarthen Priory, to the church of Charlton Adam, Somerset.[55] In the neighbouring diocese of Exeter, Edmund Lacy (bishop, 1420–55) admitted at least ten dispensed religious to benefices, among them three Benedictines, two Cistercians, and one each Carthusian, Premonstratensian, Augustinian canon, Carmelite and Franciscan.[56] And so it was for other dioceses in fifteenth-century England, this routine institution of dispensed religious to benefices.

An important distinction must be made. These dispensed religious were not in the same situation as Premonstratensian and Augustinian canons who had the care of souls in benefices appropriated to their monasteries: such pastoral care had for centuries been part of the work of these orders. Such canons, although ministering in parish churches, remained under the obedience of their religious superiors and were subject to recall to their religious houses. Nor was this dispensation a mere relaxation of the traditional prohibition against monks exercising pastoral care in parishes. The dispensed religious were in an entirely different situation. Once they received a benefice, they were no longer subject to the authority of their superiors and could not be recalled: they had severed the ties that bound them to their order. To all intents and purposes they were no longer religious.

The assault on the fabric of the religious order in England by the large-scale dispensing of professed religious met with resistance. What could religious superiors do when faced with papal bulls? It was no doubt at the urging of influential abbots that a clause was inserted in the Statute of Provisors of 1401 (mainly a repetition of the statute of 1390), a clause which rendered a religious obtaining such letters subject to prosecution.[57] Despite this threat, only one case of prosecution by use of the writ *praemunire facias* has been found. It is clear that the parliamentary statute did not slow down the entry of papal letters of dispensation into England.[58]

Moreover, by the century's end, the Cistercians judged the

---

[54] Ibid., no. 1291. The papal dispensation had been granted over a year previously (*CPL* 11. 528).

[55] *Reg. Beckington* 1. nos. 1535–6. He had received papal dispensation about four months previously (*CPL* 11. 642).

[56] *Reg. Lang, Exeter* 5. 348–9.   [57] 2 Henry IV, c.3 (*Statutes* 2. 121).

[58] The single case is discussed below, p. 64.

exodus of monks by way of papal dispensation so serious a problem that two letters were sent to the abbot of Cîteaux in an attempt to stop the haemorrhage. The abbots-commissary for England – the abbots of Fountains (Yorkshire), Stratford Langthorn (Essex) and St Mary Graces (London) – wrote in March 1496:

We marvel and, indeed, everyone marvels, Father, that brothers of our order approach the Roman curia and quickly receive capacities to the great loss and dishonour of our order. Bishops are indignant, fathers [abbots] are troubled and laymen are murmuring. Unless a remedy is promptly provided, it will disgrace our order. Wherefore we humbly beg your fatherhood in the Lord to persuade the proctor of the order that, if such monks come to him, either they be imprisoned or they withdraw such requests, since the honour of holy religion they daily defame.[59]

Marmaduke Huby, abbot of Fountains, one of these three abbots-commissary, wrote individually to Cîteaux, apparently at about the same time. He was exercised over the scandal caused as a result of these capacities, which the proctor general of the order in Rome was assisting English monks to obtain.

Many capacities are granted to our English monks, and on the pretext of these capacities our monks wander in the world, giving great scandal to our order. They even appear before bishops in towns and in other conspicuous places, where they are seen in strange habits and tonsures, thus lying to God. The bishops are astonished at this, particularly the archbishop of Canterbury, who excels the rest in prudence, authority and religious zeal and who desires the reform of our order in such matters. Such monks, whether wandering about or serving in churches or chapels, reply to the reformers that they first conferred with the proctor general and obtained his permission. Some reported – truly or falsely I know not – that they received his permission in writing and under his seal.[60]

The concerns of the English Cistercians were well founded: in the ten years before they wrote to Cîteaux at least twenty-four Cistercians had received capacities. Yet the efforts of the abbots, however much they may have curbed the complicity of their proctor general, were without success in stopping this process: at least twenty-one further Cistercians received capacities in the next ten years. Their futile efforts do underscore the negative attitude

---

[59] Author's translation from Talbot, *Letters*, pp. 187–8.
[60] Ibid,. pp 188–9.

of the official leadership of one of England's largest orders to defections resulting from dispensations.[61]

At another level, individual superiors tried to put obstacles in the way of dispensed religious. The Augustinian prior of Merton Priory in Surrey apparently threatened William Hay, a canon of that house who received a papal dispensation in 1406, but Innocent VII told Hay that he had nothing to fear since the prior's permission was not required.[62] Routinely, a clause appears to have been inserted into the dispensation to the effect that no one could prevent the dispensed religious from accepting a benefice. Yet a religious brandishing newly acquired papal letters of dispensation might understandably arouse hostility, particularly if he announced that he was merely waiting for a patron and removed himself from the active life of his house. Perhaps few religious superiors went as far as the Augustinian prior of Bridlington in Yorkshire, who persuaded Nicholas Duke, a canon of that house, to renounce his dispensation and who then proceeded to cut off the leaden bull from the papal letters.[63] Yet abbots and priors had frequently to be reminded that, although dispensed, these religious were still members of their communities and were not to be ill treated: they were to keep their place in choir, have their voice in chapter and receive support, while awaiting presentation to a benefice. Hugh Forster, a dispensed monk of Glastonbury, was reassured by the pope in 1451 that, as long as he lived there, he should be treated as a full member of that community.[64] Even the powerful abbot of St Albans failed to prevail when confronted with dispensed monks. Two of his monks, Henry Halstead, prior of Wallingford Priory, a cell of St Albans, and Robert Morpath, cellarer at Wallingford, were dispensed, but their abbot, John Stoke (1441–51), in 1448 secured royal writs for their arrest on the grounds that they were apostates.[65] Halstead returned to St Albans in 1454. Morpath, however, appealed to the pope, who ruled that, although St Albans was an exempt abbey, the dispensation was valid and Morpath could continue in peaceful possession of the church of Aldworth, Berkshire, to which he had been

---

[61] These figures derive from an examination of *CPL* 16–18.

[62] *CPL* 6. 74, 77–8.

[63] Ibid., 13. 28. Duke later regretted his deed and got a new dispensation.

[64] Ibid., 10. 111–12. He was an honorary chaplain and had been dispensed in 1448 (ibid., 10. 352).

[65] See *VCH, Herts.* 4. 403. For the request for the writs, see C81/1788/36.

instituted.[66] At about the same time, the bishop of Bath and Wells secured the arrest of a monk of Bath Priory, Robert Vise, who, he said, had lived as a secular and rector of Stokecurry for many years. Vise later escaped and returned to Stokecurry, perhaps with the connivance of the prior.[67] Although he does not appear in the surviving papal registers, it is difficult to suppress the suspicion that he had received papal letters of dispensation.

In some cases it appears that the religious with his dispensation in hand simply left without having secured a patron, treating the dispensation (wrongly) as an immediate release. Canonical visitors of religious houses in the sixteenth century were told of religious with dispensations – by that time called 'capacities' – wandering about in the world unbeneficed. The prior of the Augustinian priory at Maxstoke in Warwickshire complained to the visitor about Richard Carter, a canon with a dispensation, who left and refused to return.[68] At Caldwell Priory in Bedfordshire Bishop Atwater of Lincoln was told that Robert Hag wandered through the countryside, saying he had a capacity.[69] Similarly, at Woodbridge Priory in Suffolk, another Augustinian house, the visitor found that William Furton had obtained a dispensation but not a benefice and was wandering in the world.[70] And a strange thing happened to a monk of Christ Church, Canterbury. Robert Molash, as he later stated, sued for such a dispensation, probably in 1464, through Peter Courtenay, papal nuncio to England, and was thereupon expelled by the prior. Courtenay led him to believe that the dispensation had been granted – which, in fact, it had not – and Molash was instituted to the church of St John's, Margate. Realizing, he said, the truth of the situation, he resigned and begged readmission to the priory.[71] Similarly, in 1491, Peter Lynn, a Premonstratensian canon of West Dereham, begged absolution for having left his monastery forty years earlier on the basis of a non-existent papal privilege.[72] These few cases represent, at best,

---

[66] *CPL* 10. 49.

[67] *Reg. Beckington, Bath and Wells* 1. nos. 39, 54, 115, 123, 184; 2. no. 1639; C85/41/9, where it is misfiled.

[68] *Blythe's Vis.*, p. 11.

[69] *Vis. Dioc. Linc.* 2. 93.   [70] *Vis. Norwich*, p. 135.

[71] *Lit. Cant.* 3. 272–4. He was professed in 1439 and left in 1464 (Searle, *Lists*, p. 188). For Margate parish see *Reg. Bourgchier, Canterbury*, pp. 274, 284. For Courtenay, later bishop of Exeter and Winchester, see *BRUO* 1. 499–500.

[72] *CAP* 2. 219. In a somewhat similar case, John Spenser, a monk of Muchelney, arranged with agents to receive this dispensation, but they provided him with a forged document.

a misunderstanding or, at worst, misbehaviour; they were aberrancies in a system that, by and large, worked fairly smoothly.

On the eve of the decade that saw the end of the religious orders in England the higher clergy appeared troubled by this system of capacities. When they gathered in 1529, they lamented that some religious, claiming capacities, had renounced the observance of the regular life and wandered about in the world. They decreed that no religious, even if he had a papal bull, should leave his religious house or accept a benefice or chantry unless he first appeared before the local bishop or his abbot or prior and proved that the reasons for which the dispensation was granted were, in fact, true. The local bishop should give a declaration that the reasons had been found true. If any religious acted contrariwise, he could be declared apostate by his superior and subject to the canonical penalties.[73] What specifically provoked this statute is unknown, but clearly there was a sentiment among the clergy that capacities were being given for spurious reasons. It was clearly not foreseen that the procedure of granting capacities would be domesticated by Henry VIII in 1534, when he established the Faculty Office, which in its first three years was to grant 181 capacities, i.e., before the dissolution. This dispensation was soon to be seized upon to effect the departure of the religious of the dissolved houses. What began as a papal procedure to augment income had become a royal procedure to terminate the religious life itself.[74]

Other questions were raised during the fifteenth century. What should a dispensed religious wear once he was beneficed? Should he continue to wear the religious habit in which he had been professed or could he wear the garb of a secular priest, which, in effect, he was? In 1455 Archbishop Bourgchier complained that some professed religious who had obtained benefices by means of papal letters discarded their religious habits and were dressing like secular priests; he threatened them with excommunication.[75] The drafters of papal dispensations were equal to the task of rescuing dispensed religious from any hint of apostasy because of their laying aside the religious habit. The papal officials had perhaps

---

Acting on the basis of this 'dispensation', he left his monastery and took up employment as chaplain to a noble family. Fearing taint of apostasy, he applied for authentic papal letters, which were duly granted in 1426 (*Reg. Stafford, Bath and Wells*, p. xli and no. 65).

[73] Wilkins, *Concilia* 3. 723–4.
[74] This procedure is described fully below, pp. 157–60. See *Fac. Off. Reg.*, pp. xlii–lviii.
[75] *Reg. Bourgchier, Canterbury*, p. 21.

anticipated Bourgchier's objection. From the 1450s onward it was possible for a religious to have included in his dispensation a clause that allowed him, once beneficed, to wear the garb of a secular priest provided he wore his religious habit underneath. The earliest instance for England may have been John Wynton, an Augustinian canon of St Osyth in Essex, who, by virtue of papal dispensation, held the parish church of Claxton in Norfolk for twelve years and then Rickmansworth in Hertfordshire, where, the pope allowed in 1452, he could wear a priest's garb of dark colour over his canon's robes.[76] By the end of the century the inclusion of such a clause in the papal letters appears to have become fairly common. What was this all about? A Cistercian monk, Thomas Garforth formerly of Kirkstead Abbey (Lincolnshire), simply stated in his request that he wanted 'to live among secular clerics more honestly and without scandal to the people'.[77] One suspects that this clause simply meant that a dispensed, beneficed religious could dress like a secular priest. A religious habit worn under a full priest's garb would probably not have been visible, yet, because of the symbolic function of the habit as a sign of a professed religious and its abandonment a sign of apostasy, the apostolic see would have been loath to say explicitly that it could be abandoned. A hint of this meaning can be seen in the terms of the dispensation granted in 1500 to Geoffrey Louuyn, a Cluniac monk of Castle Acre (Norfolk), who was dispensed to wear his habit *or a mark of his religious profession* under the garb of a secular priest.[78] Of course, it was quite possible that beneficed religious wore the heavy wool of priest's clothes over the heavy wool of their religious habit under the midsummer sun, but it seems unlikely.

A profile of those religious who received papal dispensations to live as secular priests in fifteenth-century England would be a profile of the religious orders in fifteenth-century England. They were from the large monastic houses such as Westminster, Glastonbury, St Albans and Ramsey. They were from small hospitals and dependent cells. There were even two Carthusians from different parts of the country. There were friars from the four great orders of Franciscans, Dominicans, Carmelites and Austins as well as from the Crutched (so-called) Friars. Many of the friars had university degrees, like Thomas Derby, the Franciscan theologian,

---

[76] *CPL* 10. 240.   [77] Dispensation granted 5 Dec. 1500 (ibid., 17. 1. 447).
[78] 'sive signum illius' (ibid., 17. 1. 287).

who, in 1452, pleaded that old age was overtaking him after having taught the Sentences and preached for over thirty years.[79] Jacke Upland in his 'Songs against the Friars' asked,

> Why get ye your dispensations
> to have it more easie?[80]

There seem to have been runs of dispensations in some houses: three monks, for example, of Dover Priory in the mid-1460s, three monks of Ely Cathedral Priory in one day in 1476, two monks of Milton Abbey in Dorset on the same day in 1478.[81] Of the 810 dispensed religious who appear in the surviving papal registers 225 were Augustinian canons, not surprisingly since it was the largest order in England at this time. Next came the Benedictines with 181, the Cistercians with 122 and then the other major orders ranging from 36 (for the Dominicans) down to 16 (for the Gilbertines). Although dispensations were granted throughout the fifteenth century, about 85 per cent were granted after 1440, at the average of about 12 per year. Again, it should be emphasized that these are conservative figures owing to the non-survival of crucial papal registers.

It remains to place this matter of papal chaplaincies and dispensations in the general history of the religious orders. Taken together – and, indeed, there is some overlapping – the number of religious receiving papal chaplaincies and the number of religious receiving papal dispensations to live as secular priests must have been at least one thousand out of a total male religious population in England for the long fifteenth century of probably close to 35,000.[82] This represented a clear flight from the religious life by a substantial number of professed religious, a flight free from apostasy and within the law. The religious orders were not unaware of what was happening: so alarmed were the English Cistercians that they complained in 1496 of the great harm being done to their order, yet matters proceeded as before and in the next dozen years at least twenty-one Cistercians received capacities.[83] This legal exodus of

---

[79] *CPL* 10. 109.

[80] Thomas Wright, ed., *Political Poems and Songs* (RS; 2 vols.; London 1859–61) 2. 20.

[81] For Dover see *CPL* 11. 657, 674–5; for Ely ibid., 13. 493, 495; and for Milton ibid., 13. 618. One cannot assume, given the path of petitions through the curia, that rescripts granted at the same time resulted from petitions made at the same time, although such might well have been the case.

[82] Calculations based on estimates in KH, p. 494.   [83] Talbot, *Letters*, nos. 92, 93.

religious from the religious life, whether viewed as a debilitating haemorrhage or as a salutary bloodletting, must be considered a significant feature of the late medieval church.

THE CASE OF THE MUSICAL MONK OF ST ALBANS

This is the twenty-year saga of William Pouns (or Powns). We first see Pouns in 1422, when, as a monk of St Albans, he approached his abbot, John Wethamstede, and requested permission to transfer to the Benedictine priory at Canterbury Cathedral. He claimed that he had heard from a former monk of St Albans, now at Canterbury, how sweet the music was there.[84] Wethamstede was most reluctant, but somehow Pouns secured the intervention of Archbishop Chichele, and, in the face of this intervention, Abbot Wethamstede grudgingly granted permission.[85] His displeasure he displayed in a letter of extravagant language – Pouns, he wrote, was guilty of the greatest perfidy[86] – and in Latin verses of intemperate language and almost impenetrable versification (I translate freely):

> Like spoiled crop in the field at harvest
>   which no plough can save,
> Like the issue of a mother's womb,
>   viper-like devouring her innards,
> Like a dog returning to its vomit,
> Stands our apostate, who prefers the food of pigs
>   for the saving food of monastic life.
> You may say in your post-claustral hiding
> 'Here and there the garb is the same;
> 'Witness I no fraud confect.'
> But, my brother, by the sameness of the garb
>   in new cloister
> You self-deceiving can be and the monk's hood can
>   conceal a vagabond.
> If to migrate is your desire, it is lawful
> When all things are equal, ritual and rule.
> Yet remember, if in these they are not equal,
> You apostate do become.[87]

---

[84] Geoffrey Bonde, who seems to have gone to Canterbury in 1408; he died in 1447. See John Stone, *Chronicle* (ed. W. G. Searle; Cambridge Antiquarian Soc., octavo ser., 34, 1902), p. 40.

[85] Amundesham, pp. 90–1.   [86] Ibid., pp. 91–7.

[87] Ibid., p. 98. E. F. Jacob said that Wethamstede wrote 'almost untranslatable verses' and that his letter regarding Pouns was 'in the best homiletic style' (*Essays in the Conciliar Epoch* (3rd edn; Manchester, 1963), pp. 189, 191–2).

So disturbed was he by this defection from his community that Wethamstede required that henceforth at the time of profession each monk would formally swear, 'I shall not procure migration to any religion, equal or unequal, except with the express knowledge and permission of my abbot.'[88] How this would have stopped Pouns's defection, made indeed with the abbot's permission, defies explanation.

The musical monk was welcomed into the community of Christ Church, Canterbury, on the feast of St Andrew (30 November), 1422.[89] One might expect that he would then – his musical tastes now satisfied – recede into the anonymous life of a contented monk. Such was the case, but only for nineteen years. Had the music gone flat? We may never know. But in 1441 William Pouns, monk of Christ Church, reappears in the light of history. It was perhaps fitting that it was while the other monks were actually singing Vespers on the day of All Souls (2 November) that Pouns fled Canterbury without benefit of permission and made his way to London. Why? He was prompted by papal letters which he had received: they were dated 2 August 1441 and dispensed Pouns so that he could hold for life and even exchange a benefice usually held by secular or religious clergy.[90] Pouns took himself and his dispensation to the city of London, and there in the parish of St Nicholas Shambles he had the letter read and publicly pronounced. The volume of the music was now to reach a mighty roar.

The prior of Christ Church, John Woodnesburgh, procured issuance of a writ *Praemunire facias* against William Pouns.[91] The writ stated that Pouns had violated the Statute of Provisors of 1401 by introducing into England papal letters. Between 1401 and 1441 at least ninety-eight similar letters had been introduced into England in apparent violation of the clause of the statute of 1401 which specifically prohibited their introduction, yet this is the only known case in which the statute was invoked, and here at the request not of the secular authority but of the prior of Christ Church.[92] Henry Chichele, still archbishop of Canterbury, again

---

[88] Amundesham, p. 98.   [89] Searle, *Lists*, pp. 186–7.

[90] *CPL* 9. 206. Interestingly enough, another monk of Christ Church, John Clement, was issued papal letters to the same effect on the same day (ibid.), but he apparently did not avail himself of the dispensation and died as a monk of Canterbury in 1457 (Searle, *Lists*, p. 187).

[91] *Lit. Cant.* 3. 172–3.

[92] For statute see 2 Henry IV, c.3 *(Statutes* 2. 121). The writ is in *Lit. Cant.* 3. 172–3.

intervened on Pouns's behalf as, indeed, did the dean of St Martin-le-Grand, London, to both of whom Pouns had gone for assistance.[93] Both the archbishop and the dean, in addition to letters for the prior, sent oral messages to him by the precentor of Christ Church, who fittingly enough had gone to London to retrieve his musical monk. On 17 November, a fortnight after his flight, William Pouns was welcomed back into his order and stall in the choir of Canterbury Cathedral, contrite, to resume singing the praises of the Lord at Canterbury and perhaps, too, the lord of Canterbury. Yet Pouns did not sing long in the choir at Canterbury: within a year and a half of his return he transferred to the Cistercian monastery at Boxley in Kent. Why? The abbot of Boxley said that he recognized Pouns's desire to lead a stricter life and thus agreed to receive him.[94] A contemporary list of those who left Christ Church Priory tells another story: it reveals the bitter truth that Pouns, in fact, was expelled from Canterbury.[95] As far as is known, the final chants of William Pouns were sung with the White Monks of Boxley.

---

[93] The dean was patron of St Nicholas Shambles. At this time the rectorship was not vacant – not until 1455. See Hennessy, *Novum repertorium ecclesiasticum parochiale Londinense* (London, 1898), p. 352. The archbishop and dean wrote letters to the priory on 17 Nov. (*Lit. Cant.* 3. 173–5).

[94] Letter dated 25 Apr. 1443 (*Lit. Cant.* 3. 175–6).

[95] Oxford, Corpus Christi College MS 256, fo. 168v.

Chapter 3

TWO QUESTIONS:
HOW MANY? AND WHY?

In almost every year in the three hundred years here under study, discontented members of religious orders found the alternative means of departure inadequate or unavailable and personal reasons impelled them to abandon the religious life, cast aside their religious habits, take flight and return to the dress and life of the world. The incidence of religious apostasy and the reasons for it demand our attention. Women religious, while sharing similar motivations with male religious, as will be seen, also encountered problems peculiar to themselves, and these demand special attention. These issues of monastic demography and human motivation pose problems for the historian, who recognizes here the clash between questions which, of necessity, must be asked and sources which, of their nature, are limited. A search through royal and papal records, through episcopal registers, through visitation records and through the more anecdotal accounts in monastic chronicles provides a substantial, if necessarily incomplete, account of defections from the religious life. It is from these plus more marginal sources that answers to questions concerning numbers and motivation can be attempted.

THE NUMBER OF RUNAWAYS

Any attempt to answer the question about how many religious left their houses inevitably confronts the larger question of how many religious comprised the religious orders in England during this period. Professor Knowles once observed that 'every student of English medieval history will have sought at one time or another an answer to the question: What was the total number of religious houses and of the religious themselves?'[1] Estimates are now available to us. What researchers tend to provide us with are

[1] KH, p. 45.

glimpses – snapshots – of the religious population at a moment in time (e.g., Domesday survey, the poll taxes of 1377 to 1381, the suppression of the 1530s) and then by extrapolations and comparisons, using information contained in such sources as visitation records and lists of recipients of royal alms, they are able to provide reliable estimates for other periods.[2] The estimates given by Hadcock identify the population of a generation at the beginning and at the end of periods of different lengths of time. Professor Russell similarly identifies generational populations and occasionally more. A question that confronts us in attempting to estimate the religious population in England between 1240 and 1540 concerns the length of a generation: a generation is measured by the average years in the monastery after profession. At Christ Church, Canterbury, at the end of the thirteenth and the beginning of the fourteenth century, a generation was about 30 years; for those entering between 1415 and 1432 it was 27 years and for those entering between 1457 and 1471 it was 33.2 years.[3] Durham Priory in the fifteenth century lost slightly more than one-third of its monks every decade: its generations were of about 30 years' duration.[4] Calculating 30 years as a reasonable definition of a monastic generation and using the figures provided by Hadcock, which are more serviceable for this purpose and, in any case, closely parallel Russell's, we arrive at an estimate for this 300-year period of about 140,000. More meaningful for our purposes would be the period from 1270 to 1530, since the number of apostates appearing in extant sources for the years from 1240 to 1270 are not statistically significant and since, on the other end, the decade of the 1530s was the most unstable and uncertain in the history of the English church and will be discussed in the final chapter. For this shorter period of 260 years an estimate of nearly 120,000 can be reasonably used. The general pattern of development reveals growth during the thirteenth century, a high point (about 18,000) in the early

---

[2] The two principal studies are by Josiah Cox Russell in 'The Clerical Population of Medieval England', *Traditio* 2 (1944) 177–212, and by R. Neville Hadcock in KH, pp. 488–95. A discussion of the findings of these studies is in Knowles, *RO* 2. chap. 20. Also useful are H. M. Colvin, *The White Canons in England* (Oxford, 1951), pp. 358–9; Joan G. Greatrex, 'Some Statistics of Religious Motivation', *Studies in Church History* 15 (1978) 179–86; D. M. Owens, *Church and Society in Medieval Lincolnshire* (Lincoln, 1971), pp. 77, 144–5; and A. Savine, *English Monasteries on the Eve of the Dissolution* (Oxford, 1909), pp. 218–25.

[3] Russell, *British Medieval Population*, pp. 189–92.

[4] R. B. Dobson, *Durham Priory, 1400–1450* (Cambridge, 1973), pp. 55–6.

fourteenth century, a reduction by half as a consequence of the Black Death, and a fairly quick recovery to about three-quarters of the pre-plague level, at which new level the numbers tended to stay.[5] The number of religious houses also reached its highest point in the first half of the fourteenth century and, depending on whether one includes small cells and hospitals, was just above or just below one thousand. It is within this context that the estimates of runaways must be seen.

All references to runaways drawn from the various sources used in preparing this study have been drawn together for this analysis. It should be emphasized that what are discussed here are incidents of alleged apostasy. To the modern student of monasticism some of the allegations of apostasy appear spurious and not consistent with canonical apostasy. Yet the truth or falseness of apostasy, at this remove in time, despite one's suspicions must be largely left to one side. A later chapter will show that about 100 apostates were involved in internal disputes, generally involving elections, where the charge of apostasy was a weapon used by one side against another.[6] Alleged apostates, then, constitute the subject matter of this discussion.

One further caveat. The alleged apostates here referred to are those who have been found in extant sources. The archival historian is constantly reminded of the incompleteness of records: sometimes merely a glimpse here and a glimpse there, a decade of plenty and a decade of near silence, an abbey with full records and another abbey with few or none. Patterns of record survival are difficult, virtually impossible, to detect, principally because random factors have been at work. How much of the iceberg is visible we may never know with certitude. The result, quite clearly, is a statistical report which is a statement of archival survival and of a true historical minimum. In addition, although the net has been cast quite widely in a search for apostates, it would be a rash historian, indeed, who would suggest that all apostates have been caught in his net. New names will, no doubt, surface, but their number should not be so considerable as to distort the general picture painted here.

The total number of apostates in England for the period 1270 to 1530 who were detected in the preparation of this study is 1,088: they are listed in the register of apostates (Appendix 5). They

[5] KH, pp. 46–7.   [6] See below, pp. 118–20.

amount to 0.91 per cent of the estimated population of religious for this period. This figure includes men and women of every order, large and small, from every part of England and from some places in Wales, who departed the religious life in every decade of this 260-year period. Of the thousand or so religious houses in England and Wales we have reference to apostates from 379 houses (more than one-third of the total). Apostates are known to have fled from houses in every county of England (save Rutland and Westmorland) and from houses in Denbighshire, Flintshire, Monmouthshire and Pembrokeshire in Wales.[7] Monks left from at least seven of the ten cathedral churches which had monastic priories.[8] Nuns abandoned nunneries like Romsey and Shaftesbury, whose communities at times numbered near 100. Yet religious also apostasized from small and often obscure houses, many of which, on limited incomes, were struggling for survival: from leper hospitals like Burton Lazars, from monasteries like St Dogmells of the tiny Order of Tiron in remote Pembrokeshire, from scores of nunneries (e.g., Thicket in Yorkshire, Wallingwells in Nottinghamshire, Littlemore in Oxfordshire) with no more than the traditional thirteen members, if that. No pattern of house size or wealth appears in the houses from which religious departed in apostasy.

Moreover, religious generally fled from religious orders in relative proportion to the size of the orders. Although there were shifting patterns in the size of the orders, during our period the orders tended to rank in size, from larger to smaller, as follows: Augustinian canons, Benedictine monks (including alien priories), Cistercian monks, Premonstratensian canons, Benedictine nuns, Cluniac monks with the friars and other orders trailing after. In the table presented here are listed the orders and the numbers of apostates appearing for each. Although hospitals were not an order – most followed the Rule of St Augustine without belonging to the order – it seems reasonable to treat them here collectively.

The three largest orders not surprisingly produced the largest number of alleged apostates in the surviving records. A word

---

[7] Rutland had a priory of Augustinian canons at Brooke, with probably three canons at any one time, and an alien priory at Edith Weston, with about the same number of monks (KH, pp. 150, 88). Westmorland had Shap Abbey (Premonstratensian), with perhaps twenty canons before the Black Death and only six after, a Carmelite priory at Appleby, with twelve friars in 1300, and a few small hospitals (ibid., pp. 191, 234).

[8] Bath, Canterbury, Coventry, Durham, Norwich, Rochester and Worcester.

Table 1. *Numbers of apostates by religious orders*

Augustinian canons	226	Templars	11
Benedictine monks	201	Cluniac nuns	8
Cistercian monks	180	Trinitarians	8
Premonstratensians	91	Crutched friars	7
Benedictine nuns	57	Order of Tiron	7
Cluniac monks	49	Knights Hospitallers	6
Carmelite friars	37	Carthusians	6
Hospitals	35	Pied friars	5
Cistercian nuns	30	Hospital nuns	4
Dominican friars	29	Fontevrault monks	1
Franciscan friars	26	Kts Hospitaller nuns	1
Austin friars	23	Gilbertine nuns	1
Gilbertine canons	20	monks (no order given)	4
Augustinian canonesses	13	nuns (no order given)	2
		Total	1,088

should be said about what might seem a disproportionately small number of friar apostates: although they comprised somewhere in the vicinity of 25 per cent of the total religious during most of our period, they account for about 12 per cent of the known apostates. One of the major sources for our knowledge of apostates is the material found in the records for the use of the secular arm against apostates.[9] As will be seen, the mendicant orders were privileged during much of this period to approach local royal officials directly to secure the arrest of their apostates, thus bypassing the central administration and leaving no records of these apostates. It should also be noted that only six Carthusian apostates have come to light. Of these, three were from Witham Priory (Somerset): John Russell, a lay brother, in 1340; William de Standish, who, probably in 1341, went to Avignon without permission; and the curious Richard Vyell, who, in an apparent dispute over the priorship, was signified for arrest and who, in 1459, became bishop of Killala in Ireland.[10] Although circumstances peculiar to nuns will be referred

---

[9] See next chapter.

[10] For Russell and Standich see *CPL* 2. 549, 552. For Vyell see C81/1787/25; *CPR, 1452–61*, p. 116; *CPL* 12. 92–3. The others were two monks of Hinton Priory (Somerset), who, in 1391, were ordered arrested (C81/1787/24), and a monk of Hull Priory, who, without permission, went to the Roman curia and was absolved in 1477 (*CPL* 13. 55). For the reception of returned Carthusians see E. Margaret Thompson, *The Carthusian Order in England* (London, 1930), pp. 127–8.

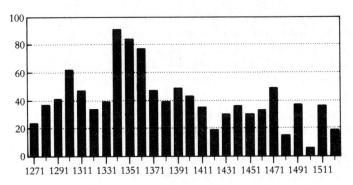

Fig. 1. *Alleged apostates, 1271–1530, by decades.*

to later in this chapter, it should be mentioned here that a total of only 116 nuns has appeared and that, whereas religious women constituted about 18 per cent of the total number of religious, they constitute only 10.6 per cent of the apostates of whom we have knowledge. Even allowing for greater loss of records for women religious, the discrepancy does pose questions. Were women religious simply more faithful to the vows of their profession? Were the difficulties for women finding another life outside the nunnery so great as to constitute a considerable deterrent to apostasy? Were other factors at play here which are now hidden from us? Whatever the explanation, the existing evidence does suggest fewer apostate nuns in relation to their numbers.

The chart above indicates the number of known apostates decade by decade from 1271 to 1530 (Figure 1). The date used is the date of apostasy, when known, or, more frequently, the date when the apostate first appears in the sources.

While acknowledging that the decennial figures derive from surviving records, the fact that about 23 per cent of the known apostates appear in the thirty years between 1341 and 1370 merits our attention. Excepting these three decades, the average for the other decades hovers near 36. What is remarkable about these mid-fourteenth-century decades is the substantial excess relative to the general decennial average: they average at 84 per decade, more than twice the average for the other decades. Two comments need be made about this mid-century increase in apostasy. In the first place, Hadcock indicates that in the generation or so before 1350 the religious orders reached their largest numbers, and it is thus in the context of a larger body of religious that these figures should be read.[11] Secondly, if we focus on the period from the summer of 1348, when the Plague first reached England, through the decade of the 1360s, when the consequences of the Plague of 1361 were being felt, we find that 183 apostates (16.7 per cent of all known apostates) appear. Should we not, then, in assessing the consequences of the Black Death on the religious orders in England, consider not only the mortalities suffered but also the apostasies experienced in the turmoil of those years? Whether increased economic opportunities – tenancies now available in the countryside – would have been a factor we may doubt, but we can never be certain. The loss of about half the population of the religious houses to the Plague must surely have had a profoundly unsettling effect for those religious who survived. How many were there like Agnes de Bowes, the sole survivor of the Black Death at Wothorpe Priory, who, in 1359, was reported to be wandering in apostasy?[12] How many houses were like Ivychurch Priory (Wiltshire)? There the prior and twelve canons died in the Plague, leaving only one canon alive; other canons came from elsewhere, but trouble ensued, leading to seven canons and two lay brothers – possibly the whole commuity – being charged in 1356 with robbery and assault and, in 1358, with apostasy.[13]

Another period which requires comment is the late fifteenth century. One hundred and one apostates appear for the last thirty years of the century – a figure near the decennial average – yet 54 of these 101 (and 12 of the 15 from the 1480s) were from one order (Premonstratensians) and are known to us by the survival of the visitation records of Bishop Redman, who, it will be remembered, frequently used the word 'apostate' in a preter-canonical sense.[14]

How common was apostasy from the religious life in medieval England? The statistical analysis which has just been presented shows that apostasy existed in every decade and in most years and that at least one-third of the religious houses had experience with apostasy. Yet the proportion of known apostates to the whole

---

[11] KH, p. 494.

[12] Lincs. Archives Office, Episc. Reg, VIII, fo. 116. Dr David Smith has drawn this case to my attention.

[13] See *VCH, Wilts.* 2. 292; C81/1789/15; *CPR, 1354–58*, p. 386; ibid., *1358–61*, p. 81. One canon was subsequently reconciled by papal letters (*CPL* 3. 594).

[14] See above, pp. 32–3.

religious population was less than 1 in 100. Accepting that the surviving records are incomplete and that many apostates have escaped modern notice, we must ask what is the proportion of known apostates to the actual historic total. Since no external controls can assist us, we find ourselves here on the thin ice of assumptions, which of their nature cannot be demonstrated. Different assumptions lead to different conclusions. If we were to assume *ex hypothesi* that only 1 in 4 actual apostates is now known to us, then the proportion would be about 4 apostates per 100 religious. If, more conservatively, we assume that only 1 in 8 is now known to us and that, therefore, 7 out of 8 apostates do not appear in surviving records, we would have a proportion of about 7 apostates per 100. If the reader would take these estimates as reasonable parameters, then the percentage of apostates would be between 3.6 per cent and 7.3 per cent of the whole. Yet even such estimates should discount those alleged apostates who were not actually apostates as well as those to whom the term was applied loosely. The conclusion that would emerge from these estimates is that apostasy occurred neither frequently nor rarely, that the apostate took his – and, to a lesser extent, her – place in the catalogue of marginal persons who constituted a permanent feature of the English population, more numerous than lepers and less numerous than fugitives from the king's justice, no more than 600 or 700 at any one time and probably much less. For religious superiors, apostasy constituted a cause of continuing concern, born from the awareness that, at any time, a member of the community might flee. Yet the picture of fugitive monks hiding in every village or on the run from village to village, peopling the roads of medieval England, clearly exaggerates. Apostasy constituted a perennial but not dominant characteristic of medieval English religious life.

THE REASONS WHY

Over a thousand religious are known to have allegedly fled from their religious houses, abandoned their vows, divested themselves of their distinctive habits and, in practice, reverted to the lay state. What led them to do so? What prompted them to defy canon law and expose themselves to humiliating punishments? What were the motives for apostasy? No area of past human conduct presents such difficulties for the historian as individual human motivation. The difficulties in understanding the motivation of one's own contemporaries and, indeed, even of one's self, are greatly compounded here by the distances of time and the exiguity of sources, where then as now monocausality cannot be assumed. Individual human motivation is to be distinguished from reasons behind policies of states and other institutions, which political and institutional historians define by time-tested traditional methods. What impelled a specific human being to perform a specific human act – what impelled a specific Cistercian monk to flee his monastery in remotest Yorkshire on a winter's night or what impelled a specific nun to flee her nunnery in Sussex ten years after her profession – we may never know with the degree of historical certitude with which we know broader policies of the church or religious orders. The question of specific human motivation may provide the final frontier of history. Facing such questions, the historian may find himself forced to use the subjunctive mood and to be satisfied with probabilities. Nevertheless, the reasons for apostasy are integral to this enquiry and command our attention.

In the overwhelming majority of the incidents of alleged apostasy, the records stand silent about the reasons. They tell us, for example, that in 1394 John de Leicester, a Cluniac monk of Bermondsey Priory (Surrey), was apostate or that in 1440 John Payne, an Augustinian canon of Woodspring Priory (Somerset), was apostate.[15] Beyond name, date and house only rarely is further information provided which suggests the reason for an individual's flight. Why John de Leicester left Bermondsey and John Payne left Woodspring it is unlikely that we shall ever know. Yet the two score or so cases in which reasons are given provide actual instances from which possible patterns can be suggested, albeit subjunctively.

Only once does heresy or near-heresy appear connected with apostasy from the religious life. In 1387, the prior of the Austin friars, Bankyn, an ardent anti-Wyclifite, sought the arrest of four apostate friars. Among them were William Pattishall and Robert Stokesley, known Wyclif supporters; the other two – Thomas Beauchamp and John Lude – may, by association, be considered Wyclifites.[16] Affairs of state only rarely can be seen in matters

---

[15] C81/1787/3; C81/1789/67.

[16] C81/1794/10. Only writs against Pattishall and Stokesley were enrolled (*CPR, 1385–89*, pp. 324, 386). In another case, the Carmelite Nicholas Weston was accused (1392 x 1396) of violating the rule by preaching, writing treatises and taking several wives in the town of Northampton (C81/1793/29).

touching religious apostasy. There was the Gilbertine canon of Malton Priory (Yorkshire), serving as rector of Rosesare in Wales, who was reported by his abbot as having left at the time of Scrope's Rebellion (1405), possibly, it seems, in support of Glendower.[17]

Religious, by their profession, vowed themselves to a lifetime lived without property of their own, without marriage and a family and in strict obedience to the authority of others. In return they could expect a secure life with shelter, clothing, food and, on a higher level, the fulfilment of a quest for a fuller spiritual life. The three vows of poverty, chastity and obedience gave context to a life lived in a community. They obviously also provided limitations to human actions: they stood in this respect like the limitations placed on human activity by employment, serfdom, marriage, actual poverty and the other social and economic restraints existing in medieval society. Yet, even in this context, the restrictions of the religious life no doubt proved more than some could bear, and apostasy resulted.

What motivated entry into the religious life was ideally a desire to live a fuller Christian life, to spend one's life in service to God, to be dedicated to personal spiritual perfection without the distraction of the world – without the encumbrance of property and the distraction of family – in the setting of a community sharing these ideals. And for some, particularly the friars and those religious in hospitals, there was the added desire to serve others. That such a pure vocation existed in the middle ages is beyond doubt; that it did not exist universally is equally beyond doubt. We shall never know how determinative such spiritual reasons were in recruitment to the religious life. That pure vocations existed seems true enough, but what other reasons were there in fact? There were parents who directed sons and daughters into religious houses just

---

[17] C81/1791/10. He was John Rays (Rase). Similarly, Glanmor Williams describes Welsh monks of Margam Abbey wandering vagabond in 1412 after the Glendower rebellion (*The Welsh Church from Conquest to Reformation* (Cardiff, 1962), p. 229). The Welsh connection can be seen in another case. Not apostasy but suspicion of it provoked Bishop Beckington of Bath and Wells, in 1444, to enquire why two monks of Goldcliff Priory (Monmouths.) were at the parish church of Bridgwater (Somerset). He was satisfied and allowed them to remain there when they explained that they had been violently expelled from their priory and were supporting themselves by saying Masses at Bridgwater (*Reg. Beckington, Hereford* 1. no. 61). In 1440 there were only a prior and two canons at Goldcliff, and they were shortly thereafter driven out by the Welsh, two of them apparently finding a safe haven in Bridgwater (KH, p. 67).

as they directed sons and daughters into marriages.[18] In the latter love might have followed the wedding; so too in the former vocation might have followed profession. The religious life had the attraction of providing security: the promise of food and shelter and the tenure that came with profession. It was a life not only approved by society but highly valued, and entrance was socially acceptable, even – especially – for the upper classes. Such worldly concerns could be mixed with an attraction to the externals of the religious life (e.g., the ceremonies, chant, habit and veil) and perhaps even an attraction to the ideal of spiritual perfection. Spiritual, worldly and mixed reasons no doubt induced young men and women to enter the religious life. Contentment, personal maturity and a sense of belonging (a vocation) might then occur. If they did not, apostasy would not necessarily follow any more than abandonment of a spouse would follow in a loveless, unhappy marriage, but the way was open for apostasy. The absence of commitment and of a sense of vocation provided the fertile ground for apostasy. Here we are dealing with remote causes. Our question must be: what drove a discontented nun, monk, friar or canon to depart in flight from the religious life?

The renunciation of personal property, the inability to call something one's own, clearly posed a problem for some individual religious. Thus, John de Coventry fled from Kenilworth Priory (Warwickshire) in the late fourteenth century, taking with him goods and chattels of the priory and £10, which belonged to a lay resident of the monastery.[19] Similarly, in 1304, Henry Howden, a Cistercian of Kirkstall Abbey (Yorkshire), was said to have apostasized, stealing some chalices and other property of the monastery.[20] Also, two Premonstratensian canons of Halesowen Abbey (Worcestershire) fled in 1324 or 1325 with books and other goods belonging to the house.[21] St Mary's Abbey, York, had a spate of such thefts by apostates. In 1299 William de York took with him a gold chalice and two silver basins.[22] Eleven years later Adam de Dalton, jnr, the *refectorius* of the monastery and collector of the king's tenth, fled York and headed for Wales, the money collected for the king in his bags, and, two years after that, another

---

[18] For a discussion of individual choice see the perceptive remarks in Penelope D. Johnson, *Equal in Monastic Profession: Religious Women in Medieval France* (Chicago, 1991), pp. 13–18.

[19] SC8/251/12547. His pardon is dated 1 May 1389 (*CPR, 1388–92*, p. 34).

[20] *Reg. Corbridge, York* I. no. 273.

[21] *Reg. Cobham, Worcester*, p. 181.   [22] *Chron. S. Mary's York*, pp. 30–1.

monk, Peter de Wakefield, apostasized with £60, a small fortune, that he stole from the bursar.[23] A trusted canon of Rocester Abbey (Staffordshire) found the temptation too strong when he was sent to the royal court with a sum of money, which, becoming fugitive, he spent instead.[24] These various examples, to which many others could be added, show the apostate leaving and taking with him money, goods or chattels from the monastery, yet we cannot be certain in every case whether the theft was the reason for the apostasy or merely an insurance against future want in the world. How many were there like John Fulstow of Louth Park (Lincolnshire), who said he took a small amount of money for his necessary expenses?[25] The issue of which precipitated which – flight or theft – could become blurred when, for example, Christ Church Priory, Canterbury, would not readmit Thomas Sandwich, a thieving apostate, until he returned what he had stolen.[26]

Other issues were involved in the obligation of poverty than the requirement that individual religious not own anything as their own. There was the concomitant obligation of religious superiors to provide their members with the necessities of life. A failure to do so violated poverty just as much as thievery. Such a failure by a prior motivated an Augustinian canon (according to his testimony) to leave Maxstoke Priory (Warwickshire) in 1518.[27] In the complex case involving William de Somerton, prior of Binham (Norfolk), a dependency of St Albans, he was said to have fled, being unable to take care of the needs of his monks and satisfy the demands of the abbot, who had provided large sums of money towards a Franciscan friar's experiments in alchemy.[28]

---

[23] Ibid., pp. 47, 53.

[24] Salter, *Chapters*, pp. 147–51, where he is called 'G. S.'. See *VCH, Staffs.* 3. 249, where Geoffrey Spurgnel is suggested. In this context should be seen the case of Richard Schelfkyng, Master of Strood Hospital (Kent), who, about 1350, left without rendering an account *(Reg. Hethe, Rochester* 2. 909–10); he was probably a Benedictine (see KH, p. 395).

[25] *CPL* 3. 607.

[26] *Lit. Cant.* 1. 232. To this can be added the case of John Spencer, Augustinian canon of Studley Priory (Warwicks.), who was said to have fraudulently extorted the enormous sum of 640 marks (£426 13s 4d) for his friends and stole precious jewels belonging to the priory; he twice apostasized and, in 1446, was imprisoned at St Augustine's Abbey, Bristol, for his crimes (Salter, *Chapters*, pp. 114–15).

[27] *Blythe's Vis.*, p. 12.

[28] *Gesta abbatum* 2. 132–3. For more on Somerton see the summaries in *VCH, Herts.* 4. 386–7; *VCH, Norf.* 3. 344; also see below, p. 145.

More subtly than the temptation for a religious to satisfy a greed for material possessions was the need of some religious to find their sense of personal identity in specific material possessions that were their own and not 'ours' and not merely *ad usum*. The sense of personal individuality – the sense of self as separate from the community – might require a religious to hold on to something not for its inherent value but simply because it was his alone. The desire for privacy emphasized this need. For example, among the demands made by Richard de Foston, a Benedictine monk of Rochester Priory in 1535, was that he should have a room of his own.[29] Not by greed alone could a religious violate the obligations of poverty but also by a desire for self-expression.

The celibate life professed by the religious clearly proved at times too difficult to sustain and led to apostasy but not with the frequency that the modern reader might expect. Stereotypes of monks running off with nuns are simply not justified by the surviving evidence. Only three such cases have appeared in the preparation of this study. The Benedictine monk John Bengeworthy of Eynsham Abbey (Oxfordshire) in 1445 broke out of the monastic prison and went apostate with a nun of nearby Godstow Abbey.[30] Also, a Cluniac monk of Pontefract Priory (Yorkshire), John Metal, in 1303, admitted that he had carnal knowledge of Constance de Daneport (alias de Pontefract) of the Cluniac nunnery in Arthington (Yorkshire) before and after his apostasy.[31] Also in this category is the nun Agnes Butler (alias Pery or Northampton) of St Michael's Priory, Stamford (Northampton-shire), who was led into 'apostasy' by the Austin friar John Harryes for a day and a night and who, when Bishop Alnwick visited in 1440, was known to have run away with a harp-player, one Robert Abbott, to Newcastle upon Tyne.[32]

Other lapses from chastity do appear in cases involving apostasy, and, in the unfairness of record survival, religious women appear perhaps disproportionately, but even here we are dealing with less than twenty instances, even including instances of pregnancy,

---

[29] Christopher Harper-Bill, 'Monastic Apostasy in Late Medieval England', *JEH* 32 (1981) 11. On this subject Jane Sayers remarks, 'For many the greatest aggravation may have been the inability to call anything one's own' ('Violence in the Medieval Cloister', *JEH* 41 (1990) 537).

[30] He was brought back to undergo penance (*Linc. Vis.* 2. 91, 116).

[31] *Reg. Corbridge, York*, nos. 255, 259.

[32] *Linc. Vis.* 2. 348. See Power, *Nunneries*, p. 449.

which will be discussed separately in the following section. A Cistercian nun of Keldholme Priory (Yorkshire) was said, in 1321, to have apostasized and besmirched herself with sins of the flesh.[33] In 1405, the pope ordered an inquiry into Wintney Priory (Hampshire) where 'two immodest nuns' – one an apostate – were reported.[34] Elsewhere nuns like Joan Horncastle of Rothwell Priory (Northamptonshire) in 1414 and Alice Hubbart of Ankerwyke Priory (Buckinghamshire) in 1519 had allegedly established adulterous relationships.[35] Male religious, again not in large numbers, apostasized for similar reasons. Archbishop Giffard of York diocese (1266–79) ordered the reconciliation of Robert Barry, an apostate canon of Felley Priory (Nottinghamshire), who had impregnated a concubine at Nottingham.[36] What happened in the parish of Dorton (Buckinghamshire) in 1447 we may never know fully, but the Augustinian canon Thomas Ewelme of nearby Notley Abbey, exercising the care of souls there, was said to be apostate, wearing secular clothes and unwilling to leave his lover at night to administer the last rites.[37] At Wigmore Abbey (Herefordshire) the canon John Eaton fled, fearing for his life, after being warned not to consort with Agnes, wife of John Barbour, nor to give her food intended for the poor. Was he fleeing the wrath of John Barbour?[38] More than unchaste behaviour seemed the problem at Barton Priory, a small house on the Isle of Wight, which was composed of an archpriest, five chaplains and a clerk, where the conduct of the archpriest, William Love, was the subject of an inquiry in 1403 'concerning apostasy, sacrilege, adultery, fornication and other grave and enormous crimes'.[39] In all this, the focus is on reasons for apostasy and, in the kaleidoscope of apostasy, we catch only fleeting glimpses of unchaste apostates.

The submission of one's will to the will of a superior, the

---

[33] *Reg. Melton, York* 2. no. 157.

[34] *CPL* 6. 55.

[35] Horncastle lived with William Luffewyk for three years (*Reg. Repingdon, Lincoln* 3. no. 15; for her reconciliation see below, p. 154) and Hubbart with a man called Sutton (*Vis. Dioc. Linc.* 2. 70).

[36] *Reg. W. Giffard, York*, nos. 666, 916.

[37] *Linc. Vis.* 2. 257. His apostasy may have consisted merely in his refusal to return to Notley when recalled by the prior.

[38] *Reg. Spofford, Hereford*, pp. 69–70.

[39] 'de apostasia, sacrilegio et fornicacione et aliis criminibus magnis et enormis' (*Reg. Wykeham, Winchester* 2. 550). He had been in the Fleet prison in 1394 (ibid., pp. 403–4, 423, 455–8). See *VCH, Hants.* 2. 180–1.

obedience to the orders of another, the daily adherence to a prescribed regimen may have constituted the greatest obstacle to a fulfilled life in a religious house. By the vow of obedience the professed religious was bound not merely to the direct mandates of superiors but also to the mandates of the rule itself, portions of which would normally be read aloud daily and which soon became memorized. The very act of apostasy was an act of disobedience. The ultimate act of disobedience was committed by a Cistercian monk of Buildwas Abbey (Shropshire), Thomas de Tonge, who in 1342 killed his abbot.[40] Not as extreme but clearly disrespectful of authority was the action of Ralph de Byker, another Cistercian (of Swineshead Abbey, Lincolnshire), who allegedly laid violent hands on the person of his abbot and then fled to London, where, remaining silent about his past, he became a monk of St Mary Graces.[41]

Conversely, the abbot was obliged, by this same obedience, to maintain a secure place in which his monks could live the religious life. There was something less than peace at Whitby Abbey (Yorkshire) in 1366. Central to the dispute was Thomas de Hauksgard, a monk of Whitby Abbey, who was living at the dependent cell at Middlesborough. The abbot charged him with incontinence with three married women and with having sired sons by them. At the correction of his faults in the chapter house at Whitby, Hauksgard bolted the abbey, taking with him perhaps a majority of the monks. To the abbot visitor Hauksgard denied leaving without permission and said that a threefold fear forced him to flee. He feared imprisonment; he feared Thomas Maulay, the abbot's friend and the local power; and, what is more, he feared the armed men in the cloister. More was involved in these matters than a monk allegedly yielding to the temptations of the flesh.[42] Similarly, a rebellion or close to it occurred at the Augustinian priory at Christchurch (Hampshire) in 1402. One wonders what could have provoked seven of the canons to swear on the Blessed Sacrament to remove the prior and other superiors. Could they have been mere discontents, brought to this point of conspiracy by the feverish demagoguery of a ringleader? Or had there been

---

[40] *CPL* 3. 137; *CPR, 1343–45*, p. 400. Other alleged murderers appear among the apostates. For example, in 1268, Robert de Cambridge, a monk of St Mary's Abbey, York, was charged with homicide (*Chron. S. Mary's York*, p. 11).

[41] He was absolved in 1409 and remained at the London monastery (*CPL* 5. 346–7).

[42] Pantin, *Chapters* 3. 277–309.

flagrant, persistent, arbitrary use of power which had gone beyond the limits of human tolerance? They fled in apostasy and – their conspiracy discovered or failed – were subsequently punished.[43] A similar breakdown of authority led to apostasy at the Benedictine priory at Littlemore (Oxfordshire), where, in 1518, there resided a prioress and five other nuns (three surnamed Wynter). Elizabeth Wynter refused to obey the prioress and continued to play and wrestle with boys in the cloister. When the prioress confined Elizabeth to the parlour and put her in stocks, three of the other nuns (including the two other Wynters) broke into the parlour, released Elizabeth and set fire to the hated stocks. The prioress sought the aid of servants and neighbours in Oxford, but, before they could assist her, the four nuns broke a window and fled into the night and into apostasy. Elizabeth Wynter, upon her return, was severely beaten by the prioress in the chapter house with punches and kicks. At least, that was the prioress's story. Only months earlier, during the bishop's visitation, she herself had been reported to the visitor by her nuns for having stolen goods of the priory to provide a dowry for her daughter, whom she had by a priest from Kent, who still visited. Was she now having her revenge?[44]

Nothing perhaps better illustrates the significance of obedience as an issue in apostasy than what followed the election of the saintly Thomas de la Mare as abbot of St Albans in 1349. Intent on reforming the monastic life by insisting on the rigorous observance of the rule, de la Mare alienated a considerable part of his monastery. The sympathetic chronicler recounts how many monks, faced with these unaccustomed severities, left in apostasy. Eight of these are named and are said never to have returned. Others did return, so many in number that, to avoid public scandal, not all were reconciled in the chapter house at St Albans, and those who had left from dependent cells were reconciled at their cells.[45] Similar changes possibly lay behind the decisions of long-professed religious at other monasteries to leave, the most

---

[43] *Reg. Wykeham, Winchester*, pp. 535–6, 542; *VCH, Hants.* 2. 157–8. John Andrew, one of the rebels, had been pursued by a writ for his capture in 1399 (C81/1789/6; *CPR, 1396–99*, p. 221).

[44] Bishop Longland of Lincoln was told that Juliana Wynter had a child two years before and would not refrain from *colloquium* with men. See *Vis. Dioc. Linc.* 3. 11; Power, *Nunneries*, pp. 595–6.

[45] *Gesta abbatum* 2. 415; see *CPR, 1340–43*, p. 444.

conspicuous example of whom is perhaps the monk of Reading Abbey who, in 1286, abandoned the religious life after thirty years.[46] One suspects that below the surface in such cases there lie submerged the reality of a new abbot, a new prior, a new cellarer, some changing circumstance to motivate the extreme action of apostasy.

The daily living of the rule, the daily following of the *horarium*, the repetitions of formularies – how many times 'Deus, in adiutorium meum intende' was said each day – could start a chain reaching from repetition to monotony to boredom to *acedia*, and at some point the chain might be broken by apostasy. As early as the fifth century the dangers to the life of a monk that resulted from *tristitia* and *acedia* were seen by John Cassian.[47] And in our period the reforming de la Mare recognized the existence of monastic tedium at St Albans and enacted reforms in his constitutions of 1351 to counteract it.[48] Later, in his abbotship, in 1384, many of his monks wished to take up the cross to follow Bishop Despenser in his ill-fated crusade to Flanders, because, in the words of the chronicler, 'quibus quies claustri displicuerat': they were bored.[49] A similar note was sounded by another chronicler, the anonymous author of the *Eulogium*, a monk of Malmesbury Abbey, who confessed that he wrote his history in the hope of relieving the tedium of his life in the monastery:

I often sit bored in the cloister, my senses dull and faculties idle, plagued with wicked thoughts, because of the length of the lessons and the monotony of the prayers, and because of the vain boastings and evil ways of the world (their pleasure and general acceptance, and what is worse their numerousness). Therefore I wondered how I could extinguish such burning darts which try to inflict a multitude of wounds on the meditations of a monk. And I decided, at the request of my superiors, to prepare a work from various authors for the information of posterity.[50]

---

[46] *Epp. Jo. Peckham* 3. 933–4. See above, p. 52, for the elderly monk of St Albans, Ralph Whichchurche, who left after fifty years and avoided apostasy by becoming an honorary papal chaplain.

[47] *Institutiones*, bks 9, 10 (*PL* 49. 351–69). He even recalled the case of a monk who, under the influence of *acedia*, convinced another monk to leave but who then himself remained.

[48] *Gesta abbatum* 2. 421. For more on this general subject see Power, *Nunneries*, chap. 7.

[49] *Gesta abbatum* 2. 416. Seven were granted permission, and one of these died.

[50] *Eulogium (historiarum sive temporis)* (ed. F. S. Haydon; RS; 3 vols.; London, 1858–63) 1. 2; translation is Antonia Gransden's (*Historical Writing in England* (2 vols.; London, 1974–82) 2. 103).

There is no reason to think boredom peculiar to St Albans and Malmesbury and every reason to think it a constant threat wherever the regular life was lived. Not every monk who was 'bored in the cloister' was fortunate to be asked to write a work. One suspects that, behind the sparse recountings of the fact of apostasy that generally confront the historian in the sources, where no reasons are given, there frequently lie an ennui, a tiredness of the spirit, fertile ground for discontent, unhappiness, violation of vows and, in the end, flight into apostasy.

It might appear that such boredom prompted the bizarre behaviour of Marion de Rye, a nun of Romsey Abbey (Hampshire). In 1369 she allegedly put off her veil and refused to sit with the other nuns in the choir but insisted, rather, on sitting in the nave with lay women. Moreover, she also refused to attend chapter, to eat in the nuns' refectory and to sleep in the dormitory. Instead, she sought the company of lay persons, with whom she ate and gossiped. She would neither confess nor receive the Eucharist. Strange as it may seem, Marion de Rye became apostate without leaving her abbey. Is one permitted to see here, in this curious affair, not the case of a woman suffering from boredom but the tragedy of a woman in the throes of a mental breakdown?[51]

REASONS PECULIAR TO WOMEN RELIGIOUS

Throughout this study issues touching women religious have not been separated for special discussion. They have been treated as integral to the story of the apostasy of religious in medieval England. There is little to distinguish men and women apostates as this story unfolds. They were subject to the same canonical provisions defining apostasy and dispensing penalties for apostasy, to the same process for the use of the secular arm, to the same manner of reconciliation upon return and, in the end, to the same fate in the 1530s. Examples of women apostates are given in these pages at every stage, yet such integration cannot – and, indeed, should not – be total. While women religious shared with men religious similar reactions (as has just been seen) to the *onera* imposed by their vows of poverty, chastity and obedience, still the question of motivation for apostasy raises issues specific to women.

---

[51] *Reg. Wykeham, Winchester* 2. 77–9. For instances of insane nuns see Power, *Nunneries*, pp. 32–3.

Two such issues are pregnancy and abduction, and they warrant our separate attention.[52]

The pregnant nun deserves attention not as the subject of snickering ridicule but as a serious historical subject, even as a subject with a tragic dimension. A nun, finding herself pregnant, might have spent days and perhaps weeks in denial, in the irrational hope that what was true was not true, that reality was not real, that the nightmare would end with a fresh awakening. Once having accepted the reality of her situation, she knew that her violation of vows of her profession, until then private and hidden, would soon become obvious to the world. Her pregnancy convicted her, in the eyes of all, of the grossest transgression of her sacred vows. No male religious, no matter how flagrant and repeated his transgressions, would ever be so publicly exposed to the scorn and contempt of society. No wonder, then, that some such unfortunate women fled their houses, apostasy seen as the necessary price to pay for preserving self-dignity. Such a one was Beatrice de Hawkesworth, a Cistercian nun of Esholt Priory (Yorkshire). In 1303 she discovered that she was pregnant and fled to her father's house to have her baby. The archbishop of York, Thomas Corbridge, sent two different orders to the prioress: on 17 October 1303 he gave orders not to admit Beatrice and on 7 March 1304 he gave orders to admit her. Presumably, in the meantime, she had delivered her child.[53] Pregnancy may have played a part in other instances of apostate nuns. An apostate nun of Wintney Priory (Hampshire) in 1405 was said to have had children and one of the Sisters Wynter of Littlemore Priory (Oxfordshire) had a child in 1518. In these cases it is not clear that apostasy actually occurred because of their pregnancies.[54] Even including such cases and, indeed, the cases of Isabel Gervays, soon to be met, and Elizabeth Lutton, whose story is told in the final section of this chapter, the total number of

---

[52] Apostasy of nuns (i.e., the abandonment of their religious life) must be sharply distinguished from simple violation of enclosure (i.e., leaving the monastic precincts). The latter was much legislated against, most prominently by the decree *Periculoso* of Boniface VIII (1299), and enforcement, though frequently tried, had little success. See Power, *Nunneries*, chap. 9; Elizabeth M. Makowski, 'The Canon Law and Cloistered Women: *Periculoso* and Its Commentators, 1298–1545' (Unpublished Ph.D. dissertation, Columbia University, 1993); Makowski and James A. Brundage, 'Enclosure of Nuns: The Decretal *Periculoso* and its Commentators', *Journal of Medieval History* 20 (1994) 143–55.

[53] *Reg. Corbridge, York* 1. nos. 247, 269.

[54] For Wintney and for Littlemore see above, p. 81.

apostasies known to have occurred when pregnancy may have been an issue does not exceed six. That there were others now unknown to us no one would deny, but the surviving evidence does not support the suggestion that pregnancy constituted a principal factor in the defection of religious women.[55]

When one speaks of the abduction of nuns, the word 'abduction' here does not necessarily imply that the nuns in question were snatched from their nunneries against their wishes: the word has the meaning merely of 'taking away' and is neutral regarding consent.[56] In fact, if the nun was accomplice to the abduction, she was clearly apostate. The historian of English nunneries held the view that such nuns were 'always willing parties' and that 'all abductions were in reality elopements'.[57] Nothing has appeared in the preparation of this study to contradict that judgement.

The problem of the abduction of nuns was not new to the England of the thirteenth century, when legislation appeared. The *Lex Baiuvariorum* (seventh century) provided that a man seducing a nun to leave her monastery and attempting to marry her should be fined a significant amount and that the nun must be sought out and returned to her monastery.[58] Even earlier, Justinian had required that action be taken against men seizing women from their monasteries and that the women be restored.[59] This text of Justinian lived on in the middle ages not only in the Roman law collections but, perhaps more importantly, in the canon law collections, since Gratian included it in his *Decretum*.[60] In England specific legislation was enacted in the Statute of Westminster II (1285), and this action was prompted, it seems abundantly certain, by a specific case. It had to do with Sir Osbert Giffard and the Benedictine abbey of nuns at Wilton (Wiltshire). First the legislation:

---

[55] The more general subject of pregnancy among nuns awaits its historian, who will begin with Power, *Nunneries*, chap. 11.

[56] For the changing meanings of the word *raptus* see J. B. Post, 'Ravishment of Women and the Statutes of Westminster', *Legal Records and the Historian* (ed. J. H. Baker; London, 1978), pp. 150–64, and Christopher Cannon, '*Raptus* in the Chaumpaigne Release and a Newly Discovered Document concerning the Life of Geoffrey Chaucer', *Speculum* 68 (1993) 74–94.

[57] Power, *Nunneries*, p. 440.

[58] *Monumenta Germaniae Historica, Legum*, sect. 1, *Leges nationum Germanicarum* 5. 1. 283.

[59] *Novellae* (6th edn; *Corpus Iuris Civilis* 3, Berlin, 1954) 123. 43.

[60] C.27. q.1. c.30.

He that carrieth a nun from her house, although she consent, shall be punished by three years' imprisonment and shall make convenient satisfaction to the house from whence she was taken, and nevertheless shall make fine at the king's will.[61]

What had been a crime in church law became thus a crime against the laws of the realm.[62] The prelates of the Canterbury province, in their criticism of the Statute of Westminster II, objected that the abduction of a nun with her consent pertains not to the court of the king but to the church, which should impose punishment not only on the nun but on her abductor.[63] The royal response was that it was not the intention of the crown to deprive prelates of that which belonged to them regarding the punishment of abducted nuns and their abductors.[64] Two points need emphasizing. First, the statute did not deny to the church its right to punish the abductor: the imprisonment and fine were intended as additions to the ecclesiastical penalties. Second, regarding the abducted nun, the statute provided no penalty even if she consented to her abduction, whereas the bishops focused, in their complaint, on the consenting abductee and affirmed their right to punish her. The implication may be that the statute was aimed at willing abduction. Be that as it may, what seems quite clear is that this legislation was prompted by the actions of Sir Osbert Giffard in the previous year.[65]

A great knight of the West Country, Sir Osbert Giffard held lands in nine counties.[66] Two of his cousins were influential bishops: the brothers Walter Giffard, archbishop of York, who had died in 1279, and Godfrey Giffard, bishop of Worcester and no doubt a player behind the scenes in this drama. Their sister Juliana Giffard was abbess of Wilton Abbey, one of the larger and

---

[61] 13 Edw. I, c.34 (*Statutes* 1. 87).

[62] The writ *de moniali abducta* appears in some registers of writs; see, e.g., BL, Lansdowne MS 652, fo. 272; Washington, Library of Congress, Law Library MS 131, fo. 64v. Dr Paul Brand, who has drawn my attention to the latter reference, dates that register *c.* 1293.

[63] *Councils and Synods* 2. 2. 965.

[64] Ibid., 2. 2. 967.

[65] The abduction of nuns, singled out specifically by statute and writ, stands apart from the abduction of male religious such as the Dominican friar William de Pykkeworth of Thetford Priory (Norf.), who, in 1380, was abducted by scholars of Mildenhall (Suffolk) (*Reg. Wykeham, Winchester* 2. 318–19).

[66] C. Moor, *Knights of Edward I* (5 vols.; Harl. Soc., Visitations, vols. 80–4, 1929–32) 2 (1929) 115–16.

wealthier of English nunneries, which provided the *mise-en-scène* of these events. Under cover of a dark night in 1284, Sir Osbert Giffard abducted two of its nuns, Alice Russell and Anna Giffard. The enormity of the crime in the eyes of contemporaries can be seen in what followed. The abbess, cousin Juliana, reacted quickly, for in November 1284 Sir Osbert was ordered seized of lands in Oxfordshire, Somerset and Wiltshire. This royal order stated that he 'has violently taken a nun of Wylton and carried her beyond seas without licence and there detains her against her will'.[67] One might suppose that the object of his designs was Anna Giffard, no doubt a kinswoman of both the abductor and the abbess (and, too, of the bishop of Worcester).[68] In the following summer there was inserted into this great statute a chapter about the abduction of nuns. If the Osbert Giffard crime and this statutory provision were unrelated, it would have been a coincidence of the greatest sort. Six months or so after the enactment of the statute, the bishops of the southern province met at London. Present among them was Giffard's cousin, the bishop of Worcester, and Walter Scammel, bishop of Salisbury, in whose diocese the crime had occurred. Also present was a repentant Osbert Giffard, seeking absolution from his excommunication. Archbishop Pecham, presiding over the synod, declared that Osbert Giffard had caused a national scandal by his sin.[69] Having agreed to return the abducted nuns and having accepted the penance, the knight excommunicate was absolved. He returned to the West Country in disgrace, ready to undertake a most humiliating public penance.[70] On Ash Wednesday, a week after his absolution in London, Giffard was to appear barefoot and bareheaded, dressed in penitential dress, among the public sinners in Salisbury Cathedral and, with them, to be ejected, not to be readmitted until Holy Thursday. On three holydays he was to

---

[67] *Calendar of the Fine Rolls* (22 vols.; London, 1911–61) 1. 207. The use of the singular here is puzzling, since, at the time of his absolution in February 1286, the two abducted nuns were to be returned to Wilton.

[68] To complicate matters further, the will (1301) of Godfrey Giffard, bishop of Worcester, left 20s. to an Agnes Giffard, nun of Wilton (*Reg. Guisborough, Worcester*, p. 51). In addition, Mabel Giffard was abbess of Shaftesbury (elected 1291).

[69] *Epp. Jo. Peckham* 3. 916–17.

[70] Two similar but slightly different forms of the penance survive: the penance imposed by Archbishop Pecham on 21 Feb. 1286 (ibid.) and the penance imposed by Bishop Scammel of Salisbury on 22 Feb. 1286 (*Reg. Giffard, Worcester*, pp. 278–9). Pecham left the execution of the penance to Scammel, and we can infer that it was Scammel's form of the penance that was imposed.

be flogged around Salisbury Cathedral and on three Tuesdays through the marketplace at Salisbury. Similar floggings were to be thrice administered at the church and marketplace at Wilton and at the church and marketplace of Amesbury. Further, Giffard was to be deprived of the insignia of knighthood and he agreed to spend three years in the Holy Land.[71] That this high-born, well-connected, powerful, wealthy man was required to undergo such public humiliation is an indication of how serious a scandal he had caused by abducting nuns from Wilton Abbey.

Were Alice Russell and Anna Giffard apostate nuns? The answer hinges on the question of consent. If they acquiesced in Osbert Giffard's schemes, then they were clearly apostate. Why did the new legislation specifically indicate that abduction even with consent was to be punished, when the phrase 'although she consent' added nothing to the substance, since abduction was neutral to consent? Also, Bishop Scammel directed the abbess and convent of Wilton to readmit the two nuns with kindness, rejoicing that the lost had been found.[72] 'Lost', in this sense, implies wayward sheep and refers to the rejoicing over the lost sinner who repents (Luke 15. 4–7). This reference presumes fault on the part of the nuns. What human complexities lay behind our sources one can only surmise, but what was probably a family dispute gained national notoriety, brought a prominent man to public disgrace and led to new legislation, and at the core of the matter was the assisted apostasy of a nun.

The enactment of this statute and the example of Sir Osbert Giffard did not end the practice of abduction of nuns from their enclosures. In 1290 Bishop Sutton of Lincoln described how a nun of Godstow Abbey (Oxfordshire) – Agnes de Sheen – was violently dragged from the convent's carriage at Wycombe much against her will by evil men. Sutton's rage was soon directed to Agnes herself, whom he discovered had apostasized.[73] When Margaret Everingham, a nun of Broadholme Priory, a Premonstratensian

---

[71] There is no evidence that he ever went to the Holy Land (see Moor, *Knights*, pp. 115–16).

[72] *Reg. Giffard, Worcester*, pp. 279–80; see Power, *Nunneries*, p. 440. Two years later a nun of Foukeholme Priory (Yorks.) was reportedly abducted by William, a chaplain of Yarm, Yorks. (*VCH, Yorks*. 3. 116). Similarly, another chaplain (John Smith) may have been involved in the abduction of two nuns of Easebourne (Sussex) in 1478 (W. H. Blaauw, 'Episcopal Visitation of the Benedictine Nunnery of Easebourne', *Sussex Archaeol. Coll.* 9 (1857) 17).

[73] *Reg. Sutton, Lincoln*, 2. lxiii, 22–4, 132–3.

house in Nottinghamshire, was abducted in 1350, three men were allegedly involved: William Fox, parson of Lea (Lincolnshire), and two Franciscan friars of Lincoln, John Fox and Thomas de Lingiston.[74]

The issues of pregnancy and abduction were combined in the happenings at Nunnaminster (Winchester) in 1370. In January of that year the abbess complained to the crown that 'a great number of evildoers' broke into the abbey and abducted Isabel Gervays, a professed nun of that house. They also took goods of the abbess valued at £40. Commissioners of oyer and terminer were appointed, who were to punish the abductors with three years' imprisonment and to require satisfaction to Nunnaminster.[75] Five months later Bishop Wykeham instructed the abbess to receive the apostate Isabel Gervays and to treat her with kindness and sweetness, but Gervays was not permitted to resume her religious habit. The abbess should be vigilant lest Isabel run away. She was pregnant, he said, and he would come after the child was born to determine what should be done.[76] That Isabel Gervays was called apostate means that she was considered a willing accomplice to the abduction. The use of a large number of men in the abduction suggests something more, indeed, than an unhappy and lonely woman, yearning for her beloved.[77]

THE CASE OF THE DEVIANT NUN OF YEDINGHAM PRIORY

Pregnancy, abduction, landgrabbing, involvement of courts ecclesiastical and secular – all played parts in the alleged apostasy of Elizabeth Lutton, who, about 1512, professed as a Benedictine nun of Yedingham Priory in the East Riding of Yorkshire and who fled about 1531. If, at story's end, the fate of the nun at the centre of the

---

[74] R. E. G. Cole, *The Priory of Broadholme* (Associated Architectural Societies' Reports and Papers 28 (1905–6) 66–7); see Power, *Nunneries*, pp. 449–50. During the pontificate of John Gynwell, bishop of Lincoln (1347–62), Joan Bruys, a nun of Nuneaton (Warwicks.), was abducted by Nicholas Green of Isham (Northants.), with whom she attempted marriage (Power, p. 441n.).

[75] *CPR, 1367–70*, p. 353. William Wykeham, bishop of Winchester, mentioned this abduction in a letter of 24 Jan. 1370 (*Reg. Wykeham, Winchester* 2. 100–1). Nunnaminster had 39 nuns in 1381 (KH, p. 268).

[76] *Reg. Wykeham*, pp. 114–15.

[77] At Easebourne Priory (Sussex) one of the nuns reported to the bishop visitor in 1478 that two of her fellow nuns had been abducted; it was also reported that one may have had children (Blaauw, *Sussex Archaeol. Coll.* 9 (1857), pp. 17–19).

controversy is uncertain, she may represent for us, in a sense, the medieval nun, a person seen by us only in glimpses, whose conventual life was virtually unchronicled, whose religious life was lived in the historical shadows of great monasteries of men, and whose vocation frequently lacks, for us, clear definition. The issues revolving about the veiled – and, indeed, unveiled – head of Elizabeth Lutton illustrate the two reasons for departure unique to women religious, just described, and much else besides.

Who was Elizabeth Lutton?[78] Like so many girls who became religious, she came from a substantial landholding family, the Luttons of Knapton, who held the manor of Knapton and West Lutton as well as lands and tenements in eight other villages (including Flamborough) in different parts of the East Riding. Her grandfather, William Lutton, had two sons, Stephen, her father and heir apparent to the Lutton estates, and Thomas. At the age of fourteen, Elizabeth, possibly an only child but certainly the only surviving child at the time of her father's death, entered the priory of Benedictine nuns at Yedingham, only about two miles from Knapton. After a year's probation, probably in 1512, Elizabeth Lutton proceeded to her solemn profession, a day which some of those present recalled twenty years later with detail. There came to Yedingham on that day the great Cistercian abbot of Rievaulx, successor of St Ailred, with two of his monks (one of whom was later to become abbot), the prioress of the Cistercian nuns at nearby Wykeham Priory, a canon regular from Bridlington Priory (a local centre of pilgrimage) and many others, whose names the long-serving chaplain, when asked two decades later, could then no longer remember.[79] Elizabeth Lutton publicly asked the prioress for admission. There was no demurrer, no public protestation, no sign of unhappiness. On the contrary, a nun present on that day later

---

[78] The description of events in this case, unless otherwise stated, is taken from two sources: (i) the inquiry by the ecclesiastical court of York (York, Borthwick Institute, CP.G.216) and (ii) the proceedings in Star Chamber (*Yorkshire Star Chamber Proceedings*, Yorks. Archaeol. Soc., Rec. Ser., vols. 41 (1909) no. 81; 45 (1911) no. 52; 51 (1914) no. 45). I am grateful to Professor Claire Cross, who drew my attention to this case. For a useful summary see her study *The End of Medieval Monasticism in the East Riding of Yorkshire* (Beverley, 1993), pp. 15–17; see also G. W. O. Woodward, *The Dissolution of the Monasteries* (London, 1966), pp. 42–5, where this case is discussed.

[79] John Burton was abbot of Rievaulx. His monk companions were Edward Kirkby (later abbot) and Richard Scarborough. The Augustinian canon from Bridlington was Peter Hardee and the prioress of Wykeham a certain Elizabeth. The chaplain was Robert Marton.

said that Elizabeth showed every sign of happiness ('gerebat hilarem uultum et gesturam'). Her fellow nuns said that, once professed, Elizabeth entered fully into the life of the nunnery by participating in divine services, accepting the authority of the prioress and acting in all things like a nun. Events were to change this.

Elizabeth Lutton became pregnant. This happened, it would seem, in 1526, about fourteen years after entry, when she would have been about twenty-eight years old. The witnesses, later recalling these events, were virtually unanimous – the prioress alone dissenting – that Elizabeth became pregnant during the first year of Prioress Agnes Braydericke. The latter – in a possible attempt to distance herself from the accusation that the misconduct occurred on her watch – swore that it happened in the final year of her predecessor, Prioress Elizabeth Whitehead. Once it was discovered that she was with child, Elizabeth Lutton was immediately separated from the other nuns and soon placed in a house outside the cloister but within the priory precincts. There, in that house, was born her child, about whom nothing further is recorded. One presumes that the child was taken and reared by her kinsfolk or perhaps by the father. However that may be, once delivered of her child, Elizabeth wanted to return to the cloister and secured the assistance of the nuns' confessor, John Fraunces, a Franciscan friar of Scarborough Priory. He pleaded with Prioress Braydericke and the convent to receive her back into the community.[80] Elizabeth Lutton appeared personally, no doubt in chapter, and asked to be readmitted into the cloister. And so she was, and she resumed her former life, but not *usque ad mortem*.

It was probably in 1531 that Elizabeth Lutton, claiming that she was not a nun, fled Yedingham Priory and married Thomas Scaseby. She had taken profession, she said, under duress and had not given free consent. If true, then her profession was no profession and she was no nun. If untrue, Elizabeth Lutton was a nun of Yedingham Priory and an apostate. This question was brought to the attention of the ecclesiastical court of York, and on the last day of April 1532 the official of that court (its presiding judge), Dr Nicholas Evererd, went to Yedingham to hold a judicial inquiry. A draft set of articles of inquiry included, in addition to questions relating to Elizabeth Lutton, a question

---

[80] The prioress was later to say that he had pleaded immoderately ('fecit instancias non modicas').

about the general state of the house under Prioress Braydericke, a question not actually used in the inquiry. The prioress and seven nuns – the entire community? – as well as the chaplain, who had served there for about forty years, were interviewed singly, a notary recording their testimony. Only two of the senior nuns and the chaplain had been at Yedingham at the time of Elizabeth Lutton's profession – the prioress herself came later – and they concurred with the narrative just given: Elizabeth Lutton professed the religious life publicly and without protest. All but the three junior nuns (who had entered after the events) gave testimony that Elizabeth, while pregnant, was segregated from the community and pleaded to be readmitted after the child's birth. The prioress, besides differing from the other witnesses about the date of the pregnancy and birth, added significant detail surprisingly not mentioned by the other witnesses. She swore that at different times since her own profession (in 1517) and before her election as prioress (in 1526), when she and Elizabeth Lutton were fellow nuns, she heard Elizabeth say that she had not given free consent to her youthful profession. Dr Evererd pressed her on this point. To whom did Lutton say this? She was loquacious and much given to talk, the prioress responded, and said these things to her fellow nuns and to lay persons both in private conversations and in correspondence. None of the other nuns, several of whom were members of the community at that time, corroborated the prioress's account.[81] Should one detect in Prioress Braydericke's testimony a support for Lutton? Was the prioress influenced by her apparently friendly relations with Sir Robert Constable, whom we shall encounter shortly in this story?

To the experienced ecclesiastical judge Nicholas Evererd two facts would have been central to his judgement: (i) Elizabeth Lutton made public, solemn profession without protest and did so, according to the testimony of the oldest nun there, cheerfully, and (ii) Elizabeth Lutton, after bearing a child, pleaded successfully to be readmitted and, being readmitted, she accepted the punishment imposed on her. Her *post-factum* protestations, known only through the testimony of one witness, probably carried little weight. On the face of it, we might say that Elizabeth Lutton had a weak case. Although Dr Evererd's judgement has not survived, it would

---

[81] The others were not specifically asked to respond to this part of Prioress Braydericke's testimony. They merely said that Elizabeth Lutton, during that period, lived like a nun.

appear quite likely that, on the evidence, her profession would
have been judged valid and that she, therefore, would have been
declared apostate.[82]

We might well ask why Elizabeth Lutton fled Yedingham
Priory in 1531. It could be that the reasons alleged and just
rehearsed moved her to do so: after eighteen years as a nun her
conscience could no longer allow her to continue living a lie.
Perhaps, but there were family considerations of great moment
which make us pause before rushing to judgement. It will be
remembered that her grandfather, William Lutton, had considerable holdings in the East Riding and that her father, Stephen
Lutton, stood to inherit and that Elizabeth was Stephen Lutton's
sole surviving child. Yet Stephen Lutton predeceased his father,
which left Elizabeth's uncle, Thomas, as heir apparent, since by her
religious profession she had become civilly dead and unable to
inherit. In 1531, her grandfather, William Lutton, died, leaving his
son, Thomas, as heir to his lands and tenements. Thomas Lutton
alleged that Elizabeth denounced her profession as invalid, fled
Yedingham Priory with the connivance of Sir Robert Constable,
married a certain Thomas Scaseby and claimed her inheritance.[83]
That she left her convent, attempted marriage with Scaseby (the
child's father?) and claimed the Lutton lands was never in dispute.
The ecclesiastical inquiry into the validity of her profession had to
do with these issues – if not professed, she was free to leave, marry
and inherit. At this point another actor appeared on the scene, Sir
Robert Constable.

The Constables had held the lordship of Flamborough since the
time of Richard I.[84] In 1536 Sir Robert was to emerge as one of
the leaders of the Pilgrimage of Grace and, in 1537, he was
executed as a traitor. That was in the future; now, in 1532, he
became involved in the Lutton affair. He was sixty years old and at
that time came into conflict with Thomas Lutton, Elizabeth's uncle
and supposed heir of William Lutton, who filed a bill of complaint
in Star Chamber against Constable, alleging the latter's misconduct
in three matters. First, Constable, on the pretext of the uncertainty
of the inheritance, seized Lutton's lands at Flamborough and let

---

[82] See below, p. 95, where the outcome is further discussed.
[83] The date of her flight is not known precisely. The witnesses at Yedingham in April 1532
said that she had left about two years before. Her uncle, Thomas Lutton, claimed in his
Star Chamber bill that she had left after her grandfather's death.
[84] See *Dictionary of National Biography* 4. 969–70.

them, collecting the rents as if they were his own. Also, Thomas Lutton served on a jury at York that found against Constable and in favour of a royal wardship. Constable, enraged by this, entered into Lutton's lands in Lutton and discharged the tenants. A third source of conflict concerned the flight of Elizabeth Lutton from Yedingham Priory, in whose flight, according to Thomas Lutton, Constable was seriously implicated: it was Constable's servants, who, together with Thomas Scaseby, the future husband, had abducted her from the nunnery.

Alleging infirmity, Sir Robert Constable did not attend the Star Chamber proceedings but sent his response instead. He declared that the matter should be resolved by the common law and the canon law and, by implication, not in Star Chamber. Yes, he admitted, he had seized the Lutton lands, but he was merely exercising his right of lordship, since the inheritance lay in dispute between Thomas and Elizabeth Lutton. Moreover, apart from marvelling that his tenant Thomas Lutton found against him at York, he took no action against him or his tenants or farmers. Finally, neither he nor his servants enticed Elizabeth Lutton to leave Yedingham. Thomas Lutton replied by repeating his charges and by adding that, since he had made the bill of complaint, he had been assaulted by one of Sir Robert's servants and six other men in the city of York, who put his life in jeopardy and who caused him to be arrested. Constable replied that he was in no way guilty of this 'riot' at York.

In a deposition for Star Chamber (dated 30 January 1533) Sir Robert Constable gave a curious response to the charge of abducting Elizabeth Lutton from Yedingham Priory. He, of course, denied the charge, but he did more: he told a story, which bears retelling. Only once did he ever meet Elizabeth Lutton. He was riding, he said, from Flamborough to Thornton in Pickering Lythe to visit his son-in-law, Sir Roger Cholmeley, to go hunting. On the way he passed near Yedingham and decided to call 'to drink with the prioress'. Two of the nuns greeted him and told him that the prioress was not at home, but invited him to have a cup of ale, which he did. He went into the priory church, he continued, while the nuns were present, and there he saw Elizabeth Lutton 'looking out at a window on high looking into the church'. He asked if she were with child, and she answered 'ye'. In the presence of the other nuns, so he said, he further asked her if she was content to remain as a nun, and she answered that she

94

had been forced to enter the nunnery, as many of the nuns there knew. 'And the said Elizabeth spake other wordes not like a religious woman.' Constable claimed that he warned the nuns to watch out for her since she was with child and wearing lay clothes ('in seculer wede'). Whether she was now married, he had no knowledge. He did understand that Scaseby was excommunicate but that the excommunication had been lifted because Scaseby had appealed to the Court of the Arches.

Constable's deposition to Star Chamber fails to date his reputed visit to Yedingham Priory. Without necessarily accepting the truthfulness of his account, one can reasonably suggest that it was meant to apply to 1526, when we know that Elizabeth Lutton was pregnant. This engaging story was, in reality, a smokescreen: Constable was merely saying that he met her only once, while the complaint was not that he had met her at all but that he had colluded with Thomas Scaseby to abduct her from her priory. Also, it is curious that Constable knew so much about Scaseby's canonical status, even the effect of his appeal on his excommuni-cation, when at the same time he pretended to know little of the matter. It may not have gone unnoticed in Star Chamber that Constable had been involved, in 1525, in abducting a royal ward, apparently to marry her to his son.[85] Whatever our suspicions might suggest about his part in the Lutton affair, we may never know the precise outcome, yet there are clear indications that Thomas Lutton prevailed. When commissioners visited Yedingham Priory in 1536, they reported that all the nuns save one, an Elizabeth Sutton, wished to continue as religious, but the pension list of Yedingham Priory in 1539 also contains the name of Elizabeth Sutton.[86] Could this be a misspelling for Lutton? In each case her name comes at the end of the list, the appropriate place for a returned apostate. Also, the 1536 commissioners' list gave the age of Elizabeth 'Sutton' as forty, which would have been the approximate age of Elizabeth Lutton. The Star Chamber proceedings must have led to a decision in favour of Thomas

---

[85] *LP* 4. 1. 1115. He was later pardoned (ibid., 4. 1. 1136. 22).

[86] SP5/2/76, 81 (J. S. Purvis, ed., 'A Selection of Monastic Rentals and Dissolution Papers', *Yorks. Archaeol. Soc., Rec. Ser.*, 80 (1931), p. 91). For the pension list see J. M. T. Clay, ed., *Yorkshire Monasteries: Suppression Papers*, Yorks. Archaeol. Soc., Rec. Ser., 48 (1912) 171. Of the nine nuns who gave testimony in 1532, seven received pensions, and no new names are found on the pension list save Elizabeth Sutton. Also, see Cross, *The End of Medieval Monasticism*, p. 17.

Lutton, for in 1546 he bequeathed property, including the contested Flamborough lands.[87]

What was this affair all about? Like so much else in medieval history it was probably about land. A likely scenario would have Sir Robert Constable as the key. To gain possession of Lutton lands at Flamborough he chose the moment of William Lutton's death to dispossess the son and heir, Thomas, by inserting into the situation the granddaughter, Elizabeth, who he knew was a discontented nun, who had borne a child. Perhaps Thomas Scaseby was the father of her child and had raised that child, by then, in 1530, four years old. Constable, in this telling, conspired, using his men, to have Scaseby abduct Elizabeth Lutton: the nun of Yedingham but a pawn in a landgrabbing scheme, a willing abductee, who braved the consequences of apostasy.

[87] York, Borthwick Institute, Wills 13, fo. 227.

Chapter 4

THE SECULAR ARM

Hundreds of apostates became subject to arrest by the secular authorities in England.[1] Liability to arrest and to forcible return to the houses from which they had fled was a real threat to English apostates. This procedure of arrest and return of apostates resembled in many ways the procedure by which bishops used the secular arm to arrest and imprison obdurate excommunicates.[2] Apostates, from 1298, were *ipso facto* excommunicated, yet they became subject to arrest in the procedure described here not by virtue of their excommunication but by virtue of their apostasy. They were pursued not by the writ *de excommunicato capiendo* sued by a bishop but by the writ *de apostata capiendo* sued by a religious superior. The procedure that developed in England and lasted for over two and a half centuries for the arrest of apostate religious, men and women, was without parallel in medieval Europe as a highly formalized and institutionalized way of dealing with religious apostasy.

ORIGINS

When did it begin? Its beginnings are shrouded in the mist of the middle decades of the thirteenth century, a mist which lifts only in the 1270s. Precedents of a sort can be found in pre-Conquest legislation, where Cnut threatened apostates with banishment from the realm.[3] More immediately, a fairly close parallel to the

---

[1] For a useful overview see Christopher Harper-Bill, 'Monastic Apostasy in Late Medieval England', *JEH* 32 (1981) 1–18.

[2] See F. Donald Logan, *Excommunication and the Secular Arm in Medieval England* (Toronto, 1968). Quite different were the procedures used for the recovery of villeins who had fled (see Paul R. Hyams, *Kings, Lords and Peasants in Medieval England* (Oxford, 1980), especially chap. 11).

[3] II Cnut 4. 1 (F. Liebermann, ed., *Die Gesetze der Angelsachsen* (3 vols.; Halle, 1903–16) 1. 310–11).

procedure which was to emerge can be seen in the protracted case of Alice Clement. She denied being a nun of Ankerwyke nunnery in Buckinghamshire and, about 1195, was pursued by the secular arm.[4] In the English synods held in the wake of the Fourth Lateran Council (1215) there is mention, indeed, of apostate religious but no mention of the assistance of the secular power in gaining their return.

The earliest hint of what was to come occurs in 1240–1 and concerned a Dominican apostate called Siward from the Berwick priory, then in Scotland. On 15 December 1240 a royal writ ordered William de Vescy and others not to retain Siward in their service nor to impede the Dominican friars in their efforts to arrest him.[5] Their attempts to arrest Siward seemed not to have met with immediate success, for on 18 March 1241, a royal writ directed the sheriffs of Yorkshire, Cumberland, Westmorland, Northumberland and Lancaster, if they were asked by the Dominicans, to arrest Siward and deliver him to the friars.[6] This writ contains the principal elements which were later common in the writ *de apostata capiendo*: it appears to have originated in a request from a religious order; it was sent to royal officials, and it ordered them to arrest and deliver the apostate.[7] Yet the writ stands alone in the records.[8] Not until 1249 do we find the next development, and again it affects the

---

[4] This was but one episode in a case which reached the royal courts in 1208 and was not settled until 1221 *(Curia Regis Rolls* 5. 183–5; C. R. Cheney and E. John, eds., *English Episcopal Acta, 1193–1205* 3 (London, 1986), nos. 330–1). For a detailed analysis of this case see Elizabeth Vodola, *Excommunication in the Middle Ages* (Berkeley, 1986), pp. 102–10.

[5] *CPR, 1232–47*, p. 262. For Vescy see *Complete Peerage* 12 (London, 1959) 276–8. He was first founder of the Carmelite house at Hulne in Northumberland *c.* 1242 (Keith F. Egan, 'Medieval Carmelite Houses, England and Wales', *Carmelus* 16 (1969) 179–80 and Egan, 'An Essay toward a Historiography of the Origin of the Carmelite Province in England', *Carmelus* 19 (1972) 70–2.

[6] *CPR, 1232–47*, p. 248. Northumberland and Lancashire were added interlinearly on the patent rolls (C66/49/m.9).

[7] The chancery scribe gave as a marginal tag for this writ 'de quodam apostata capiendo' (ibid.).

[8] In 1236 the king had written to the sheriff of York with reference to the fact that the Dominican prior of York had caused the arrest and imprisonment of a person alleged to be speaking badly and responding poorly concerning articles of faith. The king, declaring that the prior has no jurisdiction to do this, had ordered the sheriff to arrest infidels who can be convicted of heretical pravity (*CCR, 1234–37*, p. 358). This was clearly not a writ for the capture of apostates: neither these so-called infidels nor the person arrested by the prior were apostate friars, nor is there any reason to think that they were friars. See F. Pollock and F. W. Maitland, *The History of English Law* (2nd edn; 2 vols.; reissued, Cambridge, 1968) 2. 548–9.

friars. In that year the king sent an order to his royal officials that, when called upon by the Franciscan friars, they should arrest apostates of that order and either put them in the king's prison or return them to their order, whichever the friars preferred.[9] With some changes this arrangement was extended to the Dominicans and Carmelites in 1255: mandates were issued on the same day (20 March) to sheriffs and all other bailiffs to arrest religious of the Dominican and Carmelite orders who had abandoned their habits, spurned their profession and were wandering about the country-side and to deliver them to their priors. The king, it was said, wished to suppress their insolence and, especially, to come to the assistance of the friars.[10] By October of that year the Dominicans had four forms of letters directed to royal officials for the arrest of their apostates.[11] Thus, by 1255 the three established orders of mendicant friars – the Austin friars had only arrived in England in 1248–9 – had access to the secular arm in their efforts to secure the return of their runaways. This access was extended in the following decades to other orders. In 1265 the Knights Hospitallers of St John of Jerusalem were allowed to secure the help of royal officials in returning apostates to their houses.[12] Four years later the Master of Sempringham was granted similar powers with respect to apostate canons and lay brothers of the Gilbertines, but no mention was made of the nuns and lay sisters of this order, which had eleven double houses at that time.[13] Then, in 1270, the Austin friars, now well established with perhaps as many as a dozen houses in England, received similar access to the secular arm; this was repeated in 1274 and, again, in 1275, now with a duration clause of one year.[14] By this time the grant in favour of the Carmelites had been repeated twice, in 1265 and 1267.[15] In none of these writs in favour of the religious orders before the grant to the Austin friars in 1275 was there any mention of a *tempus utile*. Yet following upon the grant to the Austin friars, others, also limited in duration, were soon given: to the Cluniacs on 11 May 1276, effective until the following Michaelmas, and to the Cistercians on 16 October

[9] *CPR, 1247–58*, p. 48. The text is in *Mon. Franc.* 1. 614.

[10] *CPR, 1247–58*, p. 405.

[11] Ibid., p. 429. [12] *CPR, 1258–66*, p. 469.

[13] *CPR, 1266–72*, p. 393. In 1281 a royal writ mentioned a similar grant lately given to the Gilbertines (*CPR, 1272–81*, p. 430).

[14] *CPR, 1266–72*, p. 403; *CPR, 1272–81*, pp. 73, 96.

[15] *CPR, 1258–66*, p. 489–90; *CPR, 1266–72*, p. 179.

1280, effective until the following Christmas, both probably connected with visitations of the houses of those orders.[16] It should be underscored that by these early grants these religious orders had immediate access to royal officials and did not need to proceed by requests to chancery for writs in individual cases. To some extent, particularly for the mendicants, this arrangement was to be used throughout much of our period: during the fourteenth century the Franciscans received this grant six times, the Carmelites five times, the Dominicans four times and the Austin friars, Crutched Friars and Gilbertines once each.[17]

Another procedure, appearing somewhat later than some of these early grants, provided a second approach to secular assistance. This parallel approach was by royal writ to royal officials to arrest specific apostates. If we put aside the writ respecting the Dominican Siward of Berwick as a proto-writ *de apostata capiendo* (1241), the earliest writ extant was issued in 1259 and concerned apostate Cistercian monks of Stoneleigh Abbey in Warwickshire: it ordered sheriffs, bailiffs and others to arrest those apostates of Stoneleigh whom the abbot would indicate to them. This was clearly not a writ for all time but pertained to difficulties of the moment.[18] In a similar instance, the Benedictine abbot of Battle Abbey, in 1265, petitioned a writ against a specific, named apostate, Stephen de Wateringbury, formerly prior of Brecon in Brecknock, a priory dependent on Battle, who was said to have recently fled and was alone, wandering through the countryside; a writ no doubt followed.[19] In the following year a writ was issued against the apostate Cistercian Henry de Norton at the request of the abbot of Croxden in Staffordshire, and in 1267 a writ against the apostate Augustinian canon Reynold de Chyvele at the request of the abbot of Missenden in Buckinghamshire.[20] Two similar writs against specific apostates appear in 1270: one not mentioning names but against apostate brothers of Flitcham Priory, a small house of Augustinian canons in Norfolk, and another against the apostate canon of the same order, John de Cotes, from the priory of St Sepulchre in Warwick.[21] With a writ for the arrest of three apostate canons of Holy Cross Waltham in Essex in the last months

---

[16] *CPR, 1272–81*, pp. 140, 399.   [17] See Appendix 3, where these are listed.
[18] C66/73/m.2 (*CPR, 1258–66*, p. 45).   [19] C81/1786/4.
[20] *CPR, 1258–66*, p. 533; *CPR, 1266–72*, p. 175.
[21] *CPR, 1266–72*, p. 421; *Reg. W. Giffard, York*, no. 623.

of the reign of Henry III, the total number of these writs *de apostata capiendo* which have come to light for the period before the accession of Edward I is six.[22] By the end of the century at least thirty more had been granted and the writ *de apostata capiendo* was in place as an instrument available to religious superiors, should they want to use it, for the return of their apostates.[23]

To summarize, the early evidence of the use of the secular arm against apostate religious reveals two ways in which the secular arm was used. Grants were given to certain religious superiors to approach local royal officials directly to effect the arrest and return of apostates, and evidence suggests that this method was used initially with respect to the friars and was then extended to some other religious orders. During this same period, starting perhaps slightly later, there developed the procedure by way of royal writ issued out of the king's chancery and sent into the counties of England. The first of these procedures (by direct access) continued to be available through the fourteenth century, principally to the friars, who also at times used the second procedure, and this second procedure (by writ) continued well into the sixteenth century.

RECORDS AND NUMBERS

When religious superiors sought the aid of local royal officials without going through the royal chancery, this way of proceeding has left no trace save the granting of the power to do so. What records survive, then, pertain to the procedure by the writ *de apostata capiendo*, and we must insistently remind ourselves that we are dealing here with the surviving records. This writ was not a returnable writ, i.e., the recipient was not required to return it to the royal chancery, indicating on the dorse what action had been taken. Thus, the records kept in the king's chancery were not returned writs. What the chancery clerks kept as records were the actual requests which were sent by the religious superiors and which led invariably to the issuance of the writ itself. These requests presently form part of the general class of chancery records

---

22 *CPR, 1266–72*, p. 668.
23 It is from the last two decades of the thirteenth century that this writ begins to appear in registers of writs. The dating of these registers is never easy, but see the following registers (both in the British Library), which seem datable to these years: Harl. MS 5213, fo. 83^{r-v}; Add. MS 5761, fo. 18.

called 'Warrants for the Great Seal' and are arranged in eleven files by religious order. These files contain 354 petitions for the writ *de apostata capiendo*. In addition, three further petitions, once with this material but now not in the files, were printed by Prynne in the seventeenth century.[24] The total number of extant petitions is thus 357. Frequently writs would be enrolled on the Patent Rolls and among these are 45 writs for which there are no surviving petitions; the total is now at 402. Two otherwise unknown writs appear in other sources, bringing the grand total of instances in which the secular arm is known from surviving records to have been used against apostates to 404.

Many of these requests and writs contain the names of more than one alleged apostate – 11 monks of Eynesham were signified by the abbot in a single petition in 1344 – and, in other instances, apostates appear on more than one request or writ. The total number of apostates appearing in these sources is 542. They represent every religious order and, in general, their numbers are in proportion to the size of the orders. The largest number of apostates signified for arrest were from the largest orders: Cistercians, Augustinian canons and Benedictines with 114, 112 and 88 respectively. Also, there were 47 Cluniacs, 35 Carmelites and 23 Premonstratensian canons. And the others followed: Franciscans and Austin friars (19), Dominicans (16), Gilbertines (13) and also some Pied Friars (6), Crutched Friars (6), Knights Hospitallers (5), Trinitarians (3) and some from small independent communities. Only 13 women religious appear being pursued by this writ: 4 Augustinian canonesses, 4 from hospitals (including 2 from St Thomas's, Southwark), 3 Benedictine nuns and one each of the Minoresses and Gilbertines.

How complete are these records? To test the completeness of the files of petitions only one control seems feasible and that is to compare the actual writs found on the Patent Rolls and elsewhere with the surviving petitions. From these external sources there appear 107 instances in which we know that the writ was issued; for these there are 62 related petitions which have survived. Thus, compared with our control group, the files of petitions are 58 per cent complete. It would be hazardous to draw too strong a conclusion from so small a sample, but the fact that for 42 per cent of our surviving references to writs our files of petitions are silent

---

[24] Prynne, pp. 640–1, 1301.

suggests that perhaps a sizeable number of petitions have failed to survive the vagaries of record keeping.

A larger question raises itself: how frequently was the secular arm used against apostates? Any attempt to answer this question must be limited to procedure by writ, and here we know that the use of the secular arm depended on the initiative of the religious superior and that this initiative was discretionary. As we shall see (chapter 5), the superiors had an obligation to seek the return of runaways, but they had no obligation to invoke the secular arm.[25] It seems safe to say that the writ *de apostata capiendo* was sought only in a minority – perhaps a small minority – of cases. One control that can be used here involves the reconciliations of apostates by papal letters between 1335, when Pope Benedict XII issued his constitution *Pastor bonus*, and 1371, when reconciliation was deputed to the papal legate in England.[26] These reconciliations were recorded in the papal registers. During this 36-year period, 104 English apostates received papal letters of reconciliation; only 5 of these apostates (less than 5 per cent) are known to have been pursued by the secular arm, a very small proportion indeed. Yet of the nearly 1,100 apostates discovered in preparing this study, the 542 against whom the secular arm was used by the writ *de apostata capiendo* comprise the most sizeable single block. And we shall never know how many apostates were signified directly to the local royal officials by the friars. Thus, we are obviously dealing here with unavoidable imprecisions, but the evidence seems to suggest that the majority of apostates, perhaps even the vast majority, were not subject to the writ *de apostata capiendo*. Nevertheless, the procedure for the capture of apostates formed an integral and important feature of the historical picture of apostasy in medieval England.

Although the surviving records about the use of the secular arm are themselves to some extent incomplete, it is still useful to see what these records say about the frequency of the invocation of the secular arm against apostates. The table presented here indicates the pattern as seen in the surviving records. Undated records have not been included.

If these records reflect the general pattern of the actual use of this

---

[25] By exception, the Augustinian chapter of 1431 ordered that every apostate canon should be captured by the secular arm and kept in the nearest house of the order until he could be restored to his own house, but the extant records show no increase of requests from the Augustinians (Salter, *Chapters*, p. 83).

[26] See below, pp. 123–31.

procedure and not merely an extant archive, then the years from 1341 to 1410 were the years when the writ was most frequently employed: 172 writs (46.9 per cent of the total) were used in this seventy-year period. One may be tempted to see the dislocation caused by the Black Death as the reason for the decade of the 1350s having such a large number of apostates against whom the writ was issued, yet, while not discounting the impact of the Plague (see preceding chapter), caution should temper our rush to conclusion in view of the fairly small numbers with which we are dealing. Still, the surviving records show that decade after decade throughout this period of over two and a half centuries the procedure by royal writ remained one weapon frequently used by the religious authorities in combating the problem of apostate members of their orders.

PROCEDURE

Now to see how it worked. The procedure was initiated by a religious superior, generally by the head of the house from which the apostate had fled. It was the abbot of Battle, the Master of St Thomas's Hospital, Southwark, the prior of Worcester Cathedral Priory, the abbess of the London Minoresses and scores of others like them who took the first step in securing the arrest of their runaways. In the case of the friars the request was often made by the English provincial of the order or by his deputy. Thus, Henry de Anna, prior provincial of the Carmelites, in 1297, requested the arrest of the Carmelite apostate John Malore.[27] Unusually, there are instances of foreign religious heads petitioning the English king to issue writs under his Great Seal. In 1275, the abbot of Marmoutier in Tours requested Edward I to arrest two monks of dependent priories in England.[28] Similarly, Giles, abbot of S. Denis, Paris, in 1310, requested the capture of Peter de Thorney, an apostate monk of Deerhurst in Gloucestershire, an alien priory dependent on S. Denis.[29] The petition of the abbot of Bec-Hellouin in 1319 was supported by the French king and was related to one of that abbey's dependent English priories.[30] Also, the abbot of S. Evroul in

---

[27] C81/1793/8.

[28] Holy Trinity Priory, York, and Tickford (Newport Pagnell) Priory, Bucks. (C81/1786/26).

[29] C81/1786/38.

[30] The apostate was Ralph de Rounceville (*CPR, 1317–21*, p. 268), who, although the abbot of Bec-Hellouin replaced him as prior of the dependent priory of Goldcliff

Table 2. *Frequency of the writ 'de apostata capiendo' from datable surviving records*

1241–50	1	1341–50	19	1441–50	5
1251–60	1	1351–60	30	1451–60	14
1261–70	5	1361–70	23	1461–70	16
1271–80	6	1371–80	26	1471–80	18
1281–90	14	1381–90	30	1481–90	1
1291–1300	11	1391–1400	25	1491–1500	1
1301–10	15	1401–10	19	1501–10	5
1311–20	22	1411–20	11	1511–20	6
1321–30	11	1421–30	10	1521–30	5
1331–40	9	1431–40	9	Total	368

Normandy sent an undated request for the arrest of Nicholas Bom, 'commonachus in regno Anglie', who was a monk of Ware Priory in Hertfordshire, a dependent priory of S. Evroul.[31] In another unusual case, the abbot of an Irish monastery asked for the writ against one of his runaways: in 1402, Adam, the Cistercian abbot of Baltinglas in Co. Wicklow, said that the monk Richard Hollkey had gone apostate, and indeed writs were issued to the sheriff of Sussex and to the constable of Dover Castle for his arrest. One wonders whether Brother Richard was headed for the continent.[32] These few cases apart, the arrest procedure was initiated by English superiors against English apostates.

The petition was addressed to the king and signified that *frater* or *soror N.*, a professed religious of this house (or order), has left without permission, wanders about outside the monastery and, having given up the religious habit ('spreto habitu ordinis sui'), wears secular clothes. The petition then asked the king to issue a writ for the arrest of the apostate and for the apostate's return for punishment ('ad castigandum'). The petition would have been authenticated by the imposition of the seal of the religious house.[33]

The petition was sent to Westminster by messenger. Only four exceptions to this appear in the records. On 26 April 1286 the Cistercian abbot of Pipewell in Northamptonshire personally

---

(Monmouthshire), refused to leave (see ibid., pp. 544–5, and *Reg. Orleton, Hereford,* p. 104).

[31] C81/1786/40.   [32] C81/1788/1.

[33] Only one seal survives, that of John Burys, prior of the Crutched friars of London, affixed to a petition dated 26 Aug. 1360 (C81/1794/13).

appeared in chancery and asked for the arrest of his monk Ingram de London, who had forged his seal and was wandering in apostasy.[34] Similarly, the Cistercian abbot of Biddlesden in Buckinghamshire was in chancery on 14 September 1369 to request the arrest of three of his monks.[35] Within ten days of each other in 1512 the Benedictine abbot of Athelney in Somerset and the Augustinian prior of Launde in Leicestershire came to chancery in person to secure writs against runaways from their houses.[36] Such appearances were obviously rare: sealed petitions were usually delivered by messenger.

The royal chancery treated these petitions as if they were warrants for the Great Seal, and the writ *de apostata capiendo* was issued without inquiry. Like its parallel, the writ *de excommunicato capiendo*, it was no doubt a writ of course (*de cursu*), i.e., a writ of set form obtainable for the asking and for the payment of a small fee.[37] Where writs consequent upon these petitions appear on the patent rolls – there are 62 instances when the dates of the petitions and the writs can be compared – the writ generally bore a date just a few days later than the date of the petition; some, in fact, bear the same date as the petition. Allowing, as one must, that dating clauses can pose problems and that we do not know the date on which a petition actually arrived at Westminster, it is still safe to say that the writ *de apostata capiendo* was issued promptly.[38]

---

[34] *CCR, 1279–88*, p. 412.

[35] C81/1788/6 dorse. The petition which he brought to chancery was dated 10 Sept., and the abbot swore to the truth of its contents.

[36] Memoranda to this effect were made and kept on file in chancery (C81/1786/2; 1789/22). These religious superiors may have been in London attending convocation, which began meeting on 6 Feb. (see E. B. Fryde *et al.*, eds., *Handbook of British Chronology* (3rd edn; London, 1986), p. 603).

[37] It fulfils the traditional definition (see Elsa de Haas and G. D. G. Hall, eds., *Early Registers of Writs* (Selden Soc. 87, 1970), pp. xix–xx, lxiv–lxv). In registers of writ it is generally associated with the writ *de excommunicato capiendo*, itself a writ *de cursu*. See, e.g., BL, Add. MS 5761, fo. 18; Add. MS 20,059, fos. 42ᵛ–43; Stow MS 409, fo. 72. A fine was charged for writs and also a sealing fee, fixed at 6d for original writs from the fourteenth century. From 1334 writs *de cursu* were subject only to a sealing fee. See H. C. Maxwell-Lyte, *Historical Notes on the Use of the Great Seal of England* (London, 1926), pp. 331, 347.

[38] There is even one instance where the petition postdates the writ: the petition of the Cluniac prior of Castle Acre (Norf.) is dated 1 Nov. 1348 (C81/1787/5) and the writ is dated 25 Oct. 1348 (*CPR, 1348–50*, p. 244). It is possible that the writ of 25 Oct. was in response to an earlier petition now lost and that the writ issued in response to the petition of 1 Nov. was not enrolled. For problems related to dating clauses in chancery documents see Maxwell-Lyte, *Historical Notes*, pp. 241–65; J. F. Willard, 'The Dating and Delivery of Letters Patent and Writs in the Fourteenth Century', *BIHR* 10 (1932) 1–11.

The text of the writ repeated the *relatio* of the petition and then directed the recipient to capture the person or persons whom he is ordered to return to the religious house for punishment. By the imposition of the Great Seal to this writ the weight of the secular power was brought to the assistance of the church. Questions remain.

To whom was the writ addressed, which is not to ask to whom was it sent? The writ *de apostata capiendo* was unlike its parallel, the writ *de excommunicato capiendo*, which was routinely addressed to the sheriffs of the shires for execution. The writ against apostates had two possible ways of being addressed. The earliest writs appear to have been given a universal address (e.g., to all the sheriffs, mayors, bailiffs, ministers and other lieges). For example, in 1274, the arrest of three apostate Augustinian canons of Llanthony in Monmouthshire was addressed to all the bailiffs, and, in 1280, the writ to arrest William de Stormesworth, apostate Benedictine monk of Selby Abbey in Yorkshire, was addressed to all the sheriffs and bailiffs of the realm; in the same year, another Augustinian canon, Robert called 'Juvenis' of Tonbridge Priory in Kent, was pursued by a writ addressed to all the bailiffs of the realm.[39] This kind of omnibus writ continued to be used throughout most of our period: in 1472, for example, certain monks of the troubled Cluniac priory of St Andrew, Northampton, were the subjects of a writ addressed to 'all the sheriffs, mayors, bailiffs, ministers and others'.[40] Such writs must surely have been given to the religious superiors; the bearer of the petition probably waited at Westminster for the writ to be executed and then took it with him back to his religious house. Of the extant 107 copies of writs which have survived, the omnibus address was used in about one-quarter of the cases over the whole period. The writ in this omnibus form served as a warrant for the arrest of the apostate. The initiative in the actual capture seemed to rest with the religious superiors, who, once they had located the apostate, could by virtue of the omnibus writ require local officials to arrest and return him.

The second procedure used a form of the writ *de apostata capiendo* which was addressed to specific persons. In some cases it was the

---

[39] For the Llanthony apostates see *CPR, 1272–81*, p. 49; for Stormesworth see C81/1786/43; *Reg. Wickwane, York*, no. 682; *CPR, 1272–81*, p. 400. For the Tonbridge apostate see ibid., p. 404.

[40] *CPR, 1467–77*, p. 358.

local sheriff. In 1290, for example, the Cistercian abbot of Bindon in Dorset asked that the writ be sent to the sheriff of Dorset.[41] In 1295 the Carmelite prior provincial asked that writs be sent to the sheriff of Norfolk and Suffolk.[42] Likewise, in 1431, a writ for the arrest of a Cluniac apostate of Prittlewell Priory in Essex was sent to the sheriffs of London.[43] Other instances could easily be added from the surviving records, yet the clear impression is that the writ addressed to sheriffs was not the most common form of the writ with specific addressees.

In most cases, particularly from the 1330s, the writ was addressed to local men, generally called sergeants-at-arms, men who often served in the county in other offices such as commissioners and justices of the peace, commissioners of array, oyer and terminer, and Statute of Labourers. The local officials to whom the writ was addressed generally numbered about four or five, yet sometimes a single such person was commissioned to make the arrest. In one unusual case in 1376 ten men (from Herefordshire, Gloucestershire and Berkshire) were ordered to arrest a single apostate, William Cary of Bruton Priory in Somerset.[44] In the trouble in the 1380s at Montacute Priory, also in Somerset, the Cluniac monk Thomas Samme was the object of a writ addressed to thirteen officials, including the earl of Salisbury and three knights.[45] Much more usual was the sort of writ sent in 1371, directing five local Yorkshire officials to arrest two Gilbertine apostates.[46] On a number of such writs directed to local men the name of the local sheriff is also included. For example, in the case just mentioned, among the ten officials ordered to arrest William Cary was the sheriff of Herefordshire. Also, in 1359, the arrest of John de Hemingbrough, a Benedictine apostate of Selby Abbey in Yorkshire, was mandated to three men and the sheriff of Yorkshire (mentioned last).[47] In a unique case, an Aragonese Dominican, Miguel de Polo, allegedly apostatized from the Oxford house in 1365 or 1366, where he had been lecturing on the Sentences, and the writ for his arrest was issued to the chancellor of Oxford

---

[41] Prynne, p. 1301. [42] Ibid. pp. 640–1.
[43] C81/1787/18; for this writ see Appendix 2.
[44] *CPR, 1374–77*, p. 415. See ibid., p. 320; C81/1789/5; *Reg. Wakefield, Worcester*, p. xvii, nos. 41, 42. He may have been recalled from Horsley, a priory in Glos. dependent on Bruton, and failed to obey.
[45] *CPR, 1385–89*, p. 317; cf. ibid., p. 165.
[46] *CPR, 1370–74*, p. 103.   [47] *CPR, 1358–61*, p. 224.

University and three sergeants-at-arms, who were apparently active on the south coast.[48]

Writs addressed to sheriffs would have been routinely sent by royal messenger to the appropriate sheriff together with other chancery and exchequer writs, as indeed may have happened for writs addressed to sergeants-at-arms. In either case, the bearer of the petition himself may have taken responsibility for the writ's delivery.[49] The almost complete lack of shrieval records does not allow us to follow the route of such a writ once it reached the shrieval office. The sheriff had his own chancery, and it would have been the function of the shrieval chancery to transmit royal mandates to the appropriate local officials.[50]

The royal chancery at Westminster knew the county or counties to which writs were to be sent either because mention was made in the petition itself or, more commonly, by the *viva voce* information from the bearer of the petition: in 129 of the extant 357 petitions (i.e., 36 per cent) the petition itself indicated either where the apostate was thought to be or the sheriff to whom the writ should be sent. A Carmelite friar was said, in 1401, to be wandering apostate, especially in Devon.[51] A Crutched Friar, probably of their London house, was reportedly wandering apostate in 1390 in the city of London.[52] Frequently there was an explicit request that the writ be sent to specific persons: in 1289, for example, the Cistercian abbot of Buildwas in Shropshire requested that the writ to capture and return an apostate to his house be sent to the sheriff of Shropshire, and, in 1512, the Master of St Leonard's

---

[48] *CPR, 1364–67*, p. 278. He was in Barcelona in 1368 as a candidate for a doctoral degree in theology, and it was explained that he had left Oxford 'propter aliquas discordias inter studentes in dicto studio exortas' (S. L. Forte, 'Robert Pynk, O.P., Provincial of England', *Archivum Fratrum Praedicatorum* 27 (1957) 407–8; see *BRUO* 3. 1493). Trouble at the Oxford Dominican house reached such a dimension in 1370 that the prior provincial requested secular aid against ten friars there (*CPR, 1367–70*, p. 425).

[49] For the delivery of writs see J. F. Willard, 'The Dating and Delivery', *BIHR* 10 (1932–3) 1–11, and Mary C. Hill, *King's Messengers, 1199–1377* (London, 1961), pp. 90–2. Writs *de excommunicato capiendo* were delivered in similar ways, although sergeants-at-arms were not involved in that procedure (see F. Donald Logan, *Excommunication and the Secular Arm in Medieval England* (Toronto, 1968), p. 99).

[50] See Mabel H. Mills, 'The Medieval Shire House (*Domus Vicecomitis*)', *Studies Presented to Sir Hilary Jenkinson* (ed. J. Conway Davies; London, 1957), pp. 254–71. For the sole surviving shrieval roll of writs see G. H. Fowler, ed., *Rolls from the Office of the Sheriff of Beds. and Bucks., 1332–1334* (Quarto Memoirs of the Beds. Historical Record Soc., 3, 1929).

[51] C81/1793/21. [52] C81/1794/16.

Hospital, York, sought the arrest of Brother Robert Downham by a writ to the sheriff of Yorkshire.[53] In the 228 instances where the petition makes no mention of the whereabouts of the apostate, the bearer of the petition must have given this information. A petition sent in 1310 by the provincial minister of the English Franciscans indicated that the writs for the capture of John de Carbrook should be sent to the sheriffs whom the bearer would name.[54] And so it undoubtedly happened: when the precise information was absent from the petition, it was supplied by its bearer.[55] Occasionally, writs were not sent to those mentioned in the petition, the petition apparently being emended by the bearer, then in possession of fresh information about the likely whereabouts of the apostates. What we should grasp in all this is that the second way of proceeding by writ was by means of a writ addressed to specific officials as distinct from the omnibus writ given to the religious superiors.

The whereabouts of the apostate was not always known. Not uncommonly, he was said to be wandering *de patria ad patriam*. In one instance, in 1464, he was described as wandering from place to place, from village to village, from market to market; in fact, the writ was sent to Norfolk.[56] More often, in cases of uncertainty, writs were issued to several counties. When the nun Joan Adeleshey of Rowney Priory in Hertforshire went apostate, writs were issued on 28 March 1401 to the sheriffs of London, Middlesex, Essex and Hertfordshire; the prioress of Rowney clearly had no precise idea where she was.[57] In another case, one wonders what information the Benedictine prior of Upholland in Lancashire had when, in 1340, he asked that writs against an apostate be sent to the sheriffs of Yorkshire, Staffordshire, Leicestershire and Middlesex: had the prior plotted the route to London?[58] Also, three members of the community of St Bartholomew's Priory, Smithfield (London), were pursued, in 1472, by writs sent to London, Middlesex, Essex, Hertfordshire, Surrey and Sussex.[59] A late example, from 1526, shows the prior of

---

[53] C81/1788/15; 1796/19.   [54] C81/1792/15.

[55] In some cases the petition gave the names of officials to whom the writ should be addressed. In one case, in 1340, the abbot of St Albans gave the names of 7 men (including 2 monks), but, in the event, the writ was addressed to 6 men (the monks being excluded and another person added). See C81/1786/35; *CPR, 1338–40*, p. 485.

[56] He was a monk of St Albans (C81/1786/37 and dorse).

[57] C81/1786/31; *CPR, 1399–1401*, p. 472. An earlier petition (12 Nov. 1401; C81/1786/30) led to a writ to officials apparently of Herts. (*CPR, 1399–1401*, p. 418).

[58] C81/1786/20.   [59] C81/1789/31 and dorse.

St Mary Overy, Southwark, pursuing Richard Titchfield by writs sent into the counties of Middlesex, Cambridgeshire, Lincolnshire, Northamptonshire and Kent.

This is the place to mention repeated writs: those sent as the result of more than one petition against the same apostates. Twenty-four instances of repeated writs are known. In 1285 and again in 1289 the Franciscans sought the arrest of their apostate Robert Trone.[60] In another case, within six weeks two writs were sought against the Cistercian Peter Denias of Biddlesden Abbey in Buckinghamshire, the second specifying that it be sent to the bailiffs of London and the sheriffs of Buckinghamshire and Northamptonshire.[61] Similarly, the Gilbertine canon Richard de Thorp was signified for arrest in 1380 and, again, in 1390, the Master of Sempringham now averring that Thorp was more than ten years apostate.[62] One might think that Thomas Olyver, a Cistercian from Buckland Abbey in Devon, was the most sought-after apostate in medieval England. At least seven writs *de apostata capiendo* were issued against him as well as four other writs between 1467 and 1474.[63] How apostate Olyver actually was will be discussed later in this chapter.[64]

WHERE THEY WENT

From what has been said so far some indication should be possible concerning where the apostates went. What is said here, of course, comes from the evidence concerning those apostates whom the secular arm was asked to arrest by writ but it may well apply to apostates more generally. There are three sources which provide us with information about where apostates went when they fled their houses. First, the text of the petition might indicate either where they were or where writs should be sent. Second, the 107 extant copies of writs bear the names of addressees, and the counties with which they were associated can often be determined. Third, a chancery scribe frequently noted on the dorse of the petition the county or counties to which the writ was to be sent. Such dorsal notations appear on 52 petitions, frequently where the text itself of

---

[60] C81/1792/11, 13. For more on this case see above, p. 17.
[61] C81/1788/6, 28.
[62] C81/1791/3, 6; *CPR, 1388–92*, p. 219 for the second writ.
[63] C81/1788/8–14; see also *CPR, 1467–77*, pp. 171–2, 251, 403, 408; *CCR, 1468–76*, p. 348.
[64] See below, p. 120.

the petition is silent about this matter and copies of the writs have not survived. From these three sources there are indications in 137 cases concerning where the apostates were thought to be. It must be admitted that this evidence is about the presumed rather than the actual whereabouts of the apostates; nevertheless, it comprises a considerable body of material which, in its bulk, provides us with a useful basis for conclusions. Excluded from this total are cases where it is clear that the religious superior was very far from·sure about where the apostate was. Examples of this have already been given,[65] but perhaps one further example might be given here. The abbot of St Albans, in 1319, faced with what was apparently a rebellion at its dependent priory at Binham in Norfolk, had writs against the formidable William de Somerton issued to the keeper of the Cinque Ports and sheriffs of London, Kent, Norfolk, Suffolk and Essex.[66] Cases such as these apart, the remaining 137 cases allow generalizations.

The first and most insistent generalization is that, in the majority of these cases, the apostates remained in the general area of the religious houses from which they had fled. In two-thirds of the cases, writs were sent to the same county or to a neighbouring county. Thus, two apostate Benedictine monks of Tavistock in Devon were pursued by a writ to that county just as two apostate Gilbertine canons of Watton, Yorkshire, were pursued by a writ to that county and three Carmelites of Nottingham were pursued by a writ to Nottinghamshire.[67] For another Carmelite the net was thrown somewhat wider: in 1313, Richard Baldwyn of Ipswich Priory was sought by writs to Suffolk and also to Essex.[68] Somewhat different was the writ issued in 1468 against an apostate lay brother of Swineshead Abbey in Lincolnshire, which was sent to the sheriff of nearby Northamptonshire.[69]

Secondly, London proved a magnet for many apostates: forty writs were sent to London. Fourteen of these concerned apostates from London houses and from houses near London, such as St Bartholomew's Priory, Smithfield, St Thomas's Hospital, Southwark, St Mary Graces Abbey, east of the Tower, and Merton Priory in Surrey. The remainder came from the rest of England and

[65] See above, pp. 110–11.
[66] C81/1786/32. He may well have been thought to be on his way to the continent and possibly to the papal curia. For more on Somerton see below, p. 145.
[67] C81/1786/52; 1791/12; 1793/30.
[68] C81/1793/18.　　[69] C81/1788/51.

even Wales. From the Home Counties there came a nun from Rowney in Hertfordshire, a monk from Reading in Berkshire, a Cistercian monk from Warden in Bedfordshire, an Augustinian canon from Missenden in Buckinghamshire and many others.[70] Yet there were apostates who travelled long distances to London. Just a few examples. The Carmelite William de Bodicote of Bishop's Lynn in Norfolk was sought in London, and indeed a Franciscan from further north, from Boston in Lincolnshire, was arrested in London.[71] And others came from the west. There was the apostate from Lechlade Hospital in Gloucestershire, another from Bodmin Priory in Cornwall and still another from Llanthony Priory in Monmouthshire.[72] And many others.

In the context of apostates travelling long distances to London, it should be added that some apostates, probably never a large number, also travelled long distances but not to London. Thus, the Cistercian abbot of Kirkstead in Lincolnshire surely thought that Hugh Frischney had fled to the south coast, for he had a writ issued to the warden of the Cinque Ports and the sheriff of Kent.[73] In another case, Richard Erbyry from the house of the Bonshommes in Edington, Wiltshire, was said to have gone to Yorkshire.[74] Others had gone to Ireland: the Carmelite William Portehors as well as the Cistercian William Worthy, who travelled from the Isle of Wight.[75]

These generalizations suggest what might reasonably be presumed to be the two major concerns of runaways. In the first place, now no longer housed and fed in their religious houses, they had the obvious need of securing the support required for daily subsistence. Since many – perhaps most – religious were recruited from the local area, their familiarity with that region of the country and the presence of relations and kinsfolk nearby would make that region attractive, and travel would not always be easy and could be hazardous.[76] The other need of apostates might best

---

[70] For the examples cited see C81/1786/30, 29; 1788/61; 1789/39.
[71] C81/1793/12; 1792/19.   [72] C81/1796/8; 1789/1, 20.
[73] *CPR, 1422–29*, p. 554.   [74] C81/1796/6.
[75] The petition for Portehors failed to indicate his house (C81/1793/13); for Worthy alias Chaunflour see C81/1788/39.
[76] For local recruitment see R. B. Dobson, *Durham Priory, 1400–1450* (Cambridge, 1973), pp. 57–8; R. V. H. Burne, *The Monks of Chester* (London, 1962), p. 101; F. Donald Logan, 'Ramsey Abbey, Last Days and After', *The Salt of Common Life: Individuality and Choice in the Medieval Town, Countryside and Church: Essays Presented to J. Ambrose Raftis* (ed. E. B. DeWindt; Kalamazoo, 1995); cf. for Westminster the remarks of

be satisfied by travel: the need, felt no doubt by many, to lose their identity, to seek anonymity and a new future in the crowded lanes of the metropolis or in faraway villages. Risks there would always have been, but those who stayed locally knew that an abbot would probably not pursue them with a royal writ if they lived a low-profile, scandal-free life, whereas those who fled to London and elsewhere, perhaps even changing their name – as did the Dominican John Cheker, who became Nicholas Corf – no doubt felt fairly safe from arrest and harassment.[77] Not all succeeded. Thomas Wytham, apostate from the Augustinian Bourne Abbey in Lincolnshire, was recognized by pilgrims from Bourne, who, on their way to the shrine at Hailes in Gloucestershire, stopped at the collegiate church of St Mary in Warwick, where they were stunned to see the runaway canon.[78] Still others were arrested, and it is to that general question we must turn, but, first, legal escape from the writ.

LEGAL APPEAL FROM THE WRIT

As with the writ for the capture of excommunicates, the writ for the capture of apostates could be avoided by legal means, although, to be sure, far less recourse in this way was had by apostates than by excommunicates.[79] In general, two routes were available: denial of the fact that gave the writ its meaning and appeal in the ecclesiastical courts.

If the person sought by the writ could establish in the royal chancery that there was no apostasy, the writ would be voided. In this way, the Augustinian canon John de Horwood of St James's Abbey in Northampton sought to thwart the writ for his arrest as an apostate (petitioned on 2 June 1309) by proving that he was indeed absent from the abbey but not apostate since he was

---

Barbara Harvey, *Living and Dying in England, 1100–1540: The Monastic Experience* (Oxford, 1993), pp. 75–7. In an unusual case, the brother of an apostate became liable for punishment for harbouring his brother: in 1340 the archbishop's court of audience fined John Messager of Newington (Kent) for giving refuge to his brother Henry, who, after 14 years as a professed monk of St Augustine's, Canterbury, had fled in apostasy (Canterbury Cathedral Archives, Ch. Ant., A 36.IV, fo. 11). I am indebted to Professor Richard Helmholz for this reference.

[77] Cheker changed his name, it was said, 'ut caucius decipiat innocentes' (C81/1792/5, 6; *CPR, 1370–74*, p. 392). Cheker was at London, but the Dominican house from which he fled was not mentioned.

[78] *Linc. Vis.* 2. 37–8. A vial of the Precious Blood was venerated at Hailes, which was an important place of pilgrimage.

[79] See Logan, *Excommunication*, pp. 120–33, 150–4.

prosecuting complaints against the abbot in the court of the archbishop of Canterbury. A letter in the name of the archbishop – no doubt from his court of audience – attested to his claim and added that Horwood was there 'non extra habitum set in habitu'. This tactic by Horwood seemed to have worked, but in the following March another writ for his arrest as an apostate was requested. Had Horwood returned to Northampton to something less than a warm welcome?[80]

The other way to avoid arrest was to make an ecclesiastical appeal. The alleged apostate could lodge an appeal in the ecclesiastical courts to the effect that apostasy and consequent excommunication had not occurred. Tuitorial appeals would have been preferred by such appellants. These were, in effect, double appeals: one to the Roman court on the substance of the matter and the other to the local archbishop's court to provide protection (*tuitio*) for a year so that the appeal of substance could be prosecuted.[81] Only a few such appeals have come to light. The successful appeal of Alice de Everyngham against the Master of Sempringham in 1366–7 has already been mentioned in another context.[82] In another case, the abbot of Whitby in 1399 alleged that Thomas Hackness, bursar of the monastery, was known to be incontinent with Agnes, wife of John des Kerr, and with other women, that he climbed out of a window of the monastic dormitory one night, took off his religious habit, donned secular clothes and became *uagabundus*, and that he took with him a considerable sum of money. Hackness countered with a tuitorial appeal to the court of Rome and the court of York. A writ entirely superseding his capture was issued, mentioning that he had four mainpernors to guarantee his good behaviour towards the abbot and monks of Whitby.[83]

The provision of mainpernors in a few other cases indicates

---

[80] C81/1786/47; *CCR, 1354–60*, p. 415; *CPR, 1354–58*, p. 449. In one register of writs there is included a writ 'pro capcione per falsam suggestionem deliberando', which bears a close similarity to the particulars of this case (BL, Royal MS ll.A.ix, fos. 44^{r-v}).

[81] On tuitorial appeals see Irene J. Churchill, *Canterbury Administration* (2 vols.; London, 1933) I. 427, 460–5; Brian L. Woodcock, *Medieval Ecclesiastical Courts of the Diocese of Canterbury* (London, 1952), pp. 64–7; Norma Adams and Charles Donahue, eds., *Select Cases from the Ecclesiastical Courts of the Province of Canterbury, c. 1200–1301* (Selden Soc., vol. 95, 1979–80), intro. pp. 64–72.

[82] See above, p. 24.

[83] York, Borthwick Institute, CPE 164; *CCR, 1399–1402*, p. 281. He became subject to arrest once again, in 1404 (*CPR, 1401–05*, p. 363).

attempts to thwart the writ, but which of the two routes the alleged apostate was taking is not clear. One concerns William Hord, a Benedictine monk of Shrewsbury Abbey, whose abbot accused him of gross crimes, including homicide and mutilation. A writ *de apostata capiendo* was issued for his capture in 1356 and, in due course, he was imprisoned at Bury. Hord then took legal action, for in 1357 a writ ordered that he be delivered to his mainpernor, Sir William Carles, a knight of Shropshire, who guaranteed Hord's appearance in the king's courts.[84] Also, the Crutched Friar Robert Stannowe was released from prison into the safe keeping of two mainpernors, and the Cistercian John Stowe had recourse to the royal courts after having been imprisoned in London.[85] The handful of cases mentioned in this section, to which only a few others could be added, indicate how infrequently legal redress was sought from the writ for the capture of apostates.

SUCCESS OF THE WRIT

It remains to be seen what effect the procedure for the use of the secular arm actually had. How successful was it, if we define success not in terms of return to the ideals of the religious life but in terms of the capture and return of apostates to their orders? In a sense, the evidence is scanty. The non-returnable nature of the writ means that we lack the routine reporting of its fate in the counties, a reporting otherwise available for returnable writs. Only in a score or so of cases can it be said with some certitude that the apostate was, in fact, arrested. Many of these are known to us because their superiors, hearing that the apostates were in custody, asked that they be returned to their houses. Thus, the abbot of Hailes in Gloucestershire, in 1290, asked that the fugitive monk, John de Evesham, who had been arrested and imprisoned by the sheriff of Worcestershire, be delivered to Hailes.[86] In a later case involving Hailes Abbey, an apostate monk, John Stowe, was arrested and held in a London prison, from which he was summoned to appear in chancery.[87] In the far north of the country the apostate

---

[84] C81/1786/47; *CCR, 1354–60*, p. 415; *CPR, 1354–58*, p. 449.
[85] For Stannowe see C81/1794/13; *CPR, 1358–61*, pp. 516–17 and below, p. 117. For Stowe see C250/2/35 and below, next paragraph.
[86] SC1/18/97.
[87] In 1402, the abbot of Hailes was called to show reason for the arrest and imprisonment of Stowe (C250/2/35).

Franciscan friar Arthur de Hartlepool of the Richmond priory was arrested in 1304 by the sheriff of Cumberland at Whitehaven and imprisoned nearby at Egremont, and the Franciscans requested that he be returned to Richmond.[88] Again, in 1361, the Austin friar Simon de Badby was imprisoned at Maidstone in Kent by petition of his prior provincial, who then wanted him handed over.[89] Two years later, the prior of the Hospital of St Mary's without Bishopsgate, London, asked that John Stapleford, an apostate, be delivered to him from Newgate prison, where he was being detained.[90] Also known to have been kept at Newgate was the Austin friar Walter de Mildenhall.[91] Another apostate, the Crutched Friar Robert Stannowe, in 1360 was detained at another London prison, the Marshalsea, and had the unpleasant experience of being released in mainprise only to be waylaid by his enemies (possibly former colleagues), beaten and brought back to London, where he was confined apparently in the house of the Crutched Friars.[92]

The Dominicans appear frequently to have taken it upon themselves to bring captured friars back to their houses. In 1338, Edmund de Lisle of their Lincoln house received safe conduct to bring back an apostate from Ipswich.[93] In a most unusual case in 1356 four Dominican apostates, all from different priories, were captured and were being kept at King's Langley Priory in Hertfordshire. The prior, John Woderove, must have been anxious to get rid of them, and the king ordered their delivery to priories at Derby, Lincoln, Chester and Oxford.[94]

The records, then, might appear rather silent about the actual arrest of apostates: about a score of arrests out of 542 apostates known to have been pursued by the secular arm. Yet, in another sense, the records are far from silent. For decade after decade for over two and a half centuries the writ *de apostata capiendo* continued to be sued out of the royal chancery, which is perhaps the best

---

[88] *CCR, 1302–07*, p. 174; Prynne, p. 1042.   [89] C81/1794/3.
[90] C81/1789/33.   [91] C81/1794/8 (undated).
[92] C81/1794/13; *CPR, 1358–61*, pp. 516–17.   [93] *CPR, 1338–40*, p. 99.
[94] *CPR, 1354–58*, p. 444. Bishop's Langley friary served as the place of novitiate for the English Dominicans (Knowles, *RO* 1. 169; 2. 260). The St Albans annalist records that in 1429 the prior canon of St Thomas in Derby., in search of an apostate canon, stopped at his monastery at Christmas time and that the apostate was found at King's Langley. There is no house of canons with that dedication in Derby. Did a possibly confused Benedictine annalist mistake a white-habited Dominican for a white canon? When the captured apostate reached Coventry, he escaped. See Amundesham, 1. 45–6.

testimony to its effectiveness. If this procedure had little chance of being effective, it is reasonable to think it would have fallen into disuse, yet religious superiors were still sending messengers to Westminster to secure this writ well into the sixteenth century.

THE WRIT AND MONASTIC DISPUTES

In examining the material discussed in this chapter, one is struck by those petitions which invoked the secular arm against large numbers of apostates. The most glaring example is the petition of Abbot Upton of Eynsham in Oxfordshire, who asked the king to arrest eleven of his monks as apostates; and shortly thereafter the arrest of four others was sought. These comprised at least half of the monastic community.[95] Again, the prior of Earls Colne in Essex, a small house, requested the arrest of six of his monks as apostates.[96] One's curiosity is even further stimulated by two petitions from the Augustinian abbey of Missenden in Buckinghamshire: in 1468, Robert Risborough, calling himself abbot, signified for arrest Henry Missenden as an apostate and, in 1472, Henry Missenden, calling himself abbot, signified for arrest Robert Risborough as an apostate.[97] It is now clear that these are three instances in which the secular arm was invoked against alleged apostates where the basic issue was not apostasy but the headship of a religious house: the writ was used as a weapon by one faction against its enemies in an internal dispute. Whatever their sins of commission or omission, they were probably not apostates, merely victims of domestic discord. At least 29 such cases involving 99 religious have been detected in this material – others may still lurk there – and they should raise the warning flag for us that not all the 542 religious against whom the secular arm was invoked were necessarily apostates. A few representative examples can illustrate this point.

Eynsham Abbey witnessed extraordinary events in 1344 and 1345, events in which the charge of apostasy played a role or, at least, made cameo appearances. The bishop of Lincoln visited Eynsham and was so disturbed by what he found that he deposed the abbot, Nicholas de Upton, and replaced him with William de Stamford, who, in 1344, appears to have secured a writ for the

---

[95] C81/1786/14, 15.
[96] C81/1786/10.
[97] C81/1789/40, 41 (in 1468 and 1472). For details of this dispute see *VCH, Bucks*. 1. 371.

arrest of two of Upton's party as apostates.[98] Upton, greatly displeased by his removal, returned (it was said) with an armed band of 1500 men, stormed the abbey and expelled Abbot Stamford. A large number of the monks fled for fear of bodily harm: five went to the pope at Avignon, and at least nine others – and probably more – remained in England. Upton labelled them all apostates and on 6 October 1344 invoked the secular arm against eleven of the monks and, later, against four others. The writs might not have been successful, for, by February 1345, Upton together with his prior and cellarer were imprisoned at Oxford Castle on charges of trespass. By no canonical use of the word 'apostate' can these monks of Eynsham be considered truly apostate.[99]

Earls Colne, a priory in Essex dependent on Abingdon Abbey, was never a large house, having in 1399 perhaps a dozen members. Yet in that year John Preston, its prior, requested the arrest of six of the monks as apostates. Among these was Henry Kebbel alias Colne, who had been prior and who had disputed the priorship with John Preston. The matter was pursued further in the papal and royal courts, but, whatever the truth of the allegations and counter-allegations, we are dealing here with something other than canonical apostasy.[100]

And there were strange happenings at Prittlewell in Essex, in which the cry of 'apostasy' was heard. Prittlewell was a Cluniac priory, usually of fifteen monks, dependent on Lewes Priory. In 1317 the prior of Lewes requested that a writ be issued for the arrest of William de Avernaz and another monk, both apostates from Prittlewell. Again, in the following year the prior of Lewes sought the arrest of Avernaz and three other apostates from Prittlewell.[101] These requests merely hint at the tumultuous situation at Prittlewell. In 1316, the prior of Lewes had replaced Avernaz with James de Cusancia because of allegations of Avernaz's incontinency in London. Later, it was said that Avernaz twice gained forceful entry into the priory, supported by an armed mob. The prior of Lewes then sent some monks to Prittlewell to evict Avernaz, which

[98] *CPR, 1343–45*, p. 387.
[99] The petitions are C81/1786/14, 15. For the story as told from the point of view of Stamford's party see *CPL* 3. 174. Glimpses of Upton's saga in Oxford Castle can be seen in *CCR, 1343–46*, pp. 518, 555. For a brief summary of this dispute see *VCH, Oxon.* 2. 66.
[100] The petition is C81/1786/10. See also *CPR, 1396–99*, pp. 420, 516–17; *CPR, 1399–1401*, pp. 412, 414–15; *CCR, 1396–99*, pp. 470–1.
[101] C81/1787/6, 15, 16.

they did (if we can believe the story told) while he was saying Mass. They dragged him from the altar, bound his hands and feet and brought him in a cart to be imprisoned at Lewes, where he died, probably of his wounds, in 1321. It is in the context of these events that the writs of capture for apostasy are to be seen.[102]

One might think Thomas Olyver, whom we met above, a most notorious apostate: between 1467 and 1473 William Breton, the Cistercian abbot of Buckland Abbey in Devon, seven times petitioned Olyver's arrest as an apostate, thus making him the most frequently sought-after apostate that we know of in medieval England.[103] What lies behind all this is a particularly nasty struggle over the abbotship of Buckland Abbey: both Breton and Olyver claimed to have been elected. The matter was brought before the General Chapter at Cîteaux and before the king's courts. When the dust finally settled, Olyver, the much-called apostate, was accepted as abbot and ruled Buckland for over thirty years.[104] Olyver was but one of the many non-apostates charged with apostasy during the course of a domestic monastic dispute.[105] The fact that England's most often called apostate was not an apostate at all should serve as a cautionary reminder that the accusation of apostasy is distinct from the fact of apostasy and that they both pertain to the history of this subject.

---

[102] *CCR, 1313–18*, p. 254; *CCR, 1318–23*, pp. 8–9, 29, 51–2, 96–7; *CPR, 1317–21*, pp. 155, 258, 261–2; *CPL* 2. 211–12. A useful summary is in *VCH, Essex* 2. 139–40.

[103] See above, p. 111 and C81/1788/8–14.

[104] *CPR, 1467–77*, pp. 171–2, 251, 403, 408; *CCR, 1468–76*, p. 348; Talbot, *Letters*, no. 7. See S. F. Hockey, *Quarr Abbey and Its Lands* (Leicester, 1970), pp. 153–5 and the more sympathetic (to Olyver) remarks of John Stephan, *A History of Buckfast Abbey from 1018 to 1968* (Bristol, 1970), pp. 169, 171. Not unlike the Buckland case was the dispute at Rievaulx where William Bramley, who in 1425 was restored as abbot by the General Chapter, then became signified as an apostate by the deposed abbot, Henry Burton (*CPR, 1422–29*, p. 300; C81/1788/41).

[105] The troubling events at St Frideswide's, Oxford, which, in 1378, led to the issuance of writs against four 'apostate' canons, charged with having overcome and shackled the steward and with having broken into the prior's chest for its treasures and jewellery, had to do with a disputed priorship (C81/1789/49–51; the story is elaborated by R. L. Storey in 'Papal Provision to English Monasteries', *Nottingham Medieval Studies* 35 (1991) 81–2 with full references).

Chapter 5

RETURN AND RECONCILIATION

The stated objective of ecclesiastical authorities was to gain the return of apostates to their religious houses. Lament, as they did, the act of apostasy and impose, as they also did, penalties for what they labelled a crime, they nevertheless had as the purpose of their policy the reconciliation of apostates. The penalty of choice for apostasy was excommunication until 1298, when it became the automatic penalty. Excommunication was, in the language of the canonists, a medicinal penalty – as distinct from a vindictive penalty – aimed at curing the apostate's moral illness and not at redressing the harm done to the Christian community. So, too, the punishment imposed on the returning apostate was viewed as a medicinal, curative aid to the moral correction of the erring religious. The distinction between medicinal and vindictive punishment is essential to our subject: the ultimate, professed purpose here was to heal, not hurt, the apostate. In individual instances, individual religious superiors may indeed have been personally motivated by vindictiveness, but their motivation must not be confused with the motivation of the legislation itself. No legal system can control in an absolute way the motives of its officials; at best, it can state the purpose of laws and give guidelines for their execution. And so it was that the medieval church legislated and acted against religious apostates. This chapter studies the return of apostates to their religious orders: the efforts, apart from the use of the secular arm (preceding chapter), taken to secure their return and reconciliation and also what lay in store for them upon their return.

PAPAL EFFORTS TO EFFECT RETURN

Despite having left a religious house, despite having discarded the religious habit and despite perhaps having begun to lead a worldly life of work and marriage, the apostate was still a religious. On the day of profession the young novice by vow entered into a life-long relationship with the religious life, and apostasy did not annul that relationship, which persisted, although it had been sinned against. When apostates fled, they did not alter their status: they remained religious, albeit sinning religious. It was this persisting two-way relationship between professed religious and the religious community that allowed or, rather, demanded action be taken to bring erring, sinful, apostate religious back to the bosom of their communities.

Pope Gregory IX addressed this issue in the Decretals (1234), and his decree *Ne religiosi vagandi* cast a long canonical shadow across the rest of the middle ages.[1] It was the key text: it concerned both the need to seek out apostates and the need to receive them back. Three points were dealt with by this decree. In the first place, Gregory IX required religious superiors (presidents of chapters, abbots, priors) annually to search for apostate and expelled religious.[2] This annual search must be conducted vigorously (*sollicite*). The commentator Hostiensis (*c.*1200–71) held that this obligation of annual search continued as long as the apostate was *in fuga* and did not lapse after a certain period of time.[3] Secondly and at greater length, the decretal required the religious superiors under threat of ecclesiastical censure to readmit apostates *salva ordinis disciplina*, a not unimportant clause. This saving clause implied that some returning apostates could disturb the good order of the house and their presence could be inimical to the regular life of the house. If such were the case, the superiors were excused from readmitting them into the community. Much depended here, according to our commentator, on the opinion of the community: if the members of the religious community felt they would rather leave than live with the returned apostate, then the danger of grave scandal was present and the community was excused. Antonio de Butrio (1338–1408) said that he had seen just such a case at a convent in Florence, where the community was unwilling to

---

[1] X.3.31.24, which dates from 1227 x 1234 (A. Potthast, ed., *Regesta pontificum Romanorum* (2 vols.; Berlin, 1874–5), no. 9651).

[2] The Rule of St Benedict explicitly allowed monasteries to expel a monk for bad conduct (chap. 28), but even then the bond between monk and monastery continued, and the abbot is here reminded to search out the *eiectus* and reconcile him.

[3] *In tertium decretalium librum commentaria* (Venice, 1581), 3.31.24.

remain if a returning nun was received back.[4] Besides the unwanted troublemakers there were recidivists, who, according to the rule, could not be received back into the community, since, the commentators added, the Rule of St Benedict allowed the return of apostates only three times. Clearly the categories of troublemakers and recidivists could overlap. In either case, although the superiors were not obliged to receive them back into their communities, they were still obliged to make provisions for them. The superiors should place them elsewhere in the community apart from the other religious (e.g., with the servants or in the monastic prison, Hostiensis suggested), if this could be done without grave scandal. If the apostate could not be readmitted into the community, even in a segregated way, then the superior should send that apostate to another house of the same order and there provide for support. Thirdly, the pope recognized that an apostate, once found and required to return, might be unwilling to render obedience; such a religious should be excommunicated. It should be noted that this was not an automatic excommunication. The law did not excommunicate the disobedient apostate; it merely ordered the superior to do so and, if, for some reason, the superior failed to do so, the disobedient apostate was not excommunicated. It remained for Boniface VIII in 1298 to make excommunication the *ipso facto* penalty for apostasy: from then it was incurred by the deed itself without the need of a positive sentence by a superior.[5] Thus, from the time of the Decretals, abbots and other superiors were bound under penalty of canonical sanction to search for apostates and to reconcile them in some way, even the difficult ones, and were further bound to excommunicate the recalcitrant.

It is interesting to note that the great canonist Joannes Andreae (*c.* 1270–1348), when commenting on the decretal *Ne religiosi vagandi*, said that there was in his time a recent papal constitution that treated this question more fully (*plenius*).[6] He was referring to the constitution *Pastor bonus* issued by Pope Benedict XII on 17 June 1335. It was the second constitution of the pontificate of this former Cistercian monk and abbot and provided the most significant papal statement in the medieval period on the

---

[4] *In librum tertium decretalium commentarii* (Venice, 1578), 3.31.24, who closely followed the teaching of Hostiensis.

[5] 3.24.2 in VI°.

[6] *In tertium decretalium librum novella commentaria* (Venice, 1581), 3.31.24.

reconciliation of religious men and women separated from their orders.[7]

The opening words, while conventional in their pastoral concern – 'the good shepherd is diligent, painstaking and ever watchful lest his wandering and straying sheep be devoured by wolves' – introduce a remarkable document aimed at easing the return and reconciliation of apostates: its tone solicitous and its provisions compassionate. There have flocked to the apostolic šee, he wrote, apostates from all parts of Christendom who claim they are unable to remain in their cloisters and religious orders. Benedict XII proceeded to propose remedies for them and for other apostates, not radical remedies (such as wholesale dispensations), but practical remedies, which could be effected within the received traditions.

Pastor bonus did more than reiterate the provisions of Gregory IX's decretal (*Ne religiosi vagandi*) that heads of religious houses should strive by annual inquiries to restore apostates to the religious life. It went beyond: if after inquiry and urging, the apostates refuse to return, then the superior should have them seized and forced to return.[8] From what follows, it is clear that this forced return – already systematized in England by the formal process described in the preceding chapter – was the option of last resort.

Recognized as belonging in a special category of apostates were religious who, without permission, left their order and habit and joined another order, where they again professed and whose habit they were now wearing. Within three months from the time that this constitution comes to their attention, the pope ordered, they must return to their first order and habit, provided that they were canonically professed in that first order.

Then there were the unwanted religious, those apostates whose houses were pleased that they had left and did not want them back. The pope ordered religious superiors to take back even the unwanted. Papal deputies were to enforce this even to

---

[7] For the constitution see *Bullarium romanum* 4. 526–8. For Benedict XII see Jean-Berthold Mahn, *Le pape Benoit XII et les Cisterciens* (Paris, 1949); Clement Schmitt, *Un pape réformateur et un défenseur de l'unité de l'église: Benoit XII et l'ordre des Frères Mineurs* (Florence, 1959); Laetitia Boehm, 'Papst Benedikt XII (1334–1342) als Förderer der Ordensstudien', *Secundum Regulam Vivere: Festschrift für P. Norbert Bachmund O. Praem.* (ed. Gert Melville; Windberg, 1978), pp. 281–310.

[8] Those who were then at the papal curia were to be seized by the auditor of the apostolic camera and returned to their religious houses.

the extent of imposing ecclesiastical penalties on reluctant superiors, from which there could be no appeal. Yet, even here, Benedict XII repeated the saving clause of Gregory IX, 'salva ordinis disciplina'.

Moreover, apostate members of the mendicant orders, it was recognized, did not have the same relationship to their houses as did monks: friars are primarily professed to their order rather than to a particular house. Thus, the constitution provided that, if friars were unable conveniently to return to their own houses, they could be received in any house of their own order or, indeed, in any house of any of the mendicant orders. The superiors of these houses were bound to receive them under threat of ecclesiastical penalty.

Furthermore, the pope continued, religious superiors must bear in mind the weakness of human nature and, consequently, must not impose severe punishments upon returning apostates. Even if apostates were guilty of grave excesses or had escaped from prison, moderation must rule: a healing (medicinal) penalty should be given. Penalties too severe might discourage apostates from being reconciled. Moderation, healing, reconciling – these define the tone of this process. To facilitate this healing reconciliation, religious superiors were given broad powers: they could absolve from the penalty of excommunication incurred by apostasy and they could dispense from any irregularity contracted, for example, by the celebration of Mass while apostate.[9]

Finally, Pope Benedict ordered that, to expedite the process, papal letters mandating the acceptance of returning apostates be issued upon request. These papal letters of reconciliation would include a sweeping *non obstantibus* clause which gave these letters priority over statutes and customs of orders, even those confirmed by papal authority: such statutes and customs must not delay the reconciliation process.

These papal letters of reconciliation appear to have been granted

---

[9] Excommunication and irregularity must be distinguished. Excommunication was a penalty imposed for an ecclesiastical offence (in our case, apostasy), which to some extent excluded the person from the Christian community. As a consequence of excommunication, a person was excluded from certain ecclesiastical acts. The excommunicated apostate was suspended from saying Mass. If he violated this prohibition, he incurred irregularity. For full rehabilitation the returning apostate needed to be absolved from his excommunication and, if necessary or, at least, as a precaution, dispensed from irregularity.

routinely in the decades that followed. They followed a common form. Those in favour of English apostates were addressed to three named English ecclesiastics, who were directed to do three things: to absolve the particular apostates from the excommunication incurred by reason of the apostasy, to dispense the apostate from irregularity incurred by excommunication and to ensure his acceptance back into his order according to the norms of *Pastor bonus*. For example, in 1339, the Benedictine apostate Robert Ingheram of Sandwell Priory in Staffordshire obtained papal letters addressed to the abbot of Combe, the prior of Hinckley and a canon of Salisbury Cathedral;[10] and in 1341 the letters on behalf of the Carthusian apostate William de Standish of Witham Priory in Somerset were addressed to the dean of Lincoln Cathedral and the archdeacons of Surrey and Totnes.[11] It is clear that in some cases the apostate was actually at the papal curia at Avignon. William de Standish, just mentioned, is said to have come to the pope without permission. And so, too, many others among the English apostates: in 1355 alone – when eight papal letters for the reconciliation of English apostates were issued – Simon de Leverton, a Cistercian of Rufford Abbey in Nottinghamshire, John de Monte, a Cistercian of Holmcultram Abbey in Cumberland and John de Wallington, an Augustinian canon of Wormegay Priory in Norfolk, were all at Avignon.[12] In general, a number of apostates were said to be the bearers of these letters, implying perhaps that they had personally obtained the letters at the papal curia. Again, for 1355 alone there were three such English apostates: William de Blanquet, a Premonstratensian of Welbeck Abbey in Nottinghamshire, Thomas de Everingham, an Augustinian canon of Newburgh Priory in Yorkshire, and Richard de Orwell, an Augustinian canon of St Bartholomew's, Smithfield, London.[13] The pope had indeed mentioned in his constitution that apostates had come to his curia seeking relief; their presence at Avignon clearly caused problems. Complaints about religious at the papal curia without permission were a common refrain throughout this whole period. It had become such a problem for the English Benedictines in 1363 that the presiding abbot, Thomas de la Mare, abbot of St Albans, appointed a proctor to seize English monks who had fled without permission to the papal court and to detain them in prison until

---

[10] *CPL* 2. 545.   [11] Ibid., 2. 552.
[12] Ibid., 3. 572–3, 575.   [13] Ibid., 3. 564, 565, 574.

their superiors gave further instructions.[14] Yet there is no reason to think that all the apostates or even a majority of them who took advantage of the provisions of *Pastor bonus* actually came in person to the papal curia. Such was clearly not what Benedict XII had in mind, and English proctors at the curia or, at least, proctors at the curia specializing in English business could handle these matters.

For thirty-six years (1335–71) such papal letters were issued for the relief of English apostates. In 1371 the procedure was altered, allowing the papal legate to England to issue letters of reconciliation.[15] As a consequence, the post-1371 reconciliations do not regularly appear in the papal registers.[16] For the period from 1335 (*Pastor bonus*) to 1371 the papal registers provide the historian of apostasy with a fairly rich vein to mine. A total of 104 English apostates returned during this 36-year period under the provisions of this papal constitution. The overwhelming majority came from the larger orders: 37 Augustinian canons and one canoness, 28 Cistercians (including one lay brother), 22 Benedictine monks, 4 Premonstratensian canons, 2 each from the Carthusians (including one lay brother), Dominicans, Carmelites and Austin friars and one each from the Cluniacs, the Order of Tiron and the Knights Hospitallers. There also was a brother from a nunnery, who apparently was following the Rule of St Benedict.[17]

One might expect that an immediate flood of requests followed the papal constitution of 1335. Such was not the case, at least as far as England was concerned. The Benedictine monk Thomas de Cobewelle of Tewkesbury Abbey in Gloucestershire must have been at Avignon at the time when the constitution was issued, for he secured papal letters of reconciliation, which the papal registrar dated three days before the date of the issuance of *Pastor bonus*.[18]

---

[14] *Gesta abbatum* 2. 457; Pantin, *Chapters* 2. 73. For other examples of such religious at the papal court see Christopher Harper-Bill, 'Monastic Apostasy in Late Medieval England', *JEH* 32 (1981), pp. 14–15.

[15] *CPL* 4. 170. Similar faculties were given in 1413 (ibid., 6. 179) and in 1451 (ibid., 10. 226). In 1461 the papal legate was given the faculty to absolve thirty apostates (ibid., 11. 690).

[16] For the period from 1371 to 1513 the author has found only 23 references to the reconciliation of English apostates in the papal registers.

[17] Walter Woodward belonged to the Benedictine nunnery at Elstow (Beds.) and received papal letters dated 17 March 1349 (*CPL* 3. 276).

[18] Ibid., 2. 529. His letters are dated 13 June 1335, four days before the papal constitution. See the cautionary words of Professor C. R. Cheney about the meaning of dating clauses (*Handbook of Dates for Students of English History* (London, 1978), p. ix).

Only one other letter for an English apostate appears in the papal registers during 1335: the Dominican Arnold Lym of Guildford Priory.[19] Not another English apostate appears in the papal register until 1338, when Richard de Guisborough of Whitby Abbey received letters of reconciliation.[20] Two apostates received letters in 1339 and three others in the following year (including Roger de Worfield, a Benedictine monk of Worcester Priory, who received two sets of papal letters).[21] Ten were reconciled in 1341 and an additional 21 before 1350. Although the combined years of 1350 and 1351 saw 23 papal letters issued to English apostates, 17 of these were on behalf of pilgrim-apostates of the Holy Year of 1350.[22]

Some of these apostates might have been travelling in pairs. For example, in 1344 two Augustinian canons of Darley Abbey in Derbyshire – John de Scelleye and Thomas de Dancaster – received letters bearing dates two days apart.[23] Yet papal letters were issued to individual religious from religious houses as far apart as Buckfast Abbey in Devon and Stocking Abbey in the North Riding of Yorkshire and from over eighty other houses the length and breadth of the kingdom.

Many of these apostates from the papal registers have been met elsewhere in this book under various headings. Perhaps here may be given some examples of the variety of apostates who sought reconciliation by papal letters. We meet in letters of 1340 the Augustinian canon William Blasi of Holy Cross Abbey, Waltham in Essex, who claimed that he had been unjustly expelled from his monastery, and in 1341 we meet another canon of the same abbey, Walter de Thame, who made a similar claim. Trouble at Waltham in the early 1340s?[24] Others also claimed expulsion, such as Richard Randulf, a Benedictine of Buckfast Abbey in Devon, and Stephen de Hethe, a Cistercian of Boxley Abbey in Kent.[25] There was even the lay brother associated with the nuns at St Mary de Pré near St Albans, who, without the permission of his superior, the abbot of St Albans, left the nunnery and entered a Cistercian community

---

[19] *CPL* 2. 530. For his subsequent troubles see above, pp. 48–9.
[20] *CPL* 2. 544.
[21] Ibid., 2. 547 (10 Nov.), 549 (22 Dec.).
[22] See above, pp. 29–31.   [23] *CPL* 3. 171.
[24] Ibid., 2. 548, 550. Blasi claimed that, although he had tried to receive absolution from excommunication, he was unsuccessful and had then renounced the monastery and returned to the world.
[25] In 1344 and 1353 (ibid., 3. 175, 489). Since they were reconciled *qua* apostates, their expulsions had obviously led to apostasy.

and lived at a hermitage at Cripplegate in London. Not satisfied, however, after a year he resumed the Benedictine habit and then journeyed to Avignon in 1341 to seek reconciliation.[26] Another was said to have murdered his abbot and, after being imprisoned, to have broken out of his monastic prison: Thomas de Tonge of the Cistercian abbey of Buildwas in Shropshire.[27] Receiving papal letters in 1350 was Thomas de Melton, an Augustinian canon of Hexham Priory in Northumberland, who, in order to leave his priory without the odium of apostasy, had told his superiors falsely that he had been married before entering the order; he had now repented and sought reconciliation.[28] In many, if not most, of these cases it is clear that the apostate felt he was unable to be received back into his community unless armed with papal letters. This procedure, then, by papal letters had an obvious attraction for apostates whose superiors might be reluctant to readmit them. One can sympathize with the new abbot of Buildwas who might not want to spend the rest of his life looking over his shoulder for the murderous monk in the shadows of the cloister.[29] Papal letters could ease re-entry, if not into Buildwas, at least into most religious houses.

Very little evidence appears of opposition or resistance by local superiors to papal letters and papal commissioners mandated to carry them out. One would expect resistance to the readmission of Thomas de Tonge at Buildwas. Only one other such case among the papally mandated reconciliations has surfaced where the local house opposed readmission, and it is instructive about how the procedure worked in practice. It concerned Thomas Forncett, an Augustinian canon of Walsingham Priory in Norfolk, who broke his iron chains, escaped from the priory prison, threw off his religious habit and fled. He appeared at Rome in 1395 as a repentant apostate, seeking readmission to his priory, and papal letters were duly issued.[30] They were addressed to the archbishop

---

[26] Ibid., 2. 544.

[27] The letter is dated 20 Nov. 1343 (ibid., 3. 137). Writs for his arrest as an apostate were issued on 12 Sept. 1342 and – papal letters notwithstanding – on 18 Aug. 1344 (*CPR, 1340–43*, p. 553; *CPR, 1343–45*, p. 400).

[28] *CPL* 3. 393. See above, p. 17.

[29] In 1529 the English clergy in synod reiterated the obligation to receive back repentant apostates but added an exception in the case of those who had conspired or would in the future conspire or strive to kill the abbot, prior or fellow monk; the local bishop would verify this exception (Wilkins, *Concilia* 3. 723).

[30] *CPL* 4. 502.

of Canterbury, the bishops of Norwich and Tuy (in Galicia in Spain). The latter absolved Forncett and ordered the priory to readmit him and to compensate him for the expenses incurred by his journey to Rome. When the prior and convent refused, a canon of Wells, deputed by Bishop Despenser of Norwich, imposed on the priory of Walsingham sentences of excommunication, suspension and interdict. The canons appealed to Rome, charging that Forncett had secured the papal letters by lying at the apostolic see. The pope's response to the appeal granted the priory absolution from these sentences, pending the appeal; it was dated 20 May 1398, over three years after the papal letters of reconciliation had been granted. And there this episode fades from our sight.[31] This exceptional case can teach us about unexceptional cases: first, that busy papal commissioners might depute their responsibilities and, second, that the threat of ecclesiastical censure was far from idle.

One looks almost in vain for references to any of these 104 apostates in the records relating to the issuance of the writ *de apostata capiendo*. Only 5 of these apostates receiving papal letters of reconciliation appear in the surviving records for the use of the secular arm. Perhaps this should not surprise us since many of them might not have been wanted back and, also, since at least some of them were out of the country, at the papal curia, and beyond the reach of English writs. Thomas de Tonge, the notorious abbot-slayer, as has been seen, had two writs issued for his arrest.[32] A single petition from the abbot of Winchcombe sought the arrest of Simon de Lega and Thomas Malmeshull, who received papal letters in 1350 and 1353 respectively.[33] Also, on 12 February 1369 six Cistercian monks of Stoneleigh Abbey were signified as apostates by their abbot; one of these, John Dancaster, had already (16 January 1369) received papal letters of reconciliation. Perhaps notice of the papal letters had not yet reached Warwickshire.[34] And, finally, there is the puzzling case of Arnold Lym, who, as an

---

[31] Ibid., 5. 157–58. The bishop of Tuy, Thuribius, apparently a papal official, appears frequently in the registers. The canon of Wells was Michael Cergeaux, who was dean of Arches (*BRUO* 1. 377–8). Forncett reappears in the records as an apostate when, in 1414, a writ for his arrest was sought (C81/1789/3). He had obviously failed to make his peace with his fellow canons of Walsingham.

[32] See above, p. 129, n. 27.

[33] The abbot's petition is undated (C81/1786/54). The papal letters are in *CPL* 3. 392, 515.

[34] C81/1788/49; *CPL* 4. 80.

apostate Dominican friar of Guildford, received papal letters and who, later, as a Benedictine monk of Hyde Abbey, Winchester, was sought for arrest.[35] These few cases – 5 out of 104 – should serve as a salutary reminder to us that superiors, although bound by papal decree to pursue runaways, did not always rush to do so by invoking the secular arm.

EFFORTS BY OTHERS TO EFFECT RETURN

Not by popes alone were efforts made to bring apostates back from their apostasy. Efforts by individual orders and by bishops and others on the local level were also made. We can get glimpses of religious superiors, visitors to religious houses as well as local bishops as they handled issues of a practical and pastoral nature in securing the return and, indeed, readmission of runaways. To convince an apostate was only one step; re-entry was not guaranteed.

The legislation of individual orders echoed the papal concerns for the return of apostates. In the very wake of *Pastor bonus* (1335) there followed reforming constitutions for the Cistercians (1335), Benedictines (1336), Franciscans (1336) and Augustinian canons (1339).[36] Yet not merely in the 1330s but throughout the period here under study religious superiors were reminded of their obligations. The General Chapter of the Cistercians in 1242 ordered abbots and priors to compel the return of apostates even to the extent of invoking the secular arm.[37] A statute of the English Benedictines in 1247 repeated the substance of *Ne religiosi* in demanding annual inquiries about apostates, and Benedictine abbots and priors were reminded periodically of this obligation.[38]

English synods joined in the demand to secure the return of runaways. Even before the issuance of *Ne religiosi* a synod at Salisbury (1217 X 1219) enacted a constitution, often repeated, that ordered archdeacons and deans to use ecclesiastical censures to

---

[35] This case is discussed above, pp. 48–9.

[36] *Bullarium romanum* 4. 330–45, 348–87, 391–415, 425–59. Clarifications of some of the Benedictine constitutions were made in 1340 (pp. 462–7). An accessible text of the Augustinian constitutions is in Salter, *Chapters*, pp. 214–67, which is to be preferred to the text in Wilkins, *Concilia* 2. 629–51.

[37] Canivez, *Statuta* 2. 247.

[38] Pantin, *Chapters* 1. 28. Reminders were given, for example, in 1343 (ibid., 2. 53) and in 1444 (ibid., 2. 192).

force apostates to return to their cloisters and, if that failed, to have them arrested and placed in prison.[39] Without substantial changes this constitution was reissued by a certain (unidentifiable) bishop (1225 x 1230), by a synod at Durham (1228 x 1236) and in statutes for the Durham Peculiar (1241 x 1249?).[40] And these represent only the known English ecclesiastical legislation of this period on the subject. When the bishops of the southern province met at Lambeth in 1281, they lamented that some religious had returned *ad vomitum* and (the bishops mixing metaphors) had returned from Jerusalem to Egypt:

We order the ordinaries of places [i.e., the bishops] to investigate these instances. If the apostates are religious in clerical orders, they are to be forced, by being deprived of offices and benefices, to return to their former state or even to a more lenient rule. If the apostates are lay religious, their return is to be compelled by the use of ecclesiastical censure.[41]

The return of apostates was to remain a matter of interest for the English bishops. In 1308, for example, the archbishop of York, William Greenfield, who concerned himself much in these matters, not only required Thomas de Sherburn, an apostate monk of Selby Abbey, to return to his own monastery or to a stricter one but also ordered Sherburn to appear before him and, when his proctor offered no defence, had him denounced as an excommunicate.[42] Also, in 1343, Richard de Bury, bishop of Durham, at the urging of the Franciscan superior at Newcastle, ordered that the excommunication of the apostate friar William de Bowes be published in all the churches of Newcastle.[43] Such interventions by English bishops appear frequently enough in the records for us to think that they were fairly common.

The visitations of religious houses by bishops and others provide us with a particularly rich source which reveals the efforts made to gain the return of apostates. Routinely, visitors inquired about the

---

[39] *Councils and Synods* 2. 1. 93.

[40] Ibid., 2. 1. 191, 444. The Durham synod repeated the Salisbury statutes verbatim (see ibid., 2. 1. 57). In addition, the council held at Westminster in 1273, for which only the headings of inquiry survive, addressed the issue of apostates: *De exeuntibus religionem post habitum professionis sumptum* (ibid., 2. 2. 806).

[41] Author's translation (ibid., 2. 2. 913).

[42] *Reg. Greenfield, York* 2. no. 812.

[43] Bowes had apparently been shown hospitality by some clergy and laity of Newcastle (*Reg. Pal. Dunelm.* 3. 513–14).

number of apostates and what was being done to secure their return. Archbishop Winchelsey included in articles of inquiry for monasteries these questions: who are the apostates? and how are they being acted against?[44] Two centuries later Archbishop Morton was asking similar questions,[45] as was Archbishop Warham two decades still later.[46]

In the diocese of Lincoln, thanks to the editions of Professor A. Hamilton Thompson, we can see successive bishops as they visited the scores of religious houses of this largest of English dioceses. Near the beginning of his pontificate, William Gray (1431–6) made known to the Augustinian prior of Caldwell Priory, who was reluctant to receive back an apostate absolved by the bishop, what he thought the prior's obligations were in such matters: 'Such fugitives should be heartily sought after by those who have authority over them and should be recalled and compelled to return to the places where they made profession.'[47] He similarly reminded the Benedictine prior of Daventry Priory: 'We enjoin upon you the prior, in virtue of obedience and under pain of contempt, that you seek out with all diligence and wariness all the monks of your said priory, who, being professed in the same, are leading a life of apostasy outside the priory, and bring them back to the cloister.'[48] Gray's successor, the long-serving William Alnwick (1436–1449), continued this practice of inquiring about apostates in his visitations. At Bardney Abbey (c. 1440), for example, he discovered that one of the monks, John Hole, had sent out of the monastery all his personal belongings, including a silver spoon and a silver-garnished drinking cup, in apparent preparation for flight.[49] At Humberston Abbey in 1440, Alnwick found only five monks in residence and was told that the house had five apostates and that, of these, one had died and another had made profession as a mendicant friar.[50] It was actually while he was at Dorchester Abbey in 1441 that two of the canons – Thomas Henreth and Nicholas

---

[44] *Reg. Winchelsey, Canterbury* 2. 1300. His predecessor, John Pecham, had reserved absolution of the sin of apostasy to himself (*Epp. Jo. Peckham* 3. 25).

[45] *Reg. Morton, Canterbury* 2. 286, 291, 293, 377, 446.

[46] Mary Bateson, 'Archbishop Warham's Visitation of Monasteries, 1511', *EHR* 6 (1891) 18–35.

[47] *Linc. Vis.* 1. 29 (Thompson's translation here and elsewhere in this section).

[48] Ibid., 1. 43.

[49] He was at Bardney when Alnwick visited at this time and was still there when Alnwick came again in 1444 (ibid., 2. 26, 32).

[50] Ibid., 2. 140. This was a house of the Order of Tiron.

Plymouth – fled in apostasy. Were they fearful of what Alnwick's visitation might discover?[51] At St Neot's Priory in Huntingdonshire the visitor was informed that Robert Bylling had left in apostasy and his whereabouts were uncertain, although he might be at Winchelsea in Sussex.[52] One of the Augustinian canons at Ulverscroft Priory complained that Thomas Flory, the subprior, had been outside the priory for twenty years – in apostasy or not, the informant did not know – and that the prior not only readmitted him without the knowledge of the other canons but had appointed him confessor.[53] At another Augustinian house, Wellow Abbey, Alnwick learned about the recidivist apostate William Elkington, whom he enjoined the abbot to seek out.[54] At Notley Abbey, yet another Augustinian house, Thomas Ewelme was reported to have sinned seriously while serving the church of Dorton in Buckinghamshire: he had committed adultery with a woman, whose bed he was unwilling to leave to give the last rites to a dying woman, and 'clothed in secular garb and having laid aside his regular habit, [he] was in apostasy, cleaving to the said woman in adultery, for three quarters of a year'.[55] Bishop Alnwick recognized that temporary, unpermitted absence was like apostasy when he said that canons of Markby Priory had gone to the town 'quasi apostando'.[56] When records reappear for the Lincoln diocese in the pontificate of William Atwater (1514–21), we see the bishop asking about apostates in his circuit of the religious house of his diocese. At Eynsham Abbey, eight monks spoke in favour of the return of the apostate Walter Harburgh, and one monk opposed.[57] Three years later at Eynsham Atwater restored another apostate to his former place in the monastery and was told that the whereabouts of still another apostate was unknown.[58]

The bishops of Lincoln were not alone. At about the same time

[51] Ibid., 2. 71.   [52] Ibid., 3. 322.
[53] Ibid., 3. 388–9.   [54] Ibid., 3. 391, 393–4.
[55] Ibid., 3. 257.
[56] Ibid., p. 223. Similarly, the prior of Huntingdon Priory *inter alia* was reported having committed apostasy for having gone out on the evening of St Bartholomew's Day in 1436, wearing secular clothes, on which occasion he broke his arm in a fight. While admitting all this, he denied being irregular for continuing to say Mass – over a thousand times – since, by inference, he felt that he had not incurred canonical apostasy (ibid., 2. 154). Also, in 1446, at Peterborough Abbey the abbot purged himself of many sins, including apostasy, which (following Professor Thompson) simply meant that he had been accused of having worn secular garb (ibid., 3. 297–9).
[57] *Vis. Dioc. Linc.* 2. 139–40.   [58] Ibid., 2. 144, 141–42.

that Atwater was visiting, his neighbour the bishop of Coventry and Lichfield, Geoffrey Blythe (1503–31), was conducting visitations of religious houses in his diocese. He learned, for example, in 1518, that the abbot of Shrewsbury Abbey had tried to effect the return of Brother David, but the abbot did not know where he was and, in 1525, that the prior of Arbury Priory had reportedly sent his servants to capture John Bradshaw, an apostate, with the words, 'Follow hym witherso ever he goo, stryke him downe and take hym so that ye hurte hym not.'[59] Also contemporary were the visitations in the Norwich diocese, whose records likewise survive, which show that in 1514 William Brigges was apostate from Thetford Priory and was living in Snoring and that John Berdon had fled three or four times from Coxford Priory.[60]

It was not as a bishop that Bishop Redman visited the thirty-two Premonstratensian houses between 1475 and 1503 but as president of the order in England, an office which he held since shortly after becoming abbot of Shap in Westmorland in 1458 and which he continued to hold even after becoming successively bishop of St Asaph in 1471 and bishop of Exeter in 1495 and which he held until his death in 1505.[61] Two houses were in Kent, two in Northumberland and the rest dotted about the country from Norfolk to Wales. Everywhere Redman asked questions about apostasy, and, although he enlarged and, perhaps, even distorted its meaning,[62] he detected those religious who had abandoned the religious life, and these he was not loath to punish. In 1482, at Newsham (or Newhouse) Abbey in Lincolnshire he excommunicated for incontinence and apostasy the canon Thomas Ulsceby, who failed to appear when cited. Strangely enough, Ulsceby in 1488 was *circator* at Newsham, and his duties were to do a nightly bed-check of the monks.[63] He was not unlike John Nym, the apostate canon of Easby Abbey in Yorkshire, whom Redman excommunicated for apostasy in 1482 and who appears as *circator* in 1488 and, indeed, as prior in 1497.[64] At Welbeck Abbey in Nottinghamshire, in 1494, the visitor excommunicated Edward

[59] *Blythe's Vis.*, pp. 33, 161–6. Not all agreed that these were the prior's words.
[60] *Vis. Norwich*, pp. 88, 111.
[61] See Knowles, *RO* 3. 39; H. M. Colvin, *White Canons in England* (Oxford, 1951), p. 224.
[62] See above, pp. 32–3.
[63] *CAP* 3. 76–9. He later apostatized, allegedly for the third time (ibid., 3. 80–1).
[64] Ibid., 2. 5–6.

Colynsone for apostasy, who, three years later, was punished for the inordinate size of his tonsure.[65] When Redman visited Bayham Abbey in Sussex in 1500, he found that Thomas Studley, who had been apostate in 1497, was still apostate.[66] And, in 1503, as a very old man, the seemingly tireless reformer declared two canons of Newsham apostate.[67]

Other orders were also diligent about apostates, although the evidence for them is not so ample as for the Premonstratensians. The glimpses we get are of a well-oiled machine, operating smoothly. We see the General Chapter of the English Black Monks in 1371 ordering the arrest of Thomas de Hauksgard, an apostate of Whitby, whom we have encountered already, and in 1397 urging the abbot of Chertsey in Surrey to secure the return of his monk Adam Marlborough.[68] We catch sight of the Cistercian abbot of Hailes in Gloucestershire, in 1433, on the orders of the abbot of Cîteaux, making sure that the abbot of Combe Abbey in Warwickshire took action to secure the capture of Thomas Ashby, an apostate of that abbey.[69] Yet the efforts of bishops and religious superiors, at times, encountered opposition not from the apostates themselves but from their communities.

RELUCTANCE TO READMIT RUNAWAYS

For reasons that seem quite understandable returning apostates were in many instances not only not welcomed warmly but not welcomed at all. Numbered among those who fled their houses were undoubtedly troublemakers, whose absence was not lamented by their community and whose departure was greeted with relief. When they reappeared at the monastic gates, avowing contrition and promising amendment of their ways, many a superior, his idealism tempered by healthy cynicism, sent the returning apostate away, judging the peace of the house preferable to the doubtful conversion of a single member. And, in any case,

---

[65] Ibid., 3. 192, 194. What happened in 1494 is unclear, for Edward Colynsone was excommunicated at Welbeck on 29 May and a canon of the same name was excommunicated at Torre Abbey in Devon on 12 June (ibid., 3. 152). Could he have been absent from Welbeck and visiting Torre without permission?

[66] Ibid., 2. 79.   [67] Ibid., 3. 86.

[68] Pantin, *Chapters* 3. 278; 2. 92.

[69] Christopher Harper-Bill, 'Cistercian Visitation in the Late Middle Ages: The Case of Hailes Abbey', *BIHR* 53 (1980) 106–7.

if they followed the rule of St Benedict, they would feel no obligation to readmit a returning apostate more than three times.[70] This provision was generally interpreted to mean that the abbot must not accept such a person more than three times.[71] In 1298, the nuns at Stainfield Priory in Lincolnshire were told to abolish the custom which they had of receiving back apostates of their house even for a fourth time.[72] The decretal *Ne religiosi vagandi* (1234) foresaw this contingency, where a rule would not always permit readmission. It did not therefore relieve the superior of responsibility: the person was to be placed in the general precincts of the house, apart from the community, or in another house. Benedict XII in *Pastor bonus* (1335) went further and threatened reluctant superiors with ecclesiastical censures without possibility of appeal. The whole procedure, described earlier in this chapter, was directed by Pope Benedict towards assuring readmission, especially in the face of unwilling communities. And unwilling communities there certainly were.

Bishop Wykeham of Winchester in 1368 encountered such resistance from the community of Augustinian canons at Christchurch Priory in Hampshire, when he attempted to reconcile the apostate John Cossham to that priory: they refused to readmit him on the grounds that he was a 'common sower of tares (*seminator zizaniorum*) who stood before them in chapter convicted of crimes of sacrilege, adultery, escape from prison and theft of goods spiritual and temporal'.[73] So adamant were the canons at Christchurch that they were willing, the bishop observed, to permit Cossham to continue on the road of apostasy without even the necessities of life. Wykeham ordered officials in the archdeaconry of Winchester to investigate and, barring any canonical obstacle, to ensure Cossham's readmission, allowing the right of the priory then to discipline him.[74] And with that Cossham

---

[70] Rudolph Hanslik, ed., *Benedicti regula (Corpus scriptorum ecclesiasticorum latinorum* 75; Vienna, 1977), chap. 29.

[71] See, e.g., the Cistercian statute of 1221 (Canivez, *Statuta* 2. 2). For the practice of other orders see below, p. 149.

[72] Archbishop Winchelsey directed the bishop of Lincoln to execute this order *(Reg. Winchelsey, Canterbury* 1. 234).

[73] Author's translation (*Reg. Wykeham, Winchester* 2. 19–21). There is here the echo of the report received by visitors in 1363 that there were serious dissensions at Christchurch Priory 'mediante sizanine [sic] seminatore' (Salter, *Chapters*, pp. 162–3).

[74] 'salvis correctionibus et disciplinis regularibus eiusdem ordinis' (Salter, *Chapters*, pp. 162–3).

passes from our view unlike a monk of York, whose tragic fate is known. In 1281, John de St Oswald, a monk of St Mary's Abbey, fled one night from Wetheral Priory in Cumberland, a dependent priory of St Mary's, and two years later sought reconciliation. Despite the intervention of Archbishop Wickwane, he was refused. Undeterred, Brother St Oswald then decided to go to Rome to pursue the matter but, tragically, was killed on the way, apparently still unreconciled.[75] Not all apostates mellowed with age, as can be seen in the case of the 80-year-old Thomas Bledlow of Dunstable Priory in Bedfordshire. Called a notorious murderer and adulterer, who had thrice apostasized (for twenty years, for half a year and for more than a year), Bledlow appeared in 1446 at Dunstable, old and impoverished, seeking readmission. He was not allowed to remain there because the monks were in fear of his violent streak, and he was moved to St Osyth's Abbey (Essex).[76]

Not only communities of male religious were sometimes reluctant to reconcile apostates; some communities of nuns were equally reluctant. For example, in the early fifteenth century, the Augustinian canoness Joan Horncastle apostasized from Rothwell Priory in Northamptonshire. Bishop Repingdon of Lincoln, while visiting the parish of Coningsby, discovered her: she had been living in sin for three years with William Luffewyk. Repingdon absolved her and sent her back to Rothwell, armed with episcopal letters. Nevertheless, the prioress refused to readmit her, and Sister Joan then wandered to remote parts without her religious habit. Repingdon had her captured and sent her back to Rothwell once again in 1414.[77] The canons at Christchurch, the monks at York and the nuns at Rothwell were scarcely alone in their attitude, and the attitude of many religious communities might be summed up in the advice given in 1442 to the prior of Durham Priory by his senior monks – advice which he accepted – that to avoid greater evil the prior should not strive to recover the incorrigible.[78] It was to counter this sort of opposition that the Augustinian canons in

---

[75] He had previously gone to Rome to receive absolution for having shed the blood of a cleric. See *Chron. S. Mary's York*, pp. 16, 21; *Reg. Wickwane, York*, p. 228.

[76] Salter, *Chapters*, p. 114.

[77] *Reg. Repingdon, Lincoln* 3. no. 15. For the punishment given her see below, p. 154.

[78] R. B. Dobson, *Durham Priory, 1400–1450* (Cambridge, 1973), pp. 76–7.

their chapter in 1434 threatened to fine offending superiors the sum of £10.[79]

It fell to the bishops of England, to a considerable extent, to pressure communities to readmit returning apostates. Thus it was that the bishop of Lincoln wrote to Abbot Sawtre of Ramsey Abbey (1285–1316) to take back an apostate who had left twice.[80] Similarly, Bishop Cobham of Worcester wrote in 1322 to the abbot of Gloucester Abbey to take pity on Vincent de Lamput, who had twice apostasized, and to receive him with kindness.[81] Another Benedictine apostate, Henry de Camel of Muchelney Abbey in Somerset, appeared before the bishop of Bath and Wells, John Droxford, at Kingsbury in July 1315, was absolved and sent back to Muchelney with a letter to the abbot to this effect.[82] Other bishops did the same. At Lincoln, Bishop Sutton in 1294 and 1295 directed the abbot of Missenden to reconcile apostate canons, and, in 1296, he wrote to the prioress of Wothorpe Priory in Northamptonshire to readmit an apostate nun named Acelina.[83] At Exeter, Bishop Lacy in 1451 ordered the prior of Bodmin Priory in Cornwall to receive back William Mullyng, a canon, who, after being convicted of crimes and imprisoned, escaped and fled in apostasy but now, repentant, wished to be reconciled.[84]

At York, more than in any other diocese, thanks to record keepers and record survival, do we see in practice the intervention of the local bishop on behalf of returning apostates. This is particularly true of the pontificates of Thomas Corbridge (1300–4), William Greenfield (1306–15) and William Melton (1317–40), when letters concerning at least twenty-three apostate religious appear in the registers, of whom only eight were men.[85] Archbishop Greenfield in 1311 instructed the abbot of Selby to

---

[79] It was to be used to help pay for construction of a college for canons at Oxford (Salter, *Chapters*, p. 83).

[80] W. D. Macray, ed., *Chronicon abbatiae Ramseiensis* (RS; London, 1886), p. 398.

[81] *Reg. Cobham, Worcester*, pp. 133–4. In 1320 Cobham had directed the abbot of St Augustine's, Bristol, to absolve the apostate canon William Barry (ibid., p. 95).

[82] *Reg. Droxford, Bath and Wells*, p. 94.

[83] *Reg. Sutton, Lincoln* 5. 30–1, 99, 167.

[84] *Reg. Lacy, Exeter* 3. 129–30.

[85] Earlier, Archbishop Giffard, *c.* 1276, ordered the prior of Felley Priory to reconcile Robert Barry, a canon who had impregnated a concubine at Nottingham (*Reg. W. Giffard, York*, nos. 666, 912, 916). His successor, John le Romeyn, in 1286 alone, acted on behalf of a Cistercian nun of Sinningthwaite Priory, a Gilbertine canon of Ellerton Priory and an unnamed nun then at Richmond (*Reg. le Romeyn, York* 1. nos. 116, 531, 964).

receive back the repentant and absolved apostate Henry de Belton and to ensure that Belton stayed within the monastic confines, did not speak to women, religious or lay, and held no monastic office.[86] Two Augustinian canons of Healaugh Priory – Richard de Doncaster and Roger de York – Greenfield ordered readmitted in 1313 and 1314 respectively; he also ordered that they be kept in secure places – York, if necessary, in irons – in order to prevent their flight.[87]

The presence of comparatively so many religious women in the York registers may reflect their greater dependence on the local ordinary. They all came from small houses numbering no more than the apostolic twelve – many perhaps fewer – with the exception of the two nuns of Nun Appleton, a Cistercian house having perhaps as many as thirty members.[88] The situation of the apostate canoness of Moxby Priory in the North Riding, Joan de Brotherton, whom Archbishop Melton sought twice to reconcile, might, in the first instance (in 1322), have been complicated by the Scottish raids of that year, which necessitated a transfer of nuns from Moxby.[89] Similarly, Isabel Dayvill, a Cistercian nun of Rosedale Priory, another North Riding house, whom Melton tried to reconcile in 1322, was sent by him to Handale Priory, at about the time that the nuns of her priory were being transferred as a consequence of the Scottish raids.[90] The raiding Scots cannot be implicated in the happenings at Thicket Priory, whose nuns, in 1303, brought an apostate to the attention of Archbishop Corbridge. Alice Darel, they wrote, had approached the gates of the nunnery, declaring that she was ready to undergo penance, but they believed that she was not ready to accept the penance which she deserved. The archbishop replied that, if Alice Darel would accept the penance, the priory should admit her, but, if she refused, she should be detained in a room in safe custody.[91] Later in the same year, Corbridge was presented with a quite different situation: Beatrice de Hawkesworth, a Cistercian nun of Esholt Priory, had

[86] *Reg. Greenfield, York* 2. nos. 701, 808, 938.
[87] Ibid., 2. nos. 995, 1071.
[88] 'one of the larger nunneries' (KH, p. 275).
[89] The archbishop wrote on her behalf on 13 Feb. 1322, and the nuns were sent elsewhere on 17 Nov. – Brotherton apparently reconciled – to the Cistercian nunnery at Hampole. In 1318, Melton, once again, sought her reconciliation. See *Reg. Melton, York* 1. no. 211 (i); 2. nos. 172, 316, 317.
[90] Ibid., 2. nos. 181–2.
[91] *Reg. Corbridge, York* 1. no. 506.

fled to her father's house where she lay pregnant. Under no circumstances should the prioress of Esholt admit Beatrice until the apostate nun received the *gratia revertendi*. That grace was apparently received – and the child born – for almost six months later the archbishop ordered that Hawkesworth should humbly submit and be readmitted as a nun of Esholt.[92] Also, in 1303, Corbridge attempted to reconcile Constance de Daneport of Pontefract to the Cluniac nuns of Arthington Priory, but his efforts did not meet with success. The Cluniac monk of Pontefract with whom Constance had sinned had been reconciled with his monastery, and the archbishop sought her reconciliation. Fearing, perhaps, an unwelcoming community, Corbridge directed them to receive her with affection and charity, and, should any of them act to the contrary, he threatened to punish them. The deadline for her return was delayed from 14 January to 16 February 1304 and she failed to appear. The archbishop wrote yet again that, even as an excommunicate, Constance, coming humble and contrite, should be received *sine murmure*.[93]

Confronted with a recidivist apostate, penitent at the monastic gate once again and pleading with the very same words heard before, a religious superior might easily close the gates of reconciliation. Yet if the pleading was reinforced with a letter from the archbishop of York, the chances of reconciliation would be greatly enhanced. In four of these York diocese cases (three nuns and one canon) we are clearly dealing with recidivists, for whom the archbishop intervened. For the nun of Moxby who fled in 1322 it was her second flight, and she was to flee again. In 1308, Agnes de Thormodby was reconciled for a third time at Baysdale Priory as was Joan de Lelom in 1319 at the same house.[94] The recidivist canon was Simon le Constable, 'who, we have learned, has for a third time meddled with illicit freedoms and worldly vanities', said Archbishop Greenfield, who required Bridlington to readmit the now repentant Constable.[95]

It should be emphasized that, when English bishops intervened to effect the successful return of apostates, we cannot assume that, in every case, the bishop was confronting an unwilling community. Yet troublemakers, undesirables, sowers of discord there surely

---

[92] Ibid., 1. nos. 247, 269.   [93] Ibid., 1. nos. 255, 259, 266.
[94] *Reg. Greenfield, York* 3. no. 1210; *Reg. Melton, York* 2. no. 77.
[95] *Reg. Greenfield, York* 5. no. 2871.

were, religious who had somehow passed their year of probation, their unsuitability undetected (or, perhaps, overlooked), religious who had undergone personality or character changes, which the passage of time and the tedium of regular life had perhaps encouraged. Popes and bishops and major superiors became their spokesmen and tried to force reluctant communities to receive them back.

FORCED RETURN: THE REASON WHY

Modern readers, pondering the efforts made by the church to secure the return of those who fled the religious life, must surely wonder why. They notice the persistent efforts of the papacy to bring back apostates, and in England efforts by bishops and religious superiors alike. They notice the willingness of the English state to give significant assistance to effect their return to the extent of permitting its arrest machinery to be used for this purpose. Modern readers will soon read about the punishments imposed on runaways upon their return. What was the reasoning that lay behind all this? Why did the medieval church take such measures against religious who no longer wanted to be religious and who wanted to return to the world? One looks almost in vain for such questions in the medieval literature. While it is true that John Wyclif opposed the imprisonment of apostates in their monasteries, he did so because this punishment, he believed, pertained not to popes but to kings, and, in any case, he held *a priori* objections to the religious life itself and even held that all religious were apostates! Erasmus of Rotterdam, an Augustinian canon, may have been the first – or, at least, among the first – to raise such questions.[96] These are questions which the modern historian must ask.

From what has just been seen, it was clearly not universally held in practice that apostates should be forced to return or, if returning, that they should be received. The numerous examples of reluctant superiors and communities demonstrate this. Yet the official

---

[96] In an *apologia*, written in 1514 to his prior, he explained his lack of suitability for the religious life and his form of dress (P. S. Allen, ed., *Opus epistolarum Des. Erasmi Roterodami* (12 vols.; Oxford, 1906–58) 1. no. 296; R. A. B. Mynors and D. F. S. Thomson, trs., *The Correspondence of Erasmus* (vols.; Toronto, 1974–) no. 296. Erasmus had received a dispensation to hold an English benefice, 4 Jan. 1506 (*CPL* 18. 587).

position of the church, witnessed by papal decrees, local legislation and the constitutions of religious orders, all agreed that apostates must be compelled to return. Even the saving clauses (*salva ordinis disciplina*) did not excuse local superiors from this obligation: they had to make other arrangements (e.g., a segregated place in their own house or exile to another house). The official position required the forced return of apostates; the willingness or unwillingness of the apostate was clearly an irrelevance. The monk or canon belonged in his monastery, the friar in his friary and the nun in her nunnery. If outside, without permission, to the point of apostasy, measures must be taken to get them back. Why this insistence?

The official position was supported by official rhetoric, and the official rhetoric voiced two reasons, almost always in this order: the danger to the salvation of the soul of the apostate and the grave scandal to the Christian people. Gregory IX's *Ne religiosi vagandi* begins (my translation), 'Lest religious who have apostasized incur the loss of their own salvation and the blame for this be on the hands of their superiors'.[97] The Cistercian pope, Benedict XII, cast himself as the good shepherd seeking to protect his wandering sheep from devouring wolves, when he was establishing ways to ease the return of fugitive religious, so that they would not be lost but saved ('ne pereant, sed salventur'). He added that other Christians, obviously disturbed by the departure of apostates from the path of righteousness, would also benefit from their reconciliation.[98] When English religious superiors requested writs of arrest, they routinely stated that the apostates were acting to the peril of their souls and causing public scandal: phrases like 'in anime sue graue periculum' and 'scandalum manifestum' were common form in the petitions and in the writs themselves.[99]

As general expressions of policy, these statements must stand: the apostate must be rescued from eternal perdition and the Christian people spared grave scandal. Whether the erring religious wanted to be saved was viewed as beside the point. Christian charity demanded that superiors not allow apostates to lose their souls. Gregory IX's concern that prelates should not incur blame for neglecting the eternal salvation of those committed to them is telling and suggests the prevailing mentality. The good shepherd

---

[97] X.3.31.24.
[98] *Bullarium romanum* 4. 326.   [99] See Appendices 1 and 2.

should not neglect his sheep even when they are wandering, sinful, rebellious, unrepentant and personally loathsome. Such an image implied leaving the ninety-nine to find the one that was lost. The modern reader must guard here against imposing a modern mentality that emphasizes an individual's freedom, even to harm himself. The ultimate loss in the medieval mind was the loss of one's soul and the greatest tragedy an eternity in hell. To avoid this fate was at the core of life in the earthly city, and to save one's subjects from it was a supreme obligation of every abbot and prior, abbess and prioress.

Public scandal implies a public whose standards are affronted by certain behaviour. Scholastic writers were to distinguish this from the scandal of the pusillanimous and pharisaical, whose standards are ignorant or mean-spirited and not reflective of those of the community. The runaway religious, it was said, affronted the standards of the Christian community. What is meant here is that the fact of apostasy itself, independent of whether the apostate was acting dissolutely, constituted a source of scandal. So insistent was the significance of the habit itself – in a society with fairly rigid sumptuary views – that putting off the religious habit and clothing one's self in the clothes of the world offended the Christian community's mores and was seen to provoke public scandal. Thus, apostasy was damaging both to the apostate, who stood in peril of damnation, and to the Christian people, whose sense of decent behaviour was gravely outraged. Apostates must be sought out and forced to return.

It may be possible to go beyond the stated reasons – the official policy reasons – and suggest further considerations. The nature of the life-long commitment made by religious profession usually at a solemn ceremony with public vows was not unlike marriage, which imposed life-long obligations on the parties and was frequently, if not always, solemnized *in facie ecclesiae*. Abandonment of one's monastery or convent was not unlike the abandonment of a spouse. Further, to return to an analogy used earlier,[100] the apostate can be compared to a soldier who has deserted: he has discarded his uniform, donned 'civvies' and does not intend to return to army life; the army would pursue him by using the military police and, if he were caught, a court martial would follow. The modern reader and, indeed, the modern historian,

---

[100] See above, p. 31.

pondering the question of the forced return of apostate religious, must be ever vigilant not to impose modern values and perceptions on the middle ages.

THE RITE OF READMISSION

There approached the great gates of St Albans Abbey on a day in 1328 the apostate William Somerton. He had opposed the abbot in courts English and papal, had enlisted noble and royal support against the abbot, had twice apostasized and now came repentant, seeking readmission. Walsingham's chronicle simply says that Somerton fell prostrate at the abbey's gates and there waited for several hours while it was decided what to do with him.[101] One might be inclined to think that the delay was a deliberate, spiteful humbling of this particularly troublesome and probably arrogant Somerton or that he was kept waiting while someone found the prior. It was, in fact, the first step in the ritual of return. Monastic constitutions and books of *ordines* prescribed, sometimes with fairly elaborate rubrics, the ceremony by which an apostate was reconciled.

Chapter 29 of the Rule of St Benedict simply states that the returning fugitive should be received back in the lowest place to test his humility. In the course of time a rite developed. The basic text in England is found in the Customs given by Archbishop Lanfranc to his monks at Christ Church, Canterbury, which was widely adopted by new foundations, and its influences can be seen in other surviving monastic rituals.[102]

---

[101] *Gesta abbatum* 2. 303. Summaries of the Somerton affair can be found in *VCH, Herts.* 4. 386–7; *VCH, Norfolk* 2. 344.

[102] David Knowles, ed., *Decreta Lanfranci in monachis Cantuariensibus transmissa* (CCM 3; Siegburg, 1967), pp. 84–5. Other texts include descriptions of the reconciliation rituals at Westminster Abbey (E. M. Thompson, ed., *Customary of the Benedictine Monasteries of St. Augustine, Canterbury, and St. Peter, Westminster* (2 vols.; Henry Bradshaw Soc., 1902–4) 2. 209–11), at Eynsham Abbey (Antonia Gransden, ed., *The Customary of the Benedictine Abbey of Eynsham in Oxfordshire* (CCM 2; Siegburg, 1963), pp. 91–3). For the Augustinian canons see Salter, *Chapters*, pp. 249–50. For a brief description of the Premonstratensian ceremony see P. F. Lefèvre, ed., *Les statuts de Prémontré réformés sur les ordres de Gregoire IX et d'Innocent IV au XIIIe siècle* (Louvain, 1946), p. 76; for the description of a similar ceremony for the Dominicans, whose constitutions were based on those of Prémontré, see G. R. Galbraith, ed., *The Constitution of the Dominican Order, 1216 to 1360* (Manchester, 1925), p. 224, and Raymond Creytens, ed., 'Les constitutions des frères prêcheurs dans la rédaction de S. Raymond de Peñafort', *Archivum Fratrum Praedicatorum* 18 (1948) 46.

Lanfranc would have the returning apostate placed in the *domus hospitalis*, where he would wait for an indeterminate period, segregated from fellow monks and cloister. At Westminster Abbey he was placed in the almonry, similarly segregated. The practice at Eynsham Abbey is more fully described. The returning fugitive waited outside the abbey gates, bewailing his offence. He hoped to catch sight of the abbot, before whom he would prostrate himself, begging mercy and forgiveness. Others entering the monastery he begged to speak on his behalf. Whereas other descriptions proceed to the central ceremony in the chapter house, the Eynsham customary interposed another ceremony. While outside the great gates to the abbey, the returning apostate was kept in the custody of the almoner. After a few days ('aliquantis diebus') he came to the abbatial church, where, standing before the crucifix and speaking so that all could hear – the monks in choir and the lay people as well – he begged mercy. Then the abbot allowed him to enter the hospital or almonry, there, as at Canterbury and Westminster, suitably separated from the community. Even then he was not actually allowed into the church without further ceremony. On a day on which the monks solemnly processed into the church, he prostrated himself at the door through which they were to enter and then, having been struck by the abbot three times, he was at last allowed to enter the church. The various descriptions relate that signs of humility and repentance were looked for at this stage before the reconciliation process could continue.

The actual reception took place not in the church but in the chapter house, the place for correction of faults. In the parlour, which in many monasteries was next to the chapter house, the returning monk divested himself of his clothes. If he had returned still wearing the monastic habit, he wore now a simple undershirt and girded his waist; over his left arm he carried a folded cowl and in his right hand whipping sticks. If he had returned wearing secular clothes, he wore these disgraceful clothes. In either case, barefoot and otherwise nude and led by one of the monks, the repentant fugitive entered the chapter house and took his regular place. There he prostrated himself, placing the cowl and sticks to his right. Questioned, he confessed his fault. At Christ Church, Canterbury, he said, 'My lord [i.e., the prior], I have offended God and my order as well as you and my convent. I hereby beg grace and mercy. I come here prepared to make satisfaction.' To which the prior responded,

Yes, my brother, holy mother church opens her bosom to the humble and contrite. Because you humbly confess your fault, contritely ask forgiveness and present yourself prepared to make satisfaction, we admit you to the bosom of the church and to the communion of your brothers. We assign to you the [named] place in choir, cloister and refectory. Your humility will be perfect according to the Rule of St Benedict.[103]

The forgiven monk then sat. The whipping sticks were used on him – the 'discipline' – and, at the order of the abbot to rise, he stood and donned the cowl. Forgiven and cowled, he returned to the parlour, where he put on shoes and fully dressed himself in monastic clothes. He entered the chapter once more, where he prostrated himself on the ground yet again, while the abbot rebuked him. He remained lying there until told to rise. A penance was then imposed, and the apostate monk was now reconciled, at least formally.

PENANCE: *AD CASTIGANDUM*

The directives to accept back an apostate routinely said that mercy and charity should be shown. Benedict XII urged moderation even towards those who had committed excesses – 'ob fragilitatem carnis humanae' – lest apostates, fearful of revenge and harsh punishment, be deterred from returning to their order and habit.[104] The pleas for charity presume, as did the ceremony of readmission, that there would almost inevitably be punishment. The petitions for the writ *de apostata capiendo* commonly stated that the apostates should be captured and returned to their houses for punishment (*ad castigandum*). And punishment, indeed, there was, medicinal by design, if not always so by individual intent.

The Rule of St Benedict simply stated that the returning apostate shall take the last place in the monastery. In a small community – even in a community with fifty or sixty monks – place of seniority would take on a large significance; it marked one's *locus* within that community, determined by date of profession. Unlike modern academic processions held once or twice a year with marshals skilfully determining places, monastic processions were held every day and, indeed, many times each day. Besides, seniority indicated where one sat in choir and in chapter

---

[103] Author's translation (*Lit. Cant.* 1. 246).   [104] *Bullarium romanum* 4. 328.

and in refectory. Loss of seniority constituted a daily reminder of one's apostasy, a daily humiliation. Seldom was this penance omitted. Few monks had powerful supporters as had William Pouns, apostate of Christ Church, Canterbury, who escaped this humiliation thanks to the intercession of Archbishop Chichele.[105] The Cistercians clarified what was meant by the last place assigned to the readmitted apostate: it was the last place in that person's order. Thus, a choir monk or nun would be last among the choir monks or nuns, and a lay brother or sister last among the lay brothers or sisters.[106] The reconciled apostates did not remain last but retained the place given at this time, and newly professed members of the community took their places after them. Theoretically, when the period for performing the other penances was completed, the new place would be retained, but exceptions were made. The Cistercians' General Chapter in 1231 ruled that, unless an apostate had returned within seven days, he would always be last.[107] The Dominicans permitted a friar to return to the former place after the period of penance only by dispensation.[108] The Gilbertines similarly allowed return if it seemed expedient to the prior.[109] In one particularly poignant case Thomas Lek, a 70-year-old Augustinian canon of Kyme Priory in Lincolnshire, in 1446, after forty years in apostasy, was permitted to reclaim his original place.[110] In practice, then, the permanence of the new place might not always have been insisted on, and, after an interval, the original place might have been regained.

The loss of seniority was a penalty common to all the religious orders. Beyond that, other penalties were imposed, similar in nature – the options were limited – among the orders, yet there were peculiarities even here. The Gilbertines, for example, proportioned the penance to the length of time the fugitive was away, distinguishing whether the return was within one week, during the period from the second week to the fifth week and, lastly, after forty days. One unusual aspect of the Gilbertine penances was the general exclusion of the second and third groups

[105] See above, pp. 64–5.   [106] Canivez, *Statuta* 2. 247.
[107] Ibid., 2. 93.   [108] Galbraith, *Constitution*, p. 224.
[109] L. Holstenius, ed., *Codex regularum monasticarum et canonicarum* (6 vols.; Augsburg, 1759) 2. 514–15.
[110] As a youth he apostasized and became a Dominican friar for a while (Salter, *Chapters*, pp. 110–11). Possibly same as Richard Lek (above, p. 46n.).

from reception of Communion.[111] The Premonstratensians, on the other hand, proportioned the penance to the number of times the apostate had fled, distinguishing penalties for second, third and even fourth and fifth absences.[112] The Dominicans made a similar distinction but only up to four absences.[113] Whatever differences in detail may have existed from order to order, the principal elements in penance were those drawn by the canonists from chapters 23–25 of the rule of St Benedict:[114]

1 *secreta monitio*
2 *publica correctio*
3 *simplex vel minor excommunicatio*
4 *ieiunii afflictio*
5 *flagellorum vapulatio*
6 *ad deum oratio*
7 *de monasterio expulsio*

The first two of these, as we have seen, were imposed at the time of the apostate's return and readmission. Excommunication had been the penalty of choice before 1298 and the automatic penalty after that date, and it was incurred not upon the return of the apostate but upon the apostasy itself. The remaining four – to which we shall soon add two others generally and another for nuns alone – constitute the penalties which were usually imposed by the superior as he pronounced the *satisfactio* over the prostrate body of the repentant apostate at the end of the ceremony in the chapter house: fasting, beating, prayer and exile.

Mentioned last, perhaps because it was viewed as the severest punishment, was the forced withdrawal from the monastery.[115] As a penalty for apostasy, this punishment must be distinguished from *eiectio*, by which an erring monk was simply expelled. The penalty occasionally imposed on repentant apostates took the form of *exsilium*: the religious was sent to another house of the same order for a specific period of time – five to seven years would not have been uncommon – there to complete the other parts of the penance. The *exsilium* pertained especially to monks and nuns who

---

[111] Holstenius 2. 514–15.   [112] Lefèvre, *Statuts*, p. 76.
[113] Galbraith, *Constitutions*, p. 224.
[114] See Joannes Andreae, *In tertium decretalium librum novella commentaria* (Venice, 1581), 3.31.24, citing earlier teaching.
[115] Benedict XII in his constitutions for the Benedictines (1336) prescribed *exsilium* as a remedy for monasteries with serious lapses of the monastic life. See *Bullarium romanum* 4. 385.

had made profession not only to an order but to a specific house of that order to such an extent that, if they transferred to another house, then a new profession was made. This penalty amounted to a humiliating and shameful banishment: the monk and nun were seen and known in their new houses as so marked by guilt that their own religious *familia* had refused to accept them and banished them from their midst.[116] In 1310, for example, a returned apostate canon of Worksop Priory in Nottinghamshire, Ralph de Grove, was sent in exile to Bridlington Priory in Yorkshire, there to perform stiff penances.[117] The Cluniac nun of Rosedale Priory, Isabel Dayvill, whom we met earlier in this chapter, was sent by Archbishop Melton to Handale Priory, where she was to perform her assigned penances.[118] Somewhat unusual was the case of William Wallewen, a Benedictine monk of Worcester Priory. In 1466, convicted of disobedience, incontinence, conspiracy, apostasy and other crimes, Wallewen was exiled to Abingdon Abbey until the next General Chapter. While there, he was particularly forbidden to go to the University of Oxford or to receive Oxford scholars at Abingdon. He returned to Worcester two years later, then, in the following year transferred (*per modum transitus*) to Eynsham Abbey, where he later became abbot, an office he was still holding in 1498.[119]

About the Premonstratensian use of penalties, especially *exsilium*, a perhaps disproportionate amount is known, owing to the survival of Redman's visitation records. There we see that routinely a returning apostate was placed on bread and water for forty days. These forty days might be spent at another monastery as happened to Walter Speyer, a canon of Torre Abbey in Devon, who was exiled to Newsham (Newhouse) Abbey in Lincolnshire for forty days' fasting and for at least three more years.[120] We know of at least six other Premonstratensian apostates exiled by Redman: two for 3 years, one for 7 years and three for 10 years. One of the latter,

---

[116] When John de Cella, abbot of St Albans, lay dying in 1214, monks gathering about his bed complained of the 'intolerabilis consuetudo' of transferring monks to remote cells (*Gesta abbatum* 1. 247–8). See, too, the comments by Jane Sayers ('Violence in the Medieval Cloister', *JEH* 41 (1990) 536).

[117] *Reg. Greenfield, York* 4. no. 1851; see also nos. 1822, 1824, 1845.

[118] See above, p. 140.

[119] Pantin, *Chapters* 3. 113–15; *BRUO* 3. 1977. In 1462 he had failed in an attempt to become abbot of Wenlock (Salop). What actually happened while he was at Abingdon is uncertain, for, in Oct. 1467, the prior of Worcester sought his arrest as an apostate (C81/1786/55).

[120] *CAP* 3.143.

Roger Walsall of Halesowen Abbey in Worcestershire, in addition to his apostasy, had counselled an abortion and had caused a rebellion of younger canons against the abbot; in 1497, he was sent to Croxton Abbey in Leicestershire, where he was to be detained in prison.[121] One wonders whether such harsh penalties were in the spirit of Benedict XII's call for mercy and charity.

The duration of exile, specified when the satisfaction was imposed, could be mitigated by good behaviour. Thus, Henry de Pecham, a canon of Tandridge Priory in Surrey, because of good behaviour, returned in 1309 from nearby Newark Priory, to which he had been exiled.[122] Financial arrangements were made between the two houses involved, if a monk-for-monk exchange was not arranged. The Council of Oxford (1222) required such payments for upkeep.[123] In 1308, a canon of St Osyth's Abbey in Essex was exiled to St Bartholomew's Priory, Smithfield (London), for a payment of 1s per week. Two years later, when a scandalous canon of Royston Priory in Hertfordshire was exiled to St Osyth's, a per weekly payment of 14d was arranged.[124] No wrangling over fees appears, although the bishop of Winchester felt he had to remind the prior of Tandridge to pay Newark Priory the sum of 1s per week for Henry de Pecham's keep.[125] Yet, if the Premonstratensians followed these payment policies, then the ten-year exile of Roger Walsall would have cost Halesowen Abbey – at the rate of 1s per week – the sum of £26.

The three other general forms of punishment – fasting, corporal punishment and additional prayers – may be better grouped together since they were almost universally imposed and were thus experienced by the religious being punished as parts of their continuing life of penance. To these three should be added two further punishments which were regularly given: restrictions about personal mobility and about communications with externs. Commonly, the religious doing penance for apostasy fasted on Wednesdays and Fridays, on the latter eating only bread, legumes and beer. The discipline was usually administered also on those two days. In addition to the psalter which was usually recited each week by male religious in choir, the recitation of another psalter was not uncommonly required each week as well as the recitation of the

[121] Ibid., 2. 258–9.   [122] *Reg. Woodlock, Winchester* 1. 285, 361, 377–8.
[123] *Councils and Synods* 2. 1. 123.
[124] *Reg. Baldock, London*, p. 133.   [125] *Reg. Woodlock, Winchester* 1. 377–8.

seven penitential psalms, perhaps prostrate and before a specified altar each day. The period of penance could extend for three years and frequently for longer.

The Carthusians and Carmelites imposed imprisonment as a usual penalty for returned apostates. The prison, actually a room set aside for troublesome monks, became a standard part of Carthusian buildings, although from the surviving English sources it appears that it was little used, at least by apostates.[126] The Carmelites, at least in their constitutions, saw imprisonment as the appropriate penalty for their fugitive friars. The constitutions of London, 1281, required that apostates be imprisoned for forty days.[127] In the order's constitutions of 1324 and 1357 the Carmelites were more precise. If the apostate returned within three days, then he would be imprisoned for twenty days. If he was away more than three days but less then forty, he would be imprisoned for forty days. If his absence was for more than forty days, he could not be freed from prison within a year save by the prior general or the provincial superiors. If he had been away for more than a year, then he must remain in prison for the same period of time as he had been absent, which could be shortened by his superiors. If, however, scandal attended his apostasy, he was to be imprisoned indefinitely and could be released only by decision of the general or provincial authorities.[128] Few cases of the penalty of imprisonment appear in the extant English sources for the Carmelites, yet the case of John Hawteyn (alias Scharynton), the fifteenth-century boy friar who ran off and was later confined in London and Oxford, might not be atypical of the treatment given to returned Carmelite apostates.[129]

A few other illustrations will allow us to see beyond customaries and constitutions to how this penance system worked in actual cases and how it affected in practice those repentant apostates who, prostrate on the chapter floor, heard their *satisfactio* announced. The scandalous Augustinian canon of St Osyth's, Robert de Stratford, who was sent to St Bartholomew's Priory in 1308,

---

[126] The order required a monastic prison in 1261. See E. Margaret Thompson, *The Carthusian Order in England* (London, 1930), p. 127.

[127] L. Saggi, ed., 'Constitutiones capituli Londinensis anni 1281', *Analecta ordinis Carmelitarum* 15 (1950) 234. Imprisonment, although the term was unspecified, was given as a penalty in the constitutions of 1294 (Saggi, 'Constitutiones capituli Burdigalensis anni 1294', *Analecta* 18 (1953) 160).

[128] Paul F. Robinson, ed., *The Carmelite Constitutions of 1357* (Rome, 1992), pp. 304–6, 378–9.

[129] *VCH, London* 1. 509. See above, p. 15.

received the following as the rest of his penance: on Mondays and Wednesday he could eat only bread, soup and beer and on Fridays only bread and water; he must attend every canonical hour day and night; he must celebrate Mass daily; he had to take the last place in choir, chapel and refectory; he should receive the discipline from the presiding canon in chapter each Wednesday and Friday; he was not allowed to leave the monastic enclosure or to meet with women; and he did not know how long it would last, for his punishment had no fixed term.[130] Similar penalties, also without fixed term, were imposed in 1309 on Thomas de Sherburn, an apostate Benedictine of Selby Abbey. He was ordered to confess twice a week to the abbot or his deputy and to recite each day the seven penitential psalms with litanies, prostrate before any altar, and to recite each week an additional psalter. Sherburn also had to fast and abstain on Wednesdays from dairy products and foods grown from seeds, and on Fridays he had to be content with bread, legumes and beer. Neither in-letters nor out-letters were allowed him, and, only in the presence of the abbot, could he speak to a lay person; and, lastly, he was not permitted to leave the monastic grounds.[131]

Moreover, besides the common restrictions, other penalties were at times added. Thus, a canon of Newstead, in 1306, was virtually placed under guard in solitary confinement: William de Dingley was to live in a separate room by himself, where he was to take all his meals and where he was to be watched at night by a servant of the monastery.[132] At Healaugh Park Priory in Yorkshire, in 1313, Richard de Doncaster was enjoined a usual penance for the period of seven years, but during that period he was forbidden to celebrate Mass or receive Communion unless in danger of death.[133]

Women religious, *mutatis mutandis*, suffered the same sorts of penalties as did religious men, but with one notable difference. Almost universally the returning apostate nun was, for a period of time, not permitted to wear the veil. The clothing ceremony at a nun's profession was a central feature, and this particular penalty, not physically taxing like the discipline, the fast and extended prayers, might have caused the greatest pain. Not untypical of the

---

[130] *Reg. Baldock, London*, p. 77.
[131] *Reg. Greenfield, York* 3. no. 1237; see also 2. nos. 812, 881, 970.
[132] Ibid., 4. no. 1675.   [133] Ibid., 2. no. 995.

reconciled nun was Joan de Lelom, a Cistercian of Baysdale Priory in Yorkshire. Thrice apostate, in 1319 she received a penance which was to last seven years, unless mitigated. She was not allowed to wear the black veil. In no way was she to leave the priory nor was she to have access to lay persons or to have correspondence. Taking last place in the convent, she could hold no office and have no voice in the community's decisions. Wednesdays and Fridays were days on which she would be beaten by her superior in chapter and on which she would have a diet of bread, legumes and beer. Further, she was expected to recite the psalter each week.[134] In addition to usual penalties like these, others were imposed. For example, in 1322, Joan de Brotherton, a nun of Moxby Priory in Yorkshire, was ordered to say the full psalter daily during Lent and weekly during the rest of the year for a period of seven years.[135] Also, when Bishop Repingdon of Lincoln reconciled Joan Horncastle, the adulterous apostate canoness of Rothwell Priory, he ordered the prioress to keep her bound in chains.[136]

Lest this chapter end with a poor shackled nun in a damp cell of a Northamptonshire priory, let it be said that penances severely imposed could be mercifully moderated. When we see that, in 1314, the penance imposed on Henry de Belton, monk of Selby Abbey, was relaxed and he was readmitted to full status at Selby, may we not take a benign view and see the *poena medicinalis* achieving its purpose?[137] Let the last apostate in this chapter be Roger de York. This Augustinian canon of Healaugh Priory in Yorkshire was given the usual sorts of punishment just described, and, in addition, steps were to be taken to prevent his flight, even to the point of his being shackled in irons. This severe sentence was imposed on 14 August 1314 but was mitigated on 4 December 1314 by the archbishop of York, moved by the tears and prayers of Roger de York's mother.[138]

Moderation, mercy and charity, shown by Archbishop Greenfield in the final case and prescribed by Pope Benedict XII three decades later, do not meet the historian at every turn on his

---

[134] *Reg. Melton, York* 2. no. 77
[135] Ibid., 2. no. 172. She probably did not persevere in her penance for this period, for she was reconciled again in 1328 (nos. 316–17). See above, p. 140.
[136] *Reg. Repingdon, Lincoln* 3. no. 15. For more on this case see above, p. 138.
[137] *Reg. Greenfield, York* 2. nos. 1061, 1086; see also nos. 701, 808, 938.
[138] Ibid., 2. no. 1085; see also nos. 995, 1071.

way through the sources. Whether, behind terse statements and officialese, there was a process informed by those most Christian of virtues, he is unable to say. Monks and nuns who daily prayed, 'dimitte nobis debita nostra sicut et nos dimittimus debitoribus nostris', one would like to think, should have been moved to receive the wayward sheep back into the fold with gentleness and kindness.

Chapter 6

THE 1530s

No other decade in English history has experienced more intensely the dynamics of change in ecclesiastical affairs than the 1530s, and, indeed, no other decade in English history has seen changes of such a magnitude carried forth with such efficient rapidity against the religious orders. Four and a half centuries and more separate us from that period, allowing us the opportunity of detachment, yet, perhaps most subtly, tempting us to think of the inevitability of it all. We may be tempted to think the religious houses doomed to extinction once Henry VIII declared himself head of the church in 1534. Yet there was nothing incompatible in a national church with religious orders: the Anglican church in modern times is proof of the contrary. Even the decision, in 1536, to dissolve the smaller houses far from promising more of the same explicitly gave the larger houses a sense of security. As we shall see, the king himself as late as December 1537 was involved in founding a religious house. And yet by March 1540 there was not a religious house left in England. One looks in vain for a master plan and an inevitability in all this.

In the blur of events of this decade meanings become obscured. What was apostasy and who were apostates in these troubled years? Are we to consider apostates the Observant Franciscans who took flight in 1534 rather than subscribe to the royal supremacy? Should we include as apostates those friars who, like Robert Barnes, Miles Coverdale and John Bale, abandoned their habits and followed the reforming ways? And what of the under-24-year-olds who, although fully professed, took the opportunity afforded them in 1535–6 and left? Does apostasy apply to nuns, never dispensed by popes, who now took advantage of 'capacities' granted by the king? What, too, of the large number – in the thousands – who assumed lives in the world without the benefit even of a royal dispensation? In a period that saw the fixed institutions of the religious life challenged, changed and, finally, destroyed, clear definitions should not be rigidly insisted upon. This chapter describes how religious left the religious life during these years and how many of them came close to what classical canonists would have called apostasy.

DISPENSATIONS AND THE FACULTY OFFICE

Previous pages of this book have described how *transitus* and *dispensatio* were two principal means available for the legal withdrawal from a religious house, in the first place, and from the religious life, in the latter.[1] *Transitus* was to be used only briefly in mid-decade for religious of the smaller houses who wished to continue as religious. It was *dispensatio* that was the general means used by Cromwell for discontented religious and, later, for religious of suppressed houses to leave their religious houses. Contemporaries frequently called such dispensations 'capacities', and the two terms were synonymous. These dispensations were in substance no different from the hundreds granted by popes since 1395: they permitted the professed religious to receive a benefice for life and, in effect, to live no longer as a religious, subject now neither to the demands of poverty nor to the yoke of obedience. Such 'exclaustrated' religious were part of the landscape of the English (and, indeed, European) church from the early fifteenth century. Cardinal Wolsey, acting by papal power as *legatus a latere*, granted such dispensations to petitioning religious. Although the register of his legateship has not survived, examples of such dispensations are sprinkled in bishops' registers and elsewhere. For example, in 1527, Wolsey granted a dispensation to Geoffrey Watts, an Austin friar of King's Lynn.[2] Also, in the following year Richard Sheperd, the Franciscan prior of Bridgnorth (Shropshire), was similarly dispensed as, in 1529, was the Florentine Nicholas de Burgo, a Franciscan theologian at Oxford.[3] Even after Wolsey's death, English religious continued to seek and receive papal dispensations. As late as 29 October 1533 an Augustinian canon of Mottisfont Priory in Hampshire, William Elmaham, was issued a papal bull of dispensation.[4] Changes in this procedure were to

---

[1] See above, chap. 2.

[2] Jane E. Sayers, *Original Papal Documents in Lambeth Palace Library* (London, 1967), no. 133a.

[3] For Sheperd see *Fac. Off. Reg.*, p. xviii n. For de Burgo see *Reg. Wolsey, Winchester*, pp. 63, 65–6.

[4] *Reg. Gardiner, Winchester*, pp. 28–9.

occur as a consequence of the king's claim to supremacy over the church.

On 7 April 1534 the king ratified 'an act for the exoneration from exaction paid to the see of Rome'.[5] This act, *inter alia*, domesticated the granting of dispensations: those previously granted to the king's subjects by the pope were to be granted now by the king. English subjects were forbidden to seek dispensations from the bishop of Rome. The legislation provided that, in future, dispensations would be granted by the king's authority through the archbishop of Canterbury. Dispensations costing more than £4 had, in addition, to receive the Great Seal from the king's chancellor. The whole range of dispensations was included: dispensations for marrying within the forbidden degrees, for being ordained although illegitimate, for holding a plurality of benefices, for being non-resident in one's benefice and so forth. And among these was the by now commonly granted dispensation for a religious to accept a benefice and, in effect, to live as a secular priest. Archbishop Cranmer set up an office – the Faculty Office – to process requests for dispensations, and the first dispensation given to a religious by the king's authority was granted on 20 May 1534 to the Augustinian canon George Greves, formerly subprior of Holy Trinity Priory, London.[6] This dispensation and the others which followed in the next year or so were unrelated to the dissolution but were the continuation of a long-standing practice, now domesticated, of dispensing religious. Thus, in similar, traditional fashion, before the end of 1534, dispensations for religious to live as secular priests were granted to a Cluniac monk

---

[5] The bill, in the unusual form of a petition, was passed by parliament on 20 March and included a proviso that delayed its taking effect until 24 June. It also had a proviso that the king could abrogate the act by that date, if he so willed (25 Henry VIII, c.21; *Statutes* 3. 464–71, which contains (p. 471) the royal ratification; H. Gee and W. J. Hardy, *Documents Illustrative of English Church History* (London, 1896), pp. 209–32; see Stanford E. Lehmberg, *The Reformation Parliament, 1529–1536* (Cambridge, 1970), pp. 191–2). It was clearly meant to be used, if the king so willed, as a bargaining chip in the marriage negotiations, but by 7 April he knew that the pope had definitively decided against him (see J. J. Scarisbrick, *Henry VIII* (London, 1968), p. 333n.).

[6] The standard work is David Chambers, *Fac. Off. Reg.* For Greve's capacity see p. 1. Holy Trinity Priory, much in debt, surrendered to the king 24 Feb. 1532 (*LP* 5. 823; see E. Jeffries Davis, 'The Beginning of the Dissolution: Christchurch, Aldgate, 1532', *Transactions of the Royal Historical Soc.*, 4th ser., 8 (1925) 127–50, and Knowles's cautionary remarks in *RO* 3. 200n.). Also, in the summer of 1534 the Faculty Office gave permission for a Cistercian nun of Stixwould Abbey in Lincolnshire and for a Dominican friar of Exeter to transfer (*Fac. Off. Reg.*, pp. 2, 10). These were the only such permissions granted by the Faculty Office.

of Lewes Priory (Sussex), an Augustinian canon of St Bartholomew's, Smithfield, London, and a Benedictine monk of St Augustine's, Canterbury.[7] There is no evidence to suggest that the Faculty Office was established in anticipation of the suppression of the religious houses.

The granting of capacities was to become the vehicle of choice for Cromwell in releasing professed religious of suppressed houses from the religious life. Thus, the Faculty Office in a five-year period was to dispense well over 3,500 religious men to live as secular priests and scores of religious women to live in the world without their habits and veils. In neither case, it must be emphasized, were the religious dispensed from living single, celibate lives. From the 1450s, as has been seen, the papal chancery frequently added to the dispensation to hold a benefice usually held by the secular clergy a clause allowing the recipient to wear the dress of a secular priest over the religious habit. As has been argued earlier, this permission about the habit apparently meant, in effect, that the religious need no longer wear his habit.[8] The Faculty Office continued this practice, and, in the thousands of dispensations given to male religious, the office routinely gave the combined dispensation to hold a secular benefice and to dress as a secular priest. The fiction of wearing the dress of a secular priest *over* the religious habit was dropped in 1536, and the dispensation merely said that the religious could dress like a secular priest. For example, on 16 April 1536, George Sneth alias Landsall, probably a Premonstratensian canon of Alnwick, was dispensed 'to leave the religion which he had professed and to go into the world and there live dressed as a secular priest'.[9] The form of the dispensation to religious women allowed them to live in the world without wearing habit and veil. The earliest such reference is to Prioress Alice Cranmer and ten nuns of Minster Thanet in Kent, who were dispensed 'to go into the world and there, from henceforth, to live without the veil and habit of their religious profession'.[10] Whatever the variations in wording, the meaning was unmistakable: the

---

[7] *Fac. Off. Reg.*, pp. 11–12.

[8] See above, pp. 60–1.

[9] 'ut religionem quam professus est exire et ad seculum se conferre ac ibidem in ueste presbiteri secularis uitam agere possit' (London, Lambeth Palace Library, F 1/Vv, fo. 65; *Fac. Off. Reg.*, p. 52).

[10] 'ut ad seculum se conferre ac ibidem de cetero extra uelem et habitum professe religionis uitam agere possit' (fo. 94v; *Fac. Off. Reg.*, p. 72).

individual religious was no longer bound by his or her profession. The office's business in granting capacities to religious gained momentum at the time of the visitation that began in 1535 and was at full throttle from 1538 to 1540, when the large houses were being dissolved.

THE VISITATION OF 1535–6

In a period of seven months from late July 1535 to late February 1536 the so-called 'visitation of the monasteries' was conducted. It was, in fact, not merely a visitation of the monasteries but a visitation of the religious houses of England and Wales, and, given the haste with which it was conducted and the absence of any reference to a considerable number of houses, there must be substantial doubt whether all the religious houses were actually visited.[11] Contrary to the usual practice of suiting the injunctions given at the end of a visitation to the state of the house revealed by the visitation, in 1535 a set of injunctions was drawn up in advance and contained rules for the running of religious houses.[12] Only one of these injunctions has relevance to the question of religious leaving the religious life and then only indirectly: 'No man be suffered to profess or to wear the habit of religion in this house 'ere he be 24 years of age complete.'[13] Straightforward and clear as this injunction was – no man under 24 can make religious profession – it left three questions unresolved, and these were to cause trouble for the visitors, particularly in the first months of their circuits. In the first place, the injunction refers only to men. What about women religious? Could they continue to enter nunneries at the age of 12 or should women be treated *a pari*? These problems were, in time, to be related to the second question, namely, what should the visitors do about those men who were professed while under 24 – as most were – and who were still under 24? Should they be turned out? allowed to leave? or forced to stay? A third general question, not emerging from what the injunctions said but from what they did not say, soon presented itself: what should the visitors do when confronted with over-24-year-olds who wished

---

[11] The *locus classicus* on this visitation remains Knowles, *RO* 3. chap. 22. On the speed and incompleteness of the visitation see pp. 286–7. In addition to the religious houses, the visitors also went to Oxford and Cambridge Universities (see F. Donald Logan, 'The First Royal Visitation of the English Universities, 1536', *EHR* 106 (1991) 861–88).
[12] Wilkins, *Concilia* 3. 789–91.   [13] Ibid., 3. 791.

to leave? Who could dispense them – Cromwell, Vicar General for the visitation, or only the Faculty Office? With copies of the injunctions in their bags and with many difficult questions to be faced, the visitors began their journeys in the summer of 1535. The principal visitors were Richard Layton, John Tregonwell, Thomas Legh and John ApRice (or Price). At times Layton and Tregonwell acted in tandem, as did Legh and ApRice.[14] The key men were clearly Layton and Legh, who from late December 1535 teamed together to visit the North and East Anglia. University-trained and with degrees in law, they were unlike in temperament as well as in their understanding of their authority, and, grappling with the problems left unresolved by the injunctions, they did not produce the same solutions.

The question of under-24-year-old religious was confronted first. By a strange mix-up two visitors arrived at Bruton Abbey in Somerset within three days of each other. The abbot, having seen Layton leave on 20 August 1536, was startled when, on 23 August, Legh arrived, announcing a visitation. Legh was persuaded to leave, a suitable *honorarium* probably easing his departure, but what he reported to the Visitor General, Thomas Cromwell, is highly instructive. Layton, he wrote disapprovingly, did not 'disinvest' those canons under 24.[15] At about the very same time John ApRice 'discharged of his coat' an underage Bonshommes monk of Edington in Wiltshire who wished to leave, and also at nearby St Michael's Kington he discharged one nun under 24 who wished to leave.[16] At this point, then, practice obviously varied: Layton apparently left the under-24-year-old religious untouched, Legh allowed them to leave and ApRice allowed even underage women to leave. A month later Legh and ApRice, now teamed up and at Wintney nunnery in Hampshire, clashed over these issues. Legh, the senior partner, prevailed by having his opinion regarding nuns included in the injunctions which their team sent to Cromwell for his approval. ApRice wrote a dissenting letter, stating that these injunctions were 'without the temperance concerning the young women under 24 which Master Doctor [Legh] would not suffer me to alter in the same as I had in the other touching monks'. The same temperance, he argued, should be shown for nuns since they mature two years earlier than males and since more scandal would

[14] For character sketches see Knowles, *RO* 3. 270–4.
[15] *LP* 9. 167; see also no. 159. [16] Ibid., 9. 160.

be caused by one woman leaving than by twenty men.[17] Thus, it appears that Legh now allowed under 24-year old religious men to leave but balked at extending this 'temperance' to women religious.

Cromwell's reply, now lost, can be reconstructed from the reactions of Legh and ApRice. The issue facing Cromwell was complex. The original injunctions sent to the visitors restricted religious profession to those over 24; it was a provision *ad futurum* and rendered invalid any such attempted professions. It did not invalidate professions already made when the person was under 24: the retroactive invalidation of such professions would probably have affected well over 90 per cent of the religious in England. Yet, among this latter group, there were in 1535 some professed religious who were still under the age of 24. The injunctions did not invalidate their professions, but they were seen to form a special category by the visitors. Cromwell now gave such religious – both men and women – the choice of leaving or remaining.[18] ApRice complained to Cromwell that his colleague, Legh, disregarded the Visitor General's instructions and was not allowing underage nuns to leave. The policy concerning under-24-year-old religious – whatever the practice of individual visitors – was set, then, in the middle of October 1535: those of both sexes could choose to remain or leave.[19] The clarified policy became recognized, and, when the prior of Christ Church, Canterbury, detained six underage monks who wished to leave, complaints were made.[20] Thus, two of the questions raised by the injunctions had been met; one remained.

---

[17] SP1/96/230 (*LP* 9. 423).

[18] ApRice wrote on 16 Oct. 1535, 'You would have all those, both men and women, that were 22 years old and between that and 24 they should choose whether they would tarry or go abroad' (SP1/98/19ᵛ; *LP* 9. 622).

[19] There is the perplexing remark by ApRice to Cromwell during the following week that the latter's will was 'for not expelling of them that are above the age of 20', which he promised to follow 'as far as it may be in me', but 'we have dismissed many above that age already' (SP1/98/56; *LP* 9. 661). This may simply refer to dismissals against the will of the affected monks.

[20] In a letter dated 25 Nov. 1535 (SP1/99/97ᵛ; *LP* 9. 879). There is an undated petition concerning some London Poor Clares: Jane Gowryng, aged 23½, Frances Somer, aged 21, Mary Philbeam, aged 21, Barbara Lark, aged 20, all professed nuns, and Bridget Strange, aged 15 and not professed, all of whom wander outside the house in secular garb. The (unnamed) petitioner asked Cromwell that they be either revested and return or be permitted to be in the cloister until they were 24, when they would profess again, if they wished (SP1/99/233; *LP* 9. 1075). In another undated petition Winchcombe Abbey (Glos.) asked Cromwell for permission to accept novices under the age of 24, who, at that age, would be free to profess or leave (SP1/100/139ᵛ; *LP* 9. 1170).

An issue of larger significance had yet to be faced: what should be done about the religious of both sexes over 24 who wished to leave? Again, policy took some time to be clarified and, again, practice varied. On 21 and 22 October 1535, each of the members of the Legh–ApRice team wrote separately to Cromwell for instructions. They were at Cambridge, fresh from having visited the Poor Clare nuns at Denny Abbey, some of whom wished to leave.[21] Several days later Legh wrote more fully:

Praying also your mastership, as my desire was in my last letter, of farther knowledge of your intent and mind as concerning these religious persons which instantly kneeling on their knees, holding up their hands, desire to be delivered of such religion as they have ignorantly taken on for lack of age, having no discretion, have been, through fair speeches and flattering enticements, yoked, saying also their living after that manner is against their conscience and might better please God and the world abroad. Whom after my opinion were better to be at large and dismissed from their bondage than so unreligiously remain against their conscience, and chiefly in Denny Abbey.[22]

But not only at Denny. Legh had reportedly found ten canons of Merton Priory in Surrey who wanted to leave.[23] Also, at Swaffham Bulbeck nunnery in Cambridgeshire 'the prioress and all would have gone forth if we suffered them'.[24] The only two Gilbertine canons at Fordham Priory (Cambridgeshire) were said to be desperate to leave.[25] Five of the monks of Bury St Edmunds 'would depart if they might and they be of the best sort in the house and of best learning and judgement'.[26] This team of Legh and ApRice wrote on 19 November, that two monks at Horsham St Faith's Priory in Norfolk 'instantly desire to be dismissed of the religion, whom I have stayed until I know further your pleasure'.[27] The visitors were clearly uncertain about what they should do in these cases and were looking for direction late in November, more than halfway through their visitation. Not always in agreement, Legh and ApRice concurred that the discontented nuns should not be discharged by them and that the matter should be left to the nuns to sue in the usual way (i.e., by dispensation). Meanwhile, other

---

[21] *LP* 9. 651, 661.   [22] SP1/98/84 (*LP* 9. 694).
[23] SP1/97/59 (*LP* 9. 472).   [24] SP1/98/110 (*LP* 9. 708).
[25] Wright, pp. 82–3 (*LP* 9. 735). In fact, besides the prior there was only an old and infirm canon. There was also a neighbour, Edward Bestney, coveting the priory's lands (ibid., 9. 761).
[26] Wright, pp. 85–6 (*LP* 9. 772).   [27] SP1/99/69 (*LP* 9. 849).

visitors were trying to cope with the same problem. When Thomas Bedyll took the surrenders of three small Kentish houses (Langdon, Dover and Folkestone), he obviously did not know what to do about the inhabitants and left them in their houses pending instructions from Cromwell. Transfers and capacities he viewed as the options.[28] Layton, ever eager to amuse his master, wrote to Cromwell on 12 December 1535 that three religious – one named Bishop – had fled from Syon Abbey by night but 'they lacked the money to buy secular apparel'. Moreover, many of their brethren were 'right weary of their habit' and would gladly leave. He added, with pretended piety, 'Such religion and feigned sanctity, God, save me from.'[29] By Christmas, Legh lost whatever reluctance he may have had, and we learn this from the still reluctant Bedyll. The latter was visiting Ramsey Abbey in Huntingdonshire in mid-January 1536, where two monks wanted to leave; if Bedyll would not allow this, they threatened simply to walk away. The discontented monks could not understand the visitor's reluctance: after all, Dr Layton at Christmas had allowed half the monks of Sawtry, only five miles away, to leave.[30] Bedyll had heard of Layton's actions only second-hand, and its accuracy defies validation: something no doubt happened at Sawtry, although the numbers could be exaggerated. No dispensations for Sawtry appear before 27 October 1537 in the register kept by the Faculty Office.[31] Legh had probably exceeded his authority, yet at some point a *modus operandi* which bypassed the Faculty Office came into use.

An alternative to dispensation by the Faculty Office was being used during the visitation, probably from December 1535 or January 1536: the Visitor General, acting by royal authority, granted dispensations. None seems to have survived, but the evidence of their existence is clear enough. The perplexed Bedyll, confronted by the two Ramsey monks, said, as if an alternative was

---

[28] Letter dated 16 Nov. 1535 (Wright, pp. 88–9; *LP* 9. 829). In the event, two monks of Dover went to Christ Church, Canterbury (*LP* 10. 13). The records of the Faculty Office, show that, from these three houses, only a monk of Dover received a capacity at this time (*Fac. Off. Reg.*, p. 38).

[29] Wright, pp. 47–9 (*LP* 9. 954).

[30] Letter dated 15 Jan. 1536 (Wright, pp. 98–100; *LP* 10. 103). The two Ramsey monks – William Brampton alias Triamell and Thomas Benson alias Burton – were granted capacities on 13 Feb. 1536 (*Fac. Off. Reg.*, p. 45).

[31] Warin Brampton alias Sawyer was dispensed then and four other monks on 28 Nov. (*Fac. Off. Reg.*, pp. 110, 116).

already in place, that they wished 'to have licence to go from their cloister by the king's gracious authority or else to have licence to repair to my lord of Canterbury to sue their capacities'. The abbot of Hailes in Gloucestershire, writing within a fortnight of Bedyll, told Cromwell that 'one [of his monks] had licence of you to depart and is gone'.[32] This departed monk does not appear in the register of the Faculty Office. When Legh visited St Osyth's in Essex on 27 October 1535, he discovered a canon, Thomas Solmes, who claimed to have entered there owing to threats from his schoolmaster, to have received the habit at the age of only thirteen and to have professed at fourteen. Legh advised him to approach Cromwell, which he did, asking for permission to leave.[33] Moreover, at Norwich Cathedral Priory, the monk Richard Underwood was allowed by royal decree to become a secular priest.[34] In other instances, the visitors dismissed religious from Merton Priory in Surrey, from the Bonshommes house at Edington in Wiltshire, from St Michael Kington also in Wiltshire and from Bury St Edmunds in Suffolk, none of whom was dispensed by the Faculty Office. These few oblique references show that there was an alternative procedure 'by the king's authority' but also suggest that it may not have been frequently used. After 1536 there is not a whisper of it.

The Faculty Office was busy, but not overly busy, in processing dispensations during the period of the visitation. Although the visitation began in late July 1535, the first capacity was not granted until 20 October.[35] Two days later another capacity was issued, then one on 1 November and 5 more on 10 November. A further 12 were granted in November, 11 in December, 9 in January, 21 in February, 14 in March and 23 in April.[36] Thus, a total of 98 dispensations were issued during the visitation. While not all can be related directly to the visitation – e.g., an Austin friar of Richmond

[32] SP1/101/203 (*LP* 10. 192).

[33] *LP* 9. 1157. His letter to Cromwell is undated but clearly is after 27 Oct. 1535, when Legh was at St Osyth's (Knowles, *RO* 3. 477). At this time Solmes was, no doubt, over 24, perhaps only 25, and might have felt that he was a special case.

[34] *Fac. Off. Reg.*, p. 63. Subsequently he received a further dispensation, the fact of the prior dispensation by royal decree being duly noted.

[35] On that day Richard Skydmore, a monk of Gloucester Abbey, was dispensed (ibid., p. 34). For the material on which this discussion is based see ibid., pp. 33–47.

[36] Although the visitation ended in late Feb. 1536, a time-lag of two months between visitation and dispensation was not unusual; thus, the figures here are reckoned through April.

was dispensed a full month before the arrival of the visitors – many, and indeed most, of the entries in the register were no doubt related to the activities of Cromwell's visitors. Rochester Cathedral Priory is a case in point. Richard Layton, in a whirlwind of activity in the southeast, visited the monks of this house in October 1535.[37] There were about twenty in number, that number having accepted the royal authority in 1534.[38] Between 10 November and 9 December, seven of the monks received capacities. Judging from their placements in the 1534 document, they must have been in the middle range of seniority, surely none under 24. What seems certain is that Dr Layton encouraged them to seek release from their vows *per modum capacitatis*. The 4 Cistercian monks of Robertsbridge Abbey in Sussex who were granted capacities on 15 January 1536 may have received similar encouragement, although the details of the visitation of that house are lacking. These 4 would have formed a substantial part of this never large monastery: only the abbot and 9 monks of Robertsbridge were there at the surrender in April 1538.[39] The evidence of these capacities and of the direct dispensing by the king's authority assist us in trying to estimate the number who left at this time, yet there is further evidence.

The *compendium compertorum* is a collection of the official findings of the visitors concerning the observance and morals of the religious.[40] The *comperta* survive only for the diocese of Coventry and Lichfield, for much of the North and also for East Anglia (i.e., the diocese of Norwich). These reports cover about 150 houses, roughly one-sixth of the religious houses of England. While their reliability has been rightly questioned, they nevertheless present valuable evidence concerning the number of religious wishing to leave their orders.[41] Only in 27 of these houses (about 20 per cent) did the visitors claim to find religious wishing to leave, and these total perhaps 90.[42] They range in number, for the northern circuit, from 1 at Repton Priory, Rievaulx Abbey, Worksop Priory,

---

[37] Knowles, *RO* 3. 477.

[38] *Seventh Report of the Deputy Keeper of the Public Records* (London, 1846), App. II, p. 299.

[39] KH, p. 124.

[40] SP1/102/91–114 (*LP* 10. 364), which provides the basis for this discussion. The names of those religious wanting capacities are not calendared.

[41] See the balanced, yet critical account in Knowles, *RO* 3. 294–303.

[42] For a full list see Appendix 4.

Grosmont Priory and Thicket nunnery to as many as 5 at Pontefract, 6 at Fountains Abbey and Rufford Abbey and 8 at Thurgarton Priory. In the eastern circuit only 4 houses were reported with religious petitioning release. At Langley Abbey almost all were said to have sought to leave, at Thetford nunnery all but the prioress and at Aldeby Priory all but 2, while, at West Dereham Abbey, 2 of the canons wanted release for all the canons who wished to marry.[43] None of these East Anglian religious was dispensed by the Faculty Office except 7 canons of West Dereham three years later at the time of its suppression. Of the 63 religious reported in the northern circuit as seeking release, nothing appears in the Faculty Office register at this time. It is always possible that some of the religious who signified a wish to leave and who were not dispensed by the Faculty Office were dispensed 'by the king's authority'. There remains the distinct possibility that the visitors' *comperta* are less than totally reliable, and, in any case, these houses were visited late in the visitation, when the legislation suppressing lesser houses was probably being prepared. These 90 or so religious, if extrapolated, would amount to about 1 per cent of the religious of England.[44]

THE SMALLER HOUSES: THE FATE OF THE RELIGIOUS

The statute (April 1536) suppressing religious houses with annual incomes not exceeding £200 had the potential of affecting about one-quarter of the religious of England. Exceptions from the statute could be made, and, indeed, many were made. The statute provided that the heads of the suppressed houses would receive pensions: they could not transfer. As to the rest,

the convents of every such religious house shall have their capacities, if they will, to live honestly and virtuously abroad and some convenient charity disposed to them towards their living, or else shall be committed

---

[43] Aldeby was, at the best of times, a small community, having, in 1481, only 3 monks (KH, p. 59). The Premonstratensian house at Langley had about 15 canons at this time (ibid., p. 190) and was suppressed in 1535. Thetford had about 10 nuns (ibid., p. 267). The unusual report about possible marriage for canons of West Dereham was made by ApRice, who coveted this house (*VCH, Norf.* 2. 417, where the author calls ApRice's report 'preposterous').

[44] It should be added that, amidst the unusual circumstances of the visitation, the visitors noted cases of traditional apostasy: a canon of Bicester (Oxon.), 2 monks of Chertsey Abbey (Surrey) and a monk of Lenton Priory (Notts.) (*LP* 9. 457; 10. 655).

to such honourable great monasteries of this realm wherein good religion is observed, as shall be limited by his highness, there to live religiously during their lives.[45]

The choice could not have been starker: leave the religious life or transfer. Two observations need be made about the statute. First, it applied only to monks, canons and nuns and not to friars. Second, the rank and file, if they chose to leave, were to receive no pensions, only an unspecified charity.[46]

Although the suppression of all the smaller houses was envisaged by the act, some received exemptions, and we may well ask how many religious houses were, in fact, suppressed by the act of 1536. As has been seen, the friars (about 2,300 living in 183 houses) were not included in the terms of the statute. Of the rest, an estimated 327 houses of monks, canons and nuns had incomes not in excess of £200. Even here, before individual exemptions are factored in, we must subtract 24 Gilbertine houses with about 200 canons, which were positively excluded in instructions given to the commissioners of the suppression.[47] Thus, somewhere in the range of 300 religious houses were touched by this legislation. Perhaps 70 or so of these houses received exemptions (only to fall later with the larger houses). The number of individual religious is more difficult to estimate, but, if we assume, perhaps conservatively, an average of 5 religious per house in the remaining 230 houses, the total would be 1,150.

Commissioners in each county during the spring and summer of 1536 visited all the houses affected by the legislation except the Gilbertines. The commissioners had a common questionnaire, whose questions mostly concerned the *materialia* of each house – bells, lead, livestock, etc. Yet one question concerned the religious inhabitants: 'the number of religious persons, with their lives, conversations, how may are priests and how many will have capacities?'[48] The surviving returns from some 80 houses in various counties provide some basis for judging the desire of religious to leave the religious life. Of the 289 religious men and 265 religious

---

[45] 27 Henry VIII c.8 (*Statutes* 3. 576; conveniently reprinted in H. Gee and W. J Hardy, *Documents Illustrative of English Church History* (London, 1896), pp. 263–4). For a discussion of this statute see Stanford E. Lehmberg, *The Reformation Parliament, 1529–1536* (Cambridge, 1970), pp. 223–9. For the dissolution of the smaller houses see Sybil Jack, 'The Last Days of the Smaller Monasteries in England', *JEH* 21 (1970) 97–124.

[46] Capacities were given gratis to the religious of suppressed houses in 1536 and later.

[47] *LP* 10. 721.   [48] SP5/4, fos. 159–61 (*LP* 10. 721).

women in the houses for which reports survive, 40.5 per cent and 10.5 per cent respectively indicated that they wished to leave and would take capacities.[49] Professor Knowles has rightly urged caution with these figures in view of the 'notable difference of population between the districts and between one religious order and another'.[50] These figures require caution for still another reason. Some of those who signified their intention of remaining religious in the event of suppression, in fact, received capacities. A case in point is the nunnery of Wroxall in Warwickshire, all 5 of whose nuns reportedly indicated to the commissioners their wish to continue as religious, yet, on 1 March 1537, 4 of these nuns took capacities.[51] At the nearby Cistercian abbey of Stoneleigh, the commissioners reported in the summer of 1536 that the 9 professed religious of that abbey, including both the abbot and the former abbot, wished to remain monks whether at Stoneleigh or elsewhere, yet, on the following 1st March, 7 of these monks received capacities.[52] One other example from Warwickshire further illustrates this point: at the Augustinian priory of Studley only 2 of the 8 canons reportedly said they wanted capacities, yet all 8 were granted them.[53] The contradictions in these cases could be explained by a superior inaccurately speaking for all or by religious simply changing their minds and desiring to return to the world in what were far from normal times. One further possibility suggests itself: religious who were transferring could have hedged their bets by having a capacity in hand just in case. This must have been what happened to certain monks of Sawley Abbey (Yorkshire) who transferred to Furness at the time of Sawley's suppression but who, the abbot of Furness said, also had capacities.[54]

The matter is further complicated by the apparent ease with which the religious who were dispossessed returned to their houses in the North during the Pilgrimage of Grace of late 1536. Five

---

[49] Partial reports for Leics., Warwicks., Rutland, Hunts., Lancs. and Sussex are calendared in *LP* 10. 1191 and 11. app. 2. Parts of those for Hants., Wilts., Glos., Surrey, Norf. and Suff. are in F. A. Gasquet, 'Overlooked Testimonies to the Character of the English Monasteries on the Eve of the Suppression', *Dublin Rev.* 114 (1894) 245–77. For Yorks. see G.W.O. Woodward, 'The Exemption from Suppression of Certain Yorkshire Priories', *EHR* 76 (1961) 385–401.

[50] *RO* 3. 310.   [51] *LP* 10. 1191 (p. 498); *Fac. Off. Reg.*, p. 89.

[52] *LP* 10. 1191 (p. 498); *Fac. Off. Reg.*, p. 88.

[53] *LP* 10, 1191 (p. 498); *Fac.Off. Reg.*, p. 89, where they are dated 28 Feb. 1537.

[54] G. W. O. Woodward, *The Dissolution of the Monasteries* (London, 1966), pp. 93–7.

months after their departure the monks returned to Sawley Abbey. Elsewhere in Yorkshire, nuns returned to their priories at Clementhorpe (York) and at Nunburnholme, Augustinian canons returned to North Ferriby and Haltemprice and Premonstratensians returned to Coverham Abbey. In Lancashire other Augustinians went back to Cartmel and Conishead Priories, having received royal permission to return until further directed by parliament.[55] Marmaduke Neville boasted, 'We have set up all the abbeys in our country, and, though it were never so late, they sang matins the same night.'[56] How exaggerated his boast we may never know. Such evidence, however, must make us pause before accepting that immediate dispersal followed upon suppression at this time.

What, then, can be said about departures from the smaller religious houses? No simple proposition can accurately describe the situation in the mid-1530s. Where uncertainty and fear existed, we should not expect to find clarity and consistency of motive and action. The historian has to wend a cautious way through this evidence about the attachment of religious to their vocations and to avoid imposing pedagogical simplicity when the reality was a muddle. Still, it is possible to calculate the number of religious of the smaller houses who were dispensed by the Faculty Office: they were regularly enregistered and, to distinguish their dispensations from others, they were marked 'suppr' (i.e., suppressed).[57] On 24 May 1536, 6 Augustinian canons of Elsing Spital Hospital, London, were thus dispensed, and in the course of the next twelve months the Faculty Office gave a total of 723 dispensations to abandon the religious life to religious from 132 houses.[58] On one day – 20 August 1536 – Archbishop Cranmer's clerks produced 58 capacities, 22 of these to the Cistercians of Garendon Abbey in Leicestershire. Not all the capacities were given to men. During the year from May 1536 to May 1537, 87 nuns from 15 nunneries

[55] See ibid., pp. 93–7. For Cartmel see S. Taylor, *Cartmel, People and Priory* (Kendal, 1955), Appendix D. For the king's permission see *LP* 11. 1279.

[56] *LP* 11. 1319.

[57] For the capacities cited in this discussion see *Fac. Off. Reg.*, pp. 57–98.

[58] These totals do not include the capacities granted to the religious of Whalley Abbey, Barlings Abbey and Hexham Priory after the failure of the Pilgrimage of Grace. Fourteen Whalley monks – their abbot and 2 other monks having been executed – received capacities dated 1 April 1537, as did 3 Augustinian canons of Hexham. Included here are the capacities given to the Cistercians of Sawley Abbey and the Premonstratensians of Easby Abbey, which were given before the uprising.

had dispensations to leave their orders, over half from only 4 nunneries: 18 from Campsey Ash Priory in Suffolk, 11 from the priory of Minster in Sheppey, Kent, and 10 each from Greenfield and Legbourne Priories, both in Lincolnshire. The northernmost of these houses was Wroxall Priory in Warwickshsire and Gokewell Priory in Lincolnshire.[59] Thus, in the swirl of conflicting evidence, we can say that about 8 per cent of all the religious in England were dispensed in the wake of the suppression of the smaller houses.[60]

Another phenomenon followed the suppression of the smaller houses: in the two years or so between the act ordering their suppression and the surrender of the greater houses a considerable number of religious voluntarily sought dispensations. In addition to monks and canons of the larger houses they included friars of every order and Gilbertines, hitherto untouched by the dissolution process. During the period from May 1536 – by which time the dispensations agreed upon during the visitation worked their way through the system – until the end of 1537 – which was near the threshold of the assault on the larger houses and the friaries – a total of 100 dispensations were granted to religious whose houses were undisturbed by the first suppression.[61] Of these, 30 were granted to individual religious in 1536 itself. They belonged to all the major orders, yet, of the hundred, nearly half (49) were friars. On 18 July 1536 alone the Franciscan Thomas Whit and the Austin friars Edmund Smyth and Robert Ranking were all dispensed. How to explain this voluntary exodus of individual religious from their orders? The handwriting-on-the-wall explanation must carry some force here. Hundreds of religious houses were being suppressed or, at the least, being challenged, and religious from these houses were going into the marketplace for benefices at this time. Events were to show that the majority of the religious who later, in 1538–40, went looking for benefices were unsuccessful and helped to swell the ranks of the unbeneficed clergy, the 'day-labourers' of their class. With a healthy cynicism many of these hundred individual religious perhaps took at less than face value the words of praise lavished on larger religious houses in the preface of the act of 1536

---

[59] Among the dispensed nuns of Wroxall was 'Joanna Shakesper'. It should be noted that the father of the poet had two of his daughters baptized with the name Joan.

[60] For further discussion of the numbers dispensed see below, pp. 174–6.

[61] The discussion here is based on *Fac. Off. Reg.*, pp. 53–118.

– 'wherein, thanks be to God, religion is right well kept and observed'[62] – and suspected that suppression of these houses would soon follow. Likewise, the ready availability of dispensations surely served to create a climate in which acquiring a dispensation was no longer a remote and difficult possibility but could now be a present and available reality. In the twenty months from May 1536 more dispensations were granted than had been granted for the whole decade of the 1480s.[63] Discontented religious who, in an earlier time, might have lived with their discontent within the cloister, now found fairly easy egress. The unforced, voluntary departures during these years are clear indications of a period of unmatched uncertainty for English religious.[64]

THE END OF THE END

Historians repeat to themselves that nothing is truly inevitable, a proposition which hindsight frequently tempts us to forget, especially when historical events follow one another and seem to display to us a pre-existing plan, which placed the dominoes in a precise pattern. And such a temptation is perhaps nowhere more evident than in the suppression of the religious orders in England. The dominoes can be seen: first, the valuation of the property of the church, then the visitation of the monasteries and nunneries, followed by the suppression of the smaller houses and the realization of their incomes. The next 'inevitable' step – the final domino – was the suppression of the greater houses. Yet the temptation must be sternly resisted, for, far from being inevitable, the dissolution of the religious orders was not fixed as a policy until very late in the day. The issue here is the *extent* of the dissolution. The voluntary surrender of Furness Abbey in April 1537 gave the precedent, later to be the vehicle, for the dissolution. Rumours that the process was to be extended beyond the smaller monasteries began to be heard later that same year. On 17 December 1537 John Hussee, Lord Lisle's London agent, wrote to his master that Warden Abbey had been suppressed and others were due to follow:

---

[62] 27 Henry VIII (*Statutes* 3. 576).
[63] For their frequency in the fifteenth century see above, p. 62.
[64] See Knowles's remarks about the decline in numbers of certain Norfolk houses between 1535 and 1536 (*RO* 3. 307).

Peterborough, Ramsey, Sawtry and St Albans.[65] Yet there were clear counter-indications even as Hussee was writing. In July 1537 Henry VIII refounded the nunnery at Stixwould in Lincolnshire (which a year earlier had moved thence from Stainfield) as 'nouum monasterium regis Henrici octaui de Stixwold'.[66] At the same time as Henry was re-establishing Stixwould, he was also beginning the process of moving the Benedictine monks of Chertsey Abbey to the buildings of the recently suppressed house of Augustinian canons at Bisham, a process not completed until 18 December 1537.[67] Six months later, on 16 June 1538, Bisham Abbey was to surrender to the crown.[68] Meanwhile, in January 1538, Richard Layton was in Norfolk denying the widespread rumours of a total suppression, a denial probably made in order to stay further alienation of monastic property.[69] Also, in a letter probably of March or April 1538 Thomas Cromwell denied the charge of 'malicious and cankered hearts' that total suppression was his policy and insisted that only surrenders of the willing and the treasonous would be received.[70] Disingenuous Layton and Cromwell no doubt were, for signs of a clear policy of forced surrender appear as early as May 1538.[71] The decision to dissolve the virtually propertyless friars seems to have evolved by the end of July 1538 out of Richard Ingworth's visitation.[72] Thus the final dissolution ran its course; and, when on 23 March 1540 Holy Cross Abbey, Waltham (Essex), signed deeds of surrender, the total suppression, which emerged as policy only early in 1538, was accomplished.[73] The last capacity was issued on 17 June 1540 to the former prior of Trentham Priory (Staffordshire).[74]

---

[65] *LP* 12. 2. 1209. Warden Abbey had surrendered on 4 Dec. (*Eighth Report of the Deputy Keeper* (London, 1847), App.II, p. 47). Hussee wrote in similar vein in the following weeks (*LP* 12. 2. 1210; 13. 1. 24).

[66] Ibid. 12. 2. 411 (27). For these royal foundations see Elizabeth M. Hallam, 'Henry VIII's Monastic Refoundations of 1536–7 and the Course of the Dissolution', *BIHR* 51 (1978) 124–31.

[67] *LP* 12. 2. 1311 (22).

[68] Ibid. 13. 1. 1218. Stixwould surrendered on 29 Sept. 1539 (KH, p. 283).

[69] *LP* 13. 1. 102.

[70] Ibid. 13. 1. 573. Knowles (*RO* 3. 353n.) suggests that this may have been a draft of a letter to be sent to abbots; the acknowledgement of such a letter was made on 1 May by the abbot of Hartland (ibid., 13. 1. 893).

[71] Ibid. 13. 1. 969. For other early signs see Knowles, *RO* 3. 353.

[72] The crucial text is in Wright, pp. 196–7 (*LP* 13.1.1484). The story of the suppression of the friars awaits its historian; for a useful summary see Knowles, *RO* 3. chap. 28.

[73] *Eighth Deputy Keeper's Report*, App. II, p. 47.   [74] *Fac. Off. Reg.*, p. 221.

With the granting of that capacity it might be thought that the door can be closed on the subject of this book, but one large question looms: was the dissolution accompanied by massive apostasy? And the answer must be yes. The simple fact of the matter is that the vast majority of the religious of the dissolved houses left their houses in canonical apostasy. Although estimates vary slightly, there were about 9,000 religious in England in 1534, yet only 3,781 received dispensations from the Faculty Office.[75] The register of that office is a complete register, its entries beginning in 1534 and extending through 1540: there are no missing folios and no evidence of any disturbance. Every dispensation granted by that office was enregistered and the fees, where applicable, duly noted. While it is true that during the visitation of 1535–6 some dispensations were probably granted by Cromwell and his visitors, there is no reason to suspect that this happened to any more than one or two hundred religious. Subtracting these from the total, we are still left with the remarkable fact that less than half the religious of England received canonical dispensations, which allowed them, despite their vows of profession, to return to the world. The situation for women religious is even more marked: of the about 1,500 nuns at this time only 101 – less than 7 per cent – left their nunneries supported by dispensations. Not so dire but still remarkable was the fate of the Benedictine monks: of the about 1,900 on the eve of these events only 591 (or less than one-third) received capacities from the Faculty Office. Professor Russell estimates that the number of friars was about 3,000, yet only 1,056 capacities were granted to friars.

It may be useful at this point to review the canonical position of the religious at this time. What must be stressed is that at no point in these events did the English state abolish the religious orders or forbid men and women to live as religious. The legislation regarding the smaller houses (1536) confiscated property and allowed transfers, while the legislation regarding the larger houses (1539) legitimized the state's confiscation of their assets. In 1534, when the religious took the oath affirming the king's supremacy over the church, they did not reject the religious life nor did the king do more than assert his authority over the religious houses.

---

[75] For population estimates see Josiah Cox Russell, 'The Clerical Population of Medieval England', *Traditio* 2 (1944) 177–212 and KH, pp. 488–94.

They were still religious and so they remained, subject now to royal rather than papal authority. They were as bound to their vows of profession as they had been. Thus, for them to leave the religious life and return to the world without apostasy they needed dispensations, now granted by royal authority through the Faculty Office. The need was clearly seen, and thousands of religious received such dispensations, yet thousands more did not and left their houses in technical apostasy. It may be urged that the traditional canon law no longer applied and the need of a dispensation to avoid apostasy was no longer applicable, but this simply is not so. The reforming statutes of the time left the traditional law in place, pending the promulgation of new laws for the church.[76] Thus, the religious of England were as bound by the law regarding profession and apostasy as were the other religious with whom this study has been concerned. Thus, according to the law still in force in England, lifelong commitments made at the time of profession could be commuted only by dispensation, now recognized by the religious as vested in the royal authority. This royal authority to dispense professed religious was only applied to less than half of the religious forced from their religious houses; the rest, leaving undispensed, became apostates. It is, of course, necessary to distinguish between objective and subjective obligations. Not even the most rigid of canonists would hold these undispensed religious subjectively (i.e., morally) responsible for their objective apostasy. What else could they do? Their communities no longer existed. They had no alternative but to leave, and no personal moral responsibility could be imputed to them. They left their houses in the expectation that, in due course, dispensations would be granted. Their expectations were not fulfilled, and canonical apostasy was the result.

Why were thousands of dispossessed religious allowed simply to apostasize, although the apparatus was in place and working? The answer quite simply is that there was a bureaucratic mix-up. The responsibility lay with the commissioners who negotiated the surrenders to secure pensions from the Office of Augmentations and dispensations from the Faculty Office. Delays between surrender of houses and the granting of capacities became almost routine particularly as the floodgates opened in 1539. For example, the monks of Tynemouth Priory in Northumberland surrendered

---

[76] See F. Donald Logan, 'The Henrician Canons', *BIHR* 47 (1974) 102–3.

on 12 January 1539 and had to wait until 26 March before dispensations were granted.[77] Similarly, the 10 canons of Kyme Priory in Lincolnshire, although having surrendered on 6 July 1539, were not dispensed until 20 October.[78] The most extreme example perhaps is that of Sherborne Abbey in Dorset, whose 17 monks waited well over a year for their dispensations.[79] In the rush of events, overworked commissioners, understandably more concerned with the practical matter of pensions, simply neglected to send the proper documents to the Faculty Office. No great conspiracy here to 'punish' the religious; merely the failure of an overstretched bureaucracy. The result, however, was that the 41 monks of Bury St Edmunds, the 16 monks of Witham Priory, the 25 monks of Westminster Abbey and thousands more were never canonically relieved of the obligations of their profession and were forced into the world in canonical apostasy.

The story of the afterlife of the dispossessed religious goes beyond the terms of this study, yet one point should be made here and that concerns former nuns. It has been said above that religious of the dissolved houses were still bound to remain celibate, and so they were, but one almost overlooked change occurred in this policy in 1539. On 16 May the duke of Norfolk introduced questions on which he hoped a consensus might be reached, and among them 'whether vows of chastity made by men and women ought be observed by divine law'.[80] When the clergy met in convocation during the first week in June, they responded in the affirmative.[81] Yet, when the bill was finally passed by parliament on 16 June, requiring sacerdotal celibacy, it made an important restriction. In fact, what the Act of the Six Articles of Religion held was that vows made to God were binding only on 'such person or persons and none other (saving priests) . . . which at the time of any of their so vowing, being thereto admitted, were or shall be of the age of twenty-one years or above.'[82] The meaning is clear: those religious who became religious before the age of twenty-one and

---

[77] *Fac. Off. Reg.*, pp. 181–2.

[78] Ibid., p. 197.

[79] They surrendered on 18 March 1539 and were dispensed on 20 May 1540 (KH, p. 76; *Fac. Off. Reg.*, p. 217).

[80] 'An vota castitatis per viros aut mulieres facta sint observanda de jure divino?' (*Journals of the House of Lords* 1 (1846) 109). See Stanford E. Lehmberg, *The Later Parliaments of Henry VIII, 1536–1547* (Cambridge, 1977), pp. 65, 68–74.

[81] Wilkins, *Concilia* 3. 845.   [82] 31 Henry VIII, c.6 (*Statutes* 3. 725).

who did not later become priests were free to marry. While this probably applied only to a small number of male religious, it applied to the overwhelming majority of women religious. This act, then, gave scope to women turned out of their nunneries to consider marriage in the world. Castillion, the French ambassador, no doubt aware of these matters, reported that the English king had ordered all the nuns back to their friends and had given them power by his pontifical authority to marry if they pleased.[83]

This book should end with two comments by commissioners concerning the final moments in the life of the English religious houses. Dr John London said that 'in every house, as well of men and as of women, they be in manner all gone that night I have taken their surrender and straightway in new apparel'.[84] In Berkshire, the scene at Bisham Abbey on a summer's day in 1538 is described by the visitor Richard Layton, who, in an attempt to amuse his master, Thomas Cromwell, tells of the last hours in a monastery's life: 'When we were making sale of the old vestments within the chapter house, they [the monks] cried a new mart in the cloister, each man bringing his cowl cast upon his neck to be sold and sold them indeed.'[85] Amused as Cromwell might have been by the report of a jumble sale in Bisham Abbey, the modern reader – even the detached historian – finds it difficult to suppress feelings of melancholy.

83 London, British Library, Add. MS 33514, fo. 14 (*LP* 14. 1. 53). How this statute affected an apostate friar was considered in the royal courts (probably Common Pleas) during the reign of Elizabeth I (J. H. Baker, ed., *Reports from the Lost Notebooks of Sir James Dyer* (2 vols.; Selden Soc., 109–10, 1993–4) 1. 163–4).

84 Wright, p. 215 (*LP* 14. 1. 1321). John London wrote to Cromwell on 27 July 1539, referring to the statute which allowed those nuns who had professed before the age of 21 to marry (Wright, p. 214; *LP* 14.1. 1321).

85 Henry Ellis, *Original Letters* (11 vols.; London, 1824–46), 3rd ser., vol. 3, no. ccclviii (*LP* 13. 1. 1239). A near contemporary, writing decades later of the last day of Roche Abbey (Yorks.), wrote, 'It would have made a heart of flint to have melted and wept to have seen the breaking up of the house and their sorrowful departing and the sudden spoil that fell the same day of their departure from the house' (Ellis, *Original Letters*, no. cclxvii).

Appendix 1

PETITION FOR WRIT
DE APOSTATA CAPIENDO

Petition of Cistercian abbot of Bindon (Dorset) for a writ to be sent to the sheriff of Wiltshire for the arrest of John le Fox, a monk of that house who had apostasized, dated 20 April 1299 (C81/1788/3).

Excellentissimo principi et magnifico domino Edwardo dei prouidencia regi Anglie, domino Hibernie et duci Aquitannie frater Willelmus dictus abbas de Bynedon reuerenciam tanto regi debitam et deuotam.

Quia quidam dictus Iohannes le Fox, diu in ordine nostro professus et sacerdos, spreto ordine et habitu, uagabundus existit in dampnacionem propriam et scandalum plurimorum, magestati uestre humiliter supplico, quantum possum, quatinus, solita clemencia qua semper ordinem nostrum diligitis et fouetis, eum precipiatis per uicecomitem Wyltschyr arestari et fratribus nostris tradi, qui saluti anime sue prouideant secundum ordinis nostri disciplinam.

Dies longos et prosperos, finem felicem et uitam eternam tribuat uobis dominus Ihesus Christus.

Datum apud Bynedon xii kalendas maii anno domini millesimo ducentesimo nonagesimo nono.

Appendix 2

WRIT *DE APOSTATA CAPIENDO*

Writ to sheriffs of London to arrest John de Raylegh (alias John Hugh) apostate Cluniac monk of Prittlewell Priory (Essex), at the petition of the prior and convent of Prittlewell, 10 Feb. 1431 (C81/1787/18).[1]

Henricus dei gracia rex Anglie, heres et regens regni Francie et dominus Hibernie, uicecomitibus Londonie salutem.

Quia frater Iohannes de Raylegh, monachus monasterii beati Marie de Pritewell ordinis Cluniacensis Londonie diocesis in ordine illo professus, spreto habitu ordinis illius, sub habitu seculari de patria in patriam uagatur et discurrit in anime sue periculum ac ordinis predicti scandalum et aliorum perniciosum exemplum manifestum, sicut dilectus nobis in Christo prior loci illius per literas suas patentes nobis significauit, uobis precipimus quod prefatum Iohannem ubicumque in balliua uestra inueniri contigerit sine dilacione arestetis et prefato priori liberetis secundum regulam ordinis illius castigandum.

Teste Iohanne duce Bedeford custode Anglie apud Westmonasterium x die Februarii anno regni nostri nono.

---

[1] The petition was dated 9 Feb. 1431 (C81/1787/17). Raylegh was arrested by 14 Feb. (C81/1787/19).

THE USE OF THE SECULAR ARM
DIRECTLY AND WITHOUT ROYAL WRIT

In addition to the procedure by the royal writ *de apostata capiendo* the secular arm was used in another way to secure the arrest of apostates. This procedure allowed religious superiors to bypass the king's chancery and to approach royal officials directly and require them to arrest and effect the return of apostates. This direct access to royal officials was not available to all religious superiors, and even those to whom access was allowed did not have this access for all time, as is clear from the repetitions seen in this list as well as from the permissions given for an explicit term. Indicated here are the instances, enrolled on the patent rolls, where direct access was granted, the duration (where stated) and the order involved.[1]

2 Oct. 1249	Franciscans	*CPR, 1247–58*, p. 48
20 March 1255	Dominicans	ibid., p. 405
20 March 1255	Carmelites	ibid.
15 Sept. 1263	Carmelites	*CPR, 1258–66*, p. 278
8 Sept. 1265	Carmelites	ibid., pp. 489–90
19 Oct. 1265	Knights Hospitallers	ibid., p. 469
6 Jan. 1267	Carmelites	*CPR, 1266–72*, p. 179
12 Nov. 1269	Gilbertines[2]	ibid., p. 393
18 Jan. 1270	Austin friars	ibid., p. 403
30 Nov. 1274	Austin friars	*CPR, 1272–81*, p. 73
20 June 1275 (for 1 year)	Austin friars	ibid., p. 96
11 May 1276 (until Michaelmas)	Cluniacs	ibid., p. 140.
16 Oct. 1280 (until Christmas)	Cistercians	ibid., p. 399

---

[1] For this procedure see above, pp. 99–100.
[2] It extended only to the canons and lay brothers of the order. This may have been repeated before 1281 (see *CPR, 1272–81*, p. 430).

24 Oct. 1308	Dominicans[3]	*CPR, 1307–13*, p. 141
21 Sept. 1314	Dominicans[4]	*CPR, 1313–17*, p. 177
7 Feb. 1315	Franciscans[5]	ibid., p. 217
7 Feb. 1315	Carmelites[6]	ibid., p. 349
14 July 1315 (for 1 year)	Crutched Friars	ibid., p. 512
2 Feb. 1332	Franciscans[7]	*CPR, 1330–34*, p. 248
3 Oct. 1333	Dominicans	ibid., p. 471
28 March 1334	Austin friars	ibid., p. 541
15 Feb. 1338	Carmelites[8]	*CPR, 1338–40*, p. 67
12 Oct. 1343	Franciscans[9]	*CPR, 1343–45*, p. 126
12 May 1348	Franciscans	*CPR, 1348–50*, p. 151
10 July 1352	Carmelites	*CPR, 1350–54*, p. 333
17 April 1353	Carmelites	ibid., p. 457
20, 28 July 1375	Dominicans	*CPR, 1374–77*, pp. 159, 134
5 Dec. 1382	Gilbertines[10]	*CPR, 1381–85*, p. 211
25 April 1383	Franciscans	ibid., p. 262
2 Dec. 1385	Franciscans[11]	*CPR, 1385–89*, p. 65
15 April 1401	Franciscans[12]	*CPR, 1399–1401*, p. 481
12 Oct. 1399	Carmelites	ibid., p. 43
18 Sept. 1411	Dominicans	*CPR, 1408–13*, p. 321
15 Sept. 1412	Dominicans	ibid., p. 429

[3] On the following 26 Aug. the king ordered his bailiffs and ministers in Ireland to arrest and effect the return of those apostate Dominicans in Ireland intimated to them by the provincial (*Foedera* (London) 2. 86; *CPR, 1307–13*, p. 82).

[4] On 18 Sept. 1314 a royal mandate ordered the mayor and sheriffs of London to arrest all apostate Dominicans found there (*CPR, 1313–17*, p. 176); also, on 1 Oct. 1314 a similar mandate was sent to the sheriff of Oxon. (ibid., p. 186).

[5] The text is in *Monumenta Franciscana* 1. 615. Confirmations were made in 1385 and 1401 (see below).

[6] On the same day a similar mandate was sent separately to the sheriffs of London, York, Suffolk, Cambridge, Huntingdon, Oxford and Berks. (*CPR, 1313–17*, p. 349).

[7] Exemplified in 1343 (see below).

[8] This applied only to the sheriffs of Cambs., Hunts., Herts. and Essex.

[9] See n. 8.

[10] It extended only to the canons and lay brothers of the order.

[11] Confirmation of writ of 7 Feb. 1315.

[12] Confirmation of the confirmation of 2 Dec. 1385.

Appendix 4

THE *COMPENDIUM COMPERTORUM* AND DISAFFECTED RELIGIOUS

This appendix lists those religious houses in the extant *comperta* (compiled by the visitors of 1535-6) in which religious allegedly sought release from their vows and the number of those religious for each house.[1] The order of the *compendium* is followed here.[2]

I. For the diocese of Coventry and Lichfield and for the North of England. Of the 114 houses in the report only 23 were reported to have religious seeking release.

Repton Priory, OSA, Derby.	1
Shelford Priory, OSA, Notts.	3
Thurgarton Priory, OSA, Notts..	8
Rufford Abbey, OCist, Notts.	6
Welbeck Abbey, OPrem, Notts.	3
Worksop Priory, OSA, Notts.	1
Guiseborough Priory, OSA, Yorks. NR	2
Grosmont Priory, OSA, Grandmontine, Yorks. NR	1
Rievaulx Abbey, OCist, Yorks. NR	1
Mount Grace Priory, OCarth, Yorks. NR	2
Byland Abbey, OCist, Yorks. NR	1
Shap Abbey, OPrem, Westmorland	3
Calder Abbey, OCist, Cumberland	2
Conishead Priory, OSA, Lancs.	2[3]
St. Werburgh Abbey, OSB, Chester	3

---

[1] See above, pp. 166–7.
[2] The *Compendium* can be found in *LP* 10. 364. The following abbreviations are used here:
OCarth = Carthusians
OCist = Cistercians
OClun = Cluniacs
OPrem = Premonstratensians
OSA = Augustinian canons
OSB = Benedictines
[3] In addition, William Harington of the dependent leper hospital of St. Leonard, Kendal, Westmorland, was dispensed 20 Jan. 1536 (*Fac. Off. Reg.*, p. 45)

Pontefract Priory, OClun, Yorks. WR	5
Selby Abbey, OSB, Yorks. WR	4
St Leonard's Hospital, York	2
Clementhorpe Priory, OSB nuns, York	2
Thicket Priory, OSB nuns, Yorks. ER	1
Holy Trinity Priory, OSB, York	2
Fountains Abbey, OCist, Yorks. WR	6
St. Agatha's Abbey, Easby, OPrem, Yorks. NR	2

II. East Anglia. Of the 31 houses in the report only 4 were reported to have religious seeking release.
Aldeby Priory, OSB, Norfolk
– all except 2 desire to be released (only 3 monks there in 1481)[4]
Langley Abbey, OPrem, Norfolk
– almost all seek release (about 15 at this time)[5]
Thetford Priory, OSB nuns, Norfolk
– all but prioress seek release (10 nuns in 1532)[6]
West Dereham Abbey, OPrem, Norfolk
– 2 canons seek release 'for all who wish to marry'[7]

---

[4] KH, p. 58.   [5] Ibid., p. 190.
[6] Ibid., p. 267.   [7] See above, p. 167.

REGISTER OF APOSTATES,
1240–1530

This list contains the names of all the allegedly apostate religious who were encountered in the preparation of this study. It is not a biographical register, but it does list biographical facts where these appear relevant. Because of the unique nature of the 1530s in the history of the English religious orders (see chapter 6), it seems reasonable not to include that decade in this register. The alleged nature of the apostasy must be noted, for, in many cases, it appears that the allegation was untrue. The apostates listed here are arranged chronologically by religious order.[1] The house to which each apostate belonged is indicated, where this is known. The reader interested in individual houses will find convenient access through the index of places. The date given is the date when the apostate appears in the records and not necessarily the date of the apostasy itself; where known, the date of apostasy is given. The indication that an apostate was 'signified for arrest' refers to the procedure explained in chapter 4. Mandates to reconcile are frequently mentioned; these were directed to the religious house and were sent by the pope, local bishop or the religious order (see chapter 5). Although the net has been cast very widely, a list of this sort cannot make any claim to completeness. The author would welcome additional names.

A. RELIGIOUS MEN

1. Benedictine monks

1251–1300
Stephen de Wateringbury. Battle Abbey (Sussex). Prior

---

[1] In this register the sequence of religious orders, in general, follows that used in KH.

of dependent Brecon Priory (Brecknock). Signified for arrest, 12 Nov. 1265.[2]

Robert de Cambridge. Infirmarian. St Mary's Abbey (York). Charged with murder, he was refused reconciliation by monastery, 1268.[3]

William de Sutton. Canwell Priory (Staffs.). Killed a man and fled, 1272.[4]

Reginald de Bernevalle. Prior of Newport Pagnell (alien) Priory (Tickford, Bucks.). Signified for arrest, 11 Feb. 1275, excommunicate now for more than two years.[5]

Haymo ———. Prior. Holy Trinity (alien) Priory (York). In dispute over priorship, he was signified for arrest, 11 Feb. 1275, excommunicate then for more than two years.[6]

Henry ———. Formerly abbot. Shrewsbury Abbey (Salop). Resigned abbotship, 1258; reported apostate, 1277.[7]

Thomas de Walley. Abbot. Selby Abbey (Yorks. WR). Probably fled, 1280, after being deposed.[8]

William de Stormesworth. Selby Abbey (Yorks. WR). Apostate now for more than three years, signified for arrest, 16 Aug. 1280; writ issued 30 Oct., but still apostate 29 March 1281.[9]

John de Oswaldkirk. St Mary's Abbey (York). Fled by night, 13 July 1281. In 1273 he had gone to Rome to seek absolution for bloodying a cleric and returned absolved. In 1283, despite the archbishop's intervention, he was not received back into the house; again he set out for Rome but was killed on the way.[10]

John de Schamelefford (Shalford?). Christ Church Priory (Canterbury). King angry that he was received back 'sine manuum injectione seu violentia qualibet', 1285.[11]

---

[2] C81/1786/4. See *CPR, 1258–66*, p. 637, where an unnamed prior of Brecon received royal protection for one year.

[3] *Chron. S. Mary's York*, p. 11.

[4] 'Plea Rolls of the Reign of Henry III', *Collections for a History of Staffs.* 4 (1883) 214. The prior was fined one mark for letting him escape.

[5] C81/1786/26; Prynne, pp. 1205–6; *VCH, Bucks.* 1. 364.

[6] C81/1786/26; Prynne, pp. 1205–6; *VCH Yorks*. 3. 390. In 1274 the pope had decided against Haymo (*CPL* 1. 447–8).

[7] *CPR, 1258–66*, pp. 7–8; Pantin, *Chapters* 1. 83. See *VCH, Salop* 2. 34.

[8] *Reg. Wickwane, York*, nos. 75, 507.

[9] C81/1786/43; *CPR, 1272–81*, p. 400; *Reg. Wickwane, York*, no. 682.

[10] *Chron. S. Mary's York*, pp. 16, 21; *Reg. Wickwane, York*, no. 554.

[11] *Epp. Jo. Peckham* 3. 875–7. He and three other monks may have been arrested by royal officials.

Appendix 5

W[illiam], son of O. de B. of Leicester. Reading Abbey (Berks.). Monk for more than thirty years, left, 1286.[12]

Simon le Chamberlain. Little Malvern Priory (Worcs.). In an inheritance dispute, he was falsely accused by his brother in 1299 of having apostasized in 1290.[13]

William de York. St Mary's Abbey (York). Fled with gold chalice and silver basins, 1299; after being returned, he escaped in 1301.[14]

1301–50

Richard de Hainton. Bardney Abbey (Lincs.). In dispute over abbotship, signified for arrest with next four entries, 29 June 1304.[15]

   John de Lysours.

   William de Barton.

   Simon de Hanworth.[16]

   Richard de Fotheringhay.

Thomas de Eyton. Selby Abbey (Yorks. WR). Having apostasized two or three times, he approached Archbishop Greenfield with papal letters and was absolved, 1307. He later (1308) transferred to the stricter Premonstratensians at Dryburgh Abbey (Berwicks.).[17]

Henry de Belton. Selby Abbey (Yorks. WR). Fled from St Bees Priory (Cumberland), 1307 x 1308.[18]

Thomas de Sherburn. Selby Abbey (Yorks. WR). An officer of the house, who was reported by the abbot to have absconded with a sum of money, 1307.[19] Denounced as excommunicated apostate,13 Dec. 1308. Detailed penance imposed by Archbishop Greenfield, 11 Sept. 1309. Sent to Monk Bretton (Cluniac) Priory,

---

[12] Ibid., 3. 933–4.
[13] *Reg. Winchelsey, Canterbury* 1. 347–8; *Reg. Giffard, Worcester* 2. 496, 499, 503–5; *CPR, 1292–1301*, p. 370. See above, p. 23.
[14] *Chron. S. Mary's York*, pp. 30–1, 32.
[15] C81/1786/3. These five alleged apostates opposed Abbot Wainfleet, who was deposed in 1303 but sought their arrest even after the appointment of his successor (*VCH, Lincs.* 2. 98, 100; *CPR, 1301–07*, p. 210).
[16] He was imprisoned by Wainfleet in a darkened room, where his feet were bound by an iron chain; he was later set free by order of the presidents of the Black Monks (*VCH, Lincs.* 2. 100n.).
[17] *Reg. Greenfield, York* 2. nos. 704, 763, 794.
[18] Ibid., 2. nos. 701, 808, 938, 1061, 1086.
[19] CP40/164, m. 197; A. J. Horwood, ed., *The Year Books of the Reign of King Edward the First* (RS; 5 vols.; London, 1863–79) 5 (33–35 Edw. I) 566–9. Dr. Paul Brand has brought these references to my notice.

8 June 1310, until Michaelmas, but was said (on 25 Nov. 1312) to have been vagabond for two years.[20]

R. de Baners. Christ Church Priory (Canterbury). Went apostate, *c.* 1310.[21]

Unnamed monk of Ramsey Abbey (Hunts.). Left *c.* 1310.[22]

Adam de Dalton, jun. St Mary's (York). Left with money collected for the royal tenth, 1310. He was mentioned again as apostate in 1312.[23]

Peter de Thorney. Deerhurst (alien) Priory (Glos.). In dispute over priorship, signified for arrest, 1310.[24]

John de Guisborough. St Mary's Abbey (York). Fled cell of Rumburgh (Suff.), 1311, and returned in 1313.[25]

Peter de Wakefield. St Mary's (York). Left with £60 stolen from the bursar, 1312.[26]

William de Walton. Peterborough Abbey (Northants.). Fled twice between 1314 and 1319 from Athelney Abbey (Somerset), to which he had been sent for penance.[27]

Henry de Camel. Muchelney Abbey (Somerset). Absolved by bishop, 21 July 1315.[28]

Thomas _____. Selby Abbey (Yorks. WR). Signified for arrest, July 1317.[29]

Robert de Thanet. Christ Church Priory (Canterbury). An apostate who was thought to be appealing at the Roman curia, 1317–18.[30]

Ralph de Rounceville. Prior of Goldcliff (alien) Priory (Monmouths.). In dispute over priorship, writ for arrest, 15 Jan. 1319.[31]

William de Somerton. St Albans (Herts.), prior of Binham (dependent) Priory (Norf.). In disputes with the abbot of St Albans;

---

[20] *Reg. Greenfield, York* 2. nos. 812, 881, 970, 1237.

[21] Searle, *Lists*, p. 169.

[22] *Chronicon abbatiae Rameseiensis* (RS; ed. W. Dunn Macray; London, 1885), p. 398.

[23] *Chron. S. Mary's York*, pp. 47, 53.

[24] C81/1786/38. For the dispute see *CCR, 1307–13*, pp. 255–6; *CPR, 1313–17*, pp. 17, 38, 94, 259.

[25] *Chron. S. Mary's York*, pp. 52, 54.   [26] Ibid., p. 54.

[27] *Reg. Drokensford, Bath and Wells*, pp. 8, 67.

[28] Ibid., p. 94.   [29] C81/1786/44 (fragment).

[30] J. Robert Wright, *The Church and the English Crown, 1305–1334* (Toronto, 1980), p. 325.

[31] *CPR, 1317–21*, p. 268. For dispute see ibid., pp. 544–5; *Reg. Orleton, Hereford*, p. 104.

signified for arrest, 15 July 1319, 8 Aug. 1337, 2 Feb. 1340 (writ issued 6 Feb.).[32]

Nicholas Spayer alias Wymondham. St Albans (Herts.). Signified for arrest, 28 March 1322.[33]

Vincent de Lamput. Gloucester Abbey. After twice apostasizing, absolved; bishop ordered abbot to receive him kindly, 23 Oct. 1322.[34]

Thomas de Sandwich. Christ Church Priory (Canterbury). Fled and readmitted on condition that he return the goods taken with him, 1327.[35]

Peter Dene. St Augustine's Abbey (Canterbury). Fled and recaptured, unsuccessfully claiming simulated profession, 1331.[36]

Thomas de Cobewelle. Tewkesbury Abbey (Glos.). Papal mandate to reconcile, 13 June 1335.[37]

Robert de Guisborough (Gisburg). Whitby Abbey (Yorks. NR). Papal mandate to reconcile, 7 July 1338.[38]

Robert Ingheram. Sandwell Priory (Staffs.). Papal mandate to reconcile, 10 June 1339.[39]

Henry Messager. St Augustine's Abbey (Canterbury). After 14 years as professed monk, he left and was taken in by his brother John Messager of Newington (Kent), who appeared before the archbishop's audience court and was fined 40d, 1340.[40]

Roger de Worfield. Worcester Cathedral Priory. Papal mandates to reconcile, 10 Nov. and 22 Dec. 1340.[41]

Walter de Kelshall (Kelleshull). St Albans Abbey (Herts.). Involved in the Somerton affair; writ for his arrest and arrest of next three entries, 6 Feb. 1340.[42]

   Thomas de Flamstead.

   John Munden.

   Thomas Barn.

---

[32] C81/1786/32, 34, 35; *CPR, 1338–40*, p. 485. For this case see above, pp. 77, 145.

[33] C81/1786/33. He was a supporter of William Somerton (previous entry).

[34] *Reg. Cobham, Worcester*, pp. 133–4.

[35] *Lit. Cant.* 1. 230, 232–5, 242–3.

[36] For full discussion see above, pp. 34–41.   [37] *CPL* 2. 529.

[38] Ibid., 2. 544. Possibly the same as the monk of the same name at Whitby who was found delinquent by the visitor in 1366 (see below).

[39] *CPL* 2. 545.

[40] Canterbury Cathedral Archives, Ch. Ant. A36. IV, fo. 11. Professor Richard Helmolz kindly drew this reference to my attention.

[41] *CPL* 2. 547, 549.

[42] *CPR, 1338–40*, p. 485. For the Somerton affair see above, n. 32.

William de Doncaster. Upholland Priory (Lancs.). Signified for arrest, 23 July 1340.[43]

Arnold Lym. Hyde Abbey (Winchester). In dispute over whether he was Dominican or Benedictine, signified for arrest, 6 Jan. 1341.[44]

Stephen Gomage. St Albans Abbey (Herts.). Writ for arrest, 18 Feb. 1342. He is also listed among those who left during the abbotship of Thomas de la Mare, 1349–96.[45]

Robert de Chimney. Sometime cellarer. Eynsham Abbey (Oxon.). Supporter of Nicholas de Upton in dispute over abbotship; writ for arrest, 4 July 1344.[46]

William de Cirencester. Sometime prior. As preceding.

Thomas le Botiler. Eynsham Abbey (Oxon.). Supporter of William de Stamford in dispute over abbotship; signified for arrest with next ten entries, 6 Oct. 1344.[47]

Nicholas de Stanlake.

John de Oxon.

Nicholas de Chelsea.

John de Nony.

Geoffrey de Lambourne.

Henry de Idbury.

John de Cost alias Saunton.

Giles de Tewkesbury.

John de Huntingdon.

Walter de Elmley.[48]

Richard Randulf. Buckfast Abbey (Devon). Papal mandate to reconcile, 1 Oct. 1344.[49]

Robert de Bloxham. Abingdon Abbey (Berks.). Papal mandate to reconcile, 2 Jan. 1345.[50]

William de Stamford. Sometime abbot. Eynsham Abbey (Oxon.). In dispute over abbotship, signified for arrest with next three entries, 18 Oct. 1345 (*erronee* for 1344?).[51]

---

[43] C81/1786/20.

[44] Ibid., 21. He had previously been apostate as a Dominican (see below, p. 241) and was reconciled. For a discussion of this case see above, pp. 48–9.

[45] *CPR, 1340–43*, p. 444; *Gesta abbatum* 2. 415.

[46] *CPR, 1343–45*, p. 387. For this dispute see above, pp. 118–19.   [47] C81/1786/14.

[48] He also was named on the signification of 18 Oct. 1345 (or 1344); see next entry but two.

[49] He may have been *eiectus* rather than *apostata* (*CPL* 3. 175).   [50] *CPL* 3. 176.

[51] C81/1786/15, which also includes Walter de Elmley, already listed. The petition is from unnamed abbot of Eynsham and is dated Tues., feast of St Lucy (= 1345), but what is known about this controversy would suggest that it was sent in 1344, 12 days after the previous petition (above, n. 48).

John Clia (?).

Hugh de Wittenham.

Robert de Worcester.

Walter Woodward. Lay brother. Elstow (nunnery) Abbey (Beds.). Papal mandate to reconcile, 17 March 1349.[52]

James de Thornham. Ramsey Abbey (Hunts.). Papal mandate to reconcile, 25 Jan. 1350.[53]

Thomas de Hurley. Reading Abbey (Berks.). Papal mandate to reconcile for Jubilee pilgrimage to Rome, 27 April 1350.[54]

Simon de Lega. Winchcombe Abbey (Glos.). Papal mandate to reconcile, 12 June 1350.[55]

Walter de Winforton. Worcester Cathedral Priory. Papal mandate to reconcile for Jubilee pilgrimage to Rome, 27 July 1350. He had been conducting monastic business at Avignon and without permission went on to Rome.[56]

Robert de Rendham. Colchester Abbey (Essex). Papal mandate to reconcile, 10 Aug. 1350.[57]

Richard de Fishwick. Sele (alien) Priory (Sussex). Papal mandate to reconcile for Jubilee pilgrimage to Rome, 23 Dec. 1350.[58]

William de Byfield. Peterborough Abbey (Northants.). Papal mandate to reconcile him and two other Peterborough monks (next entries) for Jubilee pilgrimage to Rome, 23 Dec. 1350.[59]

John de Trentham.

Simon de Jarewell.

1351–1400

Benedict de Chertsey. Prior. Westminster Abbey. Papal mandate to reconcile for Jubilee pilgrimage to Rome, 18 March 1351.[60]

Peter de Hereford. Crowland Abbey (Lincs.). Went on Jubilee pilgrimage to Rome with permission but overstayed his leave. Papal mandates to reconcile, 25 May and 20 June 1351.[61]

---

[52] *CPL* 3. 276.   [53] Ibid., 3. 353.   [54] Ibid., 3. 338.

[55] Ibid., 3. 392. He was signified for arrest in an undated signification by Abbot William [de Sherborne, 1349–52] (C81/1786/54). For troubles at Winchcombe see *VCH, Glos.* 2. 69–70. See below, n. 66.

[56] *CPL* 3. 388.

[57] Ibid., 3. 392.   [58] Ibid., 3. 382.

[59] Ibid. The three monks of Peterborough mentioned here had left their monastery in Oct. 1350.

[60] Ibid., 3. 384, 397. His apostasy may have been attributed to his having worn lay clothes while travelling.

[61] Ibid., 3. 429, 461.

Roger de Winsley. Evesham Abbey (Worcs.). Writs for arrest, 28 June 1351.[62]

Ralph de Chaddesden. St Werburgh's Abbey (Chester). A ringleader of opposition to abbot; signified for arrest, 15 Oct. 1351.[63]

Simon de Mildecombe. Coventry Cathedral Priory (Warwicks.). Writ for arrest, 2 Aug. 1352.[64]

Richard de Tileneyer (Tilney?). Norwich Cathedral Priory. Papal mandate to reconcile, 29 Jan. 1353, apostate now for two years.[65]

Thomas de Malmeshull. Winchcombe Abbey (Glos.). Papal mandate to reconcile, 30 June 1353.[66]

Andrew de Tiderinton. Malmesbury Abbey (Wilts.). Papal mandate to reconcile, 14 July 1353.[67]

Thomas de Pik. Westminster Abbey. Papal mandate to reconcile, 4 Sept. 1353.[68]

Henry de Aston. Coventry Cathedral Priory (Warwicks.). Significations for arrest, 1 May and 7 June 1355, and writ enrolled for 13 June.[69]

John de Lose. Battle Abbey (Sussex). Writ for arrest, 18 Aug. 1355.[70]

William Hord. Shrewsbury Abbey (Salop). Charged with homicide, physical mutilation, incontinence and other crimes, he fled but returned with an armed band intent on murdering the abbot and others; signified for arrest, 20 June 1356. Arrested by 15 July 1357.[71]

Richard Wyke. Christ Church Priory (Canterbury). Went apostate after 1356.[72]

John de Hemingbrough. Selby Abbey (Yorks. WR). Signified for arrest, 20 May 1359; writ issued 28 May.[73]

Richard de Tuddenham. Sandwell Priory (Staffs.). Signified for arrest with next entry, 20 Dec. 1360.[74]

    William de Dunstaple.

---

[62] *CPR, 1350–54*, p. 155.

[63] C81/1786/8. For the trouble at St Werburgh at this time see *VCH, Cheshire* 3. 139.

[64] *CPR, 1350–54*, p. 339. [65] *CPL* 3. 488.

[66] Ibid., 3. 515. Signified for arrest with Simon de Lega in undated petition (see above, n. 55).

[67] Ibid. [68] Ibid.

[69] C81/1786/11, 12; *CPR, 1354–58*, p. 289. [70] *CPR, 1354–58*, pp. 296–7.

[71] C81/1786/47; see also *CPR, 1354–58*, p. 449, and *CCR, 1354–60*, p. 415.

[72] Searle, *Lists*, p. 181. [73] C81/1786/45; *CPR, 1358–61*, p. 224.

[74] C81/1786/42. Possibly the same Richard de Tuddenham who in 1355, as an Augustinian canon, had been ordered to be reconciled (below, p. 222).

Thomas de Benstede. Bradwell Priory (Bucks.). Writ for arrest, 28 Oct. 1363.[75]

Robert de Guisborough (Gisburn). Whitby Abbey (Yorks. NR). At visitation found to have twice apostasized, to have fathered a child by woman of abbot's chamber and to have remained uncorrected by abbot, 26 June, 1366. Sent to St Mary's, York, for punishment, 12 Oct. 1366.[76]

William Ormesby. Whitby Abbey (Yorks. NR). Purged himself of apostasy, 1366.[77]

Thomas de Hauksgard. Whitby Abbey (Yorks. NR). Rebellious leader of opposition to abbot, 1366; signified for arrest, 1371. He was later (1378) prior of Middlesbrough.[78]

Ralph de Pelham. Earls Colne Priory (Essex). Papal mandate to reconcile, 31 March 1368.[79]

Richard de Seynesbury. Sometime abbot. St Werburgh's Abbey (Chester). Resigned in 1362, refused obedience to successor and left without permission in 1368. Papal mandate to compel his return, 10 May 1368.[80]

Roger de Hethton. Shrewsbury Abbey (Salop). Signified for arrest, with next four entries (as indicated), 11 April 1371 and 24 April 1372; writ of 20 Nov. 1371 enrolled.[81]

   Thomas de Ronton.

   Walter de Sordron. Signified on 11 April 1371.

   Richard de Westbury. Signified on 24 April 1372.

   John Perle (?). Signified on 24 April 1372.

Thomas de Wyke. Worcester Cathedral Priory. Went apostate, 1374.[82]

Richard de Natingdon. Faversham Abbey (Kent). Signified for arrest, 3 May 1375, apostate now for several years.[83]

Thomas Coffyn. Glastonbury Abbey (Somerset). Signified for arrest, 11 June 1380; writ for arrest, 19 Sept. 1381. He had gone to the Roman curia to oppose the appointment of the abbot; he was later prior in 1408 and 1423.[84]

[75] *CPR, 1361–64*, p. 449.
[76] Pantin, *Chapters* 3. 283–4, 292, 298. Possibly the same Robert de Guisborough who was ordered reconciled in 1338 (see above).
[77] Ibid., 3. 296, 299.
[78] Ibid., 3. 248, 279–309, *passim*. See above, p. 80.
[79] *CPL* 4. 69.   [80] Ibid., 4. 70.
[81] C81/1786/48, 49; *CPR, 1370–74*, p. 180.
[82] *Sede vacante Reg., Worcester*, p. 321; see also pp. 317, 290.   [83] C81/1786/16.
[84] C84/32/23 (where it is misfiled); *CPR, 1381–85*, p. 79; *BRUO* 1. 455.

Thomas Abingdon. Reading Abbey (Berks.). Signified for arrest, 2 March 1390; writ issued 4 March.[85]

Adam Marlborough. Chertsey Abbey (Surrey). Mandate from English chapter to abbot to secure his return, probably 1393.[86]

William Dynowe. Tavistock Abbey (Devon). Signified for arrest with next entry, 21 Sept. 1394.[87]

    Richard Haleway.

Reginald de Wearmouth. Durham Cathedral Priory. Apostate now for over a year, papal mandate to reconcile, 30 Oct. 1396.[88]

Alexander Ledsham. Sandwell Priory (Staffs.). Called an apostate, he allegedly removed prior with an armed mob, 1397.[89]

William Bekett. Battle Abbey (Sussex). Signified for arrest with next entry, 11 Jan. 1398; writ issued, 16 Feb.[90]

    William Mersshe.

Henry Kebbel alias Colne. Prior. Earls Colne Priory (Essex). In dispute over priorship, signified for arrest with next five entries, 30 April 1399. He and Sudbury (next entry) were ordered set free (8 May) in mainprise to appear in chancery on 1 July.[91]

    John Sudbury.

    John Serle.

    Martin de Colne.

    John Colne.

    John Okelee.

Thomas de Yardley (Erdeley, Yerdeley). St Werburgh Abbey (Chester). Together with next entry was said to have apostasized, *c.* 1400, and to have abducted and robbed a female pilgrim on her way home from Walsingham, for which they were arrested. Pardoned 'for treasons, felonies, misprisions, rapes, rebellions, depredations, robberies, contempts, offences, lying in ambush, murder, common larceny and other trespasses', 5 April 1412. Soon became abbot (1413–34).[92]

    Richard de Skipton.

85 C81/1786/29; *CPR, 1388–92*, p. 266.   86 Pantin, *Chapters* 2. 92.

87 C81/1786/52. He and Haleway (next entry), being called rebels, had been ordered before the king and council (29 Feb. 1392) and were pardoned (19 Oct. 1394) for failure to appear *(CPR, 1391–96*, pp. 84, 492).

88 *CPL* 4. 534.   89 *VCH, Staffs.* 3. 218.

90 C81/1786/5; *CPR, 1396–98*, p. 362.

91 C81/1786/10; *CCR, 1396–99*, pp. 470–1. For the dispute see above, p. 119.

92 R. V. H. Burne, *The Monks of Chester* (London, 1962), p. 120; *CPR, 1408–13*, pp. 388–9. For the troubled state of the abbey at this time see *VCH, Cheshire* 2. 142.

Richard de Thornton. St Mary's Abbey (York). Papal mandate to reconcile, 28 Jan. 1400.[93]

John Lynch alias Kidderminster. Shrewsbury Abbey (Salop). Left and took a benefice; papal mandate now to reconcile and dispensation to hold benefice, 21 Dec. 1400.[94]

1401–50

William George. St Neots Priory (Hunts.). Signified for arrest, 27 Oct. 1401; writ issued 30 Oct.[95]

Thomas Hackness. Whitby Abbey (Yorks. NR). Allegedly climbed out the window of the dormer at night, stole money from the monastery and committed other offences. Writ for arrest (not surviving) was superseded 20 Oct. 1400; signified for arrest again, 1 Jan. 1404, and writ issued 28 Jan.[96]

Adam Durham alias Ponne. Durham Priory. Left by April 1407; absent at election of prior, 5 Nov. 1416.[97]

John Tynemouth. Durham Priory. Professed in early 1390s; stole monastic goods and left for a while in 1408, but returned. Licensed to go to Roman curia, Jan. 1416. Murdered a fellow monk in 1420 and died within 6 months.[98]

Richard Middleton. Norwich Cathedral Priory. Dispensed to live as secular priest, became rector of Marsham (Norf.), but declared apostate by 'enemies'. Pope declared him not apostate, 9 May 1413.[99]

John Fishwick. Durham Priory. Apostate at time of election of prior, 5 Nov. 1416.[100]

Henry Methwold. Bury St Edmunds Abbey (Suff.). Signified for arrest, 20 June 1416.[101]

John Marlay. Durham Priory. Order to seize him at Hexhamshire (Northumberland), 1422. Apparently still apostate, 1442.[102]

Thomas Pomfret. Durham Priory. Scholar, Durham College, Oxford; admitted 1420–1. Failed to return to priory, 1425. Apparently still apostate, 1442.[103]

---

[93] *CPL* 5. 331.   [94] Ibid., p. 358.

[95] C81/1786/41; *CPR, 1401–05*, p. 64.

[96] York, Borthwick Institute, CP/E164; *CCR, 1399–1402*, p. 281; C81/1786/53; *CPR, 1401–05*, p. 363.

[97] R.B. Dobson, *Durham Priory, 1400–1450* (Cambridge, 1973), pp. 74–5.

[98] Ibid., p. 74.   [99] *CPL* 6. 380.

[100] Dobson, *Durham Priory*, pp. 74–5.

[101] C81/1786/39.

[102] Dobson, *Durham Priory*, pp. 75–6.   [103] Ibid.; *BRUO* 3. 1497.

Ralph Dadyngstone. Eynsham Abbey (Oxon.). Episcopal mandate that he should not be received back again without special letters, 1432.[104]

Thomas Fynden. Christ Church Priory (Canterbury). Originally a monk of Westminster; transferred to Canterbury in 1431 and left in 1438.[105]

Robert Bylling. St Neots Priory (Hunts.). Reported to visitor as apostate and probably at Winchelsea (Sussex), 1439.[106]

William Shawe. St Albans Abbey (Herts.). Went apostate 1441 x 1451.[107]

John Hawton. Bardney Abbey (Lincs.). Reported to visitor as apostate, 1444.[108]

John Bengeworthy. Eynsham Abbey (Oxon.). Escaped from monastic prison and fled with nun of Godstow. Reported to visitor that he was brought back and was now doing penance, 1445.[109]

Robert Vise (Veyse). Bath Priory (Somerset). Signified for arrest as an excommunicate, 26 July 1445. Arrested by 20 June 1445. Episcopal mandate to reconcile, 24 June 1445. Returned to former ways by 27 Dec. 1445.[110]

Richard Ashton. Abbot. Peterborough Abbey (Northants.). Purged himself at visitation, 1446.[111]

John Appleby. Bath Priory (Somerset). Absent at abbatial election by reason of longstanding apostasy, 5 July 1447.[112]

Robert Morpath alias Wachank. St Albans Abbey (Herts.). Signified for arrest with next entry, 20 Oct. 1448.[113]

   Henry Halstead.

William Strete. Glastonbury Abbey (Somerset). Signified for arrest, 1 Nov. probably 1448 or 1449.[114]

Robert Cosnet alias Cornwall. Spalding Priory (Lincs.).

---

[104] *Linc. Vis.* 1. 56.   [105] Searle, *Lists*, p. 187.

[106] *Linc. Vis.* 2. 322.

[107] H. T. Riley, ed., *Registra quorundam abbatum monasterii S. Albani* (RS; 2 vols.; 1872–3) 1. 147.

[108] *Linc. Vis.* 2. 32.   [109] Ibid., p. 91.

[110] C85/41/9; *Reg. Beckington, Bath and Wells* 1. nos. 115, 123, 184; 2. no. 1639.

[111] He seems to have done nothing other than to have gone out of the monastery wearing secular garb ('super crimine apostasie'); *Linc. Vis.* 2. 290, 297–9.

[112] *Reg. Beckington, Bath and Wells* 2. 1639.

[113] C81/1786/36. For circumstances see *VCH, Herts.* 4. 403.

[114] C81/1786/17. He had obtained papal bull to transfer to another order, for which he received a royal pardon on 24 Feb. 1449 (*CPR, 1446–52*, p. 218). On 7 Aug. 1450 he was papally dispensed to live as a secular priest (*CPL* 10. 170).

Allegedly abandoned religious habit, wore secular clothes, served as a parish chaplain, murdered a fellow monk at Snargate (Kent) and preached heterodox views on pilgrimages, 1446 x 1449.[115]

1451–1500

Richard Holiman. St Augustine's Abbey (Canterbury). Returned as repentant apostate *c*. 1436 and received papal mandate for full reconciliation, 30 April 1451.[116]

John Linby. Coventry Cathedral Priory (Warwicks.). Signified for arrest, 6 Nov. 1455.[117]

John Braye. Athelney Abbey (Somerset). Absent from abbatial election by reason of apostasy, 1458.[118]

Thomas Henton. Athelney Abbey (Somerset). Absent from abbatial election by reason of apostasy, 1458.[119]

William Suckley. Great Malvern Priory (Worcs.). Signified for arrest, 31 Jan. 1458, 20 Oct. 1463, 1 April 1466, 2 April 1472.[120]

Thomas Lodam. Muchelney Abbey (Somerset). Absent from abbatial election by reason of apostasy as were three next entries, 1463.[121]

   William Mountagu, jun.

   John Elvord.

   John Mason.

William Digswell. St Albans Abbey (Herts.). Signified for arrest, 7 Jan. 1464.[122]

Thomas Twyning. Winchcombe Abbey (Glos.). Apostasized after 18 years as monk, remained apostate for four months; papal mandate to reconcile, 19 Sept. 1466.[123]

William Wallewen. Worcester Cathedral Priory. Signified for arrest with next two entries, 12 Oct. 1467. Later (1469) abbot of Eynsham.[124]

   Richard Ludlow.

   John Smaw (or Small) alias Hereford. He later (1469) was papally dispensed to live as a secular priest.[125]

---

[115] Bishop Alnwick's court book in A. Hamilton Thompson, *The English Clergy* (Oxford, 1947), p. 245.

[116] *CPL* 10. 89–90.   [117] C81/1786/13.

[118] *Reg. Beckington, Bath and Wells* 2. 1648.

[119] Ibid.   [120] C81/1780/22–5.   [121] *Reg. Beckington, Bath and Wells* 2. 1650.

[122] C81/1786/37.   [123] *CPL* 12, 510–11.

[124] C81/1786/55; see also Pantin, *Chapters* 3. 113–15. For his career see *BRUO* 3. 1977.

[125] *CPL* 12. 675.

Robert Cope alias Barogh. Peterborough Abbey (Northants.). Signified for arrest, 5 Jan. 1476.[126]

John Yelverton. Norwich Cathedral Priory. Left without abandoning religious habit. Papal mandate to reconcile and dispensation to live as secular priest, 10 Jan. 1480.[127]

Nicholas Boston. Sometime almoner, cellarer and archdeacon. St Albans Abbey (Herts.). Prior of Tynemouth (dependent) Priory (Northumberland), but deprived and resigned. Abbot's request to bishop of Durham for arrest, 16 Sept. 1480. Reinstated as prior, 8 March 1483.[128]

Thomas Barkeley. Hyde Abbey (Winchester). Reported apostate for two years at time of archiepiscopal visitation, 3 Nov. 1492.[129]

Thomas Clerk alias Grantham. Formerly monk of Abingdon Abbey; transferred to Snelshall Priory (Bucks.), which he left. Papal mandate to reconcile and dispensation to live as a secular priest, 24 Dec. 1493.[130]

Gilbert Peston alias Conell. Westminster Abbey. Claiming his profession was irregular, he left but was convinced to return. Left again, *c.* 1495, and was collated to church of Sleaford (Lincs.). Papal bull, seeking to regularize his status, required him to resign and thus be eligible then to keep Sleaford, 12 May 1500.[131]

William Nicoll. Rochester Cathedral Priory (Kent). Reported apostate at time of archiepiscopal visitation, 21 Nov. 1496.[132]

William Sevynton. Athelney Abbey (Somerset). Episcopal order for abbot to subject him to the rule, 29 July 1498.[133]

1501–30

Robert Drysfeld. Bardney Abbey (Lincs.). Incurred apostasy by wearing his habit under garb of secular priest without dispensation; now absolved and dispensed, 13 Aug. 1507.[134]

William Saltwood. Dover Priory (Kent). Reported apostate at time of archiepiscopal visitation, as was next entry, 1511.[135]

Thomas Elham.

[126] C81/1786/28.   [127] *CPL* 13. 2. 714.
[128] Riley, ed., *Registra quorundam abbatum* 2. 214–15, 234, 254.
[129] *Reg. Morton, Canterbury* 2. 129.
[130] *CPL* 16. 245.   [131] Ibid. 17. 1. 363.
[132] *Reg. Morton, Canterbury* 2. 446.
[133] *Reg. King, Bath and Wells*, no. 113.   [134] *CPL* 18. 802.
[135] Mary Bateson, 'Archbishop Warham's Visitation of Monasteries, 1511', *EHR* 6 (1891) 24n.; C. R. Haines, *Dover Priory* (Cambridge, 1930), pp. 380, 484.

Robert Bowring. Athelney Abbey (Somerset). Signified for arrest with next entry, 27 Jan. 1512.[136]

   Philip Fylle.

Walter Harburgh. Eynsham Abbey (Oxon.). Reported apostate at visitation, 1517.[137]

David _____. Shrewsbury Abbey (Salop). Abbot reported to visitor that he had tried to effect his return but did not know where he was, 1518.[138]

John Selwood. Eynsham Abbey (Oxon.). Reported apostate and whereabouts unknown at visitation, 30 April 1520.[139]

George Adderbury. Eynsham Abbey (Oxon.). Absolved of apostasy at visitation, 30 April 1520.[140]

Christopher Townsley. Burton-upon-Trent Abbey (Staffs.). Reported apostate at visitation, as was next entry, 1524.[141]

   Thomas Pyrey.

Thomas Gloucester. Malmesbury Abbey (Wilts.). Reported at visitation as having gone in apostasy twice to Gloucester and once to Dursley, 1527.[142]

John London. Malmesbury Abbey (Wilts.). Reported at visitation as having apostasized three times in two years, 1527.[143]

Richard Ashton. Malmesbury Abbey (Wilts.). Reported at visitation as having apostasized three times, 1527.[144]

Walter Bristow. Malmesbury Abbey (Wilts.). Reported at visitation as having apostasized three or four times, 1527.[145]

Thomas Purton. Malmesbury Abbey (Wilts.). Reported with next two entries as thieves and apostates at visitation, 1527.[146]

   Robert Elmore.

   Richard Glastonbury.

Robert _____. Totnes Priory (Devon). Signified for arrest as excommunicate, 8 Nov. 1529.[147]

---

[136] C81/1786/2.   [137] *Vis. Dioc. Linc.* 2. 139–40.

[138] *Blythe's Vis.*, p. 33.   [139] *Vis. Dioc. Linc.* 2. 141–2.

[140] Ibid., 2. 144.   [141] *Blythe's Vis.*, p. 190.

[142] Pantin, *Chapters* 3. 126. Some of these monks of Malmesbury who were accused of apostasy may merely have left for brief, unauthorized visits to neighbouring villages and towns, wearing secular clothes.

[143] Ibid., 3. 126–7.   [144] Ibid., 3. 127.

[145] Ibid.   [146] Ibid.

[147] C85/82/12.

UNDATED

Elyas de Combor. Sele Priory (Sussex). Signified for arrest, temp. Edward I or II.[148]

John de Littleport. St Albans Abbey (Herts.). Left in apostasy, 1349 x 1396, as did the next six entries.[149]

> **Richard de Langley.**
> **John Smyerton.**
> **Richard Temple.**
> **John Chalgrave.**
> **Robert Forneset.**
> **John Angurtone.**

Nicholas Bom. Ware (alien) Priory (Herts.). Signified for arrest, before 1414.[150]

James Cranbrook. Christ Church Priory (Canterbury). Listed as apostate, as were next 3 entries, 1415 x 1449.[151]

> **William Faversham.**
> **John Batayle.**
> **Roger Woodchurch.** Known to have left after 1418 and to have died overseas.[152]

John Wykham. Christ Church (Canterbury). He was professed in 1495 and died in apostasy.[153]

2. Benedictine monks of order of Fontevrault

Robert Warminster alias Bodenham. Amesbury Priory. Signified for arrest, 22 Nov. 1381, and writ issued 26 Nov.; another writ for arrest, 28 Jan. 1383.[154]

3. Cluniac monks

1251–1300

William de Richale. Sometime prior. Monk Bretton Priory (Yorks. WR). Cluniac order had requested writ for his arrest, but

---

[148] C81/1786/46 (fragment).
[149] Many monks are said to have left during the abbotship of Thomas de la Mare (1349–96), but only eight are named, since they never returned (*Gesta abbatum* 2. 415). In addition to the seven listed here, also named was Stephen Gomage, who is listed above under 1342.
[150] C81/1786/40.   [151] Oxford, Corpus Christi College, MS 256, fo. 168[v].
[152] He was professed in 1418 (Searle, *Lists*, p. 186).
[153] Ibid., p. 192.   [154] C81/1786/1; *CPR, 1381–85*, pp. 82, 251.

Appendix 5

Archbishop Romeyn asked the writ be revoked since he was not an apostate, 1290.[155]

1301–50

Henry de Wangford. Thetford (alien) Priory (Norf.). Fled to nearby Augustinian house, was captured but fled again, *c.* 1300.[156]
William de Avernaz. Monk of Lewes Priory (Sussex); sometime prior, Prittlewell (dependent) Priory (Essex). Signified for arrest, 3 March 1317 and 30 Sept. 1318, in dispute over priorship.[157]
Robert de Strete. Monk of Lewes Priory (Sussex) at Prittlewell (dependent) Priory (Essex). As preceding.[158]
John de Campeworth. As preceding. Signified for arrest in dispute over priorship, 30 Sept. 1318.[159]
Henry de Southchurch. As preceding. Signified in dispute over priorship, 30 Sept. 1318; signified again 23 May 1341.[160]
John Pynant alias de Ludlow. Bermondsey Priory (Surrey). Signified for arrest with next three entries in dispute over custody of priory, 18 Sept. 1321.[161]
    Nicholas Pynant alias de Ludlow.
    John de Euere.
    Geoffrey de London.
Robert de Pyrewych (Parwich?). Lewes Priory (Sussex). Signified for arrest with the next three entries, 17 June 1330.[162]
    Robert de Lynn.
    Henry de Brom.
    Henry de Seaford.
Matthew de Arley. Lewes Priory (Sussex). Signified for arrest, 8 Nov. 1346.[163]
Henry de Morley. Bermondsey Priory (Surrey). Signified for arrest, excommunicate then for three months, 20 Dec. 1346.[164]
Bertrand de Petra Levata. Montacute Priory (Somerset). Writ for arrest, 8 May 1348.[165]
William de Warenne. Illegitimate son of the earl of Surrey. Prior.

[155] *VCH, Yorks.* 3. 93.   [156] *VCH, Norf.* 2, 366.
[157] C81/1787/6, 15; for this dispute see above, pp. 119–20 and *VCH, Essex* 2. 139–40.
[158] C81/1787/6, 16.
[159] C81/1787/16.   [160] C81/1787/8, 16.
[161] C81/1787/1. For the dispute see *CPR, 1317–21*, p. 529; *CPR, 1321–24*, p. 23; *VCH, Surrey* 2. 71.
[162] C81/1787/7.   [163] C81/1787/9.
[164] C81/1787/2.   [165] *CPR, 1348–50*, p. 82.

Castle Acre Priory (Norf.). Fled after his father's death and was signified for arrest, 1 Nov. 1348; writs of 25 Oct. 1348 and 8 Feb. 1351 enrolled.[166]

Robert Mande alias de Necton. Castle Acre Priory (Norf.). Probably fled with Warenne (previous entry); subject to arrest with Warenne, 1348, 1351.[167]

1351–1400

William de Leominster. Much Wenlock Priory (Salop). Signified for arrest, 12 Aug. 1357, 12 April 1358 (writ of 5 May enrolled).[168]

John Ixworth. Thetford Priory (Norfolk). Writ for arrest, with next six entries, 10 Oct. 1363.[169]

> **William de Lenton**.
> **Roger Shropham**.
> **William Briset**.
> **John Calcot**.
> **John Harling**.
> **Thomas Carter**.

William de Molins. Montacute Priory (Somerset). Writ for arrest, 20 Oct. 1365.[170]

Robert de Wilmington. Lewes Priory (Sussex). Signified for arrest, 14 Dec. 1366.[171]

John de Lisle. Monk Bretton Priory (Yorks. WR). Papal mandate to reconcile, 12 Sept. 1367.[172]

William de Doditon (Doddington). Much Wenlock Priory (Salop). Papal mandate to reconcile, 26 Feb. 1370.[173]

John de Stapelton. Pontefract Priory (Yorks. WR). Signified for arrest, 1 June 1372.[174]

Roger Ware. Prior. Horkesley Priory (Essex). Signified by prior of Thetford Priory (Norf.), 15 June 1374, but Ware secured supersedence by appealing tuitorially to pope on grounds that Horkeseley was not subject to jurisdiction of Thetford.[175]

---

[166] C81/1787/5; *CPR, 1348–50*, p. 244; *CPR, 1350–54*, p. 78. See also *CPL* 3. 12, 124, 139.
[167] C81/1787/5; *CPR, 1348–50*, p. 244; *CPR, 1350–54*, p. 78. His recently (21 Aug. 1348) having been made an honorary papal chaplain may have been a complicating factor (*CPL* 3. 250).
[168] C81/1787/21, 22; *CPR, 1358–61*, p. 75.
[169] *CPR, 1361–64*, pp. 447–8.
[170] *CPR, 1364–67*, p. 203.   [171] C81/1787/10.
[172] *CPL* 4. 66.   [173] Ibid., 4. 82.
[174] C81/1787/14.   [175] C81/1787/20; *CPR, 1374–77*, p. 56.

Thomas Samme. Montacute Priory (Somerset). Writs for arrest, 16 Jan. 1386 and 12 Feb. 1387.[176]

Richard Knapton (Napton). St Andrew's Priory (Northampton). Amidst considerable turmoil, signified for arrest, 24 Nov. 1390; he became prior in 1399.[177]

Henry Edington. Bermondsey Priory (Surrey). Signified for arrest, 19 April 1392.[178]

John de Leicester. Bermondsey Priory (Surrey). Signified for arrest, 5 Nov. 1394.[179]

1401–50

John de Raylegh alias John Hugh. Prittlewell Priory (Essex). Signified for arrest, 9 Feb. 1431; writ issued 10 Feb. In London prison by 14 Feb.; also detained by complaint of London merchant. Handed over to subprior, 19 Feb.[180]

1451–1500

John Hamerton. St Andrew's Priory (Northampton). Signified for arrest, 12 Nov. 1469; writ issued 16 Nov.[181]

    Thomas Grove. As preceding.[182]

Robert Rykdon. Lewes Priory (Sussex). Signified for arrest as an excommunicate, 28 Oct. 1470.[183]

John Shrewsbury. Probably the recently appointed prior. Much Wenlock Priory (Salop). Signified for arrest with next three entries, 1 Nov. 1471.[184]

    Thomas Smythe.

    Thomas Gytton.

    Richard Hale.

William Stone. St Andrew's Priory (Northampton). Signified for arrest, 30 Sept. 1472.[185]

---

[176] *CPR, 1385–89*, pp. 165, 317.

[177] C81/1786/27; see *CPR, 1388–92*, pp. 501, 504; *CPL* 4. 454–5; *VCH, Northants*. 2. 1. 107.

[178] C81/1787/4.   [179] C81/1787/3.

[180] C81/1787/17–19.

[181] C81/1787/12; *CPR, 1467–77*, pp. 194–5. The four apostates from Northampton in the years 1469–72 reflect the troubled state of the priory (see *VCH, Northants*. 2. 1. 107).

[182] He failed to appear in chancery, when cited, 1473 (*CCR, 1468–76*, p. 301).

[183] C81/1787/11.

[184] C81/1787/23. The four monks of Much Wenlock listed here were signified four months after the appointment of John Shrewsbury as prior, who received temporalities 9 July 1471 (*CPR, 1467–77*, p. 274).

[185] C81/1787/13. A writ was issued 16 Nov. 1469 for the arrest of certain unnamed monks of this priory (*CPR, 1467–77*, p. 358).

William Brekenok (Brekenose). St Andrew's Priory (Northampton). Claimant to priorship, signified for arrest, 30 Sept. 1472.[186]

1501–30

Myles Grendon. Daventry Priory (Northants.). Reported at visitation as apostate for four years, 21 June 1520.[187]

Roland Gosnell alias Bridgnorth. Prior. Much Wenlock Priory (Salop). Some monks opposed his election, 1521, claiming *inter alia* that he was considered an apostate, which he denied.[188]

4. Order of Tiron

John Bareth. St Dogmells Abbey (Pembroke). Papal mandate to reconcile, 30 April 1346.[189]

David Lloyd. St Dogmells Abbey (Pembroke). Bishop's order to abbot to seek him out and reconcile him, 14 Jan. 1402.[190]

William Kele. Humberston Abbey (Lincs.). Reported with next four entries as apostate at visitation, 1440.[191]

John Clee. Known to be dead in 1440.

Thomas Gretham.

Richard Halle.

John Grouxhille. Reportedly had entered a mendicant order.

5. Order of Grandmontine[192]

Richard de Stretton. Prior. Alberbury Priory (Salop). Accused of murder, he fled priory, incurred outlawry and after many years – another prior having been appointed in the meantime – received royal pardon, 12 June 1363.[193]

---

[186] See preceding note. He had himself appointed prior by the abbot of Cluny, but Prior Thomas Stubury appealed to the pope, who, on 12 Nov. 1475, appointed a commission of inquiry (*CPL* 13. 2. 485–6).

[187] *Vis. Dioc. Linc.* 2. 112.

[188] Rose Graham, 'Roland Gosenell, Prior of Wenlock, 1521–1526', *English Ecclesiastical Studies* (London, 1929), pp. 127–9; *VCH, Salop* 2. 44.

[189] *CPL* 3. 231.

[190] R. F. Isaacson, ed., *The Episcopal Registers of the Diocese of St David's, 1397 to 1518* (2 vols.; Cymmrodorion Rec. Ser., 6, 1917–20) 1. 251.

[191] *Linc. Vis.* 2. 140. The visitor found only five monks in residence.

[192] For this order see Rose Graham, 'The Order of Grandmont and Its Houses in England', *English Ecclesiastical Studies* (London, 1929), pp. 209–46.

[193] Ibid., pp. 237–8; *VCH, Salop* 2. 49.

Appendix 5

6. Cistercian monks

1251–1300

Some (unnamed) apostates. Stoneleigh Abbey (Warwicks.). Subject to arrest, 19 Oct. 1259.[194]

Roger de Botelstan. Conversus. Newminster Abbey (Northumberland). Went apostate, 1258 x 1273. His status unknown to the prior of Durham, Roger had become a servant at the priory but later confessed.[195]

Henry de Norton. Croxden Abbey (Staffs.). Writ for arrest, 12 Jan. 1266.[196]

William de Modlether. Jervaulx Abbey (Yorks. NR). Murdered Abbot Philip and fled; declared outlaw, 1279.[197]

William de Acton. Rievaulx Abbey (Yorks. NR). Claiming to be a leper, he stabbed the monk examining him and fled into the woods. Two monks caught and beat him; he died of his wounds, 1279.[198]

Alexander. Conversus. Vaudey Abbey (Lincs.). Signified for arrest, probably early 1280s.[199]

Reginald de Bristol. Tintern Abbey (Monmouths.). Signified for arrest, in 1280s.[200]

Godfrey Darel. Rievaulx Abbey (Yorks. NR). Archbishop's order to search for him, probably 1286.[201]

Ingram de London. Pipewell Abbey (Northants.). Allegedly in apostasy and having forged abbatial seal, 26 April 1286; signified for arrest, 24 April 1287.[202]

John de Palfleteby. Cellarer. Louth Park Abbey (Lincs.). Allegedly stole substantially from monastery and was spending it in apostasy. Signified for arrest, 26 April 1287.[203]

Thomas de Farucote. Buildwas Abbey (Salop). Signified for arrest, 25 Aug. 1289.[204]

---

[194] *CPR, 1258–60*, p. 45.
[195] Frank Barlow, ed., *Durham Annals* (Surtees Soc., 154, 1945), pp. 199–200.
[196] *CPR, 1258–66*, p. 533.
[197] *VCH, Yorks.* 3. 141.   [198] Ibid., 3. 151.
[199] C81/1788/57. Quite likely the conversus Alexander de Staunford who was signified probably in the 1290s (C81/1788/59).
[200] C81/1788/53.
[201] *Reg. le Romeyn, York* 1. no. 437.
[202] *CCR, 1279–88*, p. 412; C81/1788/38. For dispute of Pipewell and Monks Kirby Priories see *VCH, Northants.* 2. 117.
[203] C81/1788/37.   [204] C81/1788/15.

Henry Sampson. Conversus. Fountains Abbey (Yorks. WR). Signified for arrest, 9 Oct. 1289.[205]

John de Hermesthorp. Vaudey Abbey (Lincs.). Signified for arrest with next three entries, probably 1290s.[206]

    Hugh de Welleby.

    Alexander de Staunford. Conversus.[207]

    Ralph Waket. Conversus.

Henry de Thurmaston. Vaudey Abbey (Lincs.) Signified for arrest with next entry, probably 1290s.[208]

    Peter de Menstern.

John de Wymfrend. Bindon Abbey (Dorset). Signified for arrest, 1 July 1290.[209]

Walter Pryket. Conversus. Swineshead Abbey (Lincs.). Allegedly disposed of monastic goods; signified for arrest, 9 April 1290.[210]

John de Evesham. Hailes Abbey (Glos.). Arrested and now to be delivered to his monastery, 2 Sept. 1290.[211]

David. Conversus. Biddlesden Abbey (Bucks.). Signified for arrest, 1 May 1294.[212]

Geoffrey de Bungay. Vaudey Abbey (Lincs.). Signified for arrest with next entry, 1 Nov. 1296.[213]

    Andrew de Swinsted.

John le Fox. Bindon Abbey (Dorset). Signified for arrest, 20 April 1299.[214]

1301–50

Walter de Thornborough. Biddlesden Abbey (Bucks.). Signified for arrest, 15 Sept. 1301.[215]

Walter de Witton. Newminster Abbey (Northumberland). Went apostate twice, *c.* 1300, and again *c.* 1311.[216]

Henry de Howden. Kirkstall Abbey (Yorks. WR). Left with chalices and other monastic goods; episcopal order to denounce as excommunicate, 29 March 1304.[217]

---

[205] C81/1788/23.   [206] C81/1788/59.

[207] Probably the same as the conversus Alexander signified in the early 1280s (C81/1788/57).

[208] C81/1788/58 (undated petition).

[209] Prynne, p. 1301.   [210] C81/1788/51.

[211] SC1/18/97.   [212] C81/1788/4.

[213] C81/1788/60.   [214] C81/1788/3.

[215] C81/1788/5.

[216] *Reg. Pal. Dunelm.* 1. 13–16. For a detailed discussion of this case see above, pp. 17–18.

[217] *Reg. Corbridge, York* 1. no. 273.

William de Smallrice. Combermere Abbey (Cheshire). Signified for arrest, 21 Sept. 1314.[218]

John de Husthwaite. Byland Abbey (Yorks. NR). Abbot's letter that he has been excommunicated for his apostasy, 22 April 1316.[219]

Thomas de Etindone(?). Stoneleigh Abbey (Warwicks.). Signified for arrest, 13 June 1317.[220]

William Pacok. Conversus. Jervaulx Abbey (Yorks. NR). Archbishop's mandate to reconcile, 23 July 1321.[221]

Thomas de Malton. Kirkstall Abbey (Yorks. WR). Signified for arrest with next entry, 18 Oct. 1324.[222]

    William de Dringhouse.

John de Kidderminster. Bordesley Abbey (Worcs.). Reconciled, 29 May 1325.[223]

William Worthy alias Chaunflour. Quarr Abbey (I.o.W.). Fled and was said to be in Ireland. Signified for arrest, 1 March 1327.[224]

John de Montacute. Claimed to be abbot. Bindon Abbey (Dorset). Allegedly broke into monastery at night with supporters and stole 100 oxen, 7,000 sheep, chalices, books, vestments and ornaments as well as the common seal. Writ for arrest, 22 March 1331. Arrested but escaped before he could be returned; new writ issued, 1 Aug. 1331.[225]

John de Well. Bindon Abbey (Dorset). Arrested with Montacute (previous entry), 1331.[226]

John Kirkeby. Rievaulx Abbey (Yorks. NR). Signified for arrest, 13 Nov. 1332, and arrested by 22 Oct. 1337.[227]

Bartholomew Ace. Cleeve Abbey (Somerset). Papal mandate to reconcile, 12 Jan. 1339.[228]

Henry de Alcester. Bordesley Abbey (Worcs.). Papal mandate to reconcile, 6 March 1341.[229]

Ives le Taylour. Conversus. Kirkstead Abbey (Lincs.). Papal mandate to reconcile, 29 Jan. 1341.[230]

John de Stickford. Swineshead Abbey (Lincs.). Papal mandate to reconcile, 14 Feb. 1341.[231]

[218] C81/1788/19.   [219] *Reg. Greenfield, York* 5. no. 2837.

[220] C81/1788/47.   [221] *Reg. Melton, York* 1. no. 31.

[222] Ibid., 1. 32.   [223] *Reg. Cobham, Worcester*, p. 186.

[224] C81/1788/39.

[225] *CPR, 1330–34*, pp. 89, 131, 142, 201; see *VCH, Dorset* 2. 84–5.

[226] *CPR, 1330–34*, p. 142.   [227] C81/1788/40; *CPR, 1334–38*, p. 578.

[228] *CPL* 2. 545.   [229] Ibid., 2. 550.

[230] Ibid., 2. 552.   [231] Ibid.

Thomas Birchvale. Merevale Abbey (Warwicks.). Papal mandate to reconcile, 4 March 1342.[232]

Thomas de Koel. Hulton Abbey (Staffs.). Led an armed band against visitors, forced resignation of abbot and succeeded in placing his candidate in abbotship, 1344.[233]

Thomas de Tonge. Buildwas Abbey (Salop). As accused murderer of abbot, placed in monastic prison, from which he broke out: writ for arrest, 12 Sept. 1342. Papal mandate to reconcile, 20 Nov. 1343, yet another writ for arrest (with next two entries), 18 Aug. 1344.[234]

Nicholas Canne.

John Wade.

Robert Cumbere. Robertsbridge Abbey (Sussex). Papal mandate to reconcile, 25 May 1344.[235]

John de Stayngrecie. Kirkstead Abbey (Lincs.). Papal mandate to reconcile, 4 Sept. 1346.[236]

John de Pernyle (Perranwell?). Dunkeswell Abbey (Devon). Signified for arrest, 1 Oct. 1346; writ issued 9 Dec.[237]

John Stauard. Kirkstead Abbey (Lincs.). Papal mandate to reconcile, 29 May 1347.[238]

John de Tadcaster. Roche Abbey (Yorks. WR). Papal mandate to reconcile, 30 Nov. 1347.[239]

Simon de Bramham. Woburn Abbey (Beds.). Signified for arrest, 5 Sept. 1348.[240]

John de Cockerham. Furness Abbey (Lancs.). Papal mandate to reconcile for Jubilee pilgrimage to Rome, 15 May 1350.[241]

1351–1400

Nicholas de Stanton. Grace Dieu Abbey (Monmouths.). Given permission for Jubilee pilgrimage, but overstayed leave; papal mandate to reconcile, 4 May 1351.[242]

---

[232] *CPL* 2. 557.

[233] Christopher Harper-Bill, 'Monastic Apostasy in Late Medieval England', *JEH* 32 (1981) 13.

[234] *CPR, 1340–43*, p. 553; *CPL* 3. 137; *CPR, 1343–45*, p. 400, where the two following apostates are also named. Dr Marjorie Chibnall suggests that the abbot's murder might have been related to a trip to Ireland (*VCH, Salop* 2. 55).

[235] *CPL* 3. 170.   [236] Ibid., 3. 230.

[237] C81/1788/22; *CPR, 1345–48*, p. 240.

[238] *CPL* 3. 251.

[239] Ibid., 3. 264.   [240] C81/1788/64.

[241] *CPL* 3. 355.   [242] Ibid., 3. 385.

Appendix 5

John de Shobnall. Bruern Abbey (Oxon.). At Avignon on business and, without permission, went to Rome for the Jubilee indulgence; papal mandate to reconcile, 4 May 1351.[243]

John Crompe. Robertsbridge Abbey (Sussex). Papal mandate to reconcile for Jubilee pilgrimage to Rome, 1351.[244]

John de Foriton. Holmcultram Abbey (Cumberland). Papal mandate to reconcile, 17 June 1352.[245]

Stephen de Hethe. Boxley Abbey (Kent). Papal mandate to reconcile, 31 July 1353.[246]

Thomas de Goffard. Furness Abbey (Lancs.). Papal mandate to reconcile, 15 March 1354.[247]

William de Levington. Holmcultram Abbey (Cumberland). Papal mandate to reconcile, 14 March 1354.[248]

Adam Sage alias de Shardeburgh (Scarborough?). Meaux Abbey (Yorks. ER). Papal mandate to reconcile, 13 Nov. 1354.[249]

John Gerard. Meaux Abbey (Yorks. ER). Papal mandate to reconcile, 12 Feb. 1355.[250]

Simon de Leverton. Rufford Abbey (Notts.). Went to Roman curia without permission; papal mandate to reconcile, 13 Feb. 1355.[251]

John de Monte. Holmcultram Abbey (Cumberland). Went to Roman curia without permission; papal mandate to reconcile, 1355.[252]

Henry Olygraunt. Conversus. Sibton Abbey (Suff.). Writ for arrest, 3 Aug. 1356.[253]

Philip de Welle. Bindon Abbey (Dorset). Writ for arrest with next two entries, 20 April 1357.[254]

   Henry de Ewyas.

   Thomas de Woodford.

Griffin Moil. Strata Florida Abbey (Cardigan). Papal mandate to reconcile, 30 April 1359; apparently exiled to Cymer Abbey.[255]

John Fulstow. Louth Park Abbey (Lincs.). Fled, taking sum of money for necessities; papal mandate to reconcile, 11 Sept. 1359.[256]

[243] Ibid., 3. 388.   [244] Ibid., 3. 396.   [245] Ibid., 3. 470.
[246] Ibid., 3. 489. He may have been *eiectus* rather than *apostata*.
[247] Ibid., 3. 521.   [248] Ibid., 3. 522.
[249] Ibid., 3. 541.   [250] Ibid., 3. 571.
[251] Ibid., 3. 572.   [252] Ibid., 3. 572–3.
[253] *CPR, 1354–58*, p. 450.   [254] Ibid., p. 554.
[255] *CPL* 3. 605; see David H. Williams, *The Welsh Cistercians* (2 vols.; Tenby, 1984) 1. 66.
[256] *CPL* 3. 607.

John de Melton. Garendon Abbey (Leics.). Signified for arrest with next three entries, 6 May 1360.[257]
    Richard de Burton.
    John de London.
    John de Hathern.
John de Wheston. Combe Abbey (Warwicks.). Signified for arrest, 22 June 1361.[258]
Richard de Eckeslay. Kirkstall Abbey (Yorks. WR). Papal mandate to reconcile, 1362.[259]
Richard Cave. House unknown. Allegedly apostate and holding a vicarage, 1363.[260]
Andrew Sergaunt. Robertsbridge Abbey (Sussex). Papal mandate to reconcile, 4 Dec. 1363.[261]
John Audenete. Hailes Abbey (Glos.). Papal mandate to reconcile, 10 June 1364.[262]
Thomas Pipe. Sometime abbot. Stoneleigh (Warwicks.). Signified for arrest, 1 May 1365; writ issued 6 May.[263]
William Banaster. Whalley Abbey (Lancs.). In struggle to become abbot, signified for arrest, 26 Oct. 1365 and 25 Oct. 1366, with next seven entries, members of his party.[264]
    John de Bolling.
    John de Baghill.
    Thomas de Halton.
    Nicholas de York.
    John de Burton.
    John de Pontefract.
    Richard de Cliderbon.
John de Stok. Bordesley Abbey (Worcs.). Writ for arrest with next four entries, 1 July 1367.[265]
    Alexander de Evesham.[266]

---

[257] C81/1788/27. For evidence of considerable unrest there at this time see *CPR, 1358–61*, p. 358.

[258] C81/1788/18.

[259] *CPL* 4. 34.   [260] *CPP* 1. 434.

[261] *CPL* 4. 42.   [262] Ibid., 4. 44.

[263] C81/1788/48; *CPR, 1364–67*, p. 145. For more on charges against him see *VCH, Warwicks*. 2. 80–1.

[264] Together with Bolling, Baghill, Halton, York and Burton in 1365 and with Halton, Pontefract and Cliderbon in 1366 (C81/1788/62, 63). For a description of the troubles at Whalley at this time see *VCH, Lancs*. 2. 1. 135.

[265] *CPR, 1364–67*, p. 446.

[266] A Cistercian monk of the same name was signified by the abbot of Stoneleigh in 1369 as fugitive from his house (below, n. 269).

Emery de Hull.

Nicholas de la Hay.

William de Wych.

William de Otley. Kirkstall Abbey (Yorks. WR). Papal mandate to reconcile, 11 Nov. 1368.[267]

Peter Denias. Biddlesden Abbey (Bucks.). Signified for arrest by abbot, 10 Sept., and by visitor, 15 Oct. 1369.[268]

John de Syresham. As preceding.

John de Kidbrooke. As preceding, but only by abbot.

Alexander de Evesham. Stoneleigh Abbey (Warwicks.). Signified for arrest with next five entries, 12 Feb. 1369; writ dated 28 Jan.[269]

William de Winterton.

Thomas Fifehead.

John de Rufford.

John Dancaster.

John de Stanlake.

Robert de Scurnton. Fountains Abbey (Yorks. WR). Left *c.* 1378 but not signified for arrest until 1 May 1392.[270]

John de Haverhill. Prior. Coggeshall Abbey (Essex). In dispute over priorship, signified for arrest, 7 Aug. 1380.[271]

Nicholas de Ackley. Tintern Abbey (Monmouths.). Signified for arrest with next three entries, 1 May 1385, and with next four entries, 6 Oct. 1387.[272]

Philip de Tintern.[273]

John Tillandre.

John de Malmesbury.

John Winchester.

Robert Olyver. Combermere Abbey (Cheshire). Accused of stealing from abbey, 1385. Writ for arrest, 30 May 1386.[274]

William de Binnington. Hulton Abbey (Staffs.). Writ for arrest, 30 May 1386.[275]

---

[267] *CPL* 4. 80.   [268] C81/1788/6, 28.

[269] C81/1788/49; *CPR, 1367–70*, p. 259. See above, n. 266.

[270] C81/1788/24.

[271] C81/1788/16. For his appointment (12 Aug. 1380) see *CPR, 1377–81*, p. 535.

[272] Of the five monks of Tintern listed here Acley, Tintern, Tillandre and Malmesbury were signified in 1385 and also, with Winchester, in 1387 (C81/1788/54–6).

[273] In one instance he is called Philip de Parva Tintern.

[274] *VCH, Cheshire* 3. 154; *CPR, 1385–89*, p. 178.

[275] *CPR, 1385–89*, p. 178.

John de Wyom. Kirkstead Abbey (Lincs.). Papal mandate to reconcile for Jubilee pilgrimage to Rome, 20 Sept. 1390.[276]

Henry Wirral. Basingwerk Abbey (Flint). Writ for arrest, 1399. Abbot of same name, 1430–54.[277]

1401–50

Ralph de Byker (Bikere). Left Swineshead Abbey (Lincs.) apostate and entered St Mary Graces (London), where status later regularized, 1 Jan. 1401, but fled from there after striking abbot, 1402.[278]

Richard Hollkey. Baltinglass Abbey (Co. Wicklow, Ireland). Signified for arrest, 2 Jan. 1402; writs issued to Constable of Dover Castle and to sheriff of Sussex.[279]

Richard Wrangle. Kirkstead Abbey (Lincs.). Signified for arrest with next entry, 16 Feb. 1402.[280]

William Lincoln.

John Stowe. Hailes Abbey (Glos.). Arrested and in a London prison, 4 Aug. 1402.[281]

Robert Hesyll. Uncertain abbey (Yorks.). Papal mandate to reconcile this recidivist, 1403.[282]

John Hollingbourne. Robertsbridge Abbey (Sussex). Exiled to Coggeshall Abbey (Essex) for carnal lapses. Fled from there, went to Rome and received absolution. Papal mandate to reconcile him, now old and penitent, 9 Feb. 1403, yet signified for arrest, 26 April 1404.[283]

Henry Alcester. Possibly abbot. Hailes Abbey (Glos.). Signified for arrest, 16 Nov. 1403; writ issued 20 Nov.[284]

John Whitwood. Roche Abbey (Yorks. WR). Professed for nine years and apostate for three years, now signified for arrest, 9 Oct. 1410.[285]

---

[276] *CPL* 4. 328.

[277] *CPR, 1396–99*, p. 511; Williams, *Welsh Cistercians* 1. 98.

[278] Details of this case can be seen in *CPL* 5. 346–7, 517, 602, and a summary is in *VCH, London* 1. 462–3.

[279] C81/1788/1 and dorse.   [280] C81/1788/33.   [281] C250/2/35.

[282] *CPL* 5. 543–4. The editor suggests Furness or Jervaulx for 'Benoys'.

[283] Ibid., 5. 553; C81/1788/43.

[284] C81/1788/30; *CPR, 1401–05*, p. 359. He may have been the Henry Alcester who had been elected abbot in 1397 (*VCH, Glos.* 2. 98). John Stowe, who is mentioned above under 1402, could have been involved in these troubles. Abbot Robert Alcester proceeded against both of these apostates and was himself later (1419) implicated in unseemly behaviour (*sede vacante, Reg. Worcester*, pp. 403–5).

[285] C81/1788/45.

Nicholas Sampson. St Mary Graces Abbey (London). Signified for arrest with next entry, 3 July 1411; writ issued 8 July.[286]

    Thomas Broun.

Roger Frank. Abbot claimant. Fountains Abbey (Yorks. WR). Dispute (Frank *v.* Rypon) over election lasting from 1410 to 1416; at one point John Rypon, calling himself abbot, had writs of caption issued against Frank and twelve other monks of Fountains (next entries), 1 June 1414, but writ superseded .[287]

    Robert Thornour.
    William Tunstall.
    John Rothom.
    Thomas Hertwyth.
    William del See.
    John Ryvax (Rievaulx?).
    Richard de Wakefield.
    John Martyn.
    Thomas de Tanfield.
    Robert Helmesley.
    William Estby.
    Richard Newhall.

John Aconbury (Alkemondbury). Sawtry Abbey (Hunts.). Signified for arrest, 12 Dec. 1422.[288]

William Doore. Croxden Abbey (Staffs.). Signified for arrest, 6 Nov. 1425.[289]

William Bramley. Rievaulx Abbey (Yorks. NR). Recently restored abbot, now signified by Henry Burton, deposed predecessor, 18 March 1426.[290]

Thomas Hamerton. Rievaulx Abbey (Yorks. NR). Signified for arrest, 5 Sept. 1426, by Henry Burton, deposed former abbot.[291]

Paschal Gilot. 'Abbas intrusus'. St Mary Graces Abbey (London). Signified for arrest with next four entries, 23 March 1428.[292]

---

[286] C81/1788/35; *CPR, 1408–13*, p. 320.

[287] *CPR, 1413–16*, p. 221. For this celebrated case see E. F. Jacob, 'One of Swan's Cases: The Disputed Election at Fountains Abbey, 1410–16', *Essays in Later Medieval History* (Manchester, 1968), pp. 79–97; for these alleged apostates, p. 89.

[288] C81/1788/46.   [289] C81/1788/20.

[290] C81/1788/41. See *CPR, 1422–29*, p. 300, where it is said *inter alia* that Burton had seized the common seal.

[291] C81/1788/42.

[292] Signified by Abbot John Pecche (C81/1788/36). For the troubles at this house see *VCH, London* 1. 463, and Harris Nicolas, ed., *Proceedings and Ordinances of the Privy Council of England* (7 vols.; London, 1834–7) 3. 269.

Roger Bolton.
Robert Benet.
John Stacy.
John Minehead.
Hugh Frischney. Kirkstead Abbey (Lincs.). Signified for arrest, 19 June 1429; writ issued 28 June.[293]
Thomas Ashby. Combe Abbey (Warwicks.). Mandate by visitor to seek out and reconcile, 1433; signification for arrest, 1 Feb. 1434; papal permission to live in his habit at Rome until king's 'ban' – the writ *de apostata capiendo?* – was lifted, 30 March 1436.[294]
William Roos. Warden Abbey (Beds.). Signified for arrest, 4 Dec. 1440.[295]
Thomas Swyfte. Robertsbridge Abbey (Sussex). Signified for arrest, 24 Nov. 1447.[296]
William Downam. Fountains Abbey (Yorks. WR). Left Fountains in apostasy but later repentant before abbots of Newminster and Kirkstead, 11 May 1448. Apostasized again, and abbot of Fountains (whom he allegedly tried to poison) was ordered to have him captured, 2 June 1449.[297]

1451–1500

John Bray. Coggeshall Abbey (Essex). Signified for arrest, 9 Nov. 1452.[298]
William Hull. Fountains Abbey (Yorks. WR). Signified for arrest, 25 Jan. 1452 and 29 Jan. 1456.[299]
Thomas Shelford. Stratford Langthorn Abbey (Essex). Signified for arrest with next entry, 5 Oct. 1455.[300]
  Hugh Watford.[301]
Robert Cornwell alias Burton. Kirkstead Abbey (Lincs.). Left *c.* 1462 and wore the garb of a secular priest and without dispensation was instituted as rector of Broughton near Kettering (Northants.); later dispensed and still later (5 Sept. 1492) appealed

---

[293] C81/1788/34; *CPR, 1422–29*, p. 554. The writ was issued to the lieutentant of the constable of Dover Castle, the warden of the Cinque Ports and the sheriff of Kent: Frischney may have been at the coast on his way to the continent.
[294] Christopher Harper-Bill, 'Cistercian Visitation in the Late Middle Ages', *BIHR* 53 (1980) 106–7; C81/1788/66; *CPL* 8. 602–3.
[295] C81/1788/61.   [296] C81/1788/44.   [297] Talbot, *Letters*, no. 2.
[298] C81/1788/17. See Harper-Bill, 'Cistercian Visitation', p. 107.
[299] C81/1788/25, 26.   [300] C81/1788/50.
[301] A monk of the same name was abbot of Stratford Langthorn in 1466 and still in 1480 (*VCH, Essex* 2. 133).

to the pope because the bishop of Lincoln had another candidate.[302]

Thomas Olyver. Buckland Abbey (Devon). Signified for arrest seven times between 1467 and 1473 in dispute over abbatial election, which he won.[303]

Thomas Wortley alias Tilson. Swineshead Abbey (Lincs.). Signified for arrest, 12 July 1468.[304]

John Neyd. Woburn Abbey (Beds.). Signified for arrest, 11 Feb. 1469.[305]

Thomas Ley. Buckland Abbey (Devon). Signified for arrest with Thomas Olyver (see above) and next entry, 2 Dec. 1472.[306]

   John Harry.

Robert Forde. Sometime abbot. Abbey Dore (Herefs.). Signified for arrest, 2 May 1472.[307]

John Bustett. Hailes Abbey (Glos.). Having left to take a benefice, he was required by his order to return to be punished, 1480. Probably the John Breystow (Bristol) who was dispensed to hold a benefice, 12 May 1468.[308]

John Tyrrell. Fountains Abbey (Yorks. WR). Letter of rehabilitation from Abbot John [Darneton] (1478–94).[309]

Thurston Lofthous alias Watson. Kirkstall Abbey (Yorks. WR). Allegedly apostate for transferring to Carthusians; papal mandate to reconcile as Cistercian, 23 Feb. 1489, yet, in 1490, allowed to continue as Carthusian.[310]

_____ **Lucy**. Warden Abbey (Beds.). Said to have lapsed into detestable apostasy, 26 Sept. 1492.[311]

John Stotesbury. Biddlesden Abbey (Bucks.). Papal dispensation to wear secular priest's garb over religious habit, which he had been doing and for which he had incurred apostasy, 28 Jan. 1497.[312]

1501–30

William Milton. Boxley Abbey (Kent). Signified for arrest with next 3 entries, 9 Feb. 1513.[313]

---

[302] *CPL* 16. 6.
[303] See above, pp. 111, 120.
[304] C81/1788/52.   [305] C81/1788/65.
[306] C81/1788/12.   [307] C81/1788/21.
[308] Canivez 5. 404; *CPL* 12. 632; Talbot, *Letters*, no. 25.
[309] Talbot, *Letters*, no. 138.   [310] For fuller discussion of this case see above, p. 49.
[311] Talbot, *Letters*, no. 79.   [312] *CPL* 16. no. 762.
[313] These four monks listed here were said to have been apostate 'per multum tempus' (C81/1788/7).

William Sandwich.
Robert Blechenden.
John Farham.
Richard Rotter. Grace Dieu Abbey (Monmouths.). Reported in 1518 as being apostate.[314]

UNDATED

Henry de Radelegh. Hailes Abbey (Glos.). Signified for arrest, temp. Edward I or II.[315]
Roger Milton. Beaulieu Abbey (Hants.). Signified for arrest, 15th cent.[316]
William Hull. Meaux Abbey (Yorks. ER). Letter of rehabilitation from Abbot Marmaduke [Huby] of Fountains (1494–1526).[317]

7. Carthusians

John Russell. Lay brother. Witham Priory (Somerset). Papal mandate to reconcile, 10 Jan. 1339.[318]
William de Standish. Witham Priory (Somerset). Papal mandate to reconcile, 13 Sept. 1341.[319]
John Parlebien. Hinton Priory (Somerset). Signified for arrest with next entry, 14 April 1391; writ issued 9 May.[320]
Richard Barbour.
Richard Vyell (Viel). Sometime prior. Witham Priory (Somerset). Signified for arrest, 20 May 1451. Later (1459) appointed bishop of Killala in Ireland.[321]
William Cuerton. Hull Priory (Yorks. ER). Left priory, alleging persecution, and went to Roman curia, still wearing his habit.

---

314 Williams, *Welsh Cistercians* 1. 98, where Rotter is said to be a chantry priest at St Briavels (Glos.).
315 C81/1788/29.   316 C81/1788/2.
317 Talbot, *Letters*, no. 140.
318 *CPL* 2. 549.   319 Ibid., 2. 552.
320 C81/1787/24; *CPR*, 1388–92, p. 441.
321 C81/1787/25. In 1447 he was referred to as prior in Cardinal Beaufort's will (J. F. Nichols, ed., *A Collection of All the Wills Now Known to be Extant of the Kings and Queens of England* (London, 1780), p. 331), and in 1453, as prior, he received a royal pardon for all offences (*CPR, 1452–61*, p. 116). As bishop of Killala in Ireland he received papal permission to reside in England (*CPL* 12. 92–3, 210–11); his appointment did not take effect (E. B. Fryde *et al.*, eds., *Handbook of British Chronology* (3rd edn; London, 1986), p. 360). He was appointed to the vicarage of Woolavington (Somerset) in 1465, which he still held in 1479 (*Reg. Stillington, Bath and Wells*, pp. xxiii, xxvi).

Absolved and allowed either to return or to transfer, 6 March 1477.[322]

8. *Augustinian canons*[323]

1251–1300

Reynold de Chyvele (Chavel?). Missenden Abbey (Bucks.). Writ for arrest, 20 Dec. 1267.[324]

Unnamed canons. Flitcham Priory (Norf.). Writ for arrest, 17 April 1270.[325]

John de Cotes. St Sepulchre Priory (Warwick). Writ for arrest, 2 June 1270.[326]

Richard de Vallibus. Waltham Abbey (Essex). Writ for arrest with next two entries, 30 July 1272.[327]

   Hilary de St Edmund.

   Richard de Paris.

Nicholas de Feckenham. Llanthony Prima Priory (Monmouths.). Writ for arrest with next two entries, 3 May 1274.[328]

   Leonard de Llanthony.

   John de Ros.

Robert Barry. Felley Priory (Notts.). Archbishop's mandate to reconcile, *c.* 1276.[329]

William, son of Henry de Belgrave. Chipley Priory (Suff.). Certified as apostate in testamentary dispute, Michaelmas term, 1276.[330]

William de Brudicot. Dorchester Abbey (Oxon.). Signified for arrest with next entry, 24 May 1278.[331]

   Richard de Chartham.

Robert *called* Juvenis. Tonbridge Priory (Kent). Writ for arrest, 15 Nov. 1280.[332]

---

[322] *CPL* 13. 55.
[323] Hospitals with religious following the Augustinian rule are difficult to categorize. Two London hospitals with fairly large communities of canons – St Mary's without Bishopsgate and St Mary's within Cripplegate (Elsing Spital) – and St Bartholomew's, Gloucester, are placed under hospitals.
[324] *CPR, 1266–72*, p. 175.   [325] Ibid., p. 421.
[326] *Reg. Giffard, York*, no. 623.
[327] *CPR, 1266–72*, p. 668.   [328] *CPR, 1272–78*, p. 49.
[329] *Reg. Giffard, York*, no. 666; see also nos. 912, 916.
[330] He had claimed his father's inheritance but had professed twenty years earlier (CP40/17/m.69d).
[331] C81/1789/8.   [332] *CPR, 1272–81*, p. 401.

Robert de Whitwell. Hexham Priory (Northumberland). Archbishop's mandate to reconcile, 1281 or 1282.[333]

William de Thornton. Brinkburn Priory (Northumberland). Signified for arrest as excommunicate by bishop of Durham, 15 June 1288.[334]

Thomas de York. Kirkham Priory (Yorks. ER). Allegedly stole books and other property belonging to the priory; signified for arrest, 26 July 1289.[335]

Nicholas de Temedsbury(?). Wigmore Abbey (Herefs.). Signified for arrest, 1289 or 1290.[336]

Robert de Wetwang. Newburgh Priory (Yorks. NR). Archbishop's mandate to reconcile, 29 Dec. 1292; yet signified for arrest as excommunicate by archbishop, 23 April 1293.[337]

Richard de Rutland. Missenden Abbey (Bucks.). Bishop's mandate to reconcile, 29 Sept. 1294.[338]

Richard de Chalfont. Missenden Abbey (Bucks.). Bishop's mandate to reconcile, 23 July 1295.[339]

John Gourda. St Augustine's Abbey (Bristol). Signified for arrest, 9 Aug. 1295.[340]

Robert de Weston. Lay brother. Catesby Priory, cell dependent on Catesby nunnery (Northants.). Bishop of Lincoln in 1307 wrote to bishop of London to help gain his return from London, where he had been living with a woman for ten years (i.e., since *c.* 1297).[341]

Peter de Alazun (All Saints?). Thornton Abbey (Lincs.). Went to Oxford where he wore secular habit and was excommunicated by chancellor, 1298. Apparently returned repentant, not before 1309.[342]

1301–50

Hugh de Farndon. Thurgarton Priory (Notts.). Archbishop's mandate to reconcile, 2 Aug. 1302.[343]

---

[333] *Reg. Wickwane, York*, no. 552.   [334] C85/198/29.

[335] C81/1789/18. He may be the same person as the unnamed apostate of that house who, in 1289, was apprehended in Norwich 'cum bonis monasterii' (*Reg. le Romeyn, York* 1. no. 585).

[336] C81/1789/66.

[337] *Reg. Romeyn, York* 1. no. 495; C85/175/77.

[338] *Reg. Sutton, Lincoln* 5. 30–1.   [339] Ibid., 5. 99.

[340] Prynne, p. 641.   [341] *VCH, Northants*. 2. 123.

[342] *VCH, Lincs*. 2. 164.   [343] *Reg. Corbridge, York* 1. no. 662.

John de Tickhill. Newstead Priory (Notts.). Recently left; archbishop's mandate to seek out, 11 April 1303.[344]

Richard de Sherburn. Marton Priory (Yorks. NR). Archbishop's mandate to reconcile, 12 Nov. 1303.[345]

William de Dingley. Newstead Priory (Notts.). Penance to be imposed on him, now returned, 27 June 1306.[346]

Robert de Greatworth. Catesby Priory, cell dependent on Catesby nunnery (Northants.). Apostasized on pretext of going to Rome; excommunication pronounced, 1307.[347]

Henry de Pecham. Tandridge Priory (Surrey). Episcopal order to seek him out, 8 July 1308; penance to be imposed on him, now returned, 27 May 1309.[348]

Ralph de Grove. Worksop Priory (Notts.). To be denounced as excommunicate (apostate for nearly a year) by bishop of Lincoln, in whose diocese he is thought to be, 24 May 1310. Archbishop's mandate to his prior to find out his whereabouts, 17 June 1310. In royal prison by 25 July 1310. Penance to be imposed given in detail, 5 Sept. 1310. Sent *in exsilium* to Bridlington Priory.[349]

John de Horwood. St James Abbey (Northampton). Signified for arrest, 2 and 30 June 1309, 1 March 1310.[350]

Robert de Killum. Thornholme Priory (Lincs.). Bishop ordered him denounced, 2 and 14 May 1311.[351]

Richard de Doncaster. Healaugh Priory (Yorks. WR). Archbishop's mandate to reconcile, 13 June 1313.[352]

Roger de York. Healaugh Priory (Yorks. WR). Archbishop's mandate to reconcile, 14 Aug. 1314; at his mother's tearful intervention penance mitigated, 4 Dec. 1314.[353]

William de Thorp. Sometime prior. Newnham Priory (Beds.). Signified for arrest, 23 May 1317.[354]

---

[344] Ibid., 1. no. 694.   [345] Ibid., 1. no. 252.
[346] *Reg. Greenfield, York* 4. no. 1675.
[347] *VCH, Northants.* 2. 123.
[348] *Reg. Woodlock, Winchester* 1. 285, 361, 377–8.
[349] *Reg. Greenfield, York* 4. nos. 1822, 1824, 1845, 1851.
[350] C81/1789/44, 45, 48. Horwood attempted to thwart, by appeal, the writ of 1309 (no. 45). For his excommunication by the bishop of Lincoln in 1309 see Lincs. Archives Office, Episc. Reg. III, fo. 160.
[351] Episc. Reg. III, fos. 214, 215.
[352] *Reg. Greenfield, York* 2. no. 995. He had come to the archbishop with letters of absolution from the papal nuncio.
[353] Ibid., 2. nos. 995, 1071, 1085.
[354] C81/1789/43. He had resigned as prior in 1315 (*VCH, Beds.* 1. 381).

Simon le Constable. Bridlington Priory (Yorks. ER). Thrice apostate. Archbishop's mandate to reconcile, 26 July 1317.[355]

William Barry. St Augustine's Abbey (Bristol). Returned penitent, 1319; bishop's mandate to absolve, 22 Sept. 1320.[356]

Roger de Badwell. St James Abbey (Northampton). Signified for arrest, 18 Oct. 1320.[357]

William de Wedon. Canons Ashby (Northants.). Episcopal mandate to receive back, 30 June 1322.[358]

Geoffrey de le Hull. Bushmead Priory (Beds.). Bishop's mandate to receive back, 11 Feb. 1323, but prior refused and was ordered (16 March 1323) to obey the mandate or to appear before the bishop.[359]

Henry de Leicester. Notley Abbey (Bucks.). Bishop's mandate to reconcile, 2 May 1323.[360]

Lawrence de Tonbridge. St Osyth Abbey (Essex). Possibly an apostate: imprisoned in the Tower and ordered to be taken to monastery, where he was to be kept in the enclosure, 1325.[361]

John de Dumpleton. Ranton Priory (Staffs.). Because he wore lay clothes while away on business, he was required by bishop to seek papal absolution, 1325. Sent *in exsilium* to Burscough Priory (Lancs.).

Stephen de Auckland. Guisborough Priory (Yorks. NR). Archbishop's mandate to a reluctant priory to reconcile, 3 Jan. 1328.[362]

Robert Hode. Plympton Priory (Devon). Prior was ordered thrice to readmit him, now returned, 17 May and 19 Aug. 1329, 4 July 1330.[363]

Odo de Denzell. Bodmin Priory (Cornwall). Bishop's mandate to denounce as excommunicated apostate, 7 Sept. 1330.[364]

G. S. (possibly Geoffrey de Spagurnel). Rocester Abbey (Staffs.). Reported at General Chapter to have apostasized while on business trip to king's court, 1334.[365]

William Boydyn. Kenilworth Priory (Warwicks.). Probably of

---

[355] *Reg. Greenfield, York* 5. no. 2871.

[356] *Reg. Cobham, Worcester*, pp. 35, 95.

[357] C81/1789/47.

[358] Lincs. Archives Office, Episc. Reg. VI, fo. 318r–v.

[359] Ibid., fos. 332v, 334v   [360] Ibid., fo. 338.

[361] *CCR, 1323–27*, p. 437.   [362] *Reg. Melton, York* 2. no. 300.

[363] *Reg. Grandisson, Exeter* 1. 565–7.   [364] Ibid., 1. 581.

[365] Salter, *Chapters*, nos. 60–4. For Spurgnel see *CPR, 1334–38*, p. 450.

cell at Calwich (Staffs.). Signified for arrest, 8 April 1336; writ issued 12 Aug.[366]

William Blasi. Waltham Abbey (Essex). Expelled and excommunicated by abbot; unable to be absolved, renounced the religious life. Papal mandate to reconcile, 10 Jan. 1340.[367]

Robert de Threngestan. Repton Priory (Derby.). Papal mandate to reconcile, 6 March 1341.[368]

Bertrand de Donington. Charley Priory (Leics.). Papal mandate to reconcile, 6 March 1341.[369]

John de Sueyllewelle (Swailwell?). Spinney Priory (Cambs.). Papal mandate to reconcile, 7 March 1341.[370]

John de Alconbury. St James Abbey (Northampton). Papal mandate to reconcile, 9 July 1341.[371]

John de Hodeston. Sometime abbot. Lesnes Abbey (Kent). Signified for arrest, 11 July 1341.[372]

Walter de Thame. Waltham Abbey (Essex). Papal mandate to reconcile, 10 Jan. 1342.[373]

Walter de Wadenhoe. Repton Priory (Derby.). Papal mandate to reconcile, 12 Feb. 1343.[374]

William de Stoke. Maiden Bradley Priory (Wilts.). Papal mandate to reconcile, 28 Feb. 1343.[375]

Robert de Coderugge (Cobridge?). St Sepulchre's Priory (Warwick). Escaped from the priory prison; papal mandate to reconcile, 28 Nov. 1343.[376]

Edmund Baudri. Lesnes Abbey (Kent). Signified for arrest, 1344.[377]

Alan de Coddington. Llanthony Secunda Priory (Glos.). Papal mandate to reconcile, 28 Sept. 1344.[378]

Alan de Wainfleet. Markby Priory (Lincs.). Papal mandate to reconcile, 4 Oct. 1344.[379]

John de Toseland (Thoulislond). Huntingdon Priory (Hunts.). Papal mandate to reconcile, 4 Oct. 1344.[380]

---

[366] C81/1789/16; *CPR, 1334–38*, p. 358.
[367] *CPL* 2. 548.   [368] Ibid., 2. 550.
[369] Ibid.   [370] *CPL* 2. 550–1.
[371] Ibid., 2. 554.
[372] C81/1789/23. He was elected abbot in 1327 but deposed by the bishop of Rochester at a visitation in 1340 (*VCH, Kent* 2. 166–7).
[373] *CPL* 2. 550.   [374] Ibid., 2. 139.
[375] Ibid., 3. 70.   [376] Ibid., 3. 117.
[377] C81/1789/24.   [378] *CPL* 3. 170.
[379] Ibid.   [380] *CPL* 3. 171.

Thomas de Dancaster. Darley Abbey (Derby.). Papal mandate to reconcile, 24 Nov. 1344.[381]

John de Scelleye. Darley Abbey (Derby.). Papal mandate to reconcile, 26 Nov. 1344.[382]

Henry de Buckingham. Missenden Abbey (Bucks.). Signified for arrest with next entry, 21 June 1347.[383]

   John de London.

Stephen de Ketton. Kenilworth Priory (Warwicks.). Signified for arrest, *c*. 1347.[384]

Thomas de Melton. Hexham Priory (Northumberland). Left after falsely declaring himself married; papal mandate to reconcile, 29 Aug. 1350.[385]

Nicholas de Beckingham. Worksop Priory (Notts.). Papal mandate to reconcile, 12 Oct. 1350.[386]

Richard de Ashwell. Royston Priory (Herts.). Papal mandate to reconcile for Jubilee pilgrimage to Rome, 30 Nov. 1350.[387]

1351–1400

Ralph de Missenden. Missenden Abbey (Bucks.). Papal mandate to reconcile for Jubilee pilgrimage to Rome, 27 Jan. 1351.[388]

Thomas de Warwick. Studley Priory (Warwicks.). Papal mandate to reconcile for Jubilee pilgrimage to Rome, 20 Feb. 1351.[389]

Robert Worthen. Haughmond Abbey (Salop). Papal mandate to reconcile, 31 March 1352.[390]

Henry de Quenton (Quinton). Kenilworth Priory (Warwicks.). Papal mandate to reconcile, 25 April 1352.[391]

William Homet. Lanercost Priory (Cumberland). Papal mandate to reconcile, 2 June 1352.[392]

Thomas de Crudewell. Llanthony Prima Priory (Monmouths.). Papal mandate to reconcile, 2 May 1354.[393]

Robert de Waltham. Markby Priory (Lincs.). Papal mandate to reconcile, 22 June 1354.[394]

---

[381] Ibid.
[382] Ibid. He had been ejected, and he then dressed as a secular priest.
[383] C81/1789/38.   [384] C81/1789/17.
[385] *CPL* 3. 393.   [386] Ibid.
[387] Ibid.   [388] *CPL* 3. 383.
[389] Ibid., 3. 383.   [390] Ibid., 3. 433.
[391] Ibid., 3. 461.   [392] Ibid., 3. 470.
[393] Ibid., 3. 522.   [394] Ibid., 3. 540.

Appendix 5

Richard de Orwell. St Bartholomew's Priory (London). Papal mandate to reconcile, 27 May 1355.[395]

John de Wallington. Wormegay Priory (Norf.). Papal mandate to reconcile, 29 July 1355.[396]

Richard de Tuddenham. St Kynemark's Priory (Monmouths.). Broke out of monastic prison and fled; papal mandate to reconcile, 3 Aug. 1355.[397]

Thomas de Everingham. Newburgh Priory (Yorks. NR). Papal mandate to reconcile, 10 Nov. 1355.[398]

Nicholas de Ravenstone. Southwark Priory (Surrey). Papal mandate to reconcile, 23 Dec. 1355.[399]

Vincent de Caldecote. Pentney Priory (Norf.). Signified for arrest with next two entries, 30 July 1356; writ issued 11 Aug.[400]

    Geoffrey de Walsingham.

    Richard Potter alias de Stratton.

John Wittenham. Missenden Abbey (Bucks.). Signified for arrest, 1356.[401]

Henry de Lisle. Deposed prior of Horsley (Glos.), cell of Bruton Priory (Somerset). In controversy over Horsley priorship, signified for arrest, 20 March 1357; writ issued 25 March.[402]

John de Langford. Sometime prior. Ivychurch Priory (Wilts.). Signified for arrest with next two entries, 8 July 1358.[403]

    John de Salisbury.

    Peter Sele (Ottesele, Rossal). Also, papal mandate to reconcile, 7 March 1358.[404]

John Malley. Dodford Priory (Worcs.). Papal mandate to reconcile, 17 Oct. 1359.[405]

---

[395] Ibid., 3. 574. [396] Ibid., 3. 575.

[397] Ibid., 3. 575. Possibly same as the Benedictine monk (Sandwell Priory, Staffs.) of the same name who was signified for arrest in 1360 (C81/1786/42); see above, p. 191.

[398] CPL 3. 565. [399] Ibid.

[400] C81/1789/52; CPR, 1354–58, p. 452.

[401] C81/1789/39.

[402] C81/1789/4; CPR, 1354–58, pp. 553–4. For more on this case see ibid., pp. 244, 266, and CCR, 1354–60, p. 469. In an earlier episode de Lisle went on pilgrimage to Rome (and Venice) with permission of the prior of Worcester Cathedral (*sede vacante*), but a jury in 1355 found he had spent £60 on this journey and had failed to receive permission of the prior of Bruton Priory (*VCH, Glos.* 2. 92).

[403] C81/1789/15; CPR, 1358–61, p. 81. After the Black Death the priory was 'refounded' with new canons; in 1357 Langford resigned. He and the other two canons named here had allegedly stolen goods in West Grimstead (Wilts.); see CPR, 1354–58, p. 386, and, for a general account, *VCH, Wilts.* 2. 292.

[404] CPL 3. 594. [405] Ibid., 3. 607.

John de Garton. Lesnes Abbey (Kent). Signified for arrest, 4 March 1360; writ issued same date.[406]

Thomas de Ellingham. Thremhall Priory (Essex). After leaving Thremhall, apostate for two years before entering Ixworth Priory (Suff.), where, silent about his past, he reprofessed and was reordained subdeacon. Papal mandate to reconcile, 16 Sept. 1363.[407]

Richard de Hexton. St Bartholomew's Priory (London). Signified for arrest with next entry, 27 May 1363.[408]

    John Kayso.

John Cossham. Christchurch Priory (Hants.). Bishop's mandate to require reluctant community to readmit, 20 Jan. 1368.[409]

William de Selby. Haltemprice Priory (Yorks. ER). Papal mandate to reconcile, 12 June 1368.[410]

William Thornbury. Keynsham Abbey (Somerset). Papal mandate to reconcile, 21 Dec. 1368.[411]

Richard de Kirkby. Felley Priory (Notts.). Papal mandate to reconcile, 24 June 1369.[412]

Simon de Digby. Ulverscroft Priory (Leics.). Papal mandate to reconcile, 23 March 1370.[413]

William Meke. Arbury Priory (Warwicks.). Signified for arrest with next five entries, 29 July 1373.[414]

    John de Coventry.

    William de Tamworth.

    Robert de Oulghton (Oulton?).

    John de Coton.

    John de Hinckley.

John Wellington. Llanthony Prima Priory (Monmouths.). Amidst charges of eye-plucking and murder, Wellington, Potter and Bolt (next two entries) were signified for arrest, 11 Nov. 1373. Papal mandate to reconcile Wellington, 5 March 1391.[415]

    John Potter.

    Robert Bolt.

---

[406] C81/1789/25; *CPR, 1358–61*, p. 410.
[407] *CPP* 1. 469–60.   [408] C81/1789/26.
[409] *Reg. Wykeham, Winchester* 2. 19–21.
[410] *CPL* 4. 69.   [411] Ibid., 4. 80.
[412] Ibid., 4. 81.   [413] Ibid., 4. 83.
[414] Ibid., 4. 10. They must have formed a substantial part of this small house.
[415] C81/1789/19; *CPL* 4. 223, 355. A canon named John Wellington appears as prior in 1397 (C81/1789/20).

Peter Emperour. Plympton Priory (Devon). Signified for arrest, 27 May 1374.[416]

Richard de Foston. Rocester Priory (Staffs.). Signified for arrest, 29 July 1375; two writs were issued (4 Aug. and 13 Oct. 1375).[417]

William Cary. Sometime prior of Horsley Priory (Glos.), a cell of Bruton Priory (Somerset). Absent a long time and excommunicate, he was signified for arrest, 16 April 1376; writ issued 22 April.[418]

Robert Chamberlayne. Merton Priory (Surrey). Signified for arrest with next three entries, 20 Nov. 1376.[419]

> **Thomas Scotte**.
> **Clement Tullesworth**.
> **John Warde**.

John Mentmore (Myntemoor) de Trumpington. Anglesey Priory (Cambs.). Brought before bishop of Ely, Jan. 1377.[420]

John Wallingford. Sometime prior. St Frideswide's Priory (Oxford). Signified for arrest in dispute over priorship, 16 Oct. 1377 and, with next three entries, 14 July 1378 (writ issued 15 July 1378).[421]

> **John Ryal**.
> **Richard Montagu**.
> **Richard Brackley alias Banning**. Also signified 10 Dec. 1392.[422]

Simon de Hecham. Walsingham Priory (Norf.). Signified for arrest, 20 March 1381.[423]

John Watford. St Bartholomew's Priory (London). Writ to seize from him (in prison) papal bulls which he had introduced into England, 22 April 1383; they were not found; writ to arrest, 20 June 1383.[424]

---

[416] C81/1789/53.

[417] C81/1789/54; *CPR, 1374–77*, pp. 159–60, 219. Foston reappeared in the turmoil at Rocester in the mid-1380s as a member of the party opposing the prior (*CPR, 1381–85*, p. 597; *CPR, 1385–90*, pp. 83, 597). For a summary see *VCH, Staffs*. 3. 250.

[418] *Reg. Wakefield, Worcester*, nos. 41–2; C81/1789/5; *CPR, 1374–77*, p. 320. He had probably not returned to Bruton, when recalled from Horsley.

[419] C81/1789/35.

[420] *VCH, Cambs*. 2. 232.

[421] C81/1789/49 and 50, where Ryal, Montagu and Brackley are also named as in the ensuing writ (*CPR, 1377–81*, p. 304). For the turmoil at St Frideswide's at this time see R. L. Storey, 'Papal Provision to English Monasteries', *Nottingham Medieval Studies* 35 (1991) 81–2.

[422] C81/1789/51.   [423] C81/1789/62.

[424] C202/C/81/27 (*iam remotum sed sine concordantia*); *CCR, 1381–85*, pp. 279–80.

Roger Tyshurst. Combwell Priory (Kent). Left with goods of the priory, 6 Aug. 1387. Stripped of office upon return.[425]

John Oundell. Newnham Priory (Beds.). Returned to his priory by order of bishop of Lincoln, 15 April 1388.[426]

John de Coventry. Kenilworth Priory (Warwicks.). Left with goods and chattels of house and £10 belonging to a non-religious resident. Received royal pardon, 1 May 1389.[427]

John Stury. St Osyth Abbey (Essex). Signified for arrest, 31 May 1391; writ issued 10 June.[428]

Richard Ellesmere. Haughmond Abbey (Salop). Went to Rome in matter of disputed election, there abandoned his habit, dressed as a secular priest, and now was to be reconciled, 19 April 1392.[429]

John Bolt. Ivychurch Priory (Wilts.). Found at bishop's visitation acting as chaplain of Fonthill Gifford (Wilts.), 1 April 1394.[430]

Thomas Forncett (Fornesete). Walsingham Priory (Norf.). Papal mandate to reconcile, 1395; difficulties encountered in being reconciled, 1398; signified for arrest, 4 June 1414.[431]

Adam de Worstead. Sometime prior. Thetford Priory (Norf.). Signified for arrest, 20 Jan. 1395.[432]

Henry Dawenyld. St Botolph's Abbey (Colchester, Essex). Signified for arrest, 29 Nov. 1395.[433]

William Thurgrym. Llanthony Prima Priory (Monmouths.). Claiming enormity of his sin, he received permission to go to Rome for absolution, 1395, but failed to return and was signified for arrest, 8 Nov. 1397.[434]

John Andrew alias Bozard. Christchurch Priory (Hants.). Royal assent to election as prior, 25 Oct. 1397. Signified for arrest, 9 May 1399. Part of rebellion at priory, 1402; imprisoned, but fled again. Papal mandate to reconcile, 7 March 1413.[435]

---

[425] *VCH, Kent* 2. 160.
[426] Lincs. Archives Office, Episc. Reg. XII, fo. 350.
[427] SC8/251/12547; *CPR, 1388–92*, p. 34.
[428] C81/1789/55; *CPR, 1388–92*, p. 444.
[429] *CPL* 4. 422–3.
[430] T. C. B. Timmins, ed., *The Register of John Waltham, Bishop of Salisbury, 1388–1395* (Canterbury and York Soc., 80, 1994), no. 1066.
[431] *CPL* 4. 502; 5. 157–8; C81/1789/63. See above, pp. 129–30.
[432] C81/1789/60; elected in 1378 (*VCH, Norf.* 2. 393).
[433] C81/1789/7.
[434] C81/1789/20.
[435] C81/1789/6; *CPR, 1396–99*, p. 221. See below, n. 436; also, *CPL* 6. 381.

1401–50

Roger Milton. Christchurch (Hants.). Ringleader of rebellion in association with Andrew (previous entry) and next four entries, 1402.[436]

John Portland.

John Wimborne.

Thomas Snoke.

Thomas Corfe.

Nicholas Newtimber. Shulbred Priory (Sussex). Reported absent for many years at time of election of prior as was next entry, 19 Nov. 1404.[437]

John Dene.

Name of canon and priory illegible. Signified for arrest, 8 May 1413.[438]

John More. St Bartholomew's Priory (London). Signified for arrest with next six entries, 17 Dec. 1420.[439]

John Sutton.

John Halle.

John Richard.

John Pomfret.

John Venise.

John Elys.

Reginald Colyere. Later prior. St Bartholomew's Priory (London). Signified for arrest, 22 Nov. 1423; papal mandate to reconcile, 10 Nov. 1424.[440]

John Clone. Subprior. Wigmore Abbey (Herefs.). Reported to visitors, 23 Feb. 1425, that he had fled for his life after being threatened by fellow canon.[441]

John More. Wigmore Abbey (Herefs.). Reported absent at visitation, 23 Feb. 1425, not clearly an apostate.[442]

John Aymestrey. Wigmore Abbey (Herefs.). Reported to visitors to be apostate, 23 Feb. 1425.[443]

---

[436] *Reg. Wykeham, Winchester* 2. 533–35; *VCH, Hants.* 2. 157–8. Also, see above, pp. 80–1.

[437] *Reg. Rede, Chichester* 2. 213.

[438] C81/1789/68 (a fragment).

[439] C81/1789/29.

[440] C81/1789/30; *CPL* 7. 375. About Colyere as prior (1436–71) see E. A. Webb, *The Records of St Bartholomew's Priory and of the Church and Parish of St Bartholomew the Great* (2 vols.; Oxford, 1921) 1. 211–19.

[441] *Reg. Spofford, Hereford*, pp. 69–70.

[442] Ibid., p. 67.   [443] Ibid., pp. 65, 67.

Richard Yurll (Yerll). Launceston Priory (Cornwall). Opposed election of William Shyre, left to have it annulled and was said by the prior to have gone to parts unknown, 1431. Signified for arrest 20 Feb. 1433.[444]

Thomas Goldyngstone (Goldington?). Caldwell Priory (Beds.). Bishop's order for reluctant community to readmit, 1432.[445]

John Beverley. Dunstable Priory (Beds.). Visitor required prior to search him out, 1432.[446]

Unnamed prior. Huntingdon Priory (Hunts.). Charge by visitor of having gone out by night in secular garb 'in apostasy', 1439.[447]

John Overton. Huntingdon Priory (Hunts.). Charged by visitor as a companion of the prior (previous entry), 1439.[448]

Thomas Wytham. Bourne Abbey (Lincs.). Apostasized while in London on abbey business; later seen at Warwick, now at Stamford, 1440.[449]

William Elkington. Wellow Abbey (Lincs.). Recidivist. Visitor's mandate to seek him out, 1440.[450]

John Payne. Woodspring Priory (Somerset). Signified for arrest, 26 May 1440.[451]

John Pawle. Bruton Priory (Somerset). No voice in election of prior because of apostasy, 10 Oct. 1440.[452]

John Lamyet (Lamyatt). As preceding.

Thomas Henreth. Dorchester Abbey (Oxford). Departed in apostasy during visitation as did next entry, 1441.[453]

  Nicholas Plymouth.

John Dalton. Launde Priory (Leics.). Visitor's order to readmit, 1442.[454]

John Horwood. Guisborough Priory (Yorks. NR). Apostate three years; papal mandate to reconcile and dispensation to live as secular priest, 3 March 1446.[455]

Thomas Lek. Kyme Priory (Lincs.). In his youth he had left, allegedly in apostasy, joined the Dominicans and forty years later

---

[444] Salter, *Chapters*, no. 85; C81/1789/21.
[445] *Linc. Vis.* 1. 29.   [446] Ibid., 1. 47.
[447] *Linc. Vis.* 2. 154. It was said that, while out, he broke his arm in a fight.
[448] Ibid.
[449] *Linc. Vis.* 2. 37–8. See above, p. 114.
[450] Ibid., 2. 391, 393–4.   [451] C81/1789/67.
[452] *Reg. Beckington, Bath and Wells* 2. no. 1640.
[453] *Linc. Vis.* 2. 71.
[454] Ibid., 2. 183.   [455] *CPL* 9. 527.

returned to Kyme, but was given the last place in choir and had no voice in chapter. Appeared personally at General Chapter and supplicated full restoration, which was granted, 26 June 1446.[456]

Two unnamed canons. Blackmore Priory (Essex). Reported apostate to General Chapter, 26 June 1446.[457]

Three unnamed canons. Huntingdon Priory (Hunts.). Reported apostate to General Chapter, 26 June 1446.[458]

Thomas Bledlow. Dunstable Priory (Beds.). Notorious murderer and adulterer, who thrice apostasized (once for twenty years, once for half a year, once for more than a year). Returned, aged eighty, because of poverty; not in chains owing to age. General Chapter ordered that he be moved to St Osyth Abbey (Essex), 26 June 1446.[459]

John Spencer. Studley Priory (Warwicks.). Used common seal to extort 640 marks for his friends, sealed 7 other charters, apostasized, taking with him many precious jewels. Decided by General Chapter that he should remain imprisoned at St Augustine's Abbey, Bristol, 26 June, 1446.[460]

Thomas Ewelme. Notley Abbey (Bucks.). Serving the church of Dorton, put off religious habit, 1447.[461]

1451–1500

William Mullyng. Bodmin Priory (Cornwall). Imprisoned in monastery for various crimes, he escaped and later repented. Bishop's order to reconcile, 12 Oct. 1451.[462]

Thomas Wagner. Southwark Priory (Surrey). Signified for arrest, 28 Nov. 1455.[463]

John Lovekok. Keynsham Abbey (Somerset). Publicly cited with next four entries but absent from abbot's election, probably apostate, 6 Feb. 1456.[464]

  Nicholas Poye.

  John Kington.

  Richard Marchall.

  William Chew.

[456] Salter, *Chapters*, no. 53 (pp. 110–11).
[457] Ibid., p. 112.   [458] Ibid., p. 114.
[459] Ibid.   [460] Salter, *Chapters*, no. 53 (pp. 114–15).
[461] *Linc. Vis.* 2. 257. See above, p. 79.
[462] *Reg. Lacy, Exeter* 3. 129–30.
[463] C81/1789/56.
[464] *Reg. Beckington, Bath and Wells* 2. no. 1643.

Thomas Sutton. Sometime abbot. Victorine. St Augustine's Abbey (Bristol). Signified for arrest in dispute over abbotship, 29 Nov. 1456.[465]

Richard Mylyent (Mill End?). Little Dunmow Priory (Essex). Signified for arrest, 30 March 1458.[466]

William Ty. Newark Priory (Surrey). Signified for arrest, 12 May 1463.[467]

Thomas Batys. Michelham Priory (Sussex). Signified for arrest, 12 Oct. 1464.[468]

Henry Missenden. Sometime abbot. Missenden Abbey (Bucks.). Signified for arrest in dispute over abbotship, 1 June 1468.[469]

Robert Risborough alias Huberd. Sometime abbot. Missenden Abbey (Bucks.). In dispute over abbotship, writ for capture to appear before king and council, 23 July 1471, and signification for arrest, 8 April 1472.[470]

Thomas Teel alias Risborough. Missenden Abbey (Bucks.). Signified for arrest, 8 April 1472 with preceding entry, and 5 July 1473 with next two entries.[471]

    Thomas Dicheyate (Ditcheat).

    William Samon (Salmon).

Robert Pudsey. St Bartholomew's Priory (London). Signified for arrest with next two entries, 26 May 1472, and writs issued to sheriffs of London, Middlesex, Essex, Herts., Surrey and Sussex.[472]

    Nicholas Southcott.

    John Logger.

John Burton. Arbury Priory (Warwicks.). Reported in 1496 as having been apostate for 24 years (= 1472).[473]

Unnamed canon. Michelham Priory (Sussex). Apostate at time of visitation, 1478.[474]

Thomas Pittlecock. Buckenham Priory (Norf.). Although dispensed to live as a secular priest, incurred 'note of apostasy' by wearing garb of secular priest over his habit at Westgate (Kent), which he had held for twenty years; papal mandate to reconcile,

---

[465] C81/1786/7. See *CPL* 11. 132–33.   [466] C81/1789/9.

[467] C81/1789/13.   [468] C81/1789/37.

[469] C81/1789/40, where he was signified by Robert Risborough, calling himself abbot. In 1471 and 1472, Missenden, calling himself abbot, signified Robert Risborough (see next entry).

[470] *CPR, 1467–77*, p. 288; C81/1789/41.

[471] C81/1789/41, 42.   [472] C81/1789/31 and dorse.

[473] *Blythe's Vis.*, p. 168   [474] *VCH, Sussex* 2. 79.

9 Nov. 1478, and papal dispensation to wear secular priest's garb over his habit, 26 Nov.[475]

John Thomas. Bodmin Priory (Cornwall). Signified for arrest, 2 Nov. 1479.[476]

Walter Bent. Launceston Priory (Cornwall). Reportedly left in 1490; archbishop ordered search for him, 21 May 1492.[477]

John Jamys. Plympton Priory (Devon). Absent in apostasy at archbishop's visitation, 13 July 1492.[478]

Henry Tancrett. Plympton Priory (Devon). Reported to visitor as wandering on borders of Wales in apostasy, 17 July 1492.[479]

Thomas Taverner. Beeston Priory (Norf.). Reported to visitor as absent without permission, 1494, and, again in 1514, when he was said to be celebrating Mass in Norwich.[480]

John Denton. Guisborough Priory (Yorks. NR). Signified for arrest, 12 June 1498.[481]

1501–30

John Mathewe. St Sepulchre Priory (Warwick). Signified for arrest, 29 Sept. 1503 and 10 April 1509.[482]

Thomas Starky. Tonbridge Priory (Kent). Signified for arrest, 4 Nov. 1503.[483]

John Hall. Breamore Priory (Hants.). Signified for arrest, 8 May 1504.[484]

Thomas Wayne. St Thomas by Stafford Priory. Signified for arrest, 8 Feb. 1508.[485]

Thomas Langham. Launde Priory (Leics.). Signified for arrest with next entry, 7 Feb. 1512.[486]

　William Weston.

John Howper. Wormsley Priory (Herefs.). Reported to be in Wales, saying Mass, 8 June 1513.[487]

William Brigges. Thetford Priory (Norf.). Reported to visitor as apostate and living in Snoring (Norf.), 1514.[488]

---

[475] *CPL* 13. 2. 640, 641.　　[476] C81/1789/1.

[477] *Reg. Morton, Canterbury* 2. 286.　　[478] Ibid., 2. 291.

[479] Ibid., 2. 293.　　[480] *Vis. Norwich*, pp. 55, 124.

[481] C81/1789/14.　　[482] C81/1789/64, 65.

[483] C81/1789/61.　　[484] C81/1789/2.

[485] C81/1789/58.　　[486] C81/1789/22.

[487] *Reg. Mayew, Hereford*, pp. 174–5.

[488] *Vis. Norwich*, p. 88.

John Berdon. Coxford Priory (Norf.). Reported to visitor for fleeing three or four times; now imprisoned, 1514.[489]

William Furton. Woodbridge Priory (Suff.). Reported apostate at visitation, 1514.[490]

Richard Germayne. Taunton Priory (Somerset). Signified for arrest with next entry, 8 May 1515.[491]

  Robert Rakysworthy.

William Panell. Cartmel Priory (Lancs.). Report to General Chapter about his readmission, 1518.[492]

J. Borell. Hexham Priory (Northumberland). General Chapter ordered renunciation of annuity and either imprisonment or transfer for a year to Thornton Abbey (Lincs.), 1518.[493]

Richard Sheffield. Maxstoke Priory (Warwicks.). Reported apostate at visitation, 1518.[494]

Thomas Dagull. Arbury Priory (Warwicks.). Report of his return and punishment given to visitor, 1518.[495]

John Bradshaw. As preceding, but prior later sent servants out to capture him in 1525.[496]

____ Bakewell. Ulverscroft Priory (Leics.). Reported apostate at visitation, 7 May 1518.[497]

Henry Selwode. Shulbred Priory (Sussex). Reported apostate at episcopal visitation, 1524.[498]

Richard Titchfield. Southwark Priory (Surrey). Signified for arrest, 5 Feb. 1526.[499]

Thomas Augustyn. Merton Priory (Surrey). Signified for arrest, 7 Feb. 1526.[500]

UNDATED

Henry de Elsworth. St James Abbey (Northampton). Signified for arrest, early 14th century.[501]

John Blake. Conversus. St Bartholomew's Priory (London). Signified for arrest, 14th century.[502]

---

[489] Ibid., pp. 111–12.
[490] Ibid., p. 135 [491] C81/1789/59.
[492] Salter, *Chapters*, p. 140.
[493] Ibid. He may have been an *eiectus* who became assimilated to *apostata*.
[494] *Blythe's Vis.*, p. 12. [495] Ibid., p. 18.
[496] Ibid. and pp. 161–5. [497] *Vis. Dioc. Linc.* 3. 116.
[498] Chichester, West Sussex Record Office, Sherborne II, Ep.1/1/4, fo. 93.
[499] C81/1789/57. [500] C81/1789/36.
[501] C81/1789/46. [502] C81/1789/27.

Robert Tebbe. Repton Priory (Derby.). Went apostate temp. Edward III.[503]

Adam Orwell. St Bartholomew's Priory (London). Signified for arrest, temp. Henry VI.[504]

9. Premonstratensian canons

1251–1300

Roger de Wendlebury (Wendlingboro). Sulby Abbey (Northants.). Signified for arrest, 28 June 1273.[505]

Edmund Zouch. Dale Abbey (Derby.). Left during the abbotship of Abbot Lawrence, 1273–89.[506]

1301–50

William de Sandwich. St Radegund's Abbey (Kent). Signified for arrest, 6 May 1305.[507]

John de Sandwich. Bayham Abbey (Sussex). Signified for arrest, c. 1310.[508]

Thomas de Farndon. Conversus. Newbo Abbey (Lincs.). Signified for arrest, 28 April 1314.[509]

Cuthbert de Durham. Blanchland Abbey (Northumberland). Signified for arrest, 20 Sept. 1314.[510]

John de Stafford. Easby Abbey (Yorks. NR). Signified for arrest with next entry, 11 Sept. 1318.[511]

   Nigel de Irby.

William de Canterbury. Langdon Abbey (Kent). Signified for arrest, 5 Aug. 1324.[512]

Ralph de West Dereham. West Dereham Abbey (Norf.). Signified for arrest with next entry, 1 Feb. 1328.[513]

   Edmund de Lynn.

Robert de Cambridge. Hagnaby Abbey (Lincs.). Papal mandate to reconcile, 20 Feb. 1346.[514]

---

[503] *VCH, Derby*. 2. 61.
[504] C81/1789/28. [505] C81/1790/16.
[506] *VCH, Derby*. 2. 72.
[507] C81/1790/12. [508] C81/1790/2.
[509] C81/1790/8. [510] C81/1790/1.
[511] C81/1790/10. [512] C81/1790/7.
[513] C81/1790/3. [514] *CPL* 3. 231.

1351–1400

John de York. Coverham Abbey (Yorks. NR). Papal mandate to reconcile for Jubilee pilgrimage to Rome, 1 May 1351.[515]

William de Blanquet. Welbeck Abbey (Notts.). Papal mandate to reconcile, 21 March 1355.[516]

Thomas de Kyrketon. Coverham Abbey (Yorks. NR). Papal mandate to reconcile, 10 Jan. 1370.[517]

William Holt. Sometime abbot. West Dereham Abbey (Norf.). Signified for arrest, 21 Feb 1387; writ issued 5 March.[518]

John Strete. Later abbot. St Radegund's Abbey (Kent). Signified for arrest, 20 Oct. 1388.[519]

John de Kirketon. Newbo Abbey (Lincs.). Signified for arrest, 1 Nov. 1392.[520]

1401–50

Simon de Castelton. Welbeck Abbey (Notts.). Made honorary papal chaplain, 13 Dec. 1393; signified for arrest, 1401, 1402; writ of 24 Jan. 1402 enrolled.[521]

John Sumaynster(?). Torre Abbey (Devon). Signified for arrest, 26 March 1416.[522]

Thomas Tilney. West Dereham Abbey (Norf.). Signified for arrest, 15 July 1433.[523]

Walter Meone. Durford Abbey (Sussex). Entered at the age of 11, left in deacon's orders, returned, ordained priest, left again, and now was papally reconciled and received dispensation to live as secular priest, 27 April 1439.[524]

1451–1500

Peter Lynn. West Dereham Abbey (Norf.). Fled *c.* 1451 on basis of fictitious dispensation, repented 1491.[525]

---

[515] Ibid., 3. 386.
[516] Ibid., 3. 564.   [517] Ibid., 4. 82.
[518] C81/1790/4; *CPR, 1385–89*, p. 321. He had become abbot 6 April 1368 and was still abbot apparently in 1378 (see *VCH, Norf.* 2. 416; H. M. Colvin, *White Canons in England* (Oxford, 1951), p. 421).
[519] C81/1790/13. See *VCH, Kent* 2. 174.
[520] C81/1790/9. He had been a monk there as early as 1377 (A. K. McHardy, ed., *Clerical Poll-Taxes of the Diocese of Lincoln, 1377–1381* (Lincoln Record Soc., 81, 1992), no. 763).
[521] *CPL* 4. 287; C81/1790/18, 19; *CPR, 1401–05*, p. 68.
[522] C81/1790/17.   [523] C81/1790/5.
[524] *CPL* 9. 65.   [525] *CAP* 4. 219.

Thomas Haysand. Blanchland Abbey (Northumberland). Sent to Welbeck Abbey for ten years as punishment, 1460, but two months later was allowed to return.[526]

John Downham. Abbot. Beauchief Abbey (Derby.). Fled in 1462 with next seven entries rather than answer an inquiry and was thus deposed, 27 Feb. 1462. Six of the seven (Boland excepted) submitted, 29 May 1462. Downham, together with canons Boland and John Mundevile, otherwise unknown (listed below), and 17 laymen, subject to writ for arrest, 1 July 1463.[527]

    William Brotherton.

    Robert Skipton. Later subprior (1475), prior (1488).[528]

    Robert Baxby. Apostate also in 1475.[529]

    John Corbrig.

    Robert Boland (Bowland). Apostate also in 1475.[530]

    John Pomfret.

    John Ashton.

    John Mundevile.

Thomas Watsone. St Radegund's Abbey (Kent). Signified for arrest, 8 July 1464.[531]

John Ryng. Durford Abbey (Sussex). Signified for arrest as excommunicate, 6 June 1466.[532]

John Newington. Later abbot. St Radegund's Abbey (Kent). Signified for arrest, 20 Dec. 1473.[533]

Robert Alnmouth. Alnwick Abbey (Northumberland). Listed as apostate at visitation, 13 April 1475.[534]

John Norton. Beauchief Abbey (Derby.). Listed with Robert Boland and Robert Baxby (above) as apostate at visitation, 27 May 1475.[535]

John Falcle. Bayham Abbey (Sussex). Listed with next entry as apostate at visitation, 6 June 1475.[536]

    John Marston.

---

[526] Ibid., 2. 90–3.
[527] Ibid., 2. xiv, 49–50, 52–3; *CPR, 1461–67*, p. 280. See Colvin, *White Canons*, pp. 253–5; *VCH, Derby*. 2. 66. He apparently retired to Wymeswold, Leics. (Colvin, p. 255).
[528] *CAP* 2. 58, 64. He probably died between 1488 and 1491, since he is not listed among the canons in 1491.
[529] Ibid., 2. 58. [530] Ibid.
[531] C81/1790/14. [532] C81/1790/6.
[533] C81/1790/15; abbot in the 1490s (*VCH, Kent* 2. 175).
[534] *CAP* 2. 17, but he was listed among the community in 1482 (p. 20).
[535] Ibid., 2. 57–8. Both Boland and Norton were listed as absent – not necessarily apostate – at the visitation in 1478 and as absent at parishes in 1482 (pp. 59, 61–2).
[536] Ibid., 2. 73.

William Hedstede. St Radegund's Abbey (Kent). Listed as apostate at visitation, 6 June 1475.[537]

Richard Bigod. Torre Abbey (Devon). Accused of apostasy, which he did not deny, and, as a penalty, was to be sent in exile to Welbeck Abbey, but visitor relented, when intercessions were made, 1 Aug. 1478.[538]

John Sandours. Halesowen Abbey (Worcs.). Confessed to apostasy at visitation, 21 May 1478.[539]

Thomas Tattershall. Newsham (or Newhouse) Abbey (Lincs.). With next four entries accused of apostasy at visitation, but all purged selves, 3 June 1478.[540]

> **Thomas Hull**.
>
> **John Hull**.
>
> **Gilbert Egleston**. By 1488 he was prior.[541]
>
> **Thomas Ulsceby (Ulceby, Usceby)**. Also, excommunicated by visitor, 25 July 1482 and 18 Aug. 1491. He was *circator* in 1488.[542]

Thomas Barrowby. Tupholme Abbey (Lincs.). Excommunicated by visitor, 12 June 1478.[543]

Thomas Sall alias Caster. Langley Abbey (Norf.). He and next entry unable to purge themselves of apostasy; penalty imposed by visitor, 3 July 1478.[544]

> **Reginald Beverley**.

Walter Speyer. Torre Abbey (Devon). Confessed to apostasy at visitation and exiled to Newsham (or Newhouse) Abbey (Lincs.), 1 Aug. 1478.[545]

Thomas Bromsgrove. Halesowen Abbey (Worcs.). Penitent at visitation; reconciled, *c.* 1480.[546]

William Bradford. Welbeck Abbey (Notts.). With next entry found guilty of apostasy, incontinence and rebellion against the abbot, at visitation in 1482.[547]

> **Christopher Hessyl**.[548]

---

[537] Ibid., 3. 96. [538] Ibid.

[539] *CAP* 3. 241–2. [540] Ibid., 3. 68–69.

[541] See also ibid., 3. 78.

[542] See also ibid., 3. 76, 80–1, 88. The *circator*'s job was to ensure observance of the enclosure. *Quis custodiet ipsos custodes?*

[543] Ibid., 3. 158. [544] Ibid., 3. 16.

[545] Ibid., 3. 143. [546] Ibid., 3. 244–5.

[547] Ibid., 3. 185.

[548] Cellarer in 1494, 1497, 1500 (ibid., 3. 193, 195).

John Nym. Easby Abbey (Yorks. NR). Listed as apostate at visitation, 18 April 1482.[549]

John York. Dale Abbey (Derby.). Penitent and reconciled at visitation, 16 July 1482.[550]

Thomas Ledley. Tupholme Abbey (Lincs.) Restored by visitor, 30 July 1482.[551]

Three unnamed canons. Bayham Abbey (Sussex). Excommunicated by visitor, 3 Sept. 1482.[552]

William Gloucester. Titchfield Abbey (Hants.). Reported to visitor that he had gone out 'in apostasiam' by night to drink, 9 Sept. 1482.[553]

John Newton. St Radegund's Abbey (Kent). Described as 'seminator discordie'; excommunicated by visitor, 14 July 1488.[554]

John Barton. Cockersand Abbey (Lancs.). With next entry declared excommunicate at visitation, 28 April 1489.[555]

   John Presaw.

Thomas Haltone. Barlings Abbey (Lincs.). With next entry declared excommunicate at visitation, 1491.[556]

   Thomas Andrew.

Edward Seyton. Sulby Abbey (Northants.). Found guilty of rebellion and apostasy at Welbeck Abbey (Notts.), to which he had been exiled; now to be sent to St Agatha's, Easby (Yorks. NR), 14 Aug. 1491. Visitor permitted him to study at Oxford at the expense of his friends, 30 April 1492.[557]

William Hankyn. Welbeck Abbey (Notts.). Penalty imposed at visitation, 14 Aug. 1491.[558]

James Grimsby. Newsham or (Newhouse) Abbey (Lincs.). Excommunicated by visitor for apostasy with a canoness of Orford (Lincs.), 18 Aug. 1491.[559]

William Coventry. Croxton Abbey (Leics.). Reported apostate at visitation, 12 Sept. 1491.[560]

Robert Grantham. Croxton Abbey (Leics.). Absolved of apostasy at visitation, 12 Sept. 1491.[561]

---

[549] Ibid., 2. 5–6.   [550] Ibid., 2. 175.

[551] Ibid, 3. 159.   [552] Ibid., 2. 73–4.

[553] Ibid., 3. 128.   [554] Ibid., 3. 99.

[555] Ibid, 2. 116.   [556] Ibid. 2. 36–7.

[557] Ibid., 1. 171; 3. 189, but not in *BRUO*.   [558] Ibid., 3. 189–90.

[559] Ibid., 3. 80–1. He was listed as a novice 31 May 1488 (p. 79) and, later, as a member of the community in 1494, 1497, 1500 and 1503 (pp. 84–6).

[560] Ibid., 3. 160; Colvin, *White Canons*, p. 391.

[561] *CAP* 2. 159; 3. 160; Colvin, p. 391.

Robert Bredon. Sulby Abbey (Northants.). Penance imposed at visitation for introducing women into dormitory and for apostasy, but penance suspended, 15 Sept. 1491. Found guilty of apostasy at next visitation, 1494, and exiled for ten years to St Agatha's, Easby (Yorks. NR), but, in 1495, provincial chapter assigned him to Dale Abbey (Derby.), and in 1500 appeared as chaplain of Ockbrook near Derby.[562]

Edmund Scarning. Wendling Abbey (Norfolk). Reported apostate at visitation, 24 Sept. 1491.[563]

Robert Derham. Langley Abbey (Norf.). Absolved from apostasy at visitation and restored to place in monastery, 28 Sept. 1491.[564]

Robert Wolfet. Beauchief Abbey (Yorks. WR). Penalty suspended in hope of amendment, 25 May 1494.[565]

Edward Colynsone. Welbeck Abbey (Notts.). Excommunicated by visitor, 29 May 1494. Appeared before visitor at Torre Abbey (Devon), where he begged mercy, 12 June 1494, and was sent back to Welbeck. Reprimanded for enormous size of his tonsure, 3 Sept. 1497, and for his lifestyle, 22 Nov. 1500.[566]

Thomas Prestone. Bayham Abbey (Sussex). Suspended and excommunicated for apostasy, 25 June 1494.[567]

Thomas Studley. Bayham Abbey (Sussex). Listed as apostate at visitation, 25 June 1494; also, at visitations of 17 Oct. 1497 and 29 Sept. 1500.[568]

Richard Beltone alias Nutsey. St Radegund's Abbey (Kent). Found by visitor to have left without permission, but claimed permission from abbot of Langdon; penalty suspended, 28 June 1494. At provincial council, held before 23 Sept. 1495, he was called a perjurer and apostate and was excomunicated.[569]

Thomas Wedatt. Langdon Abbey (Kent). Listed as an apostate at visitation, 30 June 1494.[570]

Thomas Wakare. Egglestone Abbey (Yorks. NR). Excommunicated as an apostate at visitation, 20 April 1497.[571]

Robert Huchonson. Blanchland Abbey (Northumberland). Excommunicated at visitation, 24 April 1497.[572]

---

[562] Knowles, *RO* 3. 47–8. [563] *CAP* 3. 205.
[564] Ibid., 3. 24. [565] Ibid., 2. 66–7.
[566] Ibid., 3. 152, 192, 194–5. [567] Ibid., 3. 78–9.
[568] Ibid., 3. 79–80. [569] Ibid., 1. 172–3; 3. 101–2.
[570] Ibid., 3. 9. He was listed as a novice on 12 July 1488 (p. 5).
[571] Ibid., 2. 218. [572] Ibid., 2. 101, 103.

Roger Walsall. Halesowen Abbey (Worcs.). For many offences, including apostasy, exiled by visitor for ten years to Croxton Abbey (Leics.), 30 Aug. 1497.[573]

Robert Benet. Langdon Abbey (Kent). Listed as apostate at visitation, 11 Oct. 1497.[574]

Thomas Rubby. Titchfield Abbey (Hants.). Listed as apostate at visitation, 24 Oct. 1497.[575]

William Darntone. Beauchief Abbey (Yorks. WR). Excommunicated by visitor, 12 May 1500.[576]

Thomas Marsch. Leiston Abbey (Suff.). Called apostate for going outside monastic precincts; penalty suspended by visitor, 14 Oct. 1500.[577]

1501–30

William Curlew. Sometime abbot. Langley Abbey (Norf.). Request for writ *de excommunicato capiendo*, 4 Jan. 1509.[578]

UNDATED

Edmund Pouche. Conversus. Dale Abbey (Derby.). Letter seeking his reconciliation, post 1289.[579]

Thomas Todde. St Agatha's, Easby (Yorks. NR). Signified for arrest, temp. 15th century.[580]

10. Gilbertine canons (Order of Sempringham)

1251–1300

Richard Kirkby. York Priory. With next entry denounced as apostate, 22 Aug. 1280, at request of prior.[581]

   Alan de Thorpe.

Adam de Carlton. Lay brother. St Catherine's Hospital (Lincoln). Writ for delivery of him and next entry from prison to hospital, 1 May 1281.[582]

   William de Hykeham.

---

[573] Ibid., 2. 258–9.   [574] Ibid., 3. 9.

[575] Ibid., 3. 134.   [576] Ibid., 2. 69–70.

[577] Ibid., 3. 55. He was listed as a novice both in 1491 and in 1494 (p. 52).

[578] C85/207/2. See Knowles, *RO* 3. 43, where his earlier, checkered career is traced. He resigned or was deposed as abbot, *c.* 1509 (Colvin, *White Canons*, p. 409).

[579] *CAP* 2. 165–6; Colvin, p. 390.   [580] C81/1790/11.

[581] *Reg. Wickwane, York*, no. 97.   [582] *CPR, 1272–81*, p. 430.

H[enry] de Seyton. Ellerton Priory (Yorks. NR). Mandate to reconcile, 30 April 1286.[583]

Ralph de Richmond. Malton Priory (Yorks. NR). Left 21 Dec. 1286 and signified for arrest, 26 Dec. 1286.[584]

1301–50

John Coleman alias de Hoton. Watton Priory (Yorks. ER). Signified for arrest, 30 May and 7 Sept. 1316.[585]

1351–1400

John de Leverton. St Catherine's Priory (Lincoln). Signified for arrest, 22 Jan. 1356. A number of people were charged with having taken him (and goods and money) from Watton Priory, where he was being detained, 18 May 1356.[586]

John de Bynne. Lay brother. Watton Priory (Yorks. ER). Signified for arrest with next entry, 8 Feb. 1371; writ issued 23 Feb.[587]

    Robert Andreuson.

John de Sandesby. Ellerton Priory (Yorks. ER). Signified for arrest, 8 March 1372.[588]

Richard de Thorp alias Crosby. House unnamed. Signified for arrest, 23 Oct. 1380 and 8 Feb. 1390 (writ issued 26 Feb.).[589]

John de Whitby. House unnamed. Signified for arrest, 27 Feb. 1383 (writ issued 3 March) and 9 Oct. 1389 (writ issued 18 Oct.).[590]

1401–50

John Brigham. Malton Priory (Yorks. NR). He and next five entries were honorary papal chaplains, who put off religious habits; all six signified by Master of Sempringham for arrest, 7 Sept. 1402; writ issued, 4 Oct.[591]

    William Clotherholme. Malton Priory (Yorks. NR).

    Thomas Thurnyf. Malton Priory (Yorks. NR).

    John Barow. Watton Priory (Yorks. ER).

---

[583] *Reg. le Romeyn, York* 1. no. 531.
[584] C81/1791/1.   [585] C81/1791/8, 11.
[586] C81/1796/9; *CPR, 1354–58*, p. 402.
[587] C81/1791/12; *CPR, 1370–74*, p. 103.   [588] C81/1791/9.
[589] C81/1791/3, 6; *CPR, 1388–92*, p. 219.
[590] C81/1791/4, 5; *CPR, 1381–85*, p. 259; *CPR, 1388–92*, p. 142. The 1389 petition is printed in Hubert Hall, *A Formulary Book of English Official Historical Documents* (2 pts; Cambridge, 1908–9) 1. 87–8.
[591] C81/1791/7; *CPR, 1401–05*, p. 196. See above, p. 53.

William Pocklington. Ellerton Priory (Yorks. ER).
John de Rishyngton. Haverholme Priory (Lincs.).
John Rays (Rase). Malton Priory (Yorks. NR). Apostasized at the time of Scrope's insurrection; signified for arrest, 16 Feb. 1416.[592]

11. Bonshommes

Richard Cunelegh(?). Edington house (Wilts.). Signified for arrest, 12 Feb. 1407.[593]
Richard Standerwick. Edington house (Wilts.). Incurred apostasy by not wearing religious habit after being dispensed to live as secular priest; papal mandate to reconcile, 3 April 1477.[594]
Richard Erbyry. Edington house (Wilts.). Signified for arrest, 1515.[595]

12. Trinitarians

Robert S__kelde. Possibly Moatenden house (Kent). Signified for arrest, 29 Sept. 1315.[596]
Edmund de Pollesden. Sometime prior. Easton house (Wilts.). Departed, allegedly with embezzled revenues, and went to Hertford, *c.* 1360.[597]
John Harleston. Easton house (Wilts.). Bishop's order to denounce him and next entry, 1378.[598]
  John Salisbury.
Richard Lyming. Moatenden house (Kent). Unlawfully transferred to Boxley Abbey (Cistercian); papal mandate to reconcile, 8 Jan. 1400.[599]
Robert de York. Knaresborough house (Yorks. WR). Signified for arrest, 13 Feb. 1401.[600]
Robert Donington. Easton house (Wilts.). Recidivist, signified for arrest, 2 Aug. 1414.[601]
Thomas Bradford. Knaresborough house (Yorks. WR). Signified for arrest, 1 July 1418.[602]

[592] C81/1791/10.   [593] C81/1796/5.
[594] *CPL* 13. 1. 60.   [595] C81/1796/6.
[596] C81/1794/20.   [597] *VCH, Wilts.* 3. 325.
[598] Salisbury, Wilts. Record Office, Reg. Erghum, fo. 134.
[599] *CPL* 5. 276.   [600] C81/1794/21.
[601] C81/1796/7.   [602] C81/1794/22.

13. Dominican friars

1251–1300

_____ **Siward**. Berwick Priory (Scotland). Apostate by 15 Dec. 1240; royal writ to arrest, 18 March 1241.[603]

William de St John. Oxford Priory. Signified for arrest, 26 Feb. 1298.[604]

1301–50

William de Dunham. Cambridge Priory. Signified for arrest, 10 July 1302.[605]

Robert de Kenyton. House unnamed. Writ for arrest with next entry, 14 March 1303.[606]

Benedict de Offord.

Nicholas Sandekyn. Exeter Priory (Devon). Writ pardoning three priors of Exeter for concealing him, who had stolen money deposited there and who now was absent for long time, 11 Aug. 1305.[607]

William Bassete. House unnamed. Reportedly apostate and recently appointed subprior of the Cluniac priory of Monk Bretton (Yorks. WR); papal commission of inquiry appointed, 8 Nov. 1326. Sent by Archbishop Melton to Whitby Abbey, 20 Aug. 1331.[608]

Arnold Lym. Guildford Priory (Surrey). Papal mandate to reconcile, 6 June 1336.[609]

Robert de Gatesbury. Winchester Priory (Hants.). Signified for arrest with next two entries, 23 July 1337 or 1340.[610]

William Whitwell.

John de Norton.

John Grym. Lincoln Priory. Captured at Ipswich; protection given to his captor to return him to Lincoln, 24 June 1338.[611]

Walter de Sherborne. Formerly a Benedictine monk of Milton Abbey (Dorset) but transferred to Dominicans, from which he

---

[603] *CPR, 1232–47*, pp. 248, 262.
[604] C81/1792/1.   [605] C81/1792/2.
[606] *CPR, 1301–07*, p. 123; Prynne, p. 1014.
[607] *CPR, 1301–07*, p. 376; Prynne, p. 1110.
[608] CPL 2. 254. See *VCH, Yorks*. 3. 94.
[609] CPL 2. 530. Listed as an apostate Benedictine of Hyde Abbey in 1341 (above, p. 189). For this case see above, pp. 48–9.
[610] C81/1792/3.   [611] *CPR, 1338–40*, p. 99.

apostasized and now received bishop's mandate to return to Milton, 1344.[612]

1351–1400

Thomas Hopman. Dunwich Priory (Suff.). Writs for arrest of him and next entry issued, 10 Aug. and 12 Oct. 1355.[613]

William Jordon. Chelmsford Priory (Essex).

Hugh de Beauchamp. Derby Priory. Held at King's Langley Priory with next three entries; writ to return them to their own houses, 9 June 1356.[614]

John Lypering. Lincoln Priory.

John Pygaz. Chester Priory.

Nicholas Deneys. Oxford Priory.

Miguel de Polo. Aragonese province. Student at Oxford. Writ for arrest, 30 Jan. 1366.[615]

William Hurley. House unnamed. Signified for arrest, 1370.[616]

John Cheker alias Nicholas Corf. House unnamed. Signified for arrest, 5 Sept. 1373 and 14 March 1374; writ dated 10 Sept. 1373 enrolled.[617]

Robert Ragnell. Oxford Priory. Signified for arrest, 18 April 1387.[618]

Walter Durant. Dartford Priory (Kent). Already excommunicate for more than a year, when signified for arrest, 8 Nov. 1399.[619]

John Kettleby. Probably Oxford Priory. Writ to have him delivered from custody of Oxford Priory to prior provincial or prior of London Priory, 8 May 1400.[620]

---

[612] *VCH, Dorset* 2. 61.

[613] *CPR, 1354–58*, p. 298.   [614] Ibid., p. 444.

[615] *CPR, 1364–67*, p. 278. In 1368 Pope Urban V allowed him to take his master of theology examination at Barcelona rather than at Oxford. See Stephen L. Forte, 'Robert Pynk, O.P., Provincial of England (*c*. 1361–68)', *Archivum Fratrum Praedicatorum* 27 (1957) 407–8; *BRUO* 3. 1493.

[616] C81/1792/4.

[617] C81/1792/5, 6; *CPR, 1370–74*, p. 392. He had adopted the alias to conceal his identity.

[618] C81/1792/7. He may have been originally a member of the York priory (see A. B. Emden, *A Survey of Dominicans in England* (Rome, 1967), p. 431).

[619] C81/1792/8. He had been appointed one of the attorneys for the recluse Dominican nun of Dartford called Joan, 16 Feb. 1397 (*CPR, 1396–99*, p. 69).

[620] *CPR, 1396–99*, p. 311. See Emden, *Survey of Dominicans*, p. 399 for ordinations at Chester and Shrewsbury priories.

John Illey. Sudbury Priory. Signified for arrest, 10 Feb. 1421.[621]
Maurice Gregory. House unnamed. Entered as youth, remained 18 years; left to go to Tintern Abbey (Cistercian), where, unprofessed, he remained 8 years; papal mandate to reconcile, 3 Nov. 1438.[622]

Thomas Poworth. Thetford Priory. Signified for arrest with next entry, probably 1470s or 1480s.[623]
    Robert Galion.

14. Franciscan friars

Unless otherwise stated, the house to which the apostate friar belonged is unnamed in the sources.

Robert Trone. In 1284, after nine years as friar, he, perhaps falsely, claimed prior marriage and left. Signified for arrest, 8 Sept. 1285 and 14 March 1289.[624]
Thomas de Venables. Archbishop's mandate for denouncement in archdeaconries of Coventry, Stafford and Worcester, 6 Dec. 1284.[625]
John Russell. Signified for arrest, 12 Feb. 1287.[626]
William de Pershore. Had transferred from Benedictines, but left Franciscans to return to former order amidst Franciscan cries of 'apostasy', 1290.[627]
Thomas de Mar. Possibly of York Friary. Signified for arrest, 6 May 1294.[628]

---

[621] C81/1792/9. He had been assigned to the Cambridge Priory *c.* 1415 (*BRUC*, p. 326).
[622] *CPL* 9. 2.
[623] C81/1792/10. Is he the same friar as Thomas Powis (Poweys) of Cambridge Priory, who was ordained priest in 1474 (Emden, *Survey of English Dominicans*, p. 427)? For latter see *BRUC*, p. 459.
[624] C81/1792/11, 13; *Ann. mon.* 3. 314.
[625] *Epp. Jo. Peckham* 3. 861.
[626] C81/1792/12. He was perhaps from the West Country: the writs were to be sent to the sheriffs of Somerset, Dorset, Devon and Wilts.
[627] For details and references see above, p. 47.
[628] C81/1792/14.

1301–50

Arthur de Hartlepool. Richmond Friary (Yorks. NR). Fled, having stolen goods deposited there; arrested at Whitehaven (Cumberland); imprisoned nearby at Egremont; writ now to sheriff to deliver him to Richmond Friary (Yorks. NR), 29 Oct. 1304.[629]

John de Carbrook. Signified for arrest, 23 March 1310.[630]

Thomas de Corbridge. Shrewsbury Friary. He and next entry fled with books and other goods from Shrewsbury *studium*; bishop of Worcester ordered inquiry, March 1331.[631]

  Thomas de Harthill.

Ranulph. Heretic and apostate, put in prison by bishop of London, where he died, 1336.[632]

William de Bowes. Newcastle Friary (Northumberland). Bishop's mandate to denounce as excommunicate, 1342.[633]

1351–1400

Richard Pestel. Newcastle Friary (Northumberland). Murdered allegedly by guardian of house and others, probably 1356.[634]

John de Colney. Son of Richard atte More. Fled to Waltham to claim inheritance; attempted to contract marriage; signified for arrest, 27 Feb. and 24 March, 1358; writ issued 28 March 1358.[635]

William Howys. London Friary. Signified for arrest, 5 Feb. 1386; writ dated 3 Feb.[636]

John Dunning. Boston Friary. Arrested and imprisoned in London; petition for writ for his return to Boston, 21 Oct. 1391; writ issued 21 Oct.[637]

Robert Durham. London Friary. Apostate in 1393.[638]

---

[629] *CCR, 1302–07*, p. 174; Prynne, p. 1042.

[630] C81/1792/15.

[631] Information from Dr Michael Robson, OFM Conv.

[632] *Chronicles of Edward I and Edward II* (William Stubbs, ed.; RS; 2 vols.; 1882–3) 1. 365: he had proposed his teachings before masters of theology (religious and seculars) and before Bishop Gravesend. See H.G. Richardson, 'Heresy and the Lay Power under Richard II', *EHR* 51 (1936) 3.

[633] *Reg. Pal. Dunelm.* 3. 513–14.

[634] A pardon was issued (6 Feb. 1357) to the guardian, two other friars and a layman (*CPR, 1354–58*, p. 505).

[635] C81/1792/16, 17; *CPR, 1358–61*, p. 73.

[636] C81/1792/18; *CPR, 1385–89*, p. 169.

[637] C81/1792/19; *CPR, 1388–92*, p. 522.

[638] C. L. Kingsford, *The Grey Friars of London* (Aberdeen, 1915), p. 65.

Walter Tolny. London Friary. Signified for arrest with next three entries, 20 July 1398; writ issued 20 July.[639]
   Thomas Knyght.
   John Camel.
   John Minterne.[640]

1401–50

Robert Haunton. Friary in Coventry and Lichfield diocese. Obviously desirous of leaving his order, he became an honorary papal chaplain, 22 Aug. 1395, and secured dispensation to live as a secular priest, 3 June 1399, yet signified for arrest by prior of London house, 15 May 1403.[641]
Robert Harding. Writ for arrest of him and next two entries, 18 Sept. 1406.[642]
   Richard Bures.
   John Sarge.
Certain unnamed friars, wandering about and causing trouble in their order. Writ for arrest, 5 Aug. 1431.[643]

AFTER 1451

John Tynemouth alias Maynelyn. Doctor of theology. Claimed to have entered in his tenth year and that, when he was imprisoned by fellow friars, he fled and remained *vagans* for many years. Papal mandate to reconcile, 8 March 1491. Warden of Colchester Friary, 1493. Dispensed to live as secular priest, 30 April 1496. Transferred to Hospitallers of St John, where he made religious profession, by 1506. Became a bishop *in partibus infidelium*, 1510.[644]

UNDATED

Robert de Kouelle. Mentioned in letters of Adam Marsh, 1241 x 1255.[645]

---

[639] C81/1792/20; *CPR, 1396–99*, p. 433.
[640] He was at the Gloucester house in 1393 and at the Hereford house in 1395 (*Reg. Trefnant, Hereford*, pp. 207–8, 213).
[641] CPL 4. 290; 5. 190; C81/1792/21 (printed in Kingsford, *Grey Friars*, p. 207).
[642] *CPR, 1405–08*, p. 238.
[643] *CPR, 1429–36*, p. 132. Nor are they named on the roll.
[644] *Bullarium Franciscanum*, NS, 4 (1990) nos. 2033, 2117; CPL 16.564; 18. 37; BRUO 3. 1923–4; BRUC, p. 602.
[645] *Monumenta Franciscana* (J. S. Brewer, ed.; RS; 2 vols.; 1858–82) 1. 351–2. See C. H. Lawrence, 'The Letters of Adam Marsh and the Franciscan School at Oxford', *JEH* 42 (1991) 218–38.

A[dam] de Brangford. As preceding.[646]
Unnamed friar. As preceding.[647]

15. *Carmelite friars*

Unless otherwise stated, the house of the apostate is unknown. Also, unless otherwise stated, our knowledge of each apostate is that he was signified for arrest, and the date is the date of the signification.

1251–1300

John de Barking. 22 Nov. 1293.[648]
Philip de Beccles. 22 Nov. 1293 and 27 May 1297.[649]
William de Offington. 3 Dec. 1293.[650]
Ralph de Snytterell. Writ for arrest, 9 Aug. 1295.[651]
John Malore. 16 Aug. 1297.[652]
John de Synngham. 2 Feb. 1299.[653]
Thomas Bavent. Norwich convent. 23 March 1299. Arrested and imprisoned at Norwich, but ordered by royal writ to be released because he had become a papal chaplain, 13 Sept. 1299.[654]
William de Cobham. London convent. 9 Sept. 1299.[655]
Simon de Scaldeford. Nottingham convent. About 1300.[656]
William de Bevereford. Nottingham convent. About 1300.[657]

1301–50

William de Bodicote. Perhaps of Lynn convent (Norf.). 1308.[658]
Simon de Ringstead. 11 May 1308.[659]
William Portehors. Wandered about England and was now in Ireland; signified for arrest, *c.* 1309.[660]
William de Burford. 8 Dec. 1309.[661]
Henry Tuillet (Tuylett). Cambridge convent. 4 Oct. 1311.[662]
Robert de Saunford. At Oxford convent, 1304, 1305. Signified 28 Sept. 1312.[663]

---

[646] *Mon. Fran.* 1. 361.   [647] Ibid., 1. 374.
[648] C81/1793/4.   [649] Ibid. and 7.
[650] C81/1793/5.   [651] Prynne, pp. 640–1.
[652] C81/1793/8.   [653] C81/1793/6.
[654] C81/1793/9; *CCR, 1296–1302*, p. 271.   [655] C81/1793/10.
[656] C81/1793/1.   [657] C81/1793/2.
[658] C81/1793/12.   [659] C81/1793/11.
[660] C81/1793/13.   [661] C81/1793/14.
[662] C81/1793/15.   [663] *BRUO* 3. 1646; C81/1793/16.

John de Crodewelle. 23 July 1313.[664]
Richard Baldwyn alias de Ipswich. 26 Sept. 1313. Back by 1323, when he went on pilgrimage in fulfilment of vow.[665]

1351–1400

Richard, son of John de Thornton, citizen and spicer of York. York convent. Entered and left before the age of 14 but considered apostate by Carmelites. Royal protection given, 2 March 1358.[666]
Richard Drax. Papal mandate to reconcile, 28 Nov. 1362.[667]
Richard de Guisborough. Papal mandate to reconcile, 8 June 1363.[668]
Nicholas Sek. 16 Dec. 1375; writ for arrest of him and next entry issued 16 Dec.[669]
John Fre (Frere).
Edmund Bramton (Barnton). Maldon convent (Essex). 10 Nov. 1381; writ issued 23 Nov.[670]
Thomas Bumpstead. Cambridge convent. Signified for arrest, 18 Feb. 1390; writ issued, 1 March. Became honorary papal chaplain, 3 Nov. 1390. Signified again, 1393; writ issued, 8 Oct. 1393.[671]
Matthew Tyderle. London convent. 24 July 1390; writ issued 27 July.[672]
Nicholas Weston. Northampton convent. Became honorary papal chaplain, 31 Oct. 1392. Accused of violating rule by preaching and writing treatises and taking several wives in town of Northampton. Signified probably between 31 Oct. 1392 and 15 Sept 1396.[673]

1401–50

Richard Trenance. Sutton convent (near Plymouth, Devon). As honorary papal chaplain, wandered in Devon; signified, 24 Jan. 1408.[674]

---

[664] C81/1793/17. [665] C81/1793/18; *CPR, 1321–24*, p. 271.
[666] *CPR, 1358–61*, p. 19.
[667] *CPL* 4. 34. [668] Ibid., 4. 35.
[669] C81/1793/19; *CPR, 1374–77*, p. 228.
[670] C81/1793/28; *CPR, 1381–85*, p. 82.
[671] C81/1793/ 26, 27; *CPR, 1388–92*, p. 439; *CPR, 1391–96*, p. 357; *CPL* 4, 276, 362.. The second signification bears no day and month.
[672] C81/1793/20; *CPR, 1388–92*, p. 347. The prior provincial received a royal grant of all Tyderle's goods and chattels, 13 Oct. 1390 (ibid., pp. 306–7).
[673] C85/1793/29; *CPL* 4. 284–5. [674] C81/1793/21.

Richard Leche. Sutton convent (near Plymouth, Devon). Signified with next entry, 24 Jan. 1408.[675]
    Richard Pomflete. Back by 1413.[676]
John Worcester. York convent. 7 Nov. 1413.[677]
John Hawteyn alias Scharynton. London convent. Left perhaps before profession, 1414 x 1430. Claimed, in 1443, that he had been placed in convent at the age of 8 and that, when he fled, his mother brought him back and he was put in custody of Thomas Netter, prior provincial (1414–30). Freed of obligation of profession, 1447.[678]
Thomas Becke. 5 March 1441.[679]

AFTER 1451

Thomas Hadley. Captured; request now for delivery to London prior, 29 Oct. 1451.[680]
John Melburn. Nottingham convent. Signified with next two entries, 12 May 1453. Dispensed to live as secular priest, 31 Oct. 1454.[681]
    Robert Laknam (Lakenham?).
    John Lutton.

UNDATED

John de Lenma. Returned to world and took a *de facto* wife, before 1299.[682]

16. Austin friars

Unless otherwise stated, the apostate was signified for arrest and the date is the date of the signification.

1301–50

Henry Meweys. London Priory. Apostate for over a year. 30 July 1329.[683]
William de Bury. London Priory. 30 July 1329.[684]
Richard de Lichfield. York Priory. 8 Feb. 1335.[685]

[675] C85/1793/22.
[676] Ordained deacon, 23 Sept. 1413 (*Reg. Stafford, Exeter*, p. 456).
[677] C81/1793/23.   [678] *VCH London* I. 509.
[679] C81/1793/24.   [680] C85/1793/25.
[681] C85/1793/30; *CPL* 10. 157.
[682] C81/1793/3.   [683] C81/1794/6.
[684] C81/1794/7.   [685] C81/1794/12.

1351–1400

John de Chasetown. London Priory. Papal mandate to reconcile for Jubilee pilgrimage to Rome, 17 April 1351.[686]

Nicholas de Waddington. Yarmouth Priory (Norf.). 22 July 1356 and 5 Jan. 1360; writ issued 26 May 1357.[687]

John de Snettisham. Lynn Priory (Norf.). 5 Jan. 1360.[688]

Simon de Badby. House unknown. Imprisoned for apostasy at Maidstone; petition to deliver him to bearer of petition, 1 March 1361; writ issued 2 March.[689]

William de Raby. Warrington Priory (Lancs.). Papal mandate to reconcile, 11 Dec. 1362.[690]

William de Barrow. House unknown. Writ for arrest of him and next entry, 15 June 1364.[691]

  Robert de Brunby.

William Pattishall. Wyclifite sympathizer. London Priory. Signified with next entry for arrest, 26 May 1387; writ issued 23 July 1387.[692]

  Robert Stokesley alias York.

Thomas Beauchamp. Probably Wyclifite sympathizer. Signified with next entry for arrest, 26 May 1387.[693]

  John Lude.

Stephen Peryn. London Priory. 22 Oct. 1387.[694]

AFTER 1401

John Paston. House unknown. Left his order and became secular priest. Received papal mandate to transfer to Augustinian canons, 5 March 1415.[695]

John Heton. Grimsby Priory (Lincs.). 29 Sept. 1419.[696]

Thomas Roysbych(?). House unknown. General of order required English provincial to seize him and next entry, 2 March 1473.[697]

  John Alden.

---

[686] *CPL* 3. 396.
[687] C81/1794/2, 9; *CPR, 1354–58*, p. 558.
[688] C81/1794/4.
[689] C81/1794/3; *CPR, 1358–61*, p. 582.
[690] *CPL* 4. 34.   [691] *CPR, 1361–64*, p. 543.
[692] C81/1794/10; *CPR, 1385–89*, p. 386.
[693] C81/1794/10.   [694] C81/1794/11.
[695] *CPL* 6. 465.   [696] C81/1794/5.
[697] Francis Roth, *The English Austin Friars, 1249–1538* (2 vols.; New York, 1961–6) 2. 904.

Thomas Stanley. House unkown. General of order required he be handed over to English provincial for punishment, 31 Jan. 1515.[698]

John de Burner. House unknown. Signified with next entry. Reign of a King Edward.[699]
    Simon de Canterbury.
Walter de Mildenhall. House unknown. Captured and detained at Newgate prison, London; request for delivery to London Priory, 3 Oct. (no year), temp. Edward III.[700]

17. Crutched friars

All the friars listed here were signified for arrest, and the date given is the date of the petition. In each case the petition was sent by the prior of the London house near the Tower, which may merely mean that he acted as the London agent for the order and not that they were necessarily members of that house. There is no specific indication of the houses to which these apostates belonged. The Crutched Friars at the hospital at Ospringe (Kent) are listed under hospitals.
John Lumbard. 6 March 1352; writ for arrest of him and next entry issued 4 March, but he appeared in chancery (12 March) to counter the writ, claiming he left while still a novice and only after 11 weeks. The order failed to challenge this, and the writ of capture was superseded, 17 March.[701]
    John de Stoke Nayland.
Robert de Stannowe (Stanhowe). 26 Aug. 1360. While being delivered from the Marshalsea prison to Essex, he was taken, beaten, returned to London, and imprisoned by his abductors; commission to investigate, 24 Nov. 1360.[702]
John Sharp. 25 Aug. 1382, 3 May 1390.[703]
Thomas Man. 14 June 1390.[704]
Richard Stapleford. 22 May 1392.[705]
Thomas Hauden. 1 Feb. 1428.[706]

[698] Ibid., p. 1016.   [699] C81/1794/1.   [700] C81/1794/8.
[701] C81/1794/18; *CPR, 1350–54*, p. 279; C47/109/6.
[702] C81/1794/13; *CPR, 1358–61*, pp. 516–17.
[703] C81/1794/14, 15.   [704] C81/1794/16.
[705] C81/1794/17.   [706] C81/1794/19.

18. Pied friars

Walter de Croxton (same as next entry?). Norwich house. Allegedly stole charters, chalices, a large sum of money and ornaments from church at Norwich and was signified for arrest, 1 May 1287.[707]

Walter de Norwich (same as preceding?). Westminster house. Allegedly stole books and other goods of this house and was wandering about London; signified with next two entries for arrest, 22 Sept. 1288.[708]

> **Thomas de Wyk.**
> **Hugh de York.**

John _____. Signified for arrest with next entry, temp. Edward III.[709]

> **John** _____.

19. Knights Templars

Roger Loveday. Temple Bruer (Lincs.). Allegedly a religious for ten years and apostasized in 1289, two years after his father's death; dispute over inheritance in King's Bench, 1303.[710]

Richard de Feckenham. House unnamed. Writs to sheriffs of Kent, Sussex and Hants. for his arrest as apostate, 24 June 1305.[711]

William de Grafton, jun. Preceptor, Faxfleet Preceptory (Yorks. ER). Mandate by archbishop of York and bishop of Lincoln to denounce him and next seven entries (whose preceptories were unnamed) as apostates for failing to appear for trial at York, 3 July 1310.[712]

> **John de Usseflet.**
> **Edmund Latimer alias de Barville.**
> **John de Poynton.**
> **Richard Engayn.**
> **Ralph de Bulford.**

---

[707] C81/1794/24.
[708] C81/1794/25. Had Walter de Croxton become associated with the Westminster house and become known there as Walter de Norwich?
[709] C81/1794/26, a faded fragment with two apostates named John.
[710] See above, pp. 23–4, for more detail and full references.
[711] *CCR, 1302–07*, p. 339.
[712] *Reg. Greenfield, York* 4. nos. 2271, 2303. For the 'apostate' Templars, see above, pp. 26–8.

Appendix 5

Walter le Rebel.
Stephen de Staplebridge. Captured at Salisbury and reconciled at London, summer 1311.[713]

20. Knights Hospitallers

Unless otherwise indicated the house of the apostate is unknown.
Alan de Mouncens(?). For allegedly defrauding the order, signified for arrest, 12 Feb. 1331, 5 Aug. 1334.[714]
William de Boyton. Probably Battisford House (Suff.), later Carbrooke (Norf.). Signified for arrest, 15 June 1338. Papal mandate to reconcile, 12 July 1353.[715]
Name illegible. Signified for arrest, 22 Feb. 1346.[716]
Simon Dengayne. Writ for arrest, 26 Aug. 1346.[717]
William Albon. Signified for arrest, 19 Jan. 1374.[718]
John Tompson. Absent for over a year, signified for arrest, 15 Feb. 1529.[719]

21. Hospitals

1251–1300
Daniel de Boninges. Domus dei (unnamed) under Santingfeld (France). Signified for arrest, 5 April 1282.[720]

1301–50
Ralph de Southampton. St Thomas of Acon (London). Signified for arrest, 2 Nov. 1318; writ issued 16 Dec.[721]
John de Flitwick. St Mary de Pré (Herts.), associated with St Albans Abbey. Without permission, left and was admitted by the Cistercian abbot of Garendon to a hermitage at Cripplegate, London, which, after a year, he left, resumed Benedictine habit and

---

[713] *CCR, 1307–13*, pp. 316–17; *Councils and Synods* 2. 2. 1307–10. He belonged to the preceptory at Lydley, Salop (*VCH, Salop* 2. 86).
[714] C81/1795/1, 2.
[715] C81/1795/3, which was sent from Coddenham, a manor of Battisford; *CPL* 3. 515, where Carbrooke (Norf.) is given as his house.
[716] C81/1795/4.   [717] *CPR, 1345–48*, pp. 185–6.
[718] C81/1795/5.   [719] C81/1795/6.
[720] C81/1796/14. Such hospitals were at Eberthin (Monmouths.), Farley (Beds.) and Ludgershall (Bucks.); see KH, pp. 320, 326.
[721] C81/1796/10; *CPR, 1317–21*, p. 260.

went to Avignon without permission. Papal mandate to reconcile, 2 Dec. 1341.[722]

John de Welton. Milton (Kent). Papal mandate to reconcile, 18 Nov. 1344.[723]

Richard Fraunceys. Lay brother. Gaunt's Hospital (St Mark's, Bristol). Papal reconciliation for Jubilee pilgrimage to Rome, 27 April 1350.[724]

Richard Schelfkyng. Master. Strood Hospital (Kent). Left without rendering an account of his stewardship. This came to attention of bishop, 2 Oct. 1350.[725]

1351–1400

Richard de Selling. Maison Dieu, Dover (Kent). Signified for arrest, 26 Nov. 1352.[726]

Thomas Bengeworth alias de Evesham. Ospringe (Kent). Took the habit, 11 Nov. 1358; left 1362; royal inquiry, 30 Jan., 20 May 1386. Master signified him for arrest, 12 June 1387.[727]

John Stapleford. St Mary's without Bishopsgate (London). Captured and detained in Newgate prison; prior's request for delivery, 20 Oct. 1363.[728]

Peter Gynny. Order of St Anthony of Vienna. Hospital unnamed. Writ for arrest, 3 July 1365.[729]

Geoffrey de Chaddesden. Sometime master. Burton Lazars (Leics.). Signified for arrest by Nicholas de Dover (next entry), 18 Nov. 1365 (writ issued 24 Nov.), 9 March 1369 (writ issued 26 April), in dispute over mastership.[730]

Nicholas de Dover. Sometime master. Burton Lazars (Leics.). Signified for arrest with next entry by Geoffrey de Chaddesden (previous entry), 28 Sept. 1366, in dispute over mastership.[731]

Thomas de Kele. Burton Lazars (Leics.).

---

[722] *CPL* 2. 554.
[723] Ibid., 2. 171.   [724] Ibid., 3. 338.
[725] *Reg. Hethe, Rochester* 2. 209–10. He may have been a Benedictine monk, since, in 1330, the bishop had ordered that the master and four brothers be of that order (KH, p. 395).
[726] C81/1796/4.
[727] C269/7/17, 23; C81/1796/12. At this time, the hospital was apparently still run by Crutched Friars (KH, p. 210).
[728] C81/1789/33.   [729] *CPR, 1364–67*, p. 151.
[730] C81/1795/9, 10; *CPR, 1364–67*, p. 206; *CPR, 1367–70*, p. 266. Geoffrey de Chaddesden, calling himself master, had received the king's protection, 8 Feb. 1369 (*CPR, 1367–70*, p. 259); he settled the dispute by taking a pension, 9 May 1372 (*CCR, 1369–74*, pp. 432–3).
[731] C81/1795/8.

Stephen Chaumpe. Lechlade (Glos.). Signified for arrest, 17 Nov. 1376.[732]

Richard Evesham. Ospringe (Kent). Signified for arrest, 12 June 1387.[733]

William Clerk. Chaplain. Ospringe (Kent). Signified for arrest, 7 Aug. 1388.[734]

Thomas Chamberlain. Gaunt's Hospital (St Mark's, Bristol). Signified for arrest, 1 Oct. 1393.[735]

Philip Russell. St Mark's Hospital, Billeswick (Bristol). Involved in dispute over mastership. Allegedly stole 40 marks and goods valued at £20 from hospital, 13 Nov. 1389. Signified for arrest as excommunicate by bishop of Worcester, 15 July 1392 (writ issued 26 Oct. 1392), and by archbishop of Canterbury, leading to writ of 3 Feb. 1393 (calling him 'iam apostata'). Declared outlaw, 8 Feb. 1393, and by 12 March 1393 in prison at Bristol. Signified as apostate by Master of St Mark's Hospital, 18 Oct. 1393; surrendered at Marshalsea prison and, 21 Oct., royal protection restored.[736]

1401–50

Robert Norton alias Putrell. St Thomas Acon (London). Signified for arrest, 30 Dec. 1401.[737]

Thomas Maryner. St Thomas Acon (London). Admitted, 12 Nov. 1399; professed 21 Dec. 1400; left *c.* 1403; still apostate, 18 Nov. 1406.[738]

Richard _____. St Bartholomew's (Gloucester). Signified for arrest, 26 Feb. 1401 x 1407.[739]

William Worcester. St Bartholomew's (Gloucester). Signified for arrest, 30 Jan. 1433.[740]

Robert Pontwell. Chaplain. Burton Lazars (Leics.). Signified for arrest, 14 Oct. 1448.[741]

Hugh Spalding. Burton Lazar (Leics.). Dispensed to live as secular priest, 21 Nov. 1450, but, abandoning religious habit, held

---

[732] C81/1796/8.
[733] C81/1796/12. He may have been a Crutched friar (see n. 727 above).
[734] C81/1796/13. See preceding note.   [735] C81/1796/2.
[736] C81/1796/3; *CPR, 1391–96*, p. 323; C85/164/36. See F. Donald Logan, *Excommunication and the Secular Arm in Medieval England* (Toronto, 1968), p. 107n., and *VCH, Glos.* 2. 116.
[737] C81/1796/11.
[738] C270/35/24.   [739] C81/1789/11.
[740] C81/1789/12.   [741] C81/1795/7.

to be apostate by Lazars. Papally absolved of apostasy and dispensed to wear habit under garb of secular priest, 15 July 1479.[742]

1451–1500

Robert Merston. Burton Lazars (Leics.). Signified for arrest, 20 Feb. 1453.[743]

Nicholas Buckland. Sometime master. St Thomas's, Southwark (Surrey). Signified for arrest, 5 Feb. 1456.[744]

Walter Norman. St John's Hospital, Bridgwater (Somerset). Absent, as were the next 2 entries, at election of prior, 7 April 1457.[745]

    John Bevice.

    John Spencer.

Nicholas Aly. Elsing Spital (St Mary within Cripplegate, London). Went apostate with next entry, 23 Nov. 1467; both signified for arrest, 4 Feb. 1468.[746]

    Thomas Kentish.

1501–30

Robert Downham. St Leonard's, York. Signified for arrest, 7 Nov. 1512.[747]

Thomas Wilton. St Thomas's, Southwark (Surrey). Signified for arrest, 25 Jan. 1529.[748]

UNDATED

Thomas de Thurmaston. St Mary's without Bishopsgate (London). Signified for arrest, 14th century.[749]

Thomas _____. Burton Lazars (Leics.). Signified for arrest, 25 Jan. temp. Henry IV or V.[750]

22. Order unknown

John Galun. Decision that, although he had received a royal pardon on condition that he take the religious habit and subsequently apostasized, the pardon still stands, 12 Jan. 1262.[751]

---

[742] *CPL* 10. 72; 13. 1. 7–8.   [743] C81/1795/12.

[744] C81/1796/17. In the previous year he had been called to the king's court to respond to a debt owed to the late Archbishop Chichele, and he failed to appear (*CPR, 1452–61*, p. 192).

[745] *Reg. Beckington, Bath and Wells* 2. 1647.   [746] C81/1789/34.

[747] C81/1796/19.   [748] C81/1796/16.   [749] C81/1796/32.

[750] C81/1795/11 (badly faded).   [751] *CPR, 1258–66*, p. 197.

Lawrence Breton. Rector of Catmore (Berks.). Rumoured at bishop's visitation to be an apostate, 21 April 1391.[752]
Thomas ____. Letter to reconcile, 1461.[753]
William Fromond. Winchester diocese. Papal mandate to reconcile, 1492 or 1493.[754]
John Huntingen. Norwich diocese. Papal mandate to reconcile, 1492 X 1495.[755]

B. RELIGIOUS WOMEN

The order to which individual houses belonged is not always clear. Following the rule of an order did not necessarily mean membership in that order. Here the rule followed at the time of the apostasy, where this is known, is given in questionable cases.

1. Benedictine nuns

1251–1300

Hawise de Basevil. Rusper Priory (Sussex). Allegedly left to claim her inheritance from her deceased father; matter was in the church courts in 1270 and 1271, where she may have lost, for, in 1276, she was in the royal courts again, claiming her share of her late brother's Sussex manors.[756]
Godhuda, sister of Roger de Wykes. Kilburn Priory (Middlesex). Claimed inheritance at brother's death, 1274, but claim was disallowed because the abbot of Westminster certified that she had been a true nun for over thirty years.[757]
Anna Giffard. Wilton Abbey (Wilts.). With next entry consented to abduction by Sir Osbert Giffard, 1284. Abduction probably

---

[752] T. C. B. Timmins, ed., *The Register of John Waltham, Bishop of Salisbury, 1388–1395* (Canterbury and York Soc., 80, 1994), no. 951. Possibly considered suspect because he had received orders from the friar bishop of Meath (Ireland). The suspicion must have been lifted, for Bishop Waltham allowed him to exchange benefices in 1393 (ibid., no. 718).
[753] *Reg. Stanbury, Hereford*, p. 68.
[754] *CPL* 16. 1124.   [755] Ibid.
[756] Canterbury Cathedral Archives, Christ Church Letters II, no. 301; CP40/15, m. 15. Professor Charles Donahue and Dr Paul Brand have drawn these references to my attention.
[757] CP40/105, m. 142. The case surfaced again in 1294, its resolution unrecorded. Dr Paul Brand brought this case to my attention.

occasioned chapter in Statute of Westminster II (1285) about abduction of nuns. He did public penance in Lent, 1286.[758]

Alice Russell.

Agnes de Sheen. Godstow Abbey (Oxon.). Abducted with another nun from their carriage ('in proprio curru domus illius') on king's highway at Wycombe and their abductors excommunicated, 1290, but, later, Bishop Sutton of Lincoln excommunicated her and next two entries for having left willingly and abandoned their habits, 1292.[759]

Joan de Cart.

An unnamed kinswoman of Ela, countess of Warwick.

Cecily _____. Foukeholme (or Thimbleby) Priory (Yorks. NR). Having been abducted by William, chaplain of Yarm, she voluntarily returned, 1293.[760]

Acelina _____. Wothorpe Priory (Northants.). Bishop's mandate to reconcile, 10 July 1296.[761]

Cecily _____. Clementhorpe Priory (York). Met men with saddled horse at priory gate and, throwing off her habit, rode with them to Darlington and lived with Gregory de Thornton for three years, 1300.[762]

1301–50

Alice Darel alias de Queldrick. Thicket Priory (Yorks. ER). Appeared at the gate of the nunnery and begged to be readmitted. Archbishop ordered her readmission: if she would not accept penance imposed, she should be confined to a room, 5 Feb. 1303.[763]

Beatrice de Sinnington. Wallingwells Priory (Notts.). Archbishop's mandate to reconcile, 29 Feb. 1308.[764]

Agnes de Flixthorpe alias de Wissenden. St Michael's Priory, nr Stamford (Northants.). Believed to be at Nottingham; bishop's mandate to denounce as excommunicate, 1309. Aid of secular arm sought, 1310. Confined to cell for apostasy and refusal to wear religious habit, 1311. She denied validity of her profession because of prior marriage but refused to name her husband. Bishop's

---

[758] For this celebrated case see above, pp. 86–8.
[759] *Reg. Sutton, Lincoln* 3. 23–5, 132–3; Power, *Nunneries*, p. 440.
[760] William Brown, 'The Nunnery of St. Stephen's of Thimbleby', *YAJ* 9 (1886) 334–5.
[761] *Reg. Sutton, Lincoln* 5. 167.   [762] *VCH, Yorks*. 3. 129–30.
[763] *Reg. Corbridge, York* 1. no. 506.   [764] *Reg. Greenfield, York* 4. no. 1733.

inquest found that, after twenty years as a nun, she left and was found wearing a man's gown of gilt embroidery. Bishop had her placed with the Augustinian canonesses at Cornworthy Priory (Devon). In 1312, she repented and was absolved and was in solitary confinement there until 1314, when she was returned to Stamford. She left again in 1316, and in 1318 the bishop ordered the prioress to search her out and impose penance upon her when she returned.[765]

Sabina de Applegarth. Later prioress. Moxby Priory (Yorks. NR). Returned penitent; archbishop's mandate to reconcile, 24 April 1312.[766]

Clarissa de Spidon. Arden Priory (Yorks. NR). Archbishop's mandate to reconcile, 28 Feb. 1318.[767]

Joan de Leeds. Clementhorpe Priory (York). Archbishop directed that she be sent back, 11 Aug. 1318.[768]

Isabel de Studley. Clementhorpe Priory (York). Reported guilty of apostasy and other crimes at visitation; Archbishop Melton ordered that she be sent to Yedingham Priory, 1324, from which she returned to York in 1331.[769]

Elizabeth la Zouche. Brewood Priory (Staffs.). Fled with another (unnamed) nun, 1326; she was absolved and readmitted, 1331.[770]

Alice de Kynyton. Farewell Priory (Staffs.). Found to be absent in apostasy, as was next entry, by visitor, who instructed prioress to effect their return, 1331.[771]

Cecily de Gretton.

Joan de Bracebridge. Markyate Priory (Herts.). Bishop's commission to absolve, 26 Dec. 1336.[772]

Agnes de Ledbury. Godstow Abbey (Oxon.). Abducted by Elias Walewayn but absolved by bishop and returned to abbey, 4 Feb. 1340.[773]

Joan de Crakenholme. Thicket Priory (Yorks. ER). Returned with harsh penalties imposed by archbishop, 1344.[774]

[765] Her story is told in *VCH, Northants.* 2. 99, and in Power, *Nunneries*, pp. 443–5.

[766] *Reg. Greenfield, York* 3. no. 1286. She was elected prioress in 1325 but removed in 1328 (Power, p. 599).

[767] *Reg. Melton, York* 2. no. 7.

[768] *VCH, Yorks.* 3. 130n.   [769] Ibid., 3. 130.

[770] *Reg. Norbury, Coventry and Lichfield*, pp. 252, 254, 256.

[771] *VCH, Staffs.* 3. 224.   [772] Lincs. Archives Office, Episc. Reg. v, fo. 544^v.

[773] Ibid., fo. 576. For Walewayn, who was pardoned, 15 July 1343, for not appearing before justices, see *CPR, 1340–43*, p. 491, and Emden, *BRUO* 3. 1977.

[774] *VCH, Yorks.* 3. 124.

Helen de Angram. Foukeholme Priory (Yorks. NR). Returned and readmitted to habit, 1349.[775]

1351–1400

Joan Bruys, wife of Nicholas Grene. Nuneaton Priory (Warwicks.). Accused of being a religious in an inheritance dispute, but bishop of Coventry and Lichfield denied that she was ever professed, 1358.[776]

Agnes de Bowes. Wothorpe Priory (Northants.). Sole survivor of house at Black Death. Appointed prioress. Priory absorbed into St Michael's, Stamford, 13 July 1354; Bowes said to be wandering in apostasy, 30 July 1359.[777]

Anna de Raunds. Hinchingbrooke Priory (Hunts.). Absolved and given penance by bishop of Lincoln, 5 April 1359.[778]

Marion (or Margery) de Rye. Romsey Abbey (Hants.). Bishop gave permission to absolve her from apostasy, if necessary, 20 March 1369.[779]

Isabel Gervays. Nunnaminster (Winchester). Party to her own abduction, Jan. 1370; returned pregnant by June, 1370.[780]

Margaret Colville. Arden Priory (Yorks. NR). Archbishop's letter to readmit, 16 July 1372.[781]

Agnes, wife of Richard Clivedon. Shaftesbury Abbey (Dorset). Left in 1374, apparently to claim an inheritance.[782]

Katherine de Monte Acuto. Bungay Priory (Suffolk). Signified for arrest, 7 March 1377; writ issued same date.[783]

Margaret de Prestwich. Seton Priory (Cumberland). Claimed that she was forced to enter as a novice at the age of 8 and that, realizing that profession would disinherit her, she feigned illness on the day of her profession but was physically carried to the church, where her habit was blessed. Fled and married. Upon appeal to pope, bishop commissioned to examine judged her story true and pronounced her free from nunnery, 1383.[784]

---

[775] Ibid., 3. 116.

[776] *VCH, Warwicks.* 2. 68.

[777] Lincs. Archives Office, Episc. Reg. VIII, fo. 116; IX, fos. 95, 190ᵛ–191. Dr David M. Smith has kindly drawn these references to my attention.

[778] Ibid., VIII, fo. 125.

[779] *Reg. Wykeham, Winchester* 2. 77–9.

[780] See above, p. 89, for discussion and references.

[781] *VCH Yorks.* 3. 114. She had been incontinent with a layman.

[782] For this case see above, p. 16.

[783] C81/1786/6; *CPR, 1374–77*, p. 49.   [784] Power, *Nunneries*, p. 36.

Joyce _____. St Helen's Priory (Bishopsgate, London). Reported on 10 Oct. 1388 as having apostasized and attempted marriage.[785]
Margaret Cailly. St Radegund's Priory (Cambridge). Left in 1389.[786]
Katherine Fauconer. Wherwell Abbey (Hants.). Abducted with her consent, by 16 June 1393. Episcopal mandate to reconcile, 12 April 1400.[787]
Joan Adeleshey. Rowney Priory (Herts.). Signified for arrest, 12 Nov. 1400 (writ issued 6 Jan. 1401), 12 March 1401 (writ issued 28 March).[788]

1401–50

Unnamed nun, sister of prioress (probably Alice Fyshill). Wintney Priory (Hants.). Reportedly left and had children. Papal commission appointed to investigate, 17 Sept. 1405.[789]
Grace Nowers. Flamstead Priory (Herts.). With her sister (next entry) claimed to be heirs of Emery Nowers, but bishop of Lincoln, 17 May 1409, certified that they had professed the previous 21 April.[790]
   Agnes Nowers.
_____ **Pernell**. Elstow Abbey (Beds.). Reported apostate at episcopal visitation, 1432.[791]
Katherine Tyttesbury (Tisbury?). Markyate Priory (Herts.). Episcopal visitor ordered that, if she returned, she be received with kindness, 1433.[792]
Annis _____. St Bartholomew's Priory, Newcastle upon Tyne (Northumberland). Bishop ordered her denunciation in Newcastle and Durham, 19 April 1434.[793]
Agnes Butler alias Pery or Northampton. St Michael's Priory, nr Stamford (Northants.). Ran off with harp-player and was living in Newcastle upon Tyne. Episcopal mandate to effect her return, 1440.[794]

---

[785] *Ninth Report of the Royal Commission on Historical Manuscripts* (3 vols.; London, 1883–4) 1. 28.
[786] *VCH, Cambs.* 2. 219.
[787] *Reg. Wykeham, Winchester* 2. 437, 498.
[788] C81/1786/30, 31; *CPR, 1399–1401*, pp. 418, 472.
[789] *CPL* 6. 55, where she is called a Benedictine; cf. KH, p. 272, where the house is listed as Cistercian.
[790] C269/9/24.   [791] *Linc. Vis.* 1. 54.
[792] Ibid., 1. 83.   [793] *Reg. Langley, Durham* 4. no. 1091.
[794] *Linc. Vis.* 2. 348.

Alice Dalton. Nunkeeling Priory (Yorks. ER). Having undergone penance at Yedingham Priory, she was allowed to return, 1444.[795]

Six unnamed nuns. Ankerwyke Priory (Bucks.). At visitation prioress claimed ignorance that they had apostasized during her time in office, 10 Oct. 1441.[796]

Unnamed nun. Godstow Abbey (Oxon.). Left with monk of Eynsham, *c.* 1445.[797]

AFTER 1451

Elizabeth Wynter. Littlemore Priory (Oxon.). With three other nuns (next entries), fled for two or three weeks; returned by time of visitation, 1518.[798]

   Joan Wynter.

   Juliana Wynter.

   Anna Willye.

Alice Hubbart. Ankerwyke Priory (Bucks.). Reported to visitor to have left after four years and attempted marriage to a man called Sutton, 25 May 1519.[799]

2. Cluniac nuns

Isabel de Clouville. Delapré Abbey (Northampton). Bishop's order to denounce her and next two entries as excommunicates, 1300.[800]

   Maud Rychmers.

   Ermentrude de Newark.

Helen de Castleford. Arthington Priory (Yorks. WR). Archbishop's mandate to reconcile, 31 July 1301.[801]

Constance de Daneport alias Pontefract. Arthington Priory (Yorks. WR). Her return arranged by archbishop, but she failed to appear by specified date, 16 Feb. 1304.[802]

Agnes de Landwade. Delapré Abbey (Northampton). Denounced for apostasy, 1311.[803]

Isabel de Berghby (Birkby?). Prioress. Arthington Priory

---

[795] *VCH, Yorks.* 3. 121.

[796] *Linc. Vis.* 2. 3.   [797] Ibid., 2. 91.

[798] *Vis. Dioc. Linc.* 3. 11. For the disturbed state of this nunnery see above, p. 81.

[799] *Vis. Dioc. Linc.* 2. 70.

[800] *VCH, Northants.* 2. 114.   [801] *Reg. Corbridge, York* 1. no. 154.

[802] Ibid., 1. nos. 255, 259, 266.   [803] *VCH, Northants.* 2. 114.

(Yorks. WR). Inquiry about her departure with next entry, 31 Aug. 1312.[804]

Margaret de Tang. Arthington Priory (Yorks. WR). Inquiry about her departure with prioress (previous entry), 31 Aug. 1312. Sent into exile by archbishop to Nunkeeling, 7 April 1319. Left again, but begged readmission; archbishop, having absolved her, ordered her reconciliation, 5 May 1321.[805]

3. Cistercian nuns

1251–1300

Agnes de Bedal. Sinningthwaite Priory (Yorks. WR). Archbishop's mandate to reconcile, 12 June 1286.[806]

Maud de Tyverington. Keldholme Priory (Yorks. NR). Apostasized in 1287; archbishop indicated penance for her, 20 July 1321.[807]

Christine de Stillington. Keldholme Priory (Yorks. NR). Mandate from dean and chapter of York Minster, *sede vacante*, to reconcile, 1299.[808]

Joan de Finmere. Sewardsley Priory (Northants.). Bishop's mandate to reconcile, 1300.[809]

1301–50

Beatrice de Hawkesworth. Esholt Priory (Yorks. WR). Pregnant and living outside nunnery, by 17 Oct. 1303. Archbishop's mandate to reconcile, 7 March 1304.[810]

Helen de Appleton. Keldholme Priory (Yorks. NR). Archbishop's mandate to reconcile, 16 Feb. 1304.[811]

Alice Raggid. Kirklees Priory (Yorks. WR). Archbishop's mandate to reconcile, 27 Aug. 1306.[812]

Joan de Percy and other unnamed nuns. Baysdale Priory (Yorks. NR). Wandering about, by 21 Sept. 1307. Archbishop's mandate that she be sent to Sinningthwaite Priory, 13 July 1308; she returned to Baysdale by order of archbishop, 15 Aug. 1309.[813]

[804] *Reg. Greenfield, York* 2. no. 957.   [805] Ibid. and no. 963; *VCH, Yorks.* 3. 188–9.
[806] *Reg. Romeyn, York* 1. no. 116.   [807] *Reg. Melton* 2. no. 157.
[808] *VCH, Yorks.* 3. 167.   [809] *VCH, Northants.* 2. 126.
[810] *Reg. Corbridge, York* 1. nos. 247, 269.   [811] Ibid., 1. no. 381.
[812] *Reg. Greenfield, York* 2. nos. 675, 1139. See S. J. Chadwick, 'Kirklees Priory', *YAJ* 16 (1902) 354–5, 359–62.
[813] *Reg. Greenfield, York* 1. no. 251; 3. nos. 1180, 1233.

Agnes de Thormodby. Baysdale Priory (Yorks. NR). Left three times; archbishop's mandate to reconcile, 11 Dec. 1308.[814]

Alice de Pickering. Keldholme Priory (Yorks. NR). Archbishop's mandate to reconcile her and next two entries, 1309.[815]

    Maud Bigot. Sent to the Benedictine Nunkeeling Priory (Yorks. ER) for penance.[816]

    Emma de Stapleton. Confirmed as prioress, 7 March 1309.[817]

Maud de Ripon. Nun Appleton Priory (Yorks. WR). Archbishop's letter to readmit, 12 Nov. 1309.[818]

Alice de London. Pinley Priory (Warwicks.). Bishop ordered inquiry, 1 Oct. 1311.[819]

Elizabeth de Hopton. Kirklees Priory (Yorks. WR). Archbishop's mandate to reconcile, 11 Sept. 1313.[820]

Eleanor de la Roche. Nun Appleton Priory (Yorks. WR). Archbishop's mandate to reconcile, 3 Aug. 1314.[821]

Agnes de York. Nun Appleton Priory (Yorks. WR). Absolved by archbishop (by 16 May 1315), required to return by 22 May.[822]

Joan de Lelom. Baysdale Priory (Yorks. NR). Thrice apostate; absolved by archbishop; penance imposed, 23 Feb. 1319.[823]

Isabel Dayvill. Rosedale Priory (Yorks. NR). Absolved by archbishop; penance imposed, 18 May 1322.[824]

Margaret de Burton. Kirklees Priory (Yorks. WR). Archbishop's mandate to reconcile, 26 July 1337.[825]

Margaret de Fenton. Sinningthwaite Priory (Yorks. WR). Left pregnant; reconciliation with mitigated penance – her first time – ordered by archbishop, 1 Feb. 1343.[826]

Katherine de Hugate. Nun Appleton Priory (Yorks. WR). Left pregnant; archbishop ordered severe punishment should she return, Feb. 1346.[827]

Margaret _____. Nun Appleton Priory (Yorks. WR). Left pregnant; archbishop ordered nuns not to readmit her because she had on several other occasions left similarly, Feb. 1346.[828]

Ella de Mounceaux. Nun Cothan Priory (Lincs.). Received

---

[814] Ibid. 3. no. 1210. See Power, *Nunneries*, p. 445; *VCH, Yorks*. 3. 159.

[815] *Reg. Greenfield, York* 3. no. 1198.

[816] Ibid., 3. no. 1224.   [817] Ibid.

[818] *Reg. Greenfield, York* 3. nos. 858, 934.   [819] *Reg. Reynolds, Worcester*, p. 27.

[820] *Reg. Greenfield, York* 2. nos. 1008, 1137. See Chadwick, 'Kirklees Priory', pp. 358–60.

[821] *Reg. Greenfield, York* 2. no. 1068.   [822] Ibid., 2. no. 1123.

[823] *Reg. Melton, York* 2. no. 77.   [824] Ibid., 2. nos. 181, 182

[825] Chadwick, 'Kirklees Priory', pp. 363–4.   [826] *VCH, Yorks*. 3. 171.

[827] Ibid., p. 172.   [828] Ibid.

permission to leave temporarily but failed to return, becoming instead the mistress of John Haunsard. Repentant, she appeared before bishop of Lincoln, who ordered her readmission, 29 July 1349.[829]

AFTER 1351

Alice de Cawood. Swine Priory (Yorks. ER). Archbishop's letter to readmit this twice apostate nun, 1358.[830]

Katherine Thornyf. Wykeham Priory (Yorks. NR). With another nun she set out without permission on pilgrimage to Rome. When other nun died, she lived with a married man in London. Archbishop's letter to readmit, Feb. 1450.[831]

Joan Fletcher. Baysdale Priory (Yorks. NR). A nun of nearby Rosedale Priory; elected prioress of Baysdale, 12 Aug. 1524. Fearing deposition, she resigned in 1527, left the priory and wandered 'inter seculares'. Returned repentant to Rosedale, but in 1534 Archbishop Lee ordered her return to Baysdale, where she remained until dissolution, 1539.[832]

Eleanor Scaresbrig. Sewardsley Priory (Northants.). Elected prioress, 1526. Election declared void, 1530, because of her unfitness: she had borne a child and been apostate.[833]

4. Augustinian canonesses

1301–50

Unnamed canoness. Goring Priory (Oxon.). Bishop ordered her arrest, 1309.[834]

Margery de Hedsor, wife of Roger Blaket. Burnham Abbey (Bucks.). Sometime before 1289 she married Roger, but later left him and became canoness of Burnham, where she remained for 23 years, but left about 1311 and rejoined Roger, possibly to claim an inheritance. Episcopal order to have her denounced as apostate, 12 May 1311.[835]

---

[829] A. Hamilton Thompson, 'The Registers of John Gynewell, Bishop of Lincoln, for the Years 1349–50', *Archaeological Rev.*, NS, 18 (1911) 331.

[830] *VCH, Yorks*. 3. 181.   [831] Ibid., 3. 183.

[832] Janet E. Burton, 'The Election of Joan Fletcher as Prioress of Basedale, 1524', *Borthwick Institute Bulletin* 1 (1975–8) 145–53.

[833] *VCH, Northants*. 2. 126.   [834] *VCH, Oxon*. 2. 103.

[835] W. C. Bolland, ed., *Year Books of Edward II . . . 5 Edward II, AD 1312* (Selden Soc., 33, 1916), pp. xxxiv–xxxv, 211–14; Lincs. Archives Office, Episc. Reg. III, fo. 214ᵛ.

Alice Romayn. Haliwell Priory (Shoreditch, London). Signified for arrest, 3 Sept. 1314.[836]
Joan de Brotherton. Moxby Priory (Yorks. NR). Absolved by archbishop after second apostasy; her readmission was ordered, 13 Feb. 1322. Being called an apostate of Moxby, she was ordered to be admitted with specific penance at Nunkeeling (Yorks. ER), 29 July, 5 Aug. 1328.[837]
Unnamed nun. Grimsby Priory (Lincs.). Absolved of apostasy by bishop of Lincoln, 1337.[838]
Joan Blankefrontis. Moxby Priory (Yorks. NR). Papal mandate to reconcile, 17 July 1345.[839]

1351–1400

Joan de Alveton. Goring Priory (Oxon.). Bishop's mandate to reconcile, 22 March 1359.[840]
Elizabeth Arundel. Haliwell Priory (Shoreditch, London). Signified for arrest, 26 Jan. 1383; writ issued 7 Feb.[841]
Maud Huntercombe. Burnham Abbey (Bucks.). Left to claim inheritance; signified for arrest, 10 July 1391. Royal courts had recourse to bishop of Lincoln, who found that she was truly professed, 20 April 1393.[842]
Alice Broughton. Rothwell Priory (Northants.). Signified with next entry for arrest as excommunicates by bishop of Lincoln, 27 Feb. 1396.[843]
   Agnes Grene.

AFTER 1401

Joan Horncastle. Rothwell Priory (Northants.). Detected by bishop living with a man in parish of Coningsby (Lincs.), absolved, sent back but community refused her; bishop cited prioress to appear, 19 June 1414.[844]
Philippa King. Easebourne Priory (Sussex). Bishop at visitation (June 1478) found she had left with another nun (next entry) in the

[836] C81/1786/18. With the prioress and others, Alice had been accused of theft earlier in that year (*CPR, 1313–17*, p. 146).
[837] *Reg. Melton, York* 2. nos. 172, 316–17.
[838] *VCH, Lincs.* 2. 179.   [839] *CPL* 3. 188.
[840] Lincs. Archives Office, Episc. Reg. VIII, fo. 123ᵛ.
[841] C81/1786/19; *CPR, 1381–85*, p. 255.
[842] C81/1789/31; *CCR, 1389–92*, p. 363; C269/4/29.
[843] C85/109/42.   [844] *Reg. Repingdon, Lincoln* 3. no. 15.

company of a chaplain and a retainer of the earl of Arundel; each of the apostates had allegedly borne a child.[845]
Joan Portsmouth.

5. Premonstratensian canonesses

Margaret Everingham. Broadholme Priory (Notts.). Abducted by rector of Lea (Lincs.) and two Franciscan friars; indicted to appear before royal justices, 1350, at Caistor (Lincs.).[846]
Margery Buke. Orford Priory (Lincs.). Excommunicated by visitor for apostasy with canon of Newsham, 18 Aug. 1491.[847]

6. Gilbertine nuns

Alice, daughter of John de Everingham, wife of John de Huthulle. Haverholme Priory (Lincs.). Probably involved in testamentary dispute. Signified for arrest, 17 Nov. 1366; writ issued, 12 Dec., but stayed, 13 Dec., until after Easter. She appealed in royal and papal courts; bishop of Lincoln found she was not a nun, Dec. 1367.[848]

7. Sisters of the order of St John of Jerusalem (Hospitallers)

Clarissa Styl. Buckland Preceptory (Somerset). Involved in testamentary dispute. Judgement that she was truly professed, although she entered and professed at the age of 8, because she had remained until the age of 14, given 12 Oct. 1389.[849]

8. Hospitals

Joan atte Water. St Thomas's, Southwark (Surrey). Signified for arrest, 10 June 1324.[850]
Agnes Stanley. St Bartholomew's (Bristol). Signified for arrest, 20 Feb. 1389.[851]

---

[845] *VCH, Sussex* 2. 85.
[846] R. E. G. Cole, *The Priory of Broadholme* (Associated Architectural Societies' Reports and Papers 28 (1905–6) 66–7; see Power, *Nunneries*, pp. 449–50.
[847] *CAP* 3. 80–1.
[848] C81/1791/2; *CPR, 1364–67*, p. 369; C269/4/29. For discussion of this case see above, p. 24.
[849] E135/6/73.   [850] C81/1796/15.   [851] C81/1796/1.

Joan Gamele. St Nicholas (York). Signified for arrest, 16 July 1440.[852]

Elizabeth Holloway. St Thomas's, Southwark (Surrey). Signified for arrest, 27 June 1530.[853]

9. Others

Nun at Richmond (order and name unknown) who desired to return; archdeacon of Richmond instructed to assist her, 15 June 1286.[854]

Christine Carpenter. Anchoress of Shere (Surrey). Given permission by John Stratford, bishop of Winchester, to be enclosed, 19 July 1329; she left enclosure apostate but received papal absolution, 27 July 1332; bishop ordered re-enclosure, 23 Oct. 1332.[855]

---

[852] C81/1796/20.   [853] C81/1796/18.

[854] *Reg. Romeyn, York* 1. no. 964.

[855] Winchester, Hampshire Record Office, 21M65/A1/5, fo. 76. She was the subject of the film *Anchoress* (1993).

SELECT BIBLIOGRAPHY

From the mountain of literature on the subject of medieval English religious only those books and articles which have been particularly useful in the preparation of this study are included here. The sources of manuscript materials cited in this study are indicated here. Although all printed bishops' registers have been consulted, they are not indicated here: for these the reader is referred to Abbreviations (p. xviii), s.v., *Reg.*

PRIMARY SOURCES

Unprinted

Cambridge. Trinity College MS R.5.41.
Canterbury Cathedral Archives. Chartae Antiquae, Christ Church Letters.
Chichester, West Sussex Record Office. Register Sherborne II (Ep. 1/1/4).
Lincolnshire Archives Office. Episc. Regs.
London. British Library, Harl. MS 5213, Lansdowne MS 652, Royal MSS 6E.VI and 11A.IX, Stow MS 386, 409, Add. MSS 5761, 5925, 33514, 20059, 48040.
London. Lambeth Palace Library, F 1/Vv.
London. Public Record Office.
  C66, C81, C85, C269, C279, CP40, KB27, SC1, SC8, SP1, SP5, E135.
Oxford. Corpus Christi College, MS 256.
Trowbridge. Wiltshire Record Office. Register Erghum.
Winchester. Hampshire Record Office. Register Stratford (A1/5).
York. Borthwick Institute of Historical Research. Cause Papers, Wills.

Printed

Acta capitulorum generalium ordinis praedicatorum. Ed. B. M. Reichert; in *Monumenta ordinis fratrum praedicatorum historica*, vols. 3–4, 8–14, Rome, 1898–1904.
Amundesham, John. *Annales.* Ed. H. T. Riley; RS; 2 vols.; London, 1870–1.
Annales monastici. Ed. H. R. Luard; RS; 5 vols.; London, 1864–9.
Anselm of Canterbury, Saint. *Opera omnia.* Ed. F. S. Schmitt; 6 vols.; Edinburgh, 1946–51.
  The Letters of St. Anselm of Canterbury. Tr. Walter Frohlich; 2 vols.; Kalamazoo, 1990–3.

Antonio de Butrio. *In quinque decretalium libros novella commentaria*. Venice, 1581.

Benedicti regula. Ed. Rudolph Hanslik. Corpus scriptorum ecclesiasticorum latinorum 75; Vienna, 1977.

Bishop Geoffrey Blythe's Visitations, c. 1515–1525. Ed. Peter Heath; Staffordshire Record Soc., Collections, 4th ser., 7 (1973).

Boniface VIII, pope. *Liber sextus* (in *Corpus Iuris Canonici*, vol. 2). Eds. E. L. Richter and E. Friedberg; Leipzig, 1881.

Bracton on the Laws and Customs of England. Ed. G. E. Woodbine; tr. and rev. S. E. Thorne; 4 vols.; Cambridge, MA, 1968–77.

Bullarium diplomatum et privilegiorum sanctorum Romanorum pontificum Taurinensis editio. Ed. A. Tomassetti; 25 vols.; Turin, 1857–72.

Bullarium ordinis fratrum praedicatorum. Eds. E.T . Ripoll and A. Bremond; 8 vols.; Rome, 1729–40.

Calendar of Close Rolls. London, 1902– .

Calendar of Entries in the Papal Registers pertaining to Great Britain and Ireland. London, Dublin, 1894– .

Calendar of Inquisitions Post Mortem. London, 1904– .

Calendar of Patent Rolls. London, 1901– .

Carmelite Constitutions of 1357. Ed. Paul F. Robinson; Rome, 1992.

Chapters of the Augustinian Canons. Ed. H. E. Salter; Canterbury and York Soc., 29 (1922).

Christ Church, Canterbury, vol. 1, *The Chronicle of John Stone*; vol. 2, *Lists of the Deans, Priors, and Monks of Christ Church, Canterbury*. Ed. W. G. Searle; Cambridge Antiquarian Soc., octavo ser., 34 (1902).

'Chronica Guillielmi Thorne', *Historiae Anglicanae scriptores decem*. Ed. Roger Twysden; London, 1652.

Chronicle of St. Mary's Abbey, York. Eds. H. H. E. Craster and M. E. Thornton; Surtees Soc., 148, 1933.

Chronicon abbatiae Rameseiensis. Ed. W. D. Macray; RS; London, 1886.

Chronicon abbatie de Parco Lude. Ed. E. Venables; Lincoln, 1981.

Codex regularum monasticarum et canonicarum. Ed. Lucas Holstenius; 6 vols.; Augsburg, 1759.

Concilia Magnae Britanniae et Hiberniae, AD 446–1718. Ed. D. Wilkins; 4 vols.; London, 1737.

Conciliorum oecumenicorum decreta. Eds. J. Aberigo *et al.*; Basle, 1962.

'Constitutiones capituli Burdigalensis anni 1294', ed. L. Saggi, *Analecta ordinis Carmelitarum* 18 (1953) 123–85.

'Constitutiones capituli Londinensis anni 1281', ed. L. Saggi, *Analecta ordinis Carmelitarum* 15 (1950) 203–45.

'Les constitutions des Frères Prêcheurs dans la rédaction de S. Raymond de Peñafort (1241)', ed. Raymond Creytens, *Archivum fratrum praedicatorum* 18 (1948) 5–68.

Constitutions of the Dominican Order, 1216 to 1360. Ed. G. R. Galbraith; Manchester, 1925.

Corpus consuetudinum monasticarum. vols.; Sieburg, 1963– .

Councils and Synods. Vol. 1, *AD 871–1204*; eds. D. Whitelock, M. Brett and

C. N. L. Brooke; Oxford, 1981. Vol. 2, AD 1205–1313; eds. F. M. Powicke and C. R. Cheney; Oxford, 1964.

Customary of the Benedictine Abbey of Eynsham in Oxfordshire. Ed. Antonia Gransden. *CCM* 2; Sieburg, 1963.

Customary of the Benedictine Monasteries of Saint Augustine, Canterbury, and Saint Peter, Westminster. Ed. E. M. Thompson; Henry Bradshaw Soc., vols. 23 (1902), 28 (1904).

Decreta Lanfranci in monachis Cantuariensibus transmissa. Ed. David Knowles; *CCM* 3; Siegburg, 1967.

Documents Illustrating the Activities of the General and Provincial Chapters of the English Black Monks, 1215–1540. Ed. W. A Pantin; 3 vols.; Camden Soc., 3rd ser., 45 (1931), 47 (1933), 54 (1937).

Documents Illustrative of English Church History. Eds. H. Gee and W. J. Hardy; London, 1896.

Durham Annals. Ed. Frank Barlow; Surtees Soc., 154 (1945).

Faculty Office Registers, 1534–1549. Ed. David S. Chambers; Oxford, 1966.

Foedera, conventiones, literae, etc. Ed. T. Rymer; new edn; eds. Adam Clark *et al.*; 7 vols.; London, 1816–69.

Die Gesetze der Angelsachsen. Ed. F. Liebermann; 3 vols.; Halle, 1903–16.

Gregory IX, Pope. *Decretales.* In *Corpus Iuris Canonici*; vol. 2; eds. E. L. Richter and E. Friedberg; Leipzig, 1881.

Hostiensis. *In quinque decretalium libros commentaria* (Venice, 1581).
   Summa aurea (Lyons, 1548).

Innocent IV. *Commentaria . . . super libros quinque decretalium* (Frankfurt, 1570).

Ioannes Andreae. *In quinque decretalium libros novella commentaria* (4 vols.; Venice, 1581).

Letters from the English Abbots to the Chapter at Cîteaux. Ed. C. H. Talbot; Camden Soc., 4th ser., 4 (1967).

Letters and Papers Foreign and Domestic of the Reign of Henry VIII (21 vols.; London, 1862–1910).

Literae Cantuarienses. Ed. J. B. Sheppard; RS; 3 vols.; London, 1887–9.

Lyndwode, William. *Provinciale* (Oxford, 1679).

Missale ad usum ecclesie Westmonasteriensis. Ed. J. W. Legg; Henry Bradshaw Soc. 5 (1893).

Monumenta Franciscana. Eds. J. S. Brewer and R. Howlett; RS; 2 vols.; London, 1858–82.

Monumenta historica Carmelitana. Ed. Benedict Zimmerman; Lerins, 1905.

Observances in Use at the Augustinian Priory of St. Giles and St. Andrew at Barnwell, Cambridgeshire. Ed. J. Willis Clark; Cambridge, 1897.

Original Letters. Ed. Henry Ellis; 11 vols.; London, 1824–46).

Panormitanus. *Commentaria* [*in quinque libros decretalium*], Lyons, 1586.

Registrum Palatinum Dunelmense. Ed. T. D. Hardy; RS; 4 vols.; London, 1873–8.

Rotuli parliamentorum (7 vols.; London, 1793–1832).

Select Cases from the Ecclesiastical Courts of the Province of Canterbury. Eds. Norma Adams and Charles Donahue; Selden Soc., 95 (1979–80).

Statuta capitulorum generalium ordinis Cisterciensis ab anno 1116 ad annum 1786. Ed. J. M. Canivez; Louvain, 1933–41.

Bibliography

Statutes of the Realm. Eds. A. Luders *et al.*; London, 1810–29.

Les statuts de Prémontré réformés sur les ordres de Grégoire IX et d'Innocent IV au XIIIe siècle. Ed. P. F. Lefèvre; Louvain, 1946.

Three Chapters of Letters relating to the Suppression of Monasteries. Ed. Thomas Wright; Camden Soc., 26 (1843).

Tournai, Stephen of. *Die Summa des Stephanus Tornacensis* (ed. J. F. von Schulte; Giessen, 1891).

Visitations in the Diocese of Lincoln, 1517–53. Ed. A. H. Thompson; 3 vols.; Lincoln Record Soc., 33 (1940), 35 (1944), 37 (1947).

Visitations of the Diocese of Norwich, AD 1492–1532. Ed. A. Jessopp; Camden Soc., NS, 43 (1888).

Visitations of Religious Houses in the Diocese of Lincoln. Ed. A. H. Thompson; 2 vols. in 3; Lincoln Record Soc., 7 (1914), 14 (1918), 21 (1929).

Walsingham, Thomas. *Gesta abbatum monasterii S. Albani* (ed. H. T. Riley; RS; 3 vols.; London, 1867–9).

William Thorne's Chronicle of St. Augustine's Abbey, Canterbury. Tr. A. H. Davis; Oxford, 1934.

Wyclif, John. *Tractatus de apostasia* (Wyclif Soc., London, 1889).

SECONDARY SOURCES

Barber, Malcom. *The Trial of the Templars* (Cambridge, 1978).

Bateson, Mary. 'Archbishop Warham's Visitation of Monasteries, 1511', *EHR* 6 (1891) 18–35.

Binns, Alison. *Dedications of Monastic Houses in England and Wales, 1066–1216* (Woodbridge, Suffolk, 1989).

Blaauw, W. H. 'Episcopal Visitation of the Benedictine Nunnery of Easebourne', *Sussex Archaeological Collections* 9 (1857) 1–32.

Boehm, Laetitia. 'Papst Benedikt XII (1334–1342) als Förderer der Ordensstudien', *Secundum Regulam Vivere: Festschrift für P. Norbert Bachmund O. Praem.* (ed. Gert Melville; Windberg, 1978), pp. 281–310.

Bouché, J. 'Apostasie de religion', *Dictionnaire de droit canonique* 1. 564–74.

Bourdillon, A. F. C. *The Order of Minoresses in England* (Manchester, 1926).

Brown, William. 'The Nunnery of St. Stephen's of Thimbleby', *Yorks. Archaeol. Journal* 9 (1886) 334–7.

Brys, J. *De dispensatione in iure canonico praesertim apud decretistas et decretalistas usque ad medium saeculum decimum quartum* (Bruges, 1925).

Burne, R. V. H. *The Monks of Chester* (London, 1962).

Burns, Charles. 'Vatican Sources and the Honorary Papal Chaplains of the Fourteenth Century', *Römische Kurie, kirchliche Finanzen* (ed. Erwin Gatz; 2 vols.; Pontificia Universitas Gregoriana, Misc. Historiae Pontificiae, 45 and 46, 1979) 1. 65–95.

Burton, Janet E. 'The Election of Joan Fletcher as Prioress of Basedale, 1524', *Borthwick Institute Bulletin* 1 (1975–8) 145–53.

   The Yorkshire Nunneries in the Twelfth and Thirteenth Centuries (University of York, Borthwick Papers 56, 1979).

   Monastic and Religious Orders in Britain, 1000–1300 (Cambridge, 1994).

Bibliography

Cannon, Christopher. '*Raptus* in the Chaumpaigne Release and a Newly Discovered Document Concerning the Life of Geoffrey Chaucer', *Speculum* 68 (1993) 74–94.

Chadwick, S. J. 'Kirklees Priory', *Yorks. Archaeol. Journal* 16 (1902) 319–68.

Cheney, C. R. *Episcopal Visitations of Monasteries in the Thirteenth Century* (2nd edn; Manchester, 1983).

Churchill, Irene J. *Canterbury Administration* (2 vols.; London, 1933).

Coldicott, Diana. *Hampshire Nunneries* (Chichester, 1989).

Cole, R. E. G. *The Priory of Broadholme* (Associated Architectural Societies' Reports and Papers 28, 1905–6).

Coleman, Janet. 'Fitzralph's Antimendicant "proposicio" (1350) and the Politics of the Papal Court at Avignon', *JEH* 35 (1984) 376–90.

Colvin, H. M. *The White Canons in England* (Oxford, 1951).

Constable, Giles. 'The Ceremonies and Symbolism of Entering Religious Life and Taking the Monastic Habit, from the Fourth to the Twelfth Century', *Settimane di studio del centro italiano di studi sull'alto medioeva* 33 (Spoleto, 1987) 771–834.

Cotton, Charles. *The Grey Friars of Canterbury, 1224 to 1538* (Manchester, 1924).

Cowley, F. G. *The Monastic Order in South Wales, 1066–1349* (Cardiff, 1977).

Coxley, James E. *The Reformation in Essex to the Death of Mary* (Manchester, 1965).

Cross, Claire. 'Monasticism and Society in the Diocese of York, 1520–1540', *Transactions of the Royal Historical Society*, 5th ser., 38 (1988) 131–45.

The End of Medieval Monasticism in the East Riding of Yorkshire (Beverley, 1993).

Cullum, P. H. *Cremetts and Corrodies: Care of the Poor and Sick at St. Leonard's Hospital, York, in the Middle Ages* (University of York, Borthwick Papers 79, 1991).

Davis, E. Jeffries. 'The Beginning of the Dissolution: Christchurch, Aldgate, 1532', *Transactions of the Royal Historical Soc.*, 4th ser., 8 (1925) 127–50.

Dobson, R. B. *Durham Priory, 1400–1450* (Cambridge, 1973).

Dobson, R. B. and Sara Donaghey. *The History of Clementhorpe Nunnery* (York, 1984).

Duckett, G. F. *Visitations of English Cluniac Foundations* (London, 1890).

Egan, Keith J. 'Medieval Carmelite Houses: England and Wales', *Carmelus* 16 (1969) 142–226.

'An Essay toward a Historiography of the Origin of the Carmelite Province in England', *Carmelus* 19 (1972) 67–100.

Elkins, Sharon K. *Holy Women of England* (Chapel Hill, NC, 1988).

Emden, A. B. *A Biographical Register of the University of Oxford to AD 1500* (3 vols.; Oxford, 1957–59).

A Biographical Register of the University of Cambridge to AD 1500 (Cambridge, 1963).

A Survey of Dominicans in England: Based on the Ordination Lists in Episcopal Registers (1268 to 1538) (Rome, 1967).

Erikson, Carolly M. 'The Fourteenth–Century Franciscans and their Critics', *Franciscan Studies* 35 (1975) 107–35.

Fairbank, F. R. 'The Carmelites of Doncaster', *Yorks. Archaeol. Soc.* 13 (1895) 262–70.

Bibliography

Fitzgerald-Lombard, Patrick, ed. *Carmel in Britain* (2 vols.; Rome, 1992).

Forte, S. L. 'Robert Pynk, O.P., Provincial of England (*c.* 1361–68)', *Archivum Fratrum Praedicatorum* 27 (1957) 403–13.

Foster, M. R. 'Durham Monks at Oxford *c.* 1286–1381: A House of Studies and its Inmates', *Oxoniensia* 55 (1990) 99–114.

Frey, Wolfgang N. *The Act of Religious Profession* (Catholic University of America, Canon Law Studies, 63; Washington, 1931).

Gasquet, F. A. 'Overlooked Testimonies to the Character of the English Monasteries on the Eve of the Suppression', *Dublin Review* 114 (1894) 245–77.

Graham, Rose. *English Ecclesiastical Studies* (London, 1929).

Gransden, Antonia. 'Traditionalism and Continuity during the Last Century of Anglo-Saxon Monasticism', *JEH* 40 (1989) 159–207.

Graves, Coburn V. 'English Cistercian Nuns in Lincolnshire', *Speculum* 54 (1979) 492–9.

Greatrex, Joan G. 'Some Statistics of Religious Motivation', *Studies in Church History* 15 (1978) 179–86.

Guillemain, Bernard. 'Les chapelains d'honneur des papes d'Avignon', *Mélange d'archéologie et d'histoire* 64 (1952) 217–38.

Gwynn, Aubrey. *The English Austin Friars* (Oxford, 1940).

Haines, C. R. *Dover Priory* (Cambridge, 1930).

Hallam, Elizabeth M. 'Henry VIII's Monastic Refoundations of 1536–7 and the Course of the Dissolution', *BIHR* 51 (1978) 124–31.

Harper-Bill, Christopher. 'Cistercian Visitation in the Late Middle Ages: The Case of Hailes Abbey', *BIHR* 53 (1980) 103–14.

'Monastic Apostasy in Late Medieval England', *JEH* 32 (1981) 1–18.

Harvey, Barbara. *Monastic Dress in the Middle Ages: Precept and Practice* (Canterbury, 1988).

Living and Dying in England, 1100–1540: The Monastic Experience (Oxford, 1993).

Hatcher, John. 'Mortality in the Fifteenth Century: Some New Evidence', *Economic History Review*, 2nd ser., 39 (1986) 19–38.

Heales, Alfred. *The Records of Merton Priory* (London, 1898).

Hill, Mary C. *King's Messengers, 1199–1377* (London, 1961).

Hill, R. M. T. 'Fourpenny Retirement: The Yorkshire Templars in the Fourteenth Century', *Studies in Church History* 24 (1987) 123–8.

Hines, Reginald L. *The History of Hitchin* (2 vols.; London, 1927–9).

Hinnebusch, William A. *The Early English Friars Preachers* (Rome, 1951).

The History of the Dominican Order, vol. 1 (New York, 1966).

Hockey, S. F. *Quarr Abbey and its Lands* (Leicester, 1970).

Beaulieu, King John's Abbey: A History of Beaulieu Abbey, Hampshire ([London], 1976).

Hofmeister, Philipp. 'Die Strafen für den Apostata a Religione', *Studia Gratiana* 8 (1962) 423–46.

Hutchinson, Carole. *The Hermit Monks of Grandmont* (Kalamazoo, 1989).

Jack, Sybil. 'The Last Days of the Smaller Monasteries in England', *JEH* 21 (1970) 97–124.

Bibliography

Johnson, Penelope D. *Equal in Monastic Profession: Religious Women in Medieval France* (Chicago, 1991).

Kealy, Thomas M. *Dowry of Women Religious* (Catholic University of America, Canon Law Studies, no. 134; Washington, 1941).

Kingsford, C. L. *The Grey Friars of London* (Aberdeen, 1915).

Knowles, David. *The Religious Orders in England* (3 vols.; Cambridge, 1948–59).

'Gilbert of Sempringham', *David Knowles Remembered* (eds. Christopher Brooke et al.; Cambridge, 1991), pp. 141–55.

Knowles, David and R. Neville Hadcock. *Medieval Religious Houses: England and Wales* (2nd edn; London, 1971).

Lawrence, C. H. *Medieval Monasticism* (2nd edn; London, 1989).

The Friars (London, 1994).

Lecler, Joseph. 'Boniface VIII et le jubilé de 1300', *Etudes* 264 (1950), 145–57.

Lehmberg, Stanford E. *The Reformation Parliament, 1529–1536* (Cambridge, 1968).

The Later Parliaments of Henry VIII, 1536–1547 (Cambridge, 1977).

Little, A. G. 'The Administrative Divisions of the Mendicant Orders in England', *EHR* 34 (1919) 205–9.

Little, A. G. and R. C. Easterling. *The Franciscans and Dominicans of Exeter* (Exeter, 1927).

Logan, F. Donald. *Excommunication and the Secular Arm in Medieval England* (Toronto, 1968).

'The First Royal Visitation of the English Universities, 1536', *EHR* 106 (1991) 861–88.

'Ramsey Abbey, Last Days and After', *The Salt of Common Life: Individuality and Choice in the Medieval Town, Countryside and Church: Essays Presented to J. Ambrose Raftis* (ed. E. B. DeWindt; Kalamazoo, 1995).

Lynch, Joseph H. 'The Cistercians and Underage Novices', *Cîteaux* 24 (1973) 283–97.

Mahn, Jean-Berthold. *Le pape Benoit XII et les Cisterciens* (Paris, 1949).

Makowski, Elizabeth M. 'The Conjugal Debt and Medieval Canon Law', *Journal of Medieval History* 3 (1977) 99–114; reprinted in J. B. Holloway, C. S. Wright and J. Bechtold, eds., *Equally in God's Image: Women in the Middle Ages* (New York, 1990), pp. 129–43.

Maxwell-Lyte, H. 'Visitation of Religious Houses and Hospitals, 1526', *Somerset Record Soc.* 39 (1924) 207–25.

Historical Notes on the Use of the Great Seal of England (London, 1926).

Mayali, Laurent. 'Du vagabondage à l'apostasie: le moine fugitive dans la société médiévale', *Religiöse Devianz* (ed. Dieter Simon; Frankfurt, 1990), pp. 121–42.

Milis, Ludo J. R. *Angelic Monks and Earthly Men: Monasticism and its Meaning to Medieval Society* (Woodbridge, Suffolk, 1992).

Mills, Mabel H. 'The Medieval Shire House (*Domus Vicecomitis*)', *Studies Presented to Sir Hilary Jenkinson* (ed. J. Conway Davies; London, 1957), pp. 254–71.

Mollat, Guillaume. 'Le jubilé de 1350', *Journal des savants 1963.*

Moorman, J. R. H. *The Grey Friars in Cambridge, c. 1225–1538* (Cambridge, 1962).

A History of the Franciscan Order from its Origins to the Year 1517 (Oxford, 1968).

Bibliography

Franciscans in England (London, 1974).

Medieval Franciscan Houses (St. Bonaventure, NY, 1983).

Oliger, L. 'De pueris oblatis in ordine minorum', *Archivum Franciscanum Historicum* 8 (1915) 389–447.

Owens, D. M. *Church and Society in Medieval Lincolnshire* (Lincoln, 1971).

Oxley, James E. *The Reformation in Essex to the Death of Mary* (Manchester, 1965).

Pantin, W. A. 'English Monastic Letter-Books', *Historical Essays in Honour of James Tait* (eds. J. G. Edwards *et al.*; Manchester, 1933), pp. 201–22.

Parks, George B. *The English Traveler to Italy* (Rome, 1954).

Pearce, E. H. *Thomas de Cobham, Bishop of Worcester, 1317–1327* (London, 1923).

Pollock, F. and F. W. Maitland. *The History of English Law Before the Time of Edward I* (2nd edn, reissued with introduction by S. F. C. Milsom; 2 vols.; Cambridge, 1968).

Post, J. B. 'Ravishment of Women and the Statutes of Westminster', *Legal Records and the Historian* (ed. J.H. Baker; London, 1978), pp. 150–64.

Postles, David. 'The Austin Canons in English Towns, *c.* 1100–1350', *Historical Research* 66 (1993) 1–20.

Power, Eileen. *Medieval English Nunneries* (Cambridge, 1922).

Quinn, Patricia. *Better Than the Sons of Kings: Boys and Monks in the Early Middle Ages* (New York, 1989).

Riesner, Albert J. *Apostates and Fugitives from Religious Houses* (Catholic University of America, Canon Law Studies, no. 168; Washington, 1942).

Robinson, David M. *The Geography of Augustinian Settlement in Medieval England and Wales* (British Archaeological Reports 80; Oxford, 1980).

Roby, Douglas. 'Philip of Harvengt's Contribution to the Question of Passage from One Religious Order to Another', *Analecta Praemonstratensia* 49 (1973) 69–100.

Roth, Francis. *The English Austin Friars, 1249–1538* (2 vols.; New York, 1961–6).

Russell, Josiah Cox. 'The Clerical Population of Medieval England', *Traditio* 2 (1944) 177–212.

Savine, A. *English Monasteries on the Eve of the Dissolution* (Oxford, 1909).

Sayers, Jane. 'Violence in the Medieval Cloister', *JEH* 41 (1990) 533–42.

Scarisbrick, J. J. *Henry VIII* (London, 1968).

Schmitt, Clement. *Un pape réformateur et un défenseur de l'unité de l'église: Benoit XII et l'ordre des Frères Mineurs* (Florence, 1959).

Southern, R. W. *Saint Anselm: A Portrait in Landscape* (Cambridge, 1990).

Stephan, John. *A History of Buckfast Abbey* (Bristol, 1970).

Storey, R. L. 'Papal Provision to English Monasteries', *Nottingham Medieval Studies* 35 (1991) 77–91.

Sweet, Alfred H. 'Papal Privileges Granted to Individual Religious', *Speculum* 31 (1956) 602–10.

Taylor, John. 'The Dominicans and Dominican Priory', *Transactions of Bristol and Glos. Archaeol. Soc.* 3 (1878–9) 322–40.

Taylor, S. *Cartmel, People and Priory* (Kendal, 1955).

Thompson, A. Hamilton. 'The Registers of John Gynewell, Bishop of Lincoln, for the Years 1349–50', *Archaeological Review*, NS, 18 (1911) 301–60.

Bibliography

The Premonstratensian Abbey of Welbeck (London, 1938).

The English Clergy (Oxford, 1947).

Thompson, E. Margaret. *The Carthusian Order in England* (London, 1930).

Thompson, Sally. *Women Religious: The Founding of English Nunneries after the Norman Conquest* (Oxford, 1991).

Tillotson, John H. *Marrick Priory: A Nunnery in Late Medieval Yorkshire* (University of York, Borthwick Papers 75, 1989).

Traskey, J. P. *Milton Abbey: A Dorset Monastery in the Middle Ages* (Tisbury, 1978).

Valois, N. 'Un plaidoyer du XIVe siècle en faveur des Cisterciens', *Bibliothèque de l'école des chartes* 6 (1905) 788–95.

Vaughn, Sally. *Anselm of Bec and Robert of Meulan* (Berkeley, 1987).

Victoria History of the Counties of England (London, 1900–).

Vodola, Elizabeth. *Excommunication in the Middle Ages* (Berkeley, 1986).

Waddell, Helen. *The Wandering Scholars* (7th edn; London, 1934).

Wadding, Luke. *Annales minorum* (2nd edn; 25 vols.; Rome, 1731–1886).

Walsh, Katherine. *A Fourteenth-Century Scholar and Primate: Richard Fitzralph in Oxford, Avignon and Armagh* (Oxford, 1981).

Warren, Ann K. *Anchorites and their Patrons in Medieval England* (Berkeley, 1985).

Willard, J. F. 'The Dating and Delivery of Letters Patent and Writs in the Fourteenth Century', *BIHR* 10 (1932) 1–11.

Williams, David H. *The Welsh Cistercians* (2 vols.; Tenby, 1984).

Atlas of Cistercian Lands in Wales (Cardiff, 1990).

Wilson, J. M. 'The Visitations and Injunctions of Cardinal Wolsey and Archbishop Cranmer to the Priory of Worcester in 1526 and 1534 respectively', *Associated Architectural Societies' Reports and Papers* 36 (1921–2) 356–71.

Wood, Diana. *Clement VI: The Pontificate and Ideas of an Avignon Pope* (Cambridge, 1989).

Woodcock, Brian L. *Medieval Ecclesiastical Courts of the Diocese of Canterbury* (London, 1952).

Woodward, G. W. O. 'The Exemption from Suppression of Certain Yorkshire Priories', *EHR* 76 (1961) 385–401.

The Dissolution of the Monasteries (London, 1966).

Wright, J. Robert. *The Church and the English Crown, 1305–1334* (Toronto, 1980).

Youings, Joyce. *The Dissolution of the Monasteries* (London, 1971).

Zutschi, P. and R. Ombres. 'The Dominicans in Cambridge, 1238–1538', *Archivum Fratrum Praedicatorum* 60 (1990) 313–73.

INDEX OF PLACES

Index of places

INDEX OF PERSONS

The religious orders to which individual religious are known to have belonged are indicated by the following abbreviations:

AusF	Austin friars
CruF	Crutched friars
Hosp	Hospital
KtH	Knight Hospitaller Order
KtT	Knight Templar Order
OBons	Bonshommes Order
OCarm	Carmelites
OCarth	Carthusians
OCist	Cistercians
OClun	Cluniac monks
OFM	Franciscans
OFont	Order of Fontevrault
OGilb	Gilbertine canons
OGrand	Grandmontines
OP	Dominicans
OPrem	Premonstratensians
OSA	Augustinian canons
OSB	Benedictines
OTir	Order of Tiron
OTrin	Trinitarians
PiF	Pied friars
SSJJ	Sisters of Order of St John of Jerusalem

Abbott, Robert, harp-player, 78
Abingdon, Thomas, OSB, 193
Ace, Bartholomew, OCist, 206
Ackley, Nicholas de, OCist, 210
Aconbury, John, OCist, 212
Acton, William de, OCist, 204
Adam ____, OCist, abbot of Baltinglas, Ireland, 105
Adderbury, George, OSB, 198
Adeleshey, Joan, OSB, 110, 260
Ady, Robert, OCist, 55–6
Alazun, Peter de, OSA, 217
Albon, William, KtH, 252
Alcester, Henry, OCist, Bordesley Abbey, 206
Alcester, Henry, OCist, Hailes Abbey, 211

Alcester, Robert, OCist, abbot of Hailes, 211n.
Alconbury, John de, OSA, 220
Aldeburi, Nicholas de, OP, 46
Alden, John, AusF, 249
Alnmouth, Robert, OPrem, 234
Alnwick, William, bishop of Lincoln (1436–49), 133–4
Alveton, Joan de, OSA, 265
Aly, Nicholas, Hosp, 255
Andreae, Joannes, 31, 123, 149n.
Andreuson, Robert, OGilb, 239
Andrew, John, alias Bozard, OSA, 81n., 225
Andrew, Thomas, OPrem, 236
Angram, Helen de, OSB, 259
Angurtone, John, OSB, 199

Index of persons

Anna, Henry de, OCarm, prior provincial, 104
Anselm, St, 6–7
Appleby, John, OSB, 195
Applegarth, Sabina de, OSB, 258
Appleton, Helen de, OCist, 262
ApRice, John, royal visitor, 161–3
Arley, Matthew de, OClun, 200
Arundel, Elizabeth, OSA, 265
Ashby, Thomas, OCist, 136, 213
Ashton, John, OPrem, 234
Ashton, Richard, OSB, abbot of Peterborough, 195
Ashton, Richard, OSB, monk of Malmesbury, 198
Ashwell, Richard de, OSA, 221
Aston, Henry de, OSB, 191
Astone, Robert, OSB, OCist, 46n.
atte Water, Joan, Hosp, 266
Atwater, William, bishop of Lincoln (1514–21), 59, 134
Auckland, Stephen de, OSA, 219
Audenete, John, OCist, 209
Augustyn, Thomas, OSA, 231
Avernaz, William de, OClun, prior of Prittlewell, 119–20, 200
Aymestrey, John, OSA, 226

Badby, Simon de, AusF, 117, 249
Badlesmere, Bartholomew, lord of, 35n.
Badwell, Roger de, OSA, 219
Baghill, John de, OCist, 209
Bakewell, ____, OSA, 231
Baldwyn, Richard, alias de Ipswich, OCarm, 112, 247
Bale, John, OCarm, 156
Banaster, William, OCist, 209
Baners, R. de, OSB, 187
Bankyn, ____, AusF, 74
Banning, see Brackley
Banstede, Thomas, OSB, 46n.
Barbour, Agnes, wife of John, 79
Barbour, Richard, OCarth, 215
Bareth, John, OTir, 203
Barkeley, Thomas, OSB, 197
Barking, John de, OCarm, 246
Barn, Thomas, OSB, 188
Barnes, Robert, OSA, 156
Barogh, see Cope
Barow, John, OGilb, 239
Barrow, William de, AusF, 249
Barrowby, Thomas, OPrem, 235
Barry, Robert, OSA, 79, 139n., 216
Barry, William, OSA, 139n., 219

Barton, John, OPrem, 236
Barton, William de, OSB, 186
Barville, see Latimer
Basevil, Hawise de, OSB, 256
Bassete, William, OP, 241
Batayle, John, OSB, 199
Batys, Thomas, OSA, 229
Baudri, Edmund, OSA, 220
Bavent, Thomas, OCarm, 246
Baxby, Robert, OPrem, 234
Beauchamp, Hugh de, OP, 242
Beauchamp, Thomas, AusF, 74, 249
Beccles, Philip de, OCarm, 246
Becke, Thomas, OCarm, 248
Beckett, William, OSB, 193
Beckingham, Nicholas de, OSA, 221
Beckington, Thomas, bishop of Bath and Wells (1443–65), 55–6
Bedal, Agnes, de, OCist, 262
Bedyll, Thomas, royal visitor, 164–5
Belgrave, William, son of Henry de, OSA, 216
Belton, Henry de, OSB, 140, 154, 186
Beltone, Richard, alias Nutsey, OPrem, 32, 237
Benedict, St, 2, 4, 19n., 122n., 123, 145, 147, 149n.
Benedict XII, pope (1335–42), 44, 103, 123–5, 137, 143, 147, 149n.
Benedict Aniane, 5
Benet, Robert, OCist, 213
Benet, Robert, OPrem, 238
Bengeworth, Richard, alias de Evesham, Hosp, 24–5, 253
Bengeworthy, John, OSB, 78, 195
Benson, Thomas, alias Burton, OSB, 164n.
Benstede, Thomas de, OSB, 192
Bent, Walter, OSA, 230
Berdon, John, OSA, 135, 231
Berghby, Isabel de, OClun, prioress of Arthington, 261–2
Bernevalle, Reginald de, OSB, 185
Betsey, Edward, 163n.
Bevereford, William de, OCarm, 246
Beverley, Avice de, OSB, 46
Beverley, John de, novice OSB, 17
Beverley, John, OSA, 227
Beverley, Reginald, OPrem, 235
Bevice, John, Hosp, 255
Bigod, Richard, OPrem, 235
Bigot, Maud, OCist, 263
Binnington, William de, OCist, 210
Birchvale, Thomas, OCist, 207

INDEX OF SUBJECTS

Index of subjects

Crutched friars, *see also under individual
  houses in the* Index of Places *and under
  individual friars in the* Index of Persons
  direct use of secular arm, 181
  register of apostates, 250

Dispensation from religious profession,
  42–3, 54–65
  attempt of English bishops to reform
    (1529), 60
  nature of, 55–6
  numbers, 62–3
  profile of dispensed religious, 61–2
  reaction and resistance by religious
    superiors, 56–60
  use at time of dissolution, chap. 6 *passim*,
    esp. 157–60, 174–7
Dissolution of religious houses
  friars, 173–4
  greater houses, 172–7
  nuns, 160, 174, 176–7
  smaller houses, 167–72
Dominicans, *see also under individual houses
  in the* Index of Places *and under
  individual friars in the* Index of Persons
  arrival in England, 3
  direct use of secular arm, 99–100, 180–1
  penance imposed on returning apostates,
    148–9
  reaction to honorary papal chaplains,
    52
  register of apostates, 241–3
  and *transitus*, 44

Excommunication, 10, 27, 28, 44, 87, 95,
  97, 115, 121, 123, 125–6, 132, 149
Exsilium, 149–51

Faculty Office, 158–60, 164–5, 167, 174–6
Fontevrault, Order of, register of apostates,
  199
Franciscans, *see also under individual houses in
  the* Index of Places *and under individual
  friars in the* Index of Persons
  arrival in England, 3–4
  direct use of secular arm, 99–100, 180–1
  reaction to honorary papal chaplains, 52
  register of apostates, 243–6
  and *transitus*, 44

Gilbertines, *see also under individual houses in
  the* Index of Places *and under individual
  canons in the* Index of Persons
  direct use of secular arm, 99, 180–1

penance imposed on returning apostates,
  149–50
reaction to honorary papal chaplains, 53
register of apostates; canons, 238–40;
  nuns, 266
Grandmontines, register of apostates, 203

Habit, religious, abandonment of, 25–6
Hospitals, register of apostates
  female religious, 266–7
  male religious, 253–5

Imprisonment
  in ecclesiastical prisons, 15, 28, 49, 57,
    77n., 78, 102, 129, 137, 139, 151, 152,
    186n., 195, 207, 220, 222, 225, 228,
    231, 244, 245
  in royal prisons, 17–18, 79n., 86, 89,
    116–17, 123, 202, 211, 218, 219, 224,
    238, 244, 246, 249, 250, 253, 254
Inheritance, plea of religious profession
  against, 22–4

Jubilee, Holy Year of 1350, 28–31

Knights Hospitallers of St John of
  Jerusalem
  direct use of the secular arm, 99, 180
  register of apostates: brothers, 252;
    sisters, 266
Knights Templars
  dissolution and apostasy, 27–8
  register of apostates, 251–2

Lambeth, Council of (1281), 20–1

Nuns, *see also under individual orders and, in
  Index of Places, under individual
  religious houses; otherwise, under general
  headings*
  abduction, 85–9; case of Elizabeth
    Lutton, OSB, 89–96; Giffard affair,
    86–8; other examples, 88–9; Second
    Statute of Westminster (1285), 85–6
  dissolution, 174, 176–7
  penance imposed on returning apostates,
    153–4
  pregnancy, 84–5; case of Elizabeth
    Lutton, OSB, 89–96
  reasons for apostasy peculiar to women,
    83–9
  transitus, 50
  the unwanted, 138, 140–1
  visitation (1535), 160–2

Index of subjects

Papal chaplains, honorary, 51–4
  challenge by religious superiors, 52–4
  effect on professed religious, 51–2
  number in England, 51, 54
Pastor bonus, constitution (1335) of Pope
  Benedict XII, 103, 123–5, 137, 147
Penance, *see* Readmission
Pied friars, register of apostates, 251
Premonstratensians, *see also under individual*
  houses in the Index of Places *and under*
  individual canons in the Index of
  Persons
  Bishop Redman's visitations, 32–3,
   135–6
  penance imposed on returning apostates,
   149, 150–1
  register of apostates: canonesses, 266 ;
   canons, 232–8
Profession, religious, 10–25
  rite, 19
  tacit, 20–2
  underage, 12–16, 160
  unmarried requirement, 16–18

Readmission of apostates,
  penances imposed, 147–55
  provision of Rule of St Benedict, 145,
   149
  ritual, 145–7
Religious orders, *see under individual orders*
  and, in the Index of Places, *under*
  individual houses
Return of apostates
  episcopal efforts, 131–5, 139–42
  papal efforts, 121–31
  reasons for forced return, 142–5
  the unwanted, 122–3, 124–5, 129,
   136–42
  visitations by bishops and superiors of
   orders, 132–6
Rule of St Benedict, 4–5, 7, 19n., 80,
  122n., 123, 145, 147, 149

Runaway religious, *see* Apostates

Secular arm, use of, against apostates,
  97–120
  direct access to local royal officials,
   99–100, 180–1
  origins, 97–101
  procedure by writ *de apostata capiendo*,
   100–20; addressees, 107–111; appeal
   from writ, 114–16; frequency of use,
   103–5; nature of writ, 106; number of
   apostates used against, in general and
   by order, 102; origins, 100–1; petition
   for writ, 105–6; procedure, 104–11;
   repeated writs, 111; sample petition
   for writ, 178; sample writ, 179;
   surviving records, 101–3; use of, in
   monastic disputes, 118–20
Sempringham, *see* Gilbertines

Tiron, Order of, register of apostates, 203
Transitus, 43–50
  canon law, 43–4
  case of William Pouns, OSB, 63–5
  misunderstandings concerning, 47–9
  practice in England, 45–7
  reactions of rival orders, 44–5
  uncanonical practice, 49–50
  use at time of suppression, 157, 167–9
Trinitarians, register of apostates, 240

Visitation, royal, of religious houses
  (1535–6), 160–7; *see also*
   Compendium compertorum
Visitations of religious houses, 31–3,
  132–6

Writs
  de apostata capiendo, see Secular arm
  de excommunicato capiendo, 97, 106, 107,
   109n., 238

Cambridge Studies in Medieval Life and Thought
Fourth series

Titles in series